RICHARD II
THE ART OF KINGSHIP

Richard II

The Art of Kingship

Edited by
ANTHONY GOODMAN
and
JAMES GILLESPIE

CLARENDON PRESS · OXFORD
1999

Oxford University Press, Great Clarendon Street, Oxford OX2 6DP

Oxford New York

Athens Auckland Bangkok Bogota Bombay Buenos Aires
Calcutta Cape Town Dar es Salaam Delhi Florence Hong Kong Istanbul
Karachi Kuala Lumpur Madras Madrid Melbourne Mexico City
Nairobi Paris Singapore Taipei Tokyo Toronto Warsaw

and associated companies in
Berlin Ibadan

Oxford is a registered trade mark of Oxford University Press

Published in the United States
by Oxford University Press Inc., New York

British Library Cataloguing in Publication Data
Data available

Library of Congress Cataloging in Publication Data
Richard II: the art of kingship / edited by Anthony Goodman and James
Gillespie.
p.   cm.
Includes bibliographical references (p.   ) and index.
1. Richard II, King of England, 1367–1400.   2. Great Britain—
Politics and government—1377–1399.   3. Constitutional history,
Medieval.   4. Monarchy—Great Britain.   I. Goodman, Anthony, 1936–   .
II. Gillespie, James L.
DA235.R53   1998
942.03'8'092—dc21   98–7334

0–19–820189–3

1 3 5 7 9 10 8 6 4 2

Typeset by Graphicraft Limited, Hong Kong
Printed in Great Britain
on acid-free paper by Biddles Ltd.,
Guildford & King's Lynn

Acknowledgements

I am indebted to Professor George Stow, who first encouraged me when I floated the idea of this book, but gracefully declined to be my co-editor. My second debt is to Dr James Gillespie, who undertook this tricky Transatlantic task, and mightily advanced the production process as co-editor in the earlier stages. He was assisted by some of his students, who set to on bibliographical tasks with the energy of cheerleaders. I am sure that the contributors to the book—and many other American and British students of later medieval English history—share my feelings of gratitude and admiration for Jim Gillespie's foundation of The Society of the White Hart, and for his organization of sessions under its banner (sometimes with Professor Joel Rosenthal) at successive International Congresses on Medieval Studies at Western Michigan University, Kalamazoo. Like a benign magician, Jim conjured kindred spirits from all points of the compass, and genially presided over their scholarly sessions and bibulous gatherings. He has given a big boost to studies of Richard II's reign.

I owe thanks to a succession of OUP editors for helping to launch this project (notably, Sophie McCallum) and in particular to Tony Morris for raising a kindly light when it was engulfed, and a gentle breeze when becalmed. I am grateful to the patience of the contributors, who for so long scanned the horizon in vain. I owe special thanks to Dr Nigel Saul for his unfailing encouragement.

In the final stages, Mrs Doris Williamson, Secretary of the Scottish History Department, University of Edinburgh, helped in a messy careening of the manuscript with her customary word-processing skills.

A. G.

Contents

List of Contributors

Dr Caroline M. Barron, Department of History, Royal Holloway Bedford New College, University of London.

Professor Michael J. Bennett, School of History and Classics, University of Tasmania.

Dr Richard G. Davies, Department of History, University of Manchester.

Patricia J. Eberle, Research Associate, Centre for Medieval Studies, University of Toronto.

Professor Chris Given-Wilson, Department of Mediaeval History, University of St Andrews.

Professor Anthony Goodman, Department of History, University of Edinburgh.

Professor W. M. Ormrod, Department of History, University of York.

Professor Nigel Saul, Department of History, Royal Holloway Bedford New College, University of London.

Professor Eleanor Scheifele, Henry Radford Hope School of Fine Arts, Indiana University.

Mr John Taylor, School of History, University of Leeds.

Professor Emeritus Anthony Tuck, Department of Historical Studies, University of Bristol.

List of Figures

List of Abbreviations

Adam of Usk	*Chronicon Adae de Usk*, ed. E. M. Thompson (London, 1904)
Annales	*Johannis de Trokelowe, et Henrici de Blaneforde . . . necnon quorundam anonymorum Chronica et Annales* (etc.), ed. H. T. Riley (RS, London, 1866)
BIHR	*Bulletin of the Institute of Historical Research*
BJRL	*Bulletin of the John Rylands Library*
BL	British Library
BN	Bibliothèque Nationale, Paris
CCR	*Calendar of Close Rolls*
CFR	*Calendar of Fine Rolls*
Chron. Angl.	*Chronicon Angliae, 1328–1388*, ed. E. M. Thompson (RS, London, 1874)
CP	G. E. Cokayne (ed.), *Complete Peerage*, 12 vols. (London, 1910–59)
CPMR	A. H. Thomas (ed.), *Calendar of the Plea and Memoranda Rolls of the City of London: 1364–1381* (Cambridge, 1929); *1381–1412* (Cambridge, 1932)
CPR	*Calendar of Patent Rolls*
EETS	Early English Text Society
EcHR	*Economic History Review*
EHR	*English Historical Review*
English Court Culture	V. J. Scattergood and J. W. Sherborne (edd.), *English Court Culture in the Later Middle Ages* (London, 1983)
ESFDB	European State Finance Database
Foedera	T. Rymer (ed.), *Foedera, conventiones, litterae* (etc.), 20 vols. (London, 1704–35)
Froissart	*Œuvres complètes de Froissart: Chroniques*, ed. K. de Lettenhove, 25 vols. in 26 pts. (Brussels, 1867–77)
Hist. Angl.	*Historia Anglicana*, ed. H. T. Riley, 2 vols. (RS, London, 1867–9).
JBS	*Journal of British Studies*

JMH	*Journal of Medieval History*
King's Works	R. A. Brown, H. M. Colvin, and A. J. Taylor (edd.), *The History of the King's Works: The Middle Ages*, 2 vols. (London, 1963)
Knighton	*Chronicon Henrici Knighton*, ed. J. R. Lumby, 2 vols. (RS, 1889–95)
LBH	R. R. Sharpe (ed.), *Calendar of the Letter-Books of the City of London, Letter Book H, 1375–1399* (London, 1907)
Politics and Crisis	J. Taylor and W. Childs (edd.), *Politics and Crisis in Fourteenth-Century England* (Gloucester, 1990)
POPC	N. H. Nicolas (ed.), *Proceedings and Ordinances of the Privy Council of England*, 7 vols. (London, 1834–7)
PRO	Public Record Office
Reign of Richard II	F. R. H. Du Boulay and C. M. Barron (edd.), *The Reign of Richard II: Essays in Honour of May McKisack* (London, 1971)
RP	J. Strachey *et al.* (edd.), *Rotuli Parliamentorum*, 7 vols. (London, 1767–83)
RS	Rolls Series
Traison et Mort	*Chronicque de la traison et mort de Richart Deux Roy Dengleterre*, ed. B. Williams (London, 1846)
TRHS	*Transactions of the Royal Historical Society*
Vita	G. B. Stow (ed.), *Historia Vitae et Regni Ricardi Secundi* (Philadelphia, 1977)
Westm. Chron.	*The Westminster Chronicle, 1381–1394*, ed. L. C. Hector and B. F. Harvey (London, 1982)

I

Introduction

Anthony Goodman

The personality and policies of Richard II, and the long-term significance of his reign, were matters of debate and controversy among suspicious and worried contemporaries, and they have remained matters of debate and controversy ever since. Judgements by those who had known him person-ally, or who had lived under his rule, that he was a tyrant or a foolish king, have echoed long. The theme that he was, with Edward II and Henry VI, one of a trinity of notably crass and unsuccessful rulers, has had a long currency. His rule, arguably, exemplified ill governance, whose features were the stuff of bad dreams for the subjects of the later medieval English monarchy. A *locus classicus* for the indictment of this scarifying trinity is the manifesto against Edward IV's government put out in 1469 by George duke of Clarence, George Neville, archbishop of York, and the earl of Warwick.[1] Edward's rule was compared in this manifesto to theirs, which had led 'to their destruction and the great hurt and impoverishment of this land'. The three kings had estranged the great lords of their blood from their secret council, and relied on the advice of those who had no respect for the lords' interests and those of the realm in general, but who impoverished the Crown for their own enrichment, encouraged the im-position of unjust taxes and forfeitures, and generated disorder and crime through their practice of maintenance.

However, Richard II's reign was to be considered of more vital inter-est than as an awful example of corrosive elements eating into regal polity. Later generations made judgements that his reign was a turning-point in political history, or in constitutional developments, with consequences

---

[1] Modernized text in B. Wilkinson, *Constitutional History of England in the Fifteenth Century (1399–1485)* (London, 1964), 180–2, from John Warkworth's *Chronicle*.

which affected their lives and decisions. In the fifteenth century Richard's deposition was interpreted as having long-lasting and baleful political consequences. When in 1463 Henry VI's queen Margaret of Anjou, reduced to poverty, abased herself before her enemy Philip the Good, duke of Burgundy at Saint-Pol, the event was variously interpreted, according to the court chronicler Georges Chastellain:

Autres disoient que c'estoit un vrai jugement de Dieu, suspendu longuement depuis la mort du roy Richart, lequel piteusement et en grand dueil avoit esté privé de sa couronne, et confusément mis à mort par son propre sang, dont Dieu maintenant, sur la troisième hoir, envoya la vengeance du délit, en le souffrant despouillé de la couronne mal acquise, et estre expuls misérablement, et à toute povreté, sans avoir pied de terre sien et de quoy ceste royne-ici, cause et esmou veresse de tout par les parties quelle avoit prises du régnant de son mary, portoit la punition démérie.[2]

Thomas Basin, bishop of Lisieux, writing in the 1470s, said that Richard duke of York had aspired to the throne partly because he considered that his forebear Richard II had been wickedly deposed and killed by Henry of Lancaster.[3] Such views may have been stimulated by Yorkist propaganda, but they probably owed much of their force to the composition of anti-Lancastrian histories in France in the wake of Henry IV's usurpation, and their diffusion in princely libraries there. These versions reflected the indignation of Charles VI, and his kinsfolk, at the treatment of his royal son-in-law by the latter's perfidious subjects. Such outrageous *lèse-majesté*

[2] G. Chastellain, *Œuvres*, iv. *Chronique 1461–1464*, ed. K. de Lettenhove (Brussels, 1864), 295–6; cf. ibid. 285–94. The Scot Walter Bower wrote that Henry IV was told by a friar that if he did not resign the Crown, which did not belong to him, he would be succeeded by a devil, a saint, a sword, then nobody (*Scotichronicon*, ed. D. E. R. Watt, viii (Aberdeen, 1987), 28–9). The Castilian Dies de Games, writing in the 1430s, used Richard's deposition to illustrate natural English faithlessness, (*El Vitorial: Crónica de Don Pero Niño, Conde de Buelna*, ed. J. de M. Carriazo (Madrid, 1940), 183).

[3] T. Basin, *Histoire de Charles VII*, ed. and trans. C. Samaran, ii (Paris, 1944), 170–1: 'Nam ad coronam et dyadema regni anhelabat, quod suo progenitori regi Richardo suisque et sibi inique ablatum fuisse putabat per Henricum ducem Lencastrie, qui dictum Richardum regem extinxerat atque peremerat'. For Basin's career in English service in Normandy, B. Guenée, *Between Church and State: The Lives of Four French Prelates in the Late Middle Ages*, trans. A. Goldhammer, (Chicago, 1987), 288 ff. I owe thanks to Prof. Christopher Allmand for this reference. Basin owed his rapid ecclesiastical preferment in Normandy in 1441–3 to the patronage of Zenone Castiglioni, bishop of Bayeux, a leading councillor of Richard duke of York as king's lieutenant. In 1445 Castiglioni led, and Basin participated in, the duke's embassy for the marriage of his son Edward to a daughter of Charles VII (Guenée, *Between Church and State*, 290–4). Basin as a historian was not heavily reliant on literary or documentary sources: it may be that his remarks echo the duke of York's private opinions in the early 1440s: as his marriage brokers in 1445, Castiglioni and Basin would have been keenly interested in the duke's family history.

was especially shocking to the loyal vassals and servitors of the French monarchy, pre-eminently sacred and authoritarian in Christendom. When the Lancastrians tried to take over that monarchy too, the sordid origins and evil essence of their rule in England boosted pro-Valois morale.[4]

The view that the deposition had disastrous long-term consequences entered the mainstream of English historiography as a result of its propagation by the Yorkist dynasty: it was expounded in the declaration of Edward IV's right to the throne in 1461.[5] The deposition of Richard had a long historiographical life as the root cause of the civil wars of the later fifteenth century. However, in the seventeenth century the rule of Richard gained a new constitutional significance, in the context of Stuart absolutist tendencies. The impeachment of leading royal officers by the Commons in the Parliaments of 1386 and 1388, and the Appeal of Treason against the king's chief advisers and friends by the Lords Appellant in the latter Parliament, strongly supported by the Commons, were interpreted as important constitutional precedents. In particular, the Commons' adaptation of the legal process of impeachment was seen as a powerful weapon against the arbitrary use of prerogative. These perspectives were to influence the 'Whig interpretation of history'. Bishop Stubbs's modern scholarly refinement gave new and lasting impetus to views which emphasized the constitutional significance of Richard's reign. Stubbs contrasted what he saw as the king's absolutist tendencies with the 'constitutionalism' of Henry IV. The Stubbsian view was fiercely rejected by K. B. McFarlane.[6]

How can the significance of Richard's rule be interpreted now? Recent scholarship has provided illumination. Dr John Palmer showed that the pursuit of peace with the French Crown was a persistent theme in

---

[4] For French hostility to Henry IV, P. Morgan, 'Henry IV and the Shadow of Richard II', in R. E. Archer (ed.), *Crown, Government and People in the Fifteenth Century* (Stroud, 1995), 13 ff. Dr John Palmer lists 37 MSS of the pro-Ricardian *Histoire de Richart Deux* ('The Authorship, Date, and Historical Value of the French Chronicles on the Lancastrian Revolution', *BJRL* 61 (1978–9), 36–7).

[5] M. Levine, *Tudor Dynastic Problems 1460–1571* (London, 1973), 23–4, 132–3. At Prince Edward's entry into Coventry in 1474, the figure who greeted him at the first pageant station was Richard II, who assured him that 'The right lyne of the Royall blode ys now as itt schulde be' (R. W. Ingram, *Records of Early English Drama: Coventry* (Toronto, 1981), 53). See also M. E. Aston, 'Richard II and the Wars of the Roses', in *Reign of Richard II*, 280–317. Dr Philip Morgan has shown how rumours of Richard's survival spread in Henry IV's reign and added to instability ('Henry IV and Richard II', 1–31). It is unlikely that popular memories of these uncertainties had been forgotten in 1461: Edward may have set out to exploit them then.

[6] R. H. Jones, *The Royal Policy of Richard II: Absolutism in the Later Middle Ages* (Oxford, 1968), 113–20; K. B. McFarlane, *Lancastrian Kings and Lollard Knights* (Oxford, 1972), 8–12, 24–5, 28, 55–6, 58, 99.

Richard's foreign policy.[7] It was pursued with diplomatic ingenuity and at times with reckless disregard for its domestic unpopularity. Richard is likely to have been swayed in the 1390s by current international enthusiasm for making peace in Christendom, ending the Schism, and relaunching the Crusade, but arguably his policy had long been based on a shrewd appreciation of how the Anglo-French war strained relations between Crown and community, and had objectives which were beyond the realm's resources. The magnitude of Richard's achievement in making a lengthy truce, but not the compromise peace which he had aimed at, is attested by the fact that peace was attained only in 1492 by Henry VII, but even then on terms which compromised none of the English Crown's claims. On the central issue in foreign affairs, Richard's pacific policy was fundamentally realistic and prescient. It collapsed under the Lancastrians, disastrously for Christendom and eventually to the detriment of English ambitions and unity. Henry V, though committed to the ideal of uniting Christendom to free the Holy Sepulchre, dealt Christendom a body-blow by his reckless prosecution of his claim to the French throne. In the year of Agincourt, it was his Portuguese cousins who fostered the crusading traditions of the House of Lancaster, as well as of their realm, by participating in their father João I's capture of Ceuta. Its occupation set in motion the Portuguese acquisition of wealth and empire, a more lasting and creative achievement than the internecine Lancastrian pursuit of an ephemeral empire in France, inflating English pretensions and overtaxing England's resources.[8]

In domestic affairs, Richard in one key respect set a pattern for the implementation of royal authority which, with varied emphasis, was to be characteristic of fifteenth-century kingship. Dr Chris Given-Wilson has shown how he significantly enlarged the 'royal affinity', particularly in periods in the 1390s, retaining 'king's knights' systematically and in large numbers.[9] The enhanced royal affinity had the potential to increase the effectiveness of royal government and the king's influence within local élites. However, Richard's notable retaining policy has the appearance of a showy propping-up of power rather than its careful reconstruction, mainly because it was interrupted by his deposition. The policy entailed the reversal of his support for the popular campaign to curtail the abuses associated with retaining. His affinity signally failed to provide effective

---

[7] *England, France and Christendom, 1377–1399* (London, 1972).

[8] Thomas Walsingham mentioned the capture of Ceuta, which, he asserted, had English help (*The St Albans Chronicle 1406–1420*, ed. V. H. Galbraith (Oxford, 1937), 98).

[9] *The Royal Household and the King's Affinity: Service, Politics and Finance in England 1360–1413* (New Haven, 1986), pt. 4.

military support against Henry of Lancaster's invasion in 1399, and few of his former retainers rallied to support the 'Epiphany plot' in 1400, intended to restore him to the throne. However, Richard's successors (notably Henry IV) set great store on drawing influential and able gentlefolk into their affinities. The Yorkist kings anchored the loyalties of such retainers particularly in the prestigious grant of household offices. In a century of often precarious usurping dynasties, a version of the Ricardian expedient became important as a mainstay of government. It was acceptable to the political community, to a degree which Richard's experiment was probably not, because it provided a means for kings whose subjects' hearts were cool towards them to seek stability, by staking out and confidently acting through a network of more committed supporters in the ranks of the gentry across the realm.[10]

Though certain of Richard's policies have earned him a new-found respect, judgement on his rule has in recent years been negative or, at best, apologetic. Professor Anthony Tuck demonstrated how he failed to convince much of the political establishment that he had their honour and profit sufficiently at heart. In the 1380s, and even more in 1397–9, his government aroused fears among the nobility that he was threatening their vital interests by overriding law and custom, and through ruling by his will alone.[11] Dr Given-Wilson has commented on Richard's 'wilful, vengeful temperament, and his unorthodox approach to the task of kingship', which 'had a destabilising effect on the politics of the reign and made him too many enemies'.[12] On the other hand, Dr Caroline Barron has asserted that, although aspects of his rule 'were arbitrary, uncustomary and bore heavily on certain individuals', these 'formed the normal small change of English medieval kingship'; it was unlikely that they were 'widely resented, or were so unpopular as seriously to undermine Richard's government'.[13] Dr Barron stresses the positiveness and prescience of his attempts to strengthen royal authority: 'Many of his initiatives in the last years of his reign were later taken up and developed in the "new monarchy" of the Yorkists and Tudors.'[14]

[10] D. A. L. Morgan, 'The King's Affinity in the Polity of Yorkist England', *TRHS*, 5th ser. 23 (1973), 1–25; cf. R. Horrox, *Richard III: A Study of Service* (Cambridge, 1989).

[11] *Richard II and the English Nobility* (London, 1973), 225.

[12] *Chronicles of the Revolution 1397–1400: The Reign of Richard II* (Manchester, 1993), 1. Richard II was notably merciful about shedding his opponents' blood. His tally of one execution and one (probable) assassination in 1397 compares favourably with the savagery of the Lords Appellant in 1388, and Henry IV's ruthless condemnation of Archbishop Scrope, among others.

[13] 'The Deposition of Richard II', in *Politics and Crisis*, 136; cf. 145.   [14] Ibid. 145.

Judgement on Richard's rule depends on whether one accepts his apparent conviction that social harmony was threatened by a trend to disregard or undermine divinely ordained royal authority—evidenced at its worst in the treatment of the 'martyr' Edward II—a trend which imposed on him a sacred duty to take resolute, even risky, counter-measures. Professor John Gillingham has defined the period from 1369 to 1415 as a 'time of troubles' for the Crown and political establishment, of disturbances which were familiar in nature but of unusual severity.[15] However, Professor Gillingham rejects the interpretation that these were 'symptoms of a change in the balance of power between king and subjects, of a crisis from which the crown emerged weaker than before'.[16] He argues that the socio-economic upheavals of the period had little impact on the structure of government.[17] For Gillingham, the brief crisis of kingship in the late 1390s was of Richard's own making. It arose because he was a 'poor politician' who was 'trying to put royal authority on a new and more arbitrary footing', and who failed because 'he was trying to swim against the tide of English political development'.[18]

Judgement on Richard's rule depends in some measure on whether or not we accept Gillingham's interpretation of political and constitutional trends: he has raised questions worth bearing in mind whilst reading the following chapters. They are intended as a contribution to the understanding of late medieval English government and society, and of Richard's character and rule, the significance of his policies, and the nature of his kingship. Topics with which they are concerned include ideology, conciliar and financial administration, diplomacy, political relationships, and cultural patronage.

In Chapter 2, John Taylor explores the difficulties which chroniclers had in stereotyping Richard as king, and in explaining some of his policies. The bias of chroniclers, and their lacunae, have hindered historians. Nevertheless, Taylor shows how, used with caution, chronicles can provide evidence about the king's personality. Other contributors, such as Professors Patricia Eberle and Eleanor Scheifele, provide insight into his intellectual preoccupations, particularly his interest in law and history.

Some chapters highlight a hardening of political attitudes and tensions, and deteriorations in diplomatic and economic circumstances in the later

---

[15] 'Crisis or Continuity? The Structure of Royal Authority in England 1369–1422', in R. Schneider (ed.), *Das Spätmittelalterliche Königtum Im Europäischen Vergleich* (Sigmaringen, 1987), 59.

[16] Ibid. 60.   [17] Ibid. 61–80.

[18] Ibid. 80. For discussions of the so-called 'tyranny', see below, pp. 53–7.

fourteenth century, which inhibited royal policy-making. Richard's interest in political history and constitutional precedent was not eccentric but fashionable in his youth among the well-educated laity. Notably, Edward III's decline and Richard's minority prompted the dusting-down of past schemes devised to attune the executive more firmly to the needs and aspirations of the common weal. In the 1370s it seems to have become received wisdom among parliamentary knights of the shire that blueprints for the organization of the King's Council, and the monitoring of conciliar performance in Parliament, were a means to deliver good government, and to deal with worrying domestic and foreign problems. The alarm of shire knights and their concern to influence government is understandable: problems stemming from the economy's structural instability, from the tensions and disorders associated with the grant of liveries and the formation of confederacies, and from the recovery of the French Crown were, indeed, pressing. Critical and interventionist currents of opinion among nobles and gentlefolk would have made it difficult for any young prince, except one of exceptional maturity, to assert his authority without arousing opposition in the 1380s. Moreover, Richard's attempts to exercise some of his rights of patronage in the traditionally often arbitrary royal manner were likely, Dr Given-Wilson suggests, to annoy nobles more than they had done, say, under Edward I or Edward III in his prime. The growth in the fourteenth century of precedents about the nature and rights of peerage, and the exercise by nobles of increasing tenurial freedom from feudal rules, produced points of conflict between Richard and the royal and magnatial kin-networks which constituted his natural allies, among whom resentments arose about his peerage creations and bestowal of important wardships. His attempts to ride roughshod over noble susceptibilities in order to reward intimate friends and servants generated disquiet, ill-will, and protest.

When noble rebellion broke out in 1387, headed by Richard's close kinsmen and by heads of families which had been close to Edward III, men of similar rank and background failed to give him military support. His hopes of receiving it from the City of London were soon dashed. Dr Barron shows how in the later fourteenth century there was intensification of economic and social tensions in the city, and a consequent rise in faction and disorder in the 1370s and 1380s, whose causes were strongly rooted in the effects of plague and depopulation. Richard had a harder time than Edward in ruling the city and gaining its goodwill. The need for him to compel order and obedience motivated his interventionist policies, in the 1380s in support of one or another faction, and in the 1390s in a more aloof and detached fashion, critical of the citizens as a body and harmful to their exercise of cherished communal privileges. Richard's new harshness helped to resolve the long-term crisis in London by stimulating fuller social harmony and more circumspect co-operation with the Crown. However, his policies failed to make him generally popular with the Londoners. In 1400 Henry IV looked with confidence to their support against Richard's restoration in the Epiphany plot.

The adverse situation which Richard inherited in war and diplomacy from his grandfather could not easily be reversed: the failure to do so decisively in the minority and after overshadowed and exacerbated domestic problems. In the context of the alliance made in 1381 with Wenzel king of the Romans, Professor Tuck shows how Richard continued the policy pursued in the minority of seeking allies against the French Crown in the Low Countries. This was a well-tried Plantagenet policy, yet it failed to produce a reliable ally, except the duke of Guelders, vigorous but marginal, and it exposed England to threats of French invasion from Flanders in 1385 and 1386. The dire imminence of invasion in the latter year was seen by the political community as an outrageous consequence of governmental dereliction. The underlying cause of English diplomatic failure in the Low Countries was the seemingly inexorable rise there of the power of Charles VI's well-placed and astute uncle, Philip the Bold, duke of Burgundy. Richard continued to perceive Burgundian influence as a threat to English security, but he lacked in the 1380s the diplomatic leverage or military power to prevent it, and in the 1390s he could only oppose it circumspectly without endangering the Anglo-French peace processes, in which Philip the Bold was a key player. Since political circumstance as well as underlying economic interest were to draw Duke Philip's Valois and Habsburg successors into English alliances, Richard's diplomatic failures in this important sphere did not damage long-term English interests.

The difficulties which the Crown had in financing its heavy expenditure on war in the first part of the reign, up to the truce of 1389, are well known. Overseas trade was characterized throughout the reign by a lack of buoyancy, adversely affecting the yield from indirect taxation, on which fourteenth-century English kings had set such store. Professor Mark Ormrod traces positive responses to the problem by Ricardian government, in the form of attempts at fiscal reform, which were pressed with vigour and some success in the 1390s. Richard secured acquiescence in the need for special indirect taxes when there was no active warfare taking place, and for their extension to new commodities. The sums raised contributed significantly to royal revenue in the 1390s. Professor Ormrod pronounces the fiscal reforms to have been 'the last attempts before Tudor times to reform the actual base on which indirect taxation was assessed'.

Constraints and problems at home and abroad which Richard faced as a novice were not entirely novel but they formed nasty concatenations. His policy responses cannot be dismissed as merely petulant or menacing yet that is how his mien and intent were on occasion recorded by chroniclers. His personality eluded them, as it eludes us. Perhaps his greatest personal failing was that he could not generate generally the feeling (so precious an adjunct for royal wilfulness) encapsulated in Shakespeare's phrase, 'a little touch of Harry in the night'.

The dice had not been loaded at Richard's accession in his favour. As a ruler, in many respects he turned out to be a conventional player. He constituted and used his Council and Great Councils in traditional ways. He attached great importance to hallowed royal cults and ceremonies. His cultural tastes were conventional, as Professors Eberle and Scheifele demonstrate. He enjoyed kingly sports and pastimes like a true Plantagenet. Dr Richard Davies shows that, in a period when ostentatious and dangerous pieties had an appeal to bookish layfolk—including some of Richard's knightly companions—he remained stodgily orthodox in his piety. This is consistent with the centrality which the cults of the Virgin and of royal saints had to his concept of English regality. Dr Davies points out how Richard resisted anticlerical blandishments to oppress the clergy by harsh taxation or disendowment—policies which might have ingratiated him with carping shire knights. No one, from the pope downwards—not even the ill-used Archbishop Arundel in 1399—could say that Richard had tyrannized over the clergy.[19] Perhaps he missed a golden opportunity to restore the wealth and popularity of an embattled Crown by turning on a widely criticized Church. Was this the greatest political failure of his reign?

Nevertheless, despite Richard's conventional habits, the hallmark of his rule was that it had unusual and novel features. Nigel Saul argues that, especially in his last years, Richard developed a coherent and strongly authoritarian theory of kingship, based on civilian precepts, and a programme for the projection and implementation of this theory. Richard's monarchism remained a matter of show rather than substance because he failed to induce the majority of his politically involved subjects to endorse it. Their sense of alienation is a recurring theme in this book. Yet Richard was introducing ways of elaborating royal power which were to be

---

[19] Items 22 and 29, in the Articles of Deposition, charged Richard with offences against the liberties of the Church (Given-Wilson (ed. and trans.), *Chronicles of the Revolution*, 179, 181).

characteristic of the later fifteenth and early sixteenth centuries, when, in a different climate of opinion, a more authoritarian style of kingship and stiffer enforcements of royal prerogative were acceptable or even welcome. In the 1390s in forms of address to himself, Richard fostered the replacement of the more customary language of lordship by that of princeliness and majesty, which distanced himself from his subjects, and emphasized his sovereignty.[20] The trend to address the king in terms like 'prince' and 'your majesty' was to stay: such verbal exaltation of the king was to be characteristic of the florid ways in which Tudor monarchs were to be apotheosized. Costume, furnishings, and displays at Richard's court and in his public ceremonies acquired memorable magnificence, especially in the 1390s; their decorative schemes and devices emphasized the divine sanctions and terrestrial glory of kingship. The costly elaborateness of the pageants laid on for the king's reconciliatory reception in London in 1392, and their theme of the exaltation of the prince, made it the precursor of princely entries into the city on special occasions, such as the celebration of victory at Agincourt, down to Tudor times.

Yet all this glitter failed to win the hearts of Richard's subjects to him, whereas later rulers considered, with justifiable confidence, that displays of majesty would help to win theirs. Hostile insinuation and fearful rumour spread in the wake of Richard's efforts in the late 1390s to strengthen his provincial power-base, the palatine earldom of Chester, and to enforce more fully the Lordship of Ireland. His interest in increasing royal power in the Marches of Wales and in Ireland were anticipations of Tudor policies. Professor Michael Bennett argues that Richard aimed to implement more fully imperial rule over the British Isles, whose precedents could be found in Geoffrey of Monmouth's 'British History', and in the ambitions of earlier Plantagenet kings and especially of Edward I. A possible clue to Richard's imperial concepts and aspirations may have been revealed by the recent cleaning of the Wilton Diptych, which shows that within the orb surmounting the red-cross banner, held by one of the angels accompanying the Virgin Mary, is the depiction of an island. This is roughly triangular, green, with trees on the horizon, and dominated by a white castle with two imposing corner towers. In the foreground a ship sails on the silver sea.[21] The island may represent Britain or the British Isles, with

---

[20] N. E. Saul, 'Richard II and the Vocabulary of Kingship', *EHR* 110 (1995), 854–77.

[21] D. Gordon, *Making and Meaning: The Wilton Diptych* (London, 1993), 57. According to Professor Gordon Kipling, an illumination in a MS commissioned by Henry VII (BL MS Royal II Exi, 2ʳ) portrays England as a sea-girt castle (*The Triumph of Honour* (Leiden, 1977), 112 and n. 39). The significance of the Diptych is discussed by several of the contributors to this book.

English strength and hegemony symbolized by the great white tower, and English naval defences and pretensions in the Channel by the ship. The red cross was the banner of St George, a crusading saint whose cult had been promoted by Edward I and Edward III.[22] In the Ordinances of War for Richard II's expedition to Scotland in 1385, chapter 18 laid down that everyone—of whatever estate, condition, or nation—in the army was to carry the sign of the arms of St George. This was repeated in Henry V's ordinances.[23] St George was closely associated with the cult of the Virgin Mary. This association may be reflected in the mural painting formerly at the east end of St Stephen's chapel, Westminster Palace, in the upper panel of which the Magi are depicted adoring the Virgin and Child. Underneath, in a lower panel, St George leads Edward III and his sons towards the altar, St George and Edward being positioned directly under the Virgin's throne.[24] The Virgin's relationship with the realm was being viewed by the later fourteenth century as a feudal one. Archbishop Arundel, in a mandate addressed to Bishop Braybrooke of London dated 10 February 1400, encouraged devotion to the cult of the Virgin as defender and protector of the nation. We are described, he said, as the servants of her own inheritance and liegemen of her special dowry ('veluti propriae suae haereditatis servuli, ac peculiaris dotis ascriptitii'). He attributed to her protection and intercession past English victories over other nations and the recent escape from the machinations of plotters—an emotionally charged reference to the Epiphany plot: he had narrowly escaped capture by the rebels.[25] The author of the *Gesta Henrici Quinti* wrote that in 1415 the fleet at

[22] D. A. L. Morgan, 'The Cult of St George *c.*1500: National and International Connotations', in J.-M. Cauchies (ed.), *L'Angleterre et les pays bourguignons: relations et comparaisons (XVe–XVIe)*, (Centre Européen d'Études Bourguignonnes (XIVe–XVIe s.), Neuchâtel, 1995), 153.

[23] T. Twiss (ed.), *The Black Book of the Admiralty*, i (RS, London, 1871), 456, 464. On the brasses of Sir Thomas Swynbourne (1412: Little Horkesley, Essex) and Sir Thomas Felbrigg (1416: Felbrigg, Essex), the armour appears to be shown as decorated with the cross of St George (M. Clayton (ed.), *Catalogue of Rubbings of Brasses and Incised Slabs* (Victoria and Albert Museum, London, 1968), pls. 15, 17).

[24] J. Alexander and P. Binski (edd.), *Age of Chivalry: Art in Plantagenet England, 1200–1400* (London, 1987), 499–500.

[25] D. Wilkins, *Concilia Magnae Britanniae et Hiberniae* iii (London, 1737), 246–7. I owe thanks to Dr Gary Dickson for drawing my attention to the citation of this mandate in D. Atwater, *A Dictionary of Mary* (London, 1957), 70. In his article 'Dowry, Our Lady's' (ibid. 70–1), the author traces the later history of the cult. The origin of the concept that England was the Virgin's dower is unclear. Perhaps it is an extension of the ideas contained in the Virgin's prophecy to St Thomas of Canterbury (T. A. Sandquist, 'The Holy Oil of St Thomas of Canterbury', in id. and M. R. Powicke (edd.), *Essays in Medieval History Presented to Bertie Wilkinson* (Toronto, 1969), 330–44). For Arundel's letter to the monks of Canterbury describing his narrow escape, J. B. Sheppard (ed.), *Literae Cantuarienses: The Letter Books of the Monastery of Christ Church, Canterbury* 3 (RS, London, 1889), 73–5.

Southampton, assembled for Henry's expedition to France, received a favourable wind on the Vigil of the Assumption of the Blessed Virgin— 'doing so at God's command as a result of the intercession of His Mother' ('compacientis, ut pie creditur, gentis dotis sue Anglie').[26] The description of England as the Virgin's dower is found in a fifteenth-century Salve Regina poem in English.[27] St George is sometimes referred to in English sources as 'Our Lady's knight',[28] and he can be found associated with her in the protection of the realm. In one of the Coventry pageants for Prince Edward (the future Edward V) in 1474, St George declared

> So shall I be your helpe vnto your lives fine
> To Withstonde your Enemyes with the help of that blessed virgyn
> The Whiche loveth you Right wel I dar playnly it say.[29]

The Virgin's relationships with St George and with England positioned the saint as her advocate, the defender of the *imperium* whose representation apparently tops his banner in the Wilton Diptych. Protestant susceptibilities were to obscure the fact that 'St George for England' was an invocation of a Marian cult. Richard appears to have strongly embraced this particular cult. In a lost altarpiece, formerly in Rome, he was depicted as holding 'the globe or patterne of England' before the Virgin. The altarpiece bore the inscription 'Dos tua Virgo pia haec est; quare rege Maria'.[30] This painting helps to illuminate the meaning of the Diptych. On this interpretation the banner held by the angel in the Diptych signifies her rule over England, upheld by her knight, and about to be entrusted to Richard, with the blessing Christ gives him, presumably at his Mother's petition.

The Wilton Diptych, I suggest, positions Richard within the strand of English political thought and action which promoted an imperial view of England's role in the British Isles—whose *locus classicus* is found in the arguments put forward by Thomas Polton at the Council of Constance in 1417.[31] The Diptych also suggests that Richard promoted the particular

---

[26] *Gesta Henrici Quinti* ed. F. Taylor and J. S. Roskell (Oxford, 1975), 144–5. I owe thanks for this reference to Professor Allmand.

[27] C. Brown and R. H. Robbins, *The Index of Middle English Verse* (New York, 1943), no. 3074. I owe thanks for this reference to Professor Nicholas Orme.

[28] N. Orme, 'Sir John Speke and his Chapel in Exeter Cathedral', *Trans. Devon Association for the Advancement of Sciences*, 118 (1986), 37.

[29] Ingram (ed.), *Records of Early English Drama: Coventry*, 55. Cf. St George's remarks in the pageant for the reception of Henry VII at Worcester in 1486, D. N. Klausner (ed.), *Records of Early English Drama: Herefordshire and Worcestershire* (Toronto, 1990), 113–15.

[30] Gordon (ed.), *Making and Meaning: The Wilton Diptych*, 58.

[31] C. M. D. Crowder, *Unity, Heresy and Reform 1378–1460: The Conciliar Response to the Great Schism* (London, 1977), 108–26.

Marian cult which, certainly by the later fifteenth century, was the affect-
ive force in the development of a popular sense of English nationality, as
reflected in parochial plays of St George and the Dragon, in the saint's
appearances in urban pageants, depictions of scenes from his sacred life
in church windows, and the greater use of George as a baptismal name.
Richard may have impressed these concepts on the future Henry V when
the latter was in his company in 1399. Henry was to show himself to be
a great devotee of St George.[32] Since the Diptych was ideally suited for
use on a portable altar, maybe Richard took it on his Irish expedition in
1399 as well as Henry; if so, perhaps the latter became familiar with the
Diptych, and reverenced its powerful exposition of the relations of king,
realm, and the sacred. The survival of the Diptych under Lancastrian rule
has been viewed as possibly subversive; it has been seen as an icon to a
deposed, but in Henry IV's reign (as Philip Morgan has expounded) perhaps still future, king. Maybe we have become too fixated with the image
of Richard in the Diptych. Perhaps it continued to be valued and cherished because its iconography perfectly encapsulated the spiritual agenda
of the late medieval English polity.[33] Indeed, might not the possessor and
preserver of the Diptych have been Henry of Monmouth?

It can be argued that the débâcle of 1399 was either a symptom of a
general crisis of kingship or the consequence of misjudgements and mis-
takes by a king who was a poor politician and who misread and exacerbated the problems which he faced. Either way, despite his conventional
virtues as a ruler, Richard emerges as in vital respects mediocre in the art
of kingship. He failed to give his subjects confidence in him. Nevertheless, his constructive thinking about the nature of royal authority, and the
measures which he undertook to project and underpin his vision of kingship, were influential in the development of the ideology of the English
monarchy and realm, and in the practicalities of effective rule. In Yorkist
and Tudor England, the historically minded were preoccupied with the
consequences of the failure of Richard's rule. Generations, in their eyes,
had suffered as a result of his deposition. They failed to recognize the
Ricardian image and substance of rule which had shaped positively, and
continued to shape, their political lives and environment.

[32] C. Allmand, *Henry V* (London, 1992), 91, 110, 170, 220, 415–16.
[33] For Lancastrian adherence to the cults of St Edward and St Edmund, ibid. 415–16.
For MSS owned by Edward IV containing imagery and heraldry associated with these cults,
J. Backhouse, 'Founder of the Royal Library: Edward IV and Henry VII as Collectors of
Illuminated Manuscripts', in D. Williams (ed.), *England in the Fifteenth Century: Proceedings
of the 1986 Harlaxton Symposium* (Woodbridge, 1987), 27, 37.

2

Richard II in the Chronicles

John Taylor

I

Although we possess his likeness in the Westminster abbey portrait, and almost certainly in the Wilton Diptych, Richard II lives principally in the chronicles and the literary sources. What relatively few letters of his survive throw an interesting though limited light upon his character and outlook.[1] For centuries the popular view of Richard has been determined by Shakespeare's play, where the portrait of Richard is heightened by the 'dramatic bid for tragedy', and where the image of the king derives ultimately from the Lancastrian chronicles and also from the propagandist French accounts of Creton and the author of the *Traison et Mort*, accounts which were known to Shakespeare through Holinshed. In the play, which is concerned with the theme of kingship, Richard the man gradually emerges from the trappings of office. On a human level he changes from the arrogant and feckless youth to the suffering king, a change dictated in part by these sources. In view of the fact that Shakespeare's view of Richard was conditioned by his chronicle sources, we need to look at them with some care, for through Shakespeare they have immensely influenced most subsequent writings. When we turn to the contemporary chronicles, consisting of narratives written in England, in Hainault, and in France, we find that we are dealing, the French narratives apart, with accounts which were the work of monks and secular clerks situated in different parts of the country. Their work may contain first-hand information. In certain

---

[1] E. Curtis, 'Unpublished Letters from Richard II in Ireland, 1394–1395', *Proceedings of the Royal Irish Academy*, 37 (1927), 276–303; M. D. Legge (ed.), *Anglo-Norman Letters and Petitions* (Anglo-Norman Text Soc., Oxford, 1941). For further discussion of Richard's character, see below, pp. 27–31.

cases, however, their narrative is little more than an annalistic record of historical events. It has been said with some truth that such compilations are not the most rewarding sources for the portrayal of human character. We might in fact be tempted to agree with the comment of one historian that, as depicted in these accounts, 'the heroes of the humourless narratives of the fourteenth century, Edward III, the Black Prince, John of Gaunt are but shadows of men'.[2] Yet whatever the truth of that statement, the character of Richard certainly lies buried beneath the conventions of fourteenth-century chronicle-writing. In considering the image of the king as depicted in these sources, therefore, we should first examine certain problems connected with the chronicles of the period. These problems may at first sight appear considerable, and it might be thought that this chapter could more aptly have been entitled 'problems in constructing a portrait of Richard from the chronicle sources', none the less it is hoped that some positive features may emerge in the course of these comments.

II

One problem which immediately confronts us in considering the image of Richard in the chronicle sources, is the possible rewriting of these accounts after 1399, and the propagandist intention of certain of the writings. Are the majority of Richard II chronicles simply a form of Lancastrian propaganda, written after the revolution, containing the 'second thoughts' of writers about the king, and unlikely therefore to show much sympathy or understanding of Richard? An older view of the revolution of 1399 was that it did indeed produce a revolution in historical writing in the sense that all writing not pro-Lancastrian was revised in a Lancastrian sense. According to this theory we should now have no chronicles written from Richard's viewpoint were it not for the fortunate survival of Walsingham's unexpurgated 'Scandalous Chronicle' (1376–7), the Monk of Westminster's well-balanced account, and the two French narratives, the *Traison et Mort* and Creton's *Metrical History*, which are strongly partisan in Richard's cause. That view requires considerable revision. Not all chronicles were rewritten after 1399, while in the case of Walsingham some change of opinion concerning Richard is also evident during the reign.[3]

---

[2] V. H. Galbraith, 'Good Kings and Bad Kings in English Medieval History', *History*, 30 (1945), 122.

[3] The fundamental work on the St Albans MSS is found in id., 'Thomas Walsingham and the St Albans Chronicle', *EHR* 47 (1932), 19–29, and *The St Albans Chronicle, 1406–1420*, ed. id. (Oxford, 1937). For a recent view of the sequence of St Albans MSS see G. B. Stow, 'Richard II in Thomas Walsingham's Chronicles', *Speculum*, 59 (1984), 68–102. See now C. Given-Wilson (ed. and trans.), *Chronicles of the Revolution, 1397–1400: The Reign of Richard II* (Manchester, 1993).

As we can tell from references in Walsingham's *Chronica Maiora*, Richard, who began in a great outburst of popularity in 1377, had by 1386 dissipated much of the goodwill felt towards him at St Albans.[4] Although chroniclers were careful in what they said, particularly during the period of Richard's personal government, in more than one case their tone became noticeably cooler as the reign progressed.

It is true, however, that the most comprehensive account of Richard II's reign, namely that written by Thomas Walsingham, was almost certainly revised after 1399. In the final versions of his *Chronica Maiora*, Walsingham, who appears to be the sole author of the St Albans accounts of this period, is strongly pro-Lancastrian and anti-Richard. This is largely due to the fact that part of the text of Walsingham's contemporary history, that is to say the part after 1392, survives only in late manuscripts written *c.*1420. It seems more than likely that the version of events contained in these manuscripts replaced an earlier account of the late 1390s written contemporary with the events themselves. None the less we also know that Walsingham revised parts of his chronicle not only after but during the reign. By a fortunate chance we possess early drafts of his contemporary history for the years 1376–7, which he appears to have removed from his *Chronica Maiora* before 1399. These early drafts dealt, however, not with Richard II but with Edward III, and they express Walsingham's dissatisfaction with Gaunt's conduct during the years 1376–7.[5] None the less in the succeeding part of his narrative describing the years from 1377 onwards, an account which was written up some two or so years at a time, we can trace a change of opinion concerning Richard himself. By the middle 1380s Walsingham's early enthusiasm for the young king had clearly changed. There was, for example, criticism of Richard's attachment to Robert de Vere, and the charge that the king had neglected to take the advice of his natural councillors.[6]

Walsingham's chronicle shows therefore a change of opinion concerning Richard during the reign. We can also say with some certainty that not all chronicles favourable to Richard were rewritten or revised after 1399. The rewriting of history after the Lancastrian revolution was carried out in no very systematic fashion, and parts of chronicles escaped revision. Thus

---

[4] See below, pp. 26–7.

[5] See Galbraith, 'Thomas Walsingham', and J. Taylor, *English Historical Literature in the Fourteenth Century* (Oxford, 1987), 59–73. On the chroniclers' attitude to Gaunt see A. Goodman, 'John of Gaunt: Paradigm of the Late Fourteenth Century Crisis', *TRHS*, 5th ser. 37 (1987), 133 ff.

[6] *Chron. Angl.* 353–4. *Hist. Angl.* ii. 148–9. On Walsingham's outlook see A. Gransden, *Historical Writing in England*, ii (London, 1982), ch. 5.

sections of certain Cistercian narratives which were not unfavourably disposed to Richard, and which appear to have been composed immediately
before 1399, were not revised. This can be seen in the case of the short
Kirkstall Chronicle, the first part of which was composed about 1397–8.[7]
In this section of his work the author appears to be favourably disposed
towards Richard.[8] In the latter part of the narrative, however, which may
belong to the early months of 1400, there was a more cautious tone.
Richard's policy in the years 1397–9 was passed over without comment.
A section of the official, Lancastrian-inspired *Record and Process* was transcribed in the text. Only towards the very end of the chronicle did the
writer venture a general remark that in the opinion of learned men the
cause of Richard's plight was his neglect of the greater lords and the reliance
he placed upon those inexperienced in weighty decisions.[9]

In a similar manner the first part of the Dieulacres Chronicle, a Cistercian narrative from a house close to the Welsh borders, appears to be a
pre-1399 account, completed immediately after 1399, by an author sympathetic to Richard. This section of the chronicle also escaped revision.
The author of the first part of the chronicle, which extends from 1333 to
1400, told the story of the reign from the viewpoint of the king. Actions
discreditable to Richard were glossed over. According to this account the
murder of Gloucester in 1397 was a mystery. By way of contrast the second section of the chronicle, which covers the years from 1400 to 1403,
was written by a monk of the house who was a supporter of the Percies.
He commented on the first section to the effect that there was much in it
which he found to be untrue. None the less he made no attempt to revise
the earlier narrative.[10] The text of the Whalley Chronicle (BL MS Harley
3600), written as a continuation of a *Polychronicon*, also seems to contain
an account of events in north Wales which was not the subject of later
rewriting.[11] Likewise the first section of the *Vita Ricardi Secundi*, which
extends as far as 1390, appears to be a contemporary account, and preserves a narrative generally favourable to Richard.[12]

[7] On these Cistercian narratives see Gransden, *Historical Writing*, 186–7, and Taylor,
English Historical Literature, 176–7, 190–2. The most recent comment is by C. M. Barron,
'The Deposition of Richard II', in *Politics and Crisis*, 134–5.

[8] See below, p. 25.

[9] *The Kirkstall Abbey Chronicles*, ed. J. Taylor (Thoresby Soc., Leeds, 1952), 83.

[10] On the Dieulacres Chronicle see M. V. Clarke and V. H. Galbraith, 'The Deposition
of Richard II', *BJRL* 14 (1930), 125–81.

[11] On the Whalley Chronicle see Taylor, *English Historical Literature*, 87, 193.

[12] *Vita*, 1–3. Note, however, the reference to Richard at the time of the Peasants' Revolt,
ibid. 65. Pt. 1 of the chronicle was probably composed *c*.1392 by Nicholas Herford.

We do therefore possess parts of chronicles containing contemporary views on the king written *c*.1397–1400, and which seemingly escaped revision after 1399. In considering the dating of the main chronicles, however, we have to recognize the fact that, despite the survival of these narratives, some very influential writing about Richard dates to a period after 1399, and was written with a propagandist intention in mind. This applies not solely to an important part of Walsingham's text (the section after 1392) but also to the French accounts by Creton and the author of the *Traison*. In the case of Creton, the composition of his *Metrical History*, an apologia for Richard, can be dated fairly accurately. Creton wrote an open letter to Richard II, which was composed before April 1402, and which mentions the *Metrical History*. The *Metrical History* itself records an event in August 1401. It must therefore have been written after that time, and before the date of this first letter, possibly early in 1402. Although it is not possible to date the *Traison* exactly, it is possible that it was written a little later than Creton's work.[13]

III

Problems other than those of dating are encountered in connection with the chronicles. What is lacking in Richard II's reign, as indeed in the reigns of most English medieval kings, is any kind of official history. This deficiency is relevant to our understanding of Richard. An officially inspired history might well have given us a totally different picture of Richard to the one discovered in the chronicles which do survive. Why medieval England failed to produce official history on the lines of the *Grandes Chroniques* in France is a question not easily answered.[14] It may be thought that the abbey of Westminster was the place most likely to have developed into a centre of officially inspired chronicle-writing. The monastery was at the centre of political events, and was the burial place of kings such as Edward the Confessor and Henry III. Yet there was no officially inspired history at Westminster, no official historiographer, and no continuous tradition of chronicle-writing in the abbey. The excellent Westminster Chronicle which describes a part of Richard II's reign is not official history. We may even hesitate to describe it as a 'Ricardian chronicle', for

[13] On the French chronicles see J. J. N. Palmer, 'The Authorship, Date, and Historical Value of the French Chronicles of the Lancastrian Revolution', *BJRL* 61 (1978–9), 145–81, 398–421; also Taylor, *English Historical Literature*, 175–94.

[14] Taylor, *English Historical Literature*, 45–7. The comments of C. Given-Wilson, *The Royal Household and the King's Affinity: Service, Politics and Finance in England, 1360–1413* (New Haven, 1986), 262 on court chroniclers are worth noting. On the subject of official history see A. Gransden, 'Propaganda in English Medieval Historiography', *JMH* 2 (1975), 363–81.

it is in no way a consistent apologia for the king. It is, however, an excellent, well-balanced, and informative account, and one that was certainly written before 1399.[15] None the less an official history or a court chronicle might well have added a new dimension to our understanding of Richard.

In addition to these features we have to bear in mind the conventions under which fourteenth-century chronicles were composed. The writing of chronicles was often a task imposed upon a monk in a particular religious house where one important consideration was the need to keep a dated record of historical events. Although there were gifted individuals who wrote chronicles, including secular clerks like Adam of Usk, or monks such as those at Westminster whose outlook transcended what has been described as 'the hazy group consciousness' which arguably was one feature of medieval monastic life, we should not expect too much by way of individual character-drawing in their work. Renaissance historiography in England was more than a century away, and medieval chroniclers were not concerned with exploring the finer shades of human character. On the whole they saw individuals as types, 'accidents occurring in a substance', and had little notion of the development of human personality. Gaunt, for example, may have matured during his later years. To explain this Walsingham describes a dramatic repentance on the part of Gaunt after his return from Spain in 1389.[16]

In particular we should recognize that even the most talented of chroniclers lived and wrote under a different dispensation from that of modern historians. They judged rulers mainly by their military prowess and by their relationship with the Church, including in the case of chroniclers at St Albans and Westminster, the particular relationship of the king with their monastic community. By these criteria Richard, although orthodoxly pious, must have been judged, as regards his military achievements, to fall well below the standards set by Edward III and the Black Prince. The fulfilment or non-fulfilment of his kingly role in other areas, as for example, in his relationship with the magnates, must also have entered into the chroniclers' judgements. None the less loyalty to the Crown as an office was again a powerful factor, and one that might counterbalance other criticisms.

Because of the limitations in the chroniclers' outlook, some historians have fallen back in the case of Richard II upon such short-hand descriptions as 'the last of the medieval kings' and 'a man of crises who slept in

---

[15] *Westm. Chron.* For a discussion of this chronicle, see below, pp. 25–6.
[16] *Hist. Angl.* ii. 194.

their intervals', or have seen Richard as 'a mumbling neurotic sinking rapidly into a state of acute melancholia'.[17] A study of the chronicle sources lends substance to none of these views. It is, however, more difficult to say exactly what kind of person emerges from the chronicle sources. It may be that Richard fell outside the normal range of the chroniclers' types. He was neither a successful warrior like Henry V, this 'star of England', nor, although pious, a ruler of extreme piety like Edward the Confessor. To a certain extent his personality eluded the formulas of the chroniclers. None the less, it can be said that, despite the limitations inherent in fourteenth-century chronicle-writing, there is probably more evidence concerning Richard's person in these sources than is the case with either Edward II or Edward III.[18]

In emphasizing the problems inherent in evaluating the chronicle evidence, one further factor is that certain episodes concerning the king depend upon the testimony of a single source. Henry Knighton, an Austin canon of St Mary's Leicester, probably never witnessed events in the city of London. None the less his chronicle is our sole authority for certain episodes at the start of the Wonderful Parliament, when according to his narrative the king withdrew to Eltham.[19] To the demand for the removal of the chancellor and treasurer, Richard replied in a well-known comment that he would not remove the humblest scullion from his office at the request of the Commons. Rejecting the king's proposal that they send to him a deputation of forty knights, Parliament conveyed their terms to the king at Eltham in the persons of Gloucester and Thomas Arundel. The two delegates told the king that he was bound to hold Parliament once a year, and met his threat of invoking French aid by a declaration of their power, based on a non-existent statute, to depose an incompetent king. The threat produced its desired effect, and the king appeared at Westminster.[20] Thus far Knighton, in a passage which is quoted in most histories of the reign. Yet Knighton was almost certainly not an eyewitness of these events, and his reliability is often open to question.[21] None the less the transcription of several documents relating to the Wonderful Parliament in his chronicle suggests that on this occasion he had access to a well-informed source.[22]

The well-known story of Richard's demand that his subjects kneel when his glance fell upon them at court is again related in a single source.

[17] A. Steel, *Richard II* (Cambridge, 1941), 279, offers this last judgement.
[18] See below, pp. 27–31.   [19] Knighton, 215–25.   [20] Ibid.
[21] See e.g. the comments by J. J. N. Palmer, 'The Parliament of 1385 and the Constitutional Crisis of 1386', *Speculum*, 46 (1971), 490.
[22] Knighton, 215–33.

This account of Richard's behaviour belongs to the years 1398 and 1399, and appears in an individual continuation of the *Brut* known as 'An English Chronicle'. The chronicle derives much of its information from the Franciscan text found in the continuation of the *Eulogium Historiarum*. As the derivative account in *An English Chronicle* goes, Richard would sit silently in full regalia before his court from dinner to vespers. 'Aftir this, the kyng . . . (would) make in his chambir a trone, wherynne he was wont to sitte fro aftir mete unto evensong tyme, spekynge to no man, but overlokyng alle menn, and yf he loked on eny mann, what astat or degre that evir he were of, he moste knele'.[23] If this description is accurate, as it may well be, Richard's behaviour may have had its origins in memories of the court of the Black Prince. The Anonimalle Chronicle, for example, says of the Black Prince at Bordeaux in 1367 that he was 'si hauteyn et de si graunt port' that he made some suitors wait four or five days before seeing them, and would only allow them to approach him kneeling.[24]

We may take as one final example of this type of problem the story found in the Whalley Chronicle of a deposition of Richard after the battle of Radcot Bridge in 1387. This chronicle is alone in its statement that Woodstock, Arundel, and Warwick deposed Richard for three days but, failing to agree on a successor, restored him to the throne.[25] The passage should, however, be compared with the statement in the Westminster Chronicle which speaks only of a threat of deposition by the Appellants, and which goes on to say that 'the suggestion was opposed by the earl of Warwick, who hastened to recall the lords from this way of thinking'.[26] The text of Gloucester's confession in 1397 with its suggestion of an earlier renunciation of allegiance, should almost certainly be read in the light of this threat of deposition, of which the Whalley Chronicler's account may well be an exaggerated version.[27]

Problems such as these by no means exhaust the difficulties posed by the chronicles. It is clear, for example, that chroniclers vary in the amount of material which they supply concerning Richard. Walsingham and the Westminster Chronicle have, relatively speaking, a good deal to say about

---

[23] *An English Chronicle of the Reigns of Richard II, Henry IV, Henry V, and Henry VI, 1377–1461*, ed. J. S. Davies (London, 1856), 12. For the account in the *Eulogium Historiarum*, see below, p. 40.

[24] *Anonimalle Chronicle, 1333–1381*, ed. V. H. Galbraith (Manchester, 1927), 56. See the comments of P. Shaw, 'The Black Prince', *History*, 24 (1940), 9; also G. Mathew, *The Court of Richard II* (London, 1968), 15.

[25] M. V. Clarke, *Fourteenth Century Studies*, ed. L. S. Sutherland and M. McKisack (Oxford, 1937), 91–5.

[26] *Westm. Chron.* 218–19.   [27] Clarke, *Fourteenth Century Studies*, 91–5.

the king. Their accounts tend, therefore, to colour our view of Richard. On the other hand certain chronicles such as the prose *Brut* have relatively little new light to cast on the subject of Richard.[28] Concerning Froissart's information it has been said that 'it is doubtful whether an historian could analyse the character of the king on the basis of what Froissart wrote'.[29] Again there are aspects of Richard's character, such as his supposed literary and artistic interests, which find little, if any, expression in the chronicle sources.

IV

One major difficulty in considering the image of Richard in the chronicle sources is the fact that politically no common view of him emerges in these texts. 'Politics', that is to say the relations between king and magnates, were of paramount importance in fourteenth-century England and, compiling what were in effect political narratives, chroniclers viewed Richard primarily in this context. It was essentially Richard's role in the intermittent struggle with the magnates that concerned them. According to the nature of their support for the Lancastrian regime, their sympathy with the deposed king, or their involvement with the interests of some great magnate, chroniclers took opposing views of Richard, and imputed different motives to him.

Writing in the shadow of the Lancastrian revolution almost all chroniclers in England after 1399 cast Richard in an unfavourable light. It was Richard's faults of government, and in particular his reliance on unworthy advisers, that had cost him the throne. In the last analysis he had proved unworthy of the office of kingship. To buttress the Lancastrian cause such writers depicted Richard at Conway and in the Tower resigning his throne willingly, 'with a smiling face [*vultu hilari*]', as though 'bored with all this kingship'.[30] The type of libel produced against deposed monarchs in later ages was also used against Richard. Thus Adam of Usk says of the birth

---

[28] *Brut or the Chronicles of England*, ed. F. W. D. Brie (2 vols., EETS, London, 1906–8), ii. 335–59.

[29] Froissart, xvi. 54. For a view that Froissart's portrayal of Richard was generally unfavourable see G. B. Stow, 'Richard II in Jean Froissart's *Chroniques*', *JMH* 11 (1985), 333–43.

[30] The St Albans narrative is at this point a good example of Lancastrian history, *Hist. Angl.* ii. 233–7. On Lancastrian propaganda see the comments of Gransden, *Historical Writing*, 140, 186–8; id., 'Propaganda in English Medieval Historiography', 368; and Stow, 'Thomas Walsingham's Chronicles'. A useful analysis of the chronicles is found in L. D. Duls, *Richard II in the Early Chronicles* (The Hague, 1975), although her classification of the chronicles must be treated with caution.

of Richard 'that much evil report was noised abroad, as of one sprung not from a father of royal race, but from a mother given to slippery ways of life'.[31] Writing outside England, Froissart reports a dialogue between Richard and Henry in the Tower in 1399 in which it was alleged that Richard was not the son of the Black Prince, but of a clerk or canon.[32] Froissart recounts an episode to the effect that, when staying in 1361 in the manor of Berkhamsted belonging to the Black Prince, he heard an old knight called Sir Bartholomew Burghersh saying to the queen's maids-of-honour that, according to a book called the *Brut*, 'which many people believe to be the prophecies of Merlin . . . the crown of England shall not pass to the Prince of Wales, nor to the Duke of Clarence, nor to the present Duke of Lancaster, nor to the Duke of York, nor to the Duke of Gloucester, although they are sons of King Edward, but it will return to the house of Lancaster'.[33]

Despite such views Richard did not lack defenders. Writing in France, Creton, the author of the *Traison*, and the Monk of St Denys, produced a very different political profile of the king. According to their accounts, and to that of Creton in particular, Richard was not only the legitimate king, but a worthy ruler. He had been tricked into surrender at Conway, and led as a prisoner to Flint.[34] Their view of what transpired in the Tower, and in the so-called 'Deposition Parliament', conflicted with the official Lancastrian version of events.[35] Concerned as they were with demonstrating the illegitimacy of the Lancastrian cause, their narratives also sought to influence opinion through the portrait of a 'martyr king' who had fought and suffered in defence of kingship. To this end Creton and the author of the *Traison* depicted Richard at times, 'weeping most tenderly and greatly lamenting his lot', while at other times fiercely denouncing his betrayers, and offering to prove his charge against 'any four of the best of you, with my body, like a loyal knight as I am'.[36] As with the Lancastrian accounts this image of the king was fashioned in accordance with the political sympathies of the writers. Despite such writings, however, the legend of a martyr king failed to take hold in fifteenth-century England. No poems

---

[31] Adam of Usk, 180–1.   [32] Froissart, xvi. 200.

[33] Ibid. 235. On Froissart's attitude to Richard see n. 29, above.

[34] The most important study of these events is that by Clarke and Galbraith, 'Deposition of Richard II', 125–63. For a recent account see J. Sherborne, 'Perjury and the Lancastrian Revolution of 1399', *Welsh Hist. Rev.* 14 (1988), 217–41. See also Given-Wilson (ed. and trans.), *Chronicles of the Revolution 1397–1400.*

[35] For a detailed account of the contents of the chronicles for this period see Duls, *Early Chronicles,* 112–54.

[36] The first passage occurs in J. Creton, 'Translation of a French Metrical History of the Deposition of Richard II', ed. and trans. J. B. Webb, *Archaeologia,* 20 (1824), 157. The second is found in the *Traison et Mort,* 217–18.

or ballads celebrated the memory of the deposed monarch, while in England the 'afterlife' of Richard only began in the Tudor age when his overthrow was depicted as the start of the troubles of the fifteenth century.[37] Even before 1399, however, different views of Richard had prevailed. Not surprisingly some chroniclers wrote their histories with a bias in favour of the reigning king. Others gave hardly any indication of a political sympathy. Almost alone among contemporary writers, Walsingham ventured on outright criticism of Richard in the period before the Wonderful Parliament. Almost certainly representative of one important strand in contemporary opinion were the authors of the short Kirkstall Chronicle, the first part of the Dieulacres Chronicle, and the opening section of the *Vita Ricardi Secundi*, all of whom supported Richard as the reigning king. Thus in the opening section of the *Vita* events in the aftermath of the Peasants' Revolt, and during the Scottish expedition of 1385, were related from the viewpoint of the king.[38] The first part of the Dieulacres Chronicle was written by an author sympathetic to Richard.[39] In the short Kirkstall Chronicle the author wrote in support of Richard for almost the whole of his narrative. Indicative of his attitude at this time was his comment on the Parliament of 1397: 'Astonishing indeed is the long suffering of the King. Of late the sun has been concealed by a cloud, that is to say the King's majesty beneath an alien power, but now in arms he bounds on the mountains, and leaps over the hills.'[40] This account appears to be the work of a writer who was loyal to Richard, but who was obliged in 1399 to change allegiance and recognize the Lancastrian seizure of the throne. The desirability of supporting 'whatsoever king may reign' almost certainly influenced the viewpoint of other contemporaries.[41]

A more complex political treatment of Richard is found in the Westminster Chronicle. The account which covers the years from 1381 to 1394 may have been put together in its present form during the 1390s.[42] If so, it was almost certainly based in its opening sections on drafts which were composed during the previous decade. For the events of the 1380s the

---

[37] M. E. Aston, 'Richard II and the Wars of the Roses', in *Reign of Richard II*, 280–317. The very different posthumous treatment of Richard and Thomas of Lancaster in the literary sources is worth noting.

[38] *Vita*, 2.

[39] See the introd. to the Dieulacres Chronicle repr. in Clarke, *Fourteenth Century Studies*, 53–98.

[40] *Kirkstall Abbey Chronicles*, ed. Taylor 75. See above, p. 18.

[41] See Barron's remarks in 'Deposition of Richard II', to the effect that Richard had not lost all support prior to 1399.

[42] *Westm. Chron.*, pp. xxii–xxxi. See also A. Gransden, 'The Westminster Chronicles, 1381–1394', *Nottingham Medieval Studies*, 28 (1984), 95–103.

chronicle has all the hallmarks of contemporary reporting. Although the chronicle has been described as 'mildly Ricardian' we cannot say that it is either royalist or baronial in sympathy. If the early part of the narrative relates incidents not entirely to Richard's credit, the king's wise and moderating actions are stressed in the latter part of the work,[43] while even as early as 1383 the chronicler commended Richard for acting 'with great shrewdness and discernment' on the occasion of a Parliament that year.[44] It may be that a combination of influences lay behind the emergence of this narrative, including not only the royal presence at Westminster but also Thomas of Woodstock who was, too, a frequent visitor to the abbey. The result is a chronicle which, in the case of Richard, is neither over-critical nor profoundly partisan. Possibly because of the cross-currents at Westminster, the need for discretion, and also the different periods of the reign to which parts of the chronicle belong, no clear political attitude towards Richard emerges in this work.

By way of contrast Walsingham is the one chronicler who voiced outright criticism of the king early in the reign. In his attitude to Richard, Walsingham was no doubt sustained by the long and independent tradition of chronicle-writing at St Albans and possibly also by the encouragement of his abbot, Thomas de la Mare, who may well have had some association with the baronial opposition. It should also be borne in mind that St Albans did not enjoy a particularly favoured relationship with the king who, in the disputes between St Albans and Westminster, was seen as 'an especial favourer and promoter of Westminster'. As regards Walsingham's own work, if his viewpoint on the reign was not quite 'the medieval equivalent to the Whig view of history', his chronicle was the work of a man who had a viewpoint none the less and whose narrative rose significantly above the dull conformity of much contemporary writing.[45] His outspoken criticism, 'the extravagance of his prejudices', concerning not only Richard but also figures such as Gaunt and Wycliffe, render Walsingham's work of particular interest, especially for the light which his writing casts on contemporary attitudes.

As regards Walsingham's treatment of Richard, it seems that Walsingham began in 1377 with a hope for kingship, which he quickly came to see was not destined to be realized in the person of the king. When Richard

---

[43] *Westm. Chron.* 122–3.

[44] Ibid. 55. For a further discussion of this chronicler's views on Richard, see below, pp. 28–9.

[45] On the St Albans tradition of chronicle writing in the 14th cent. see Gransden, *Historical Writing*, 118–56. V. H. Galbraith's *Roger Wendover and Matthew Paris* (Glasgow, 1944) is still very much worth consulting for the earlier tradition.

came to the throne, however, Walsingham was rapturous in his comments. He spoke favourably of an attempt by Richard to reconcile Gaunt and William Wykeham, bishop of Winchester.[46] The highest expectations were held of this son of the Black Prince. None the less Walsingham's attitude soon changed. Under 1383, in a section of his chronicle which was written contemporary with events, Walsingham spoke of the 'inconstantia regis' in connection with the election of the abbot of Bury St Edmunds, adding the comment, 'vae terrae cuius rex puer est'.[47] During the 1390s Walsingham became even more critical. His comments at the time of Richard's *coup d'état* of 1397 may be taken as typical of his attitude.[48] Although this part of Walsingham's chronicle was almost certainly redrafted after 1399 and reflects a Lancastrian interest, none the less throughout most of Richard's reign Walsingham adopted a critical attitude, anticipating the views of those who, living with Richard, decided against him in the end.

V

To a considerable extent the divergence of political views on Richard in the chronicle sources is explained by the Lancastrian revolution and by factors peculiar to monasteries such as St Albans. A greater consensus of opinion is found when we consider the statements of chroniclers concerning Richard's own person. Even in the jejune accounts of the chroniclers, Richard is no stereotype, no 'cardboard cutout', but a living person, and aspects of his character come through in the chronicles with greater clarity than is the case perhaps with any other fourteenth-century ruler. Despite their differing political assessments, chroniclers often agree in fact in their impression of Richard the man. Although Richard's personality is considered elsewhere, it may be appropriate here to mention one or two features concerning the chroniclers' treatment of Richard's person.

As regards his physical appearance Richard appears to have had no obvious physical feature or disability such as might have attracted the chroniclers' attention.[49] Certain chroniclers emphasized the fact that Richard was a handsome man. Adam of Usk at the beginning of his chronicle says of Richard that he was 'si secundus Apsalon pulcherimus' ('fair among

---

[46] *Chron. Angl.* 150.   [47] *Hist. Angl.* ii, 97.

[48] *Annales*, 201. Walsingham says that Richard 'through his cunning, vanity, and insolence' threw the realm into uproar by the arrest of Gloucester, Arundel, and Warwick.

[49] The most common characteristic of Richard as noted in the chronicles was perhaps not a physical one, but his failure to take sound advice. It was a poet and not a chronicler, however, who summed him up as 'Richard the Redeles'. For portrayals of Richard, see below, pp. 263–71.

men as another Absalom').[50] A valuable description written after Richard's
deposition is found in the second part of the *Vita Ricardi Secundi*. The
author says that Richard 'was of the common stature, his hair yellowish,
his face fair, round, and feminine, sometimes flushed, abrupt and stammer-
ing in his speech, capricious in his manners'.[51] Although this description,
from a not entirely friendly source, requires some qualification (Richard
appears to have been over 6 feet tall), it conveys perhaps a not entirely
misleading impression of his physical appearance. Richard seems, for
example, to have flushed easily, and chroniclers, including Froissart, refer
to his quick change of colour.[52]

The chronicles are again our main source of evidence for the traditional
view of Richard's character. They emphasize such features as his extravagance, his attachment to favourites, and his volatile and unstable nature.
This latter characteristic appears to be well established. It is remarked on
in a number of sources, most notably in the Westminster Chronicle. If we
allow one incident to stand for many, we may take the episode related in
this chronicle concerning Richard in the Salisbury Parliament of 1384.
According to the Westminster account, in the course of this Parliament
Richard, 'white with passion [*torvo vultu*]', said to Arundel that if 'it is
supposed to be my fault that there is misgovernment in the kingdom, you
lie in your teeth. You can go to the Devil.' We are told that 'a complete
hush followed as these words were heard'.[53] How reliable is this account?
As previously mentioned, the Westminster Chronicle portrays Richard
behaving with greater moderation on later occasions. We are informed, for
example, of the king's wise and soothing reply to his half-brother, Sir John
Holand.[54] There are other instances of Richard's later moderation, and it
has been said that the 'later Richard behaves like a real person' while 'the
early Richard (the one given to outbursts) more resembles a caricature'.[55]
It is just possible therefore that the Westminster account of incidents involving the king during the early 1380s contains an element of exaggeration.
None the less evidence of Richard's intemperate nature is found elsewhere, while the Westminster account of these incidents carries a note of

[50] Adam of Usk, 1.
[51] *Vita*, 166. This famous description occurs in pt. 2 of the narrative. The description is
also found in an unpublished portion of Giles Chronicle (BL Royal 13, C.1), which at this
point is a variant of the *Vita*. It is printed in the *Traison et Mort*, 295. See Clarke, *Fourteenth
Century Studies*, 78–81. I am grateful to Prof. G. B. Stow for drawing my attention to this
reference.
[52] Froissart, xvi. 184.   [53] *Westm. Chron.* 68–9.   [54] Ibid. 122–3.
[55] Ibid., p. lxxiii. None the less, similar episodes are reported in the 1390s, see *Hist. Angl.*
ii. 215.

conviction. It seems almost certain in fact from the chronicle evidence that Richard's uncertain temper was one important factor in a life which was lived in public.

The Westminster Chronicle also provides a warning against forming an impression of Richard exclusively from a printed text. As the Westminster Chronicle first appeared in the Rolls Series edition, the text says that in 1384 a Carmelite friar approached Richard, and told him that his uncle the duke of Lancaster was plotting against his life. As the text was printed and frequently quoted, 'Richard, nervous and highly strung at all times, now completely lost self control. He behaved like a madman, took off his hat and shoes, and threw them out of the window.' Unfortunately for those who have used the incident to illustrate the king's unstable nature, the editor misread his original. From an examination of the manuscript at this point it is clear that the scribe transposed certain passages. When the narrative is rearranged it appears that it was not the king but the Carmelite friar who, shamming insanity, took off his cap and shoes, and threw them out of the window.[56]

Despite such qualifications the general reliability of the chronicle evidence concerning Richard's person is often confirmed by the record sources.[57] Aspects of Richard's character and outlook, mentioned in the chronicles, can frequently be traced in the records. Thus Richard's explosive temper is, for example, amply confirmed by the record evidence. A grant from the king to Robert de Vere in the 1380s concludes with the words, 'the curse of God, and Saint Edward and the King on any who do or attempt ought against this grant'.[58] A writ issued under the Privy Seal and dated 9 April 1395 shows that after the death of his wife Richard did destroy the buildings at Sheen as the chronicles state.[59] Richard's interest in books and literary affairs, reported by Froissart, is again confirmed by entries on the Exchequer records.[60] His fiscal policies during the period 1397–9, which are mentioned in several accounts, were no figment of

[56] H. L. Hector, 'An Alleged Hysterical Outburst of Richard II', *EHR* 68 (1953), 62–5. The MS is in Corpus Christi College, Cambridge, MS 197A.

[57] See the excellent account by G. B. Stow, 'Chronicles versus Records: The Character of Richard II', in J. S. Hamilton and P. J. Bradley (edd.), *Documenting the Past: Essays to George Peddy Cuttino* (Wolfsboro, NH, 1989), 155–76, to which several of the following comments are indebted.

[58] *CPR 1381–1385*, 542. This concerned the grant to Vere on 13 Mar. 1385 of the castle and lordship of Queenborough, where Vere was to flee later after the battle of Radcot Bridge.

[59] *King's Works*, ii. 998. The incident is related in the *Vita*, 134, and Adam of Usk, 9.

[60] Froissart, xv. 140–67. See the account in Stow, 'Chronicles versus Records', 167, and the literature quoted there. The nature of Richard's literary interests has been the subject of some debate.

the chroniclers' imagination.[61] Finally Richard's extravagance, which features prominently in several narratives, is also well attested in the record sources, which provide evidence both of his lavish use of patronage, and his personal expenditure on clothes and jewellry.[62]

Concerning Richard's views on kingship the chronicles provide only limited information.[63] Although the loyalty of religious houses to the political interests of their patrons comes through in several of these accounts (notably in the Leicester chronicle of Henry Knighton), most chronicles display a limited range of 'political ideas'. Even Walsingham in his account of the Good Parliament sees that event rather as a personal drama than as a 'constitutional crisis'.[64] As regards monarchy, chroniclers at the most took their stand on the proposition that kingship should function with the help of good counsel. Lacking any form of sophisticated political analysis, it is difficult to tell from the chronicle texts therefore whether in his policies Richard was intending to put the clock forward (and anticipate Stuart notions of Divine Right) or back (and recover what he regarded as the lost prerogatives of the Crown). None the less their essentially factual approach enabled the chroniclers to report Richard's speeches, and record his actions. From this reporting we see something of the emphasis which he placed on his regality and upon the outward marks of kingship. As early as 1381, as recorded in the Anonimalle Chronicle, Richard's words to Wat Tyler contain the phrase 'sauvant a luy la regaltee de sa corone'.[65] In 1385 the Westminster Chronicle mentions Richard's 'eagerness to have from everybody the deference properly due to his kingship'.[66] The same source says that when Richard was threatened with deposition in 1387 he yielded to the Appellants only, 'salva corona sua ac etiam regia dignitate'.[67] According to Creton Richard, in the final period of his reign, felt that he was standing for a principle, and that 'his troubles were an outrage on all kings'.[68] The particular emphasis which Richard placed on the outward

(margin annotation: Regality)

---

[61] The best account of Richard's financial measures is found in C. M. Barron, 'The Tyranny of Richard II', *BIHR* 41 (1968), 1–18. For chronicle accounts of these measures see e.g. *Annales*, 234–5; *Eulogium Historiarum sive Temporis*, ed. F. S. Haydon, 3 vols. (RS, London, 1858–63), iii. 378.

[62] *Westm. Chron.* 161–3, has a well-known passage on Richard's extravagance; see Stow, 'Chronicles versus Records', 159, 165 ff. For a study of Richard's later use of patronage see R. A. K. Mott, '*A Study in the Distribution of Patronage 1389–1399*', Ph.D. thesis (Leeds, 1974), 113–33. We should not necessarily believe, however, that Richard's personal extravagance was greater in degree than that of many of his contemporaries.

[63] For Richard's views on kingship and for a valuable study of the reign generally see V. H. Galbraith, 'A New Life of Richard II', *History*, 26 (1942), 223–39. See also below, pp. 48–50.

[64] J. Taylor, 'The Good Parliament and its Sources', in *Politics and Crisis*, 85–8.

[65] *Anonimalle Chronicle*, 147.   [66] *Westm. Chron.* 139.   [67] Ibid. 229.

[68] Creton, 'Translation of a French Metrical History', 339.

symbols of kingship was also thought worthy of record.[69] Concerning the personal arms of the king, the *Annales Ricardi Secundi* says that Richard added the arms of the Confessor to his shield after the Shrewsbury Parliament.[70] According to the *Vita Ricardi Secundi* Richard's famous livery of the white hart with a crown or gold chain was first given by the king at the Smithfield tournament in October 1390.[71] The *Annales Ricardi Secundi* notes that at the wedding of Richard and Isabella, Charles VI wore on his breast the hart as a livery of the king of England.[72]

Other evidence of Richard's interest in the sacred character of kingship is perhaps more contentious. In his chronicle Walsingham tells the story that when Richard, who was something of an antiquary, 'curiosus perscrutator rerum progenitoribus relictarum', was rummaging in the Tower in the 1390s he came across several chests. Discovering one which was locked, he ordered it to be broken open, and in it he found an eagle containing an ampulla of holy oil which according to a prophecy Becket had meant to be used for the anointing of future kings. On hearing of the prophecy Richard asked the archbishop of Canterbury to anoint him with the oil. The archbishop refused, taking the view that one anointment was sufficient for any king. Richard desisted in his attempts, but none the less carried the oil with him to Ireland. The difficulty with this passage is that it was almost certainly written by Walsingham after 1399, and carries with it the suspicion of being a form of Lancastrian propaganda. None the less, despite its use by the Lancastrians, the account may well contain some element of truth concerning Richard's own outlook.[73]

VI

Whatever the limitations of the chronicles, and the differing attitudes of chroniclers, the portrait of Richard in these sources depends in part also upon the nature of the chroniclers' acquaintance with the king. How well did the chroniclers know Richard? The extent of their knowledge inevitably coloured their descriptions and helped to form their judgements. We should therefore consider finally the extent of the chroniclers' knowledge of Richard.

At St Albans Thomas Walsingham was the most comprehensive chronicler both of Richard II's reign and of the Lancastrian revolution. Beginning his *Chronica Maiora* in 1376, and dying *c.*1420, Walsingham

---

[69] This evidence was used with great effect by Clarke in order to date the Wilton Diptych: *Fourteenth Century Studies*, 272–92. The Diptych itself is an important piece of evidence for Richard's views on kingship.

[70] *Annales*, 223.   [71] *Vita*, 132.   [72] *Annales*, 190.

[73] Ibid. 297–300. See the comments in Gransden's *Historical Writing*, 141, and the literature quoted there.

lived and wrote throughout the entire period of the reign. Yet with the exception of a perhaps not entirely successful time as prior of Wymond-ham, a dependency of St Albans, Walsingham appears to have spent the whole of his life at St Albans itself. From the evidence we possess, it seems that his first-hand acquaintance with events in London was limited. His information on the Good Parliament of 1376, for example, with which he opened his history, almost certainly came from Sir Thomas Hoo, knight of the shire for Bedfordshire.[74] Much of the general information in his chronicle is likely to have been gained from visitors to the abbey. As regards his knowledge of Richard, the king was certainly at St Albans on several occasions, at which times Walsingham would have had the opportunity of observing him at first hand or of hearing accounts about him. Richard visited St Albans in the aftermath of the Peasants' Revolt.[75] He visited St Albans again in 1383, when he borrowed a palfrey which he did not return. On this occasion Richard hastened back to London, incurring Walsingham's criticism for changing his mind too precipitately on the sub-ject of Despenser's crusade.[76] After the end of the reign Richard's body rested in the abbey church in February 1400, on its way to burial at Kings Langley.[77] Despite such episodes Walsingham's direct encounters with the king were probably limited although, as a member of one of the premier Benedictine monasteries in England which had entertained the king on several occasions, Walsingham must have had some first-hand knowledge of Richard.

The authors of the Westminster Chronicle were even more centrally placed. It has been said that 'Richard II was known at Westminster as at no other house in the kingdom'. Richard's coronation had taken place in the abbey, on which occasion one of the consecrated shoes had been lost. Throughout the reign Richard was a constant visitor to the shrine of St Edward. 'He liked to worship in the monastic church on the feast of the translation of St. Edward the Confessor (13 October), and on the patronal festivals of St. Peter and St. Paul and sometimes came on other feast days besides these.'[78] The king brought visitors to see the relics and regalia at Westminster, and on one occasion appears to have unsuccess-fully attempted to get one of the monks, John Lakingheath, elected as

---

[74] A. Goodman, 'Sir Thomas Hoo and the Parliament of 1376', *BIHR* 41 (1968), 139–49.
[75] *Chron. Angl.* 320 ff. See Gransden's *Historical Writing*, 137, 150 on this and the fol-lowing incident.
[76] *Hist. Angl.* ii. 103. On this occasion Richard rode through the night from Daventry.
[77] *Annales*, 331.
[78] *Westm. Chron.*, p. lv. See Given-Wilson, *Royal Household*, 262. For Richard's devotion to St Edward, see below, pp. 41–3, 90–1, 203, 259, 261–2, and 268–9.

abbot.[79] The monks at Westminster had therefore an unprecedented opportunity for observing Richard's moods and demeanour. The author or authors of this account almost certainly came from a small circle of Westminster monks who themselves had long associations with the Abbey.[80] It is no surprise therefore that their chronicle is in many respects the best-informed account of Richard that we possess.

Apart from Walsingham and the monks at Westminster there was yet another chronicler who might claim some first-hand knowledge of Richard: Adam of Usk. Adam, an ecclesiastical lawyer, was a native of Usk in Monmouthshire. After a distinguished career at Oxford and in the province of Canterbury, his later career placed him close to the centre of political events. In 1399 he accompanied Arundel on Henry of Lancaster's march to Chester. He was present at the Parliament of 1399, and was a member of the commission to advise on the deposition of the king. He visited Richard in the Tower in 1399. According to Usk he was on this occasion present in the Tower while Richard dined, 'and I marked his mood and bearing, having been taken there for that very purpose by Sir William Beauchamp'.[81] This famous visit appears to have taken place on 21 September. Although there is no reason to suppose that Usk knew the king well, he was none the less in a position to observe him on this and perhaps on other occasions, and he moved in circles where there would almost certainly have been some informed knowledge of Richard.

The remainder of the native English chroniclers, who were in many instances members of the religious orders, were often placed at some distance from London. Their narratives reveal, therefore, little direct knowledge of the king. The Anonimalle Chronicle, written at St Mary's, York, is perhaps something of an exception. The chronicler at St Mary's used London sources for his account of the Good Parliament of 1376, and for the Peasants' Revolt of 1381. For the period between 1376 and 1381 also his narrative has the character of a London-based account. The chronicle mentions the fact that Richard was entertained in 1377 by the citizens of London, that he was knighted at Westminster, and it contains what is perhaps the fullest account we possess of Richard's coronation.[82] Transcribed therefore in the Chronicle of St Mary's is a London narrative by an author or authors who may also have observed Richard at first hand. Yet unlike Adam of Usk's account we cannot say that its narrative provides any living impression of the king.

[79] *Westm. Chron.* 176–7.   [80] Ibid., pp. xxxi–xliii.   [81] Adam of Usk, 30, 182.
[82] *Anonimalle Chronicle*, 102, 106, 107–115.

Opposed to the native chronicles are the writings of Froissart, Creton, and the author of the *Traison*. Each of these writers was probably in a position at some time or other to observe Richard. Froissart's first-hand acquaintance with Richard has been disputed. According to Froissart's account he was in 1395 'filled with a strong desire to revisit England' which he had not seen for some twenty-seven years.[83] In preparation for his visit he prepared a copy of his romance *Meliador* as a present to the king. Froissart says that after crossing to England, and some delays, he finally met Richard at Eltham following the king's return from Ireland, and there presented the manuscript to him. 'The king asked me what it was about and I told him, "About love". He was delighted by this answer, and dipped into the book in several places, and read, for he spoke and read French very well. Then he gave it to one of his knights, called Sir Richard Credon, to take into his private room, and was more cordial than ever towards me.'[84] Did this visit take place? It has been suggested that the famous interview may not have occurred.[85] On balance, however, it appears unlikely that Froissart would have fabricated an incident of this nature. It seems probable that he did meet the king about 15 July 1395 and had therefore a limited but first-hand knowledge of him.[86]

Jean Creton, *valet de chambre* to Charles VI of France and the duke of Burgundy, whose *Metrical History* is an important source for the events of August 1399, almost certainly did set eyes on Richard. Creton travelled from Paris to join Richard's forces at the time of the second Irish expedition of 1399. He was a witness, therefore, to the events of the Irish campaign and to certain episodes in the north of Wales after Richard's return from Ireland in that year. Although his picture of Richard, 'forlorn and weeping' at times, and at other times 'pale with anger' may have a propagandist intent, it was the work of an author whose basic credibility has been defended, and who was in north Wales in 1399. His description of Bolingbroke's meeting with Richard at Flint has all the hallmarks of an eyewitness account. The author of the *Traison*, a less trustworthy writer than Creton, may likewise have observed Richard at close quarters. The writer of this account was possibly attached to the household of John Holand duke of Exeter, the king's half-brother. This could have given him the opportunity of attending gatherings at which Richard himself was present.

[83] Froissart, xv. 140–1.   [84] Ibid. xv. 167.

[85] J. W. Sherborne, 'Charles VI and Richard II', in J. J. N. Palmer (ed.), *Froissart: Historian* (Woodbridge, 1981), 62.

[86] Stow, 'Richard II in Jean Froissart's *Chroniques*', 343. For this lost volume, see also below, pp. 248–9.

He may also have travelled with Richard's French queen, Isabella, to England in 1397, and returned with her to France in 1401.

We may conclude therefore that a number of chroniclers were in a position to observe Richard closely. They came either from a small and privileged group of monks and secular clergy or, in the case of the French writers, moved in circles not too far distant from the king. How well they understood the complexities of Richard's character is of course another matter. None the less they were on occasion observers of some of the most dramatic scenes of the reign. They had access to privileged information. This alone would render them indispensable, if at times hostile, witnesses to the character and actions of Richard II.

3

The Kingship of Richard II

Nigel Saul

The governance of Richard II fits uneasily into the general pattern of constitutional development in later medieval England. In many ways it appears uncharacteristic of its age. Richard's emphasis on the prerogative recalls the Angevin world of *vis* and *voluntas*, when the king could override the common law at will; while the use that was made of Chamber officials in central and local government anticipates one of the Tudors' expedients for undermining the power of the magnates.[1] By comparison with the less doctrinaire, though still assertive, kingship of an Edward III or Henry V, Richard's appears an alien, even a provocative, style of rule—an 'absolut-ist' experiment conceived out of its time and predestined to failure.

Viewed in a solely English context, Richard's reign will always appear puzzling. Seen from a European perspective, however, much of its singularity vanishes. All over the continent in the later fourteenth century kings were moving on to the offensive. Their objective, achieved by a variety of means, was to halt and if possible to reverse the advances made at their expense by representative assemblies and movements of provincial separatism. In the Empire, where royal authority could be exercised only indirectly and with princely goodwill, the pace was necessarily slow. However, in the reign of Charles IV (1346–78) notable advances were made in repairing the damage done by the interregnum of the mid-thirteenth century and the internal strife that had followed it. Bohemia was turned into a hereditary fief of the Luxemburgs, Charles's own family, and a long and

---

[1] For *vis* and *voluntas* see J. E. A. Jolliffe, *Angevin Kingship* (2nd edn., London, 1963), chs. 3 and 4. For contrasting insights into Richard's anticipation of Tudor policy see R. H. Jones, *The Royal Policy of Richard II: Absolutism in the Later Middle Ages* (Oxford, 1968), 111–12, 191–2; D. Starkey, 'The Age of the Household: Politics, Society and the Arts, *c.*1350–*c.*1550', in S. Medcalf (ed.), *The Later Middle Ages* (London, 1981), 225–90; and N. E. Saul, *Richard II* (New Haven and London, 1997), 440–1.

ultimately successful battle was fought by the emperor to have his eldest son and heir crowned in his lifetime. At the same time, to reduce future uncertainty about the succession, the electoral procedure was regulated in the Golden Bull and an electoral vote won by the king of Bohemia.[2] In France, by contrast, a quicker tempo of reform was possible: the obstacles to royal authority were fewer, and the crisis caused by the English invasions lent a sense of urgency to political life. In a series of measures taken between 1356 and 1380 the dauphin, later Charles V, was able to reorganize the royal armies, reinvigorate national finances, and neutralize the dissident element in the nobility; and with the assistance of the papacy he was even able to extend French dominion into the county of Flanders.[3] Further to the south, in Italy, a similar momentum was maintained. Representative assemblies wilted before a sustained princely assault, and by the end of the century seigneurial rule had replaced communal in the majority of states.[4] Even in the Church, where the battle between the conciliar and authoritarian principles was fought out most clearly, the matter was resolved early in the next century in favour of the latter.[5] It was not only in Richard's England that monarchical power was advancing; it was doing so in almost every corner of Europe.

Parallel with the growth of royal power was a growing elaboration of the institutions by which that power was mediated to the world outside. In almost every kingdom royal establishments were becoming larger and more complex. In France, for example, an establishment of around 200 which had ministered to St Louis had grown into one of close on 400 half a century later, and of no less than 800 a century after that.[6] In England the rate of growth was of approximately the same order. A household of 150 in the reign of Henry I had become one of 400–700 by the fourteenth century (depending on whether or not the realm was at war) and of as many

---

[2] The best summaries in English of Charles IV's policies are to be found in the following: B. Jarrett, *The Emperor Charles IV* (London, 1935); F. R. H. Du Boulay, *Germany in the Later Middle Ages* (London, 1983), 36–42; V. Dvorakova *et al.*, *Gothic Mural Painting in Bohemia and Moravia, 1300–1378* (Oxford, 1964), 41–50.

[3] E. Perroy, *The Hundred Years War* (London, 1995), 146–74; J. B. Henneman, 'The Military Class and the French Monarchy in the Late Middle Ages', *American Hist. Rev.* 83 (1978), 946–65.

[4] P. J. Jones, 'Communes and Despots: The City State in Late-Medieval Italy', *TRHS*, 5th ser. 15 (1965), 71–96.

[5] For a brief, though useful, discussion see D. Waley, *Later Medieval Europe* (London, 1964), ch. 6.

[6] C. Given-Wilson, *The Royal Household and the King's Affinity: Service, Politics and Finance in England, 1360–1413* (New Haven and London, 1986), 258; B. Guenée, *States and Rulers in Later Medieval Europe*, trans. J. Vale (Oxford, 1985), 78.

as 800 in the time of Henry VI.[7] In Burgundy, a duchy rather than a kingdom, after a delayed start the rate of growth was not far short of that in
the kingdoms. A household of 250–300 in the time of the first Valois duke
had become one of about 400, expanding at times into 1,000 or more in
the time of his grandson.[8]

The pressure for expansion came from two main sources. The first was
the gradual abandonment of the itinerant lifestyle, which allowed establishments to settle down and become larger; while the second was a growing appreciation of the role of the king's entourage as a forum for the display
of his majesty. These two influences acted together and brought about a
fundamental change in the character of courtly life. Courts became larger
and grander; and, in proportion as they did so, they became more civil-
ized and sophisticated. Over time they acquired something of the character of the princely courts of the Renaissance. In England (though this may
not have been the case elsewhere) it does not appear that the process of
growth was accompanied by any major structural or organizational shifts;
in this respect the court altered remarkably little between the twelfth
century and the fifteenth. However, it is none the less possible to sense in
the sources a change in the purpose and character of the royal entourage.
In the 1360s, for example, a new class of knight was found in attendance
on the king—the Chamber knights, whose employments were of a more
political character than those of the long-established Household knights,
and who were to be among the chief agents of Richard's rule in the 1390s.[9]
At the same time there is evidence of a greater preoccupation with ceremony and ritual. Richard's coronation, for example, was preceded by a civic
triumph in the streets of London, which served as the model for those
staged in 1382, before the coronation of Anne of Bohemia, and in 1392,
following the king's reconciliation with the Londoners.[10] On all these occasions symbolism was employed to telling effect. In 1377, and again in 1392,
the first of the conduits which the king passed was transformed into a
Heavenly City on which angels were seated disbursing cups of wine as
if at the Eucharist, while on one of the others a throne was placed which

---

[7] Given-Wilson, *Royal Household and King's Affinity*, 258–9.
[8] Ibid. 259. For examples from other states see Guenée, *States and Rulers*, 78–9. There are
useful comments on this theme in M. Keen, *Chivalry* (New Haven and London, 1984), 246–7.
[9] Given-Wilson, *Royal Household and King's Affinity*, ch. 4.
[10] For the procession of 1377 *Chron. Angl.* 154–6; and for that of 1392, Richard
Maidstone's account in T. Wright (ed.), *Political Songs and Poems relating to English History*,
2 vols. (RS, London, 1859–61), ii. 282–300. The procession of Jan. 1382 is less well documented but hints of its character are given by *The Brut or The Chronicler of England*, ed.
F. W. D. Brie, 2 vols. (EETS, London, 1906–8), ii. 338–9, and *CPMR 1381–1412*, 3.

was surrounded by three circles of angels symbolizing the three angelic orders in attendance on the Almighty.[11] At the coronation itself a new interest was taken in the details of the ceremony. At one point the traditional *ordo* was changed, to allow the oath to be taken before and not after acclamation by the people—thus emphasizing the latter's allegiance to a king who was already their ruler *de jure*. At the end, when it was all over, John of Gaunt, who as steward of England had masterminded the proceedings, had their details recorded on the Close Roll for future reference.[12] Similarly, in the daily life of the court it appears that a greater emphasis was placed on ceremonial and formal behaviour. This was particularly so in the later 1390s. As the *Eulogium* writer relates, it became the king's practice to sit throned in state from dinner till vespers observed by his courtiers who were expected to bend the knee whenever his gaze fell on them.[13] Richard's behaviour here carries distinct echoes of that of his father, the Black Prince, who was reported to have kept the Aquitanian nobility waiting for days on end for an audience, and then only to have suffered them to approach him kneeling.[14] Richard's court was much influenced by his father's, not least because of the continuity in personnel. However, in character and style there was probably little to distinguish it from the other main courts of the day. All over Europe rulers were seeking to distance themselves more from their subjects and dependants.[15] Gervase Mathew was of the opinion that this development had its origins in the Luxemburg court at Prague, with which Richard had been brought into contact by his marriage to Anne of Bohemia. The Luxemburg court, however, is unlikely to have been the immediate source.[16] Queen Anne's attendants

---

[11] G. Kipling, 'Richard II's "Sumptuous Pageants" and the Idea of the Civic Triumph', in D. M. Bergeron (ed.), *Pageantry and the Shakespearean Theatre* (Athens, Ga., 1986), 83–103.

[12] *CCR 1377–1381*, 1–5.

[13] *Eulogium Historiarum sive Temporis*, ed. F. S. Haydon 3 vols. (RS, London, 1858–63), iii. 378; see also ibid. 376, for Archbishop Arundel preaching against the luxury of the court before leaving for exile in 1397. C. L. Kingsford, *English Historical Literature in the Fifteenth Century* (Oxford, 1913), 28, argued that this part of the chronicle was written much later than the period it describes, and was for that reason of little value as a source. In fact, as recent work has shown, it was almost certainly written fairly contemporaneously with events from the late 14th cent. onwards (A. Gransden, *Historical Writing in England*, ii. (London, 1982), 138 n. 5). E. Kantorowicz's view was that the writer was describing a 'festival crowning' (Kantorowicz, *The King's Two Bodies: A Study in Medieval Political Theology* (Princeton, 1957), 29 n. 16). From an earlier period in the reign there are already suggestions that the king liked to be treated with deference by people: see *Westm. Chron.* 138.

[14] *The Anonimalle Chronicle, 1333–1381*, ed. V. H. Galbraith (Manchester, 1927), 55–6.

[15] For the notion of a 'kingship of distance', see Starkey's, introd. in id. (ed.), *The English Court from the Wars of the Roses to the Civil War* (London, 1987), 7–8.

[16] G. Mathew, *The Court of Richard II* (London, 1968), 17. For lengthier discussion of Richard's court and his influences on it, see Saul, *Richard II*, ch. 14.

may have brought with them styles and fashions of their own—notably a preference for shoes with long curled toes which were known to the English as 'cracows' or 'pikes'[17]—but it is doubtful if they could have been the source for the broader developments in ceremonial observable at the time. These are more likely to have come from the Valois court at Paris. The Luxemburg court is known to have been influenced by that of the Valois, which Charles IV had known from childhood days, and a good many other courts were also influenced by it to a greater or lesser degree. Thus courtly styles are likely to have been disseminated along a route broadly similar to that followed by the most beautiful symbol of regality fashioned in the late fourteenth century—the crown now in the Bavarian State Museum at Munich. Made in all probability in Paris, it found its way to Bohemia, whence it came to England—probably in the baggage train of Queen Anne—only to be taken away again, back to the Empire, by Henry IV's daughter Blanche, on the occasion of her marriage to Ludwig III of Bavaria.[18] This record of journeyings can stand as a metaphor for the circulation of courtly fashions more generally in late medieval Europe.

Against the undoubted internationalism of late medieval courtly culture, however, has to be set the parallel concern of rulers to stress the local or national roots of their power. This is demonstrated by the interest that they showed in promoting dynastic cults. In Bohemia the emperor Charles IV stressed his lineage's descent from St Wenceslas, the duke who became a symbol of Bohemian nationhood and independence.[19] In France a couple of generations earlier Philip IV had secured the canonization of his predecessor Louis IX at the same time as continuing to exploit his family's association with the Emperor Charlemagne.[20] In England since the 1160s the Angevins had basked in the reflected glory of their saintly predecessor, King Edward the Confessor. The Confessor's cult was, however, by European standards one with a peculiarly chequered history to it. Its origins lay in the Angevins' desire for the sanction of dynastic legitimacy. Unlike the Norman kings, who had been happy to rule by right of conquest, the Angevins wanted to establish their rightful descent from the last legitimate ruler of the Wessex royal house. There can be little doubt that it was this desire that led to Henry II's approach to the pope which resulted

---

[17] *Vita*, 134. For the Bohemian entourage, see below, p. 219.

[18] J. Alexander and P. Binski (edd.), *The Age of Chivalry: Art in Plantagenet England 1200–1400* (London, 1987), 202–3.

[19] For Charles's interest in the saint see Dvorakova *et al.*, *Gothic Mural Painting in Bohemia*, 43. The staircase of the great tower at Karlstein was decorated with a painted cycle of the Wenceslas legend: ibid. 137.

[20] E. M. Hallam, *Capetian France, 987–1328* (London, 1980), 176–7, 312.

in the Confessor's canonization in 1161. Largely because of its dynastic associations, interest in the cult was for the most part confined to the royal family; it never attracted a widespread popular following. In the thirteenth century the cult's most enthusiastic sponsor was Henry III. Henry initiated the rebuilding of the abbey which the Confessor had founded at Westminster; he ordered scenes from the saint's life to be painted on the walls of his castles and palaces, and he supervised the translation of the saint's relics to their new shrine in 1269.[21] He even named his eldest son after the saint. For Henry's successors on the throne the cult appears to have been of lesser significance. Edward I was an Arthurian enthusiast, while Edward III actively promoted the cult of St George. Only when Richard became king in 1377 was there a major revival of royal interest. From 1389 Richard's patronage of the cult was particularly extensive. The rebuilding programme at Westminster, which had been resumed in the 1370s, was put on a firmer financial basis; a host of expensive gifts were lavished on the saint's shrine; and the Confessor's mythical arms were quartered with the king's own.[22] The reason for the king's interest in the Confessor is not difficult to find: Richard could identify with his image in a way that his immediate predecessors could not. Thus the Confessor lacked a record of success in arms; and so too did Richard. The Confessor had brought what Matthew Paris called 'a glorious peace' to his people; and in the 1390s Richard sought to bring a similar 'peace' to his.[23] Aspects of the Confessor's mythical persona which had been an embarrassment to his predecessors were to him a source of legitimization. It was surely for this reason that he chose the Confessor as one of his three sponsors in

[21] *King's Works*, i. 127; F. M. Powicke, *King Henry III and the Lord Edward*, 2 vols. (Oxford, 1947), ii. 569–76; P. Binski, 'Reflections on *La estoire de Seint Aedward le rei*: Hagiography and Kingship in Thirteenth-Century England', *JMH* 16 (1990), 333–50.

[22] For the king's support for the rebuilding programme see *CPR 1385–1389*, 188, and W(estminster) A(bbey) M(uniments) 6226. For gifts that he made specifically to the shrine of the Confessor see WAM 9473 (a ring of gold with a ruby set in it); *Cal. Charter Rolls 1341–1417*, 311 (a chasuble of gold cloth with images of St Mary, St Edward the Confessor, and St Edmund); and C. Wilson *et al.*, *Westminster Abbey* (London, 1986), 117 (a silver moveable altar enamelled with the story of the Confessor and the Pilgrim). Richard's patronage of the abbey is discussed by N. E. Saul, 'Richard II and Westminster Abbey', in W. J. Blair and B. Golding (edd.), *The Cloister and the World: Essays in Medieval History presented to Barbara Harvey* (Oxford, 1995).

[23] Matthew Paris wrote a biography of the Confessor, probably on Henry III's initiative, which was based on the 'standard' life by Ailred of Rievaulx. Ailred himself had stressed the Confessor's peace: 'Since the pacific king reigned for a long time', he wrote, 'all things met together within one bond of peace.' (D. Carpenter, 'King, Magnates and Society: The Personal Rule of King Henry III, 1234–1258', *Speculum*, 60 (1985), 61 n. 116). For further discussion of 'peace', see below, pp. 52–3. For further discussion of Richard's patronage of Westminster abbey and the cult of St Edward, see below, pp. 90–1, 203, 259, 261–2, and 268–9.

that most delicate and powerful expression of his kingship, the Wilton Diptych.

Though Richard was clearly interested in the imagery and iconography of kingship, he does not on the other hand appear to have been greatly attracted by either literature or learning. The evidence here is admittedly difficult to interpret. At no time in the late Middle Ages can we be sure of the size or composition of the royal library. A stray document from Edward III's reign shows that a collection of some 160 books was circulating in the Tower in the 1330s.[24] However, in the absence of any similar source for Richard II's reign it is impossible to say whether a collection of comparable size existed three-quarters of a century later. The only directly relevant source that exists—an inventory compiled in 1384—is almost certainly incomplete: it lists a mere dozen and a half volumes. Most of these were of fairly predictable character. One or two were works of devotion— a two-volume Bible, for example, and the 'Galaath' (a religious romance) —but most were *chansons de gestes*—like *Aimeri de Narbonne* and *Garin de Loherenc*—or Arthurian romances—like the *Romance de Roy Arthure* and the *Queste de Saint Grael*.[25] In later years further volumes were added. In 1395 the king received from Froissart a volume of love poems which, so the poet tells us, he dipped into and then ordered to be placed in his private room.[26] In the following year, when he married the daughter of the king of France, he was presented with a splendid breviary in two volumes, the *Breviaire de Belleville*.[27] At about the same time he was given by Philippe de Mézières a copy of his *Epistre d'un Viele Solitaire des Celestins de Paris* (better known as the *Letter to King Richard II*) which called on the kings of England and France to heal their differences and unite in the defence of Christendom against the infidel.[28] These were all books which came to the king as gifts or as bids for support. The one volume which he is known to have commissioned himself is the *Confessio Amantis*, which Gower tells us Richard encouraged him to write, probably in about 1390. Two others, however, can be associated in all probability with his patronage.

---

[24] J. Vale, *Edward III and Chivalry: Chivalric Society and its Context, 1270–1350* (Woodbridge, 1982), 49.

[25] E. Rickert, 'Richard II's Books', *Library*, 4th ser. 13 (1933), 144–7; R. S. Loomis, 'The Library of Richard II', in E. B. Atwood and A. A. Hill (edd.), *Studies in Language, Literature and Culture of the Middle Ages and Later* (Austin, Tex., 1969), 173–8; R. F. Green, 'King Richard II's books revisited', *Library*, 31 (1976), 235–9.

[26] Froissart, xv. 164.

[27] V. J. Scattergood, 'Literary Culture at the Court of Richard II', in *English Court Culture*, 33.

[28] P. de Mézières, *Letter to King Richard II*, ed. G. W. Coopland (Liverpool, 1975), esp. 3.

The first is the collection of treatises, now MS Bodley 581, which was probably written by John Thorpe, treasurer of Ireland in 1393-4, and which contains several references to the king; and the second, St John's College, Cambridge, MS A.7, a book of statutes of *c.*1390, on fo. 133 of which is a drawing of the king receiving a presentation copy, presumably of this volume, from a kneeling cleric.[29] For a king who presided over a court of such literary distinction the absence of more extensive patronage is surprising; yet its lack cannot be gainsaid or denied. The many talented writers who thronged the court or who found employment there, such as Chaucer, Clanvow, John Montagu, or even Gower, wrote largely for their own satisfaction and not in response to royal encouragement. Whatever expansion the royal collection underwent in Richard's reign (and it was surely greater than our sources allow) is unlikely to have owed much to royal initiative; for Richard was almost certainly no bibliophile. By comparison with the great library built up at the Louvre by Charles V the English royal book collection was small.

Partly because of the king's apparent lack of interest in books there has been a tendency in recent scholarship to play down the influence of ideas on the practice of his kingship. Anthony Tuck has conveniently summarized the case: 'there is little evidence', he writes, 'that Richard theorised about kingship. The epitaph he composed for himself, which began "He threw down whomsoever violated the royal prerogative . . ." hardly amounts to a new theory of kingship, and authentic pronouncements of his own on the nature of royal power are hard to find.'[30] There is certainly a measure of truth in Professor Tuck's view: beyond the king's famous remark that the laws of England were in his mouth or his breast, very few of Richard's *obiter dicta* are recorded. However, the reaction against the influence of ideas on his kingship has probably gone too far. R. H. Jones suggested in 1968 that Giles of Rome's *De Regimine Principum* exercised a powerful influence on the king's style of governance.[31] Comparing Giles's ideas and Richard's it is evident that this must have been so. Giles and Richard, for example, were at one in placing a strong emphasis on the subject's obligation of obedience: Giles said that strict obedience to the sovereign's will was the source from which all the values of the commonwealth were derived; Richard and his ministers both stressed the subject's duty of obedience in letters or speeches in the 1390s.[32] Giles and Richard

---

[29] For Gower's works, see below, pp. 234-6. The portrait of the king is reproduced in D. Gordon, *Making and Meaning: The Wilton Diptych* (London, 1993), 22.

[30] *Crown and Nobility, 1272-1461* (London, 1985), 222.

[31] *Royal Policy*, 154-8. For Giles's influence in England, see also below, pp. 45, 51-2.

[32] e.g. *RP* iii. 150, 329, 347.

both claimed the greatest possible authority for the king. Giles said that all privilege and nobility flowed from the king; Richard articulated a broadly similar view of relations between Crown and magnates in patents of ennoblement in 1385 and later. Giles and Richard both saw the king as the supreme lawgiver. Giles said that the king should be above the law to act with equity; Richard allegedly maintained that he could make or change the laws at will.[33] The examples of such similarities are many, and could be multiplied. All told, they bear eloquent witness to the influence on Richard of Giles's ideas. The question is how Richard and his circle came to acquire their knowledge in the first place. Jones has suggested that Richard received his first introductions to Giles as a boy. Jones was struck by the fact that Sir Simon Burley, Richard's childhood tutor and *magister*, owned a copy of the *De Regimine Principum*; and he argued that 'in view of the character of the programme of the first twenty years of his [Richard's] reign, it is tempting to suspect that Richard, like many another prince in his age, had been set to school to Giles of Rome and had learned his lessons well'.[34] The suggestion is a plausible one, but it is doubtful if it can ever be proved. Giles's treatise circulated widely in late medieval England, particularly among those with an interest in government, and it is unlikely that Burley was the only courtier to have read it. Michael de la Pole, for example, a friend of Richard's and a chancellor in the 1380s, was clearly familiar with Giles's doctrine of obedience: addressing Parliament in 1383 he said that 'obedience to the king was the foundation of all peace and quiet in the realm'.[35] Edmund Stafford, a successor of his as chancellor, expressed similar sentiments in Parliament in September 1397.[36] It is possible that there was a definite group of courtiers in Richard's entourage who found an attraction in Giles's ideas. Burley, de la Pole, Stafford, and possibly others were committed to the idea of strong royal government. Very likely in Giles's treatise they found a sort of tract for their times.

The influence of Giles's ideas on Richard and his ministers was matched by that of the Roman or civil law tradition more generally. In a sense, these two streams of influence overlapped: Giles was schooled in the civilian tradition of thought and civilian assumptions (and quotations) informed and validated his treatise. It seems reasonable to suppose that Richard gained his first acquaintance of civil law through Giles—the

---

[33] For Giles's ideas see Jones, *Royal Policy*, 156–7, and J. Dunbabin, 'Government', in J. H. Burns (ed.), *The Cambridge History of Medieval Political Thought c.1350–c.1450* (Cambridge, 1988), 483–5. Richard's policies are discussed in Saul, *Richard II*; for the king's later elaboration of obedience, see below, pp. 51–2.
[34] *Royal Policy*, 161. [35] *RP* iii. 150. [36] Ibid. 347.

civilians' emphasis on strong government was there; and so too was the notion of the king as the supreme lawgiver. By the mid- to late 1390s, however, there are signs that he was dipping into other sources. The clearest evidence of this is to be found in his *obiter dicta*. According to the Articles of Deposition he had a penchant for repeating some of the more familiar civil law maxims and adages. On one occasion, apparently, he said that the laws of England were in his mouth or, alternatively, in his breast, and on another that he alone could make or change the laws of the kingdom. These were maxims that had an obvious appeal to him because they reinforced his conception of himself as a lawgiver. Both were frequently cited by late medieval rulers and Richard could have picked them up from the standard glossarial sources—or from those who were familiar with such sources.

It is clear that Richard's knowledge of civil law went beyond the merely trite or superficial, however. There are signs that he had been delving in some depth into civilian ideas of authority. Evidence of this is to be found in the encouragement that he gave to new, and grander, forms of address. In the final decade of the reign it was common for him to be referred to in the headings to parliamentary petitions as a 'prince'.[37] The significance of this is that 'prince' implied the ruler's possession of sovereignty: the king was envisaged as a legislator acting rationally in the common interest. Again from the headings to petitions, but also from other sources— letters, for example—it is evident that Richard encouraged his subjects to address him as 'your majesty'.[38] 'Majesty' was a term that originally overlapped in meaning with sovereignty. In the later Roman Empire it referred to the sovereignty enjoyed by the emperor. When the emperors embraced Christianity, however, it acquired a religious gloss. 'Majesty' was seen as referring to the theocratic character of the king's or the prince's rule.[39] Richard's purpose in encouraging his subjects to refer to him as 'your majesty' was thus to reinforce the perception of himself as a *semideus*—as a distant, remote, all-powerful ruler—in a sense, as the king depicted in the 'Coronation' portrait.

The use that Richard made of the terms 'prince' and 'majesty', and of civilian ideas more generally, bears witness to the range and depth of his

---

[37] Ibid. 290, 305, 344. Forms of address are discussed by N. E. Saul, 'Richard II and the Vocabulary of Kingship', *EHR* 110 (1995).

[38] For some examples see M. D. Legge (ed.), *Anglo-Norman Letters and Petitions* (Oxford, 1941), nos. 24, 27; *RP* iii. 290.

[39] W. Ullmann, *Principles of Government and Politics in the Middle Ages* (4th edn., London, 1978), 136–7.

interest in the theoretical foundations of kingship. If he was not a widely read ruler, it seems that he was certainly a well-advised one. His principal mentors were probably the civilian administrators in his service. Edmund Stafford, the minister who gave the authoritarian opening address at the Revenge Parliament of 1397, was a graduate in civil law from Oxford. Richard Scrope, bishop of Lichfield, a close friend and companion in his later years, had doctorates in both canon and civil law.[40] Laymen like Simon Burley and Michael de la Pole, as we have seen, were probably also familiar with civilian concepts. It was these half-dozen or so men who were —in R. H. Jones's words—the 'architects and servants' of Richard's prerogative rule.[41]

The question arises of why Richard became so interested in the civilian repertory of ideas, and what he sought to gain from their practical application to government. It is possible to make at least a couple of suggestions. In the first place, it is clear that the king was fascinated with the law *tout court*. The first indications of that fascination are to be found in the questions that he put to the judges in 1387. A major theme underlying the questions is the nature and authority of law: who could make the law, and when the law might or might not be binding.[42] Though the questions were almost certainly drafted by a legal expert—perhaps a serjeant —they were surely prompted by the king's personal initiative. Further evidence of the king's legal interests is to be found in the book of statutes (St John's College, Cambridge, MS A.7), which he commissioned in or around 1390. The book, a presentation copy, was an unusually wide-ranging compilation: it was much larger (and more accurate), for example, than a comparable volume made for Edward III. Moreover, it was lavishly produced. Portraits of kings adorn the initial letters at the beginning of each reign and on fo. 133 Richard himself is shown enthroned and in full regalia. There is strong evidence that the book was intended for actual use as much as for ostentation: it is significant that from Edward I's and Edward II's reigns documents like the *Articuli super Cartas* and the ordinances were

[40] A. B. Emden, *A Biographical Register of the University of Oxford to A.D. 1500*, 3 vols. (Oxford, 1957–9), iii. 1749–50, 1659. It is tempting to associate John Waltham, bishop of Salisbury, with this group, although nothing is known of his educational background. Waltham was keeper of the Privy Seal from 1386 to 1389 and treasurer from 1389 till his death. Richard regarded his talents so highly that he honoured him with burial in the Confessor's chapel of Westminster Abbey—a unique privilege of which the monks of Westminster disapproved (*Annales*, 186).

[41] *Royal Policy*, 125.

[42] S. B. Chrimes, 'Richard II's Questions to the Judges, 1387', *Law Quarterly Review*, 72 (1956), 365–90.

included—suggesting that Richard had been thinking hard about king–magnate conflicts in other reigns than his own. Possibly he was inclined to see the volume as a book of precedents for use in connection with a future reassertion of power. In the past the law had been used not only to magnify but to restrain royal power. In future its function would be confined to magnifying it.

Consideration of Richard's legal obsessions leads naturally on to the other reason for his interest in scholarly writing, namely his desire to remedy what he considered the weakness of English government. An axiom of civilian thought had been the necessity to a realm of strong government. William of Ockham had written that the king should rule by will alone and Giles of Rome had said that it was better for a king to be too strong than too weak.[43] Statements like these lent authority to Richard's own instincts and prejudices. From the beginning of his reign he had been convinced that his monarchy was too weak. He could see evidence of the consequences of that weakness all around him. First, and most obviously, the traditional organization of society was breaking down. The lower orders, encouraged by rapidly rising wages and better conditions, were rejecting their traditional place in the hierarchy. Not only were they refusing to perform the services that they owed to their employers or lords; they were even challenging the authority of the government itself. Proof of their arrogance was found in their boldness in rebelling in 1381. Secondly, and still more seriously, there were the challenges to the king's authority from within political society itself. The origins of these lay in the revival of criticism of the court which began in the mid-1370s. Edward III by this time was nearing the end of his life, and those who enjoyed his confidence were abusing their position for personal gain. In the Good Parliament in 1376, a group of courtiers and hangers-on in the Household had been charged with acts of malfeasance and with accroaching the royal power for their own gain. One of them had been condemned to imprisonment and two others were dismissed from office. In the early years of Richard's reign the barrage of criticism was renewed. What particularly angered the Commons was what they saw as the excessive size of the court and the burden that it placed on the taxpayer. In 1381 a committee was appointed to examine 'the estate and governance of the king's person and his household, and to ordain sufficient remedy', and the earl of Arundel and Sir Michael de la Pole were placed in the Household 'to advise and govern' the king.[44] Four years later

---

[43] Dunbabin, 'Government', 482–93.   [44] *RP* iii. 101, 104.

another commission was appointed 'to survey the king's estate, to enquire into his revenues and diminish his expenses'.[45] Neither of these commissions had been able to effect much improvement, and when the attack was renewed in 1386 the chancellor, Michael de la Pole, now earl of Suffolk, was impeached and removed from office, and yet another reforming commission appointed with supervisory control over the Household. Richard's reaction to this last initiative was immediate. He abandoned Westminster and, as Knighton said, 'gyrated' around the realm to escape the commission's scrutiny.[46] At the same time his friend Robert de Vere began mobilizing a force for the king in Cheshire and the north-west. By mid-December de Vere and his men were heading southwards to London, but at Radcot Bridge near Burford they were met by a force under the earl of Derby and defeated. Richard had no alternative but to submit. When Parliament was summoned early in the next year, he was powerless to prevent the judicial destruction of his friends and former servants.

The vigorous new kingship that Richard styled in the 1390s obviously originated as a response to the setbacks and humiliations of the 1380s. Richard's general aim was to enhance the prestige and authority of his office—to raise himself above, and to distance himself from, his subjects. In that way, he believed, he could strengthen his claims to his subjects' obedience. In the doctrines of Giles and the civilians Richard found the conceptual and legal framework that he needed. Civil law conceived of the king as a prince—in other words, it saw him as a supreme legislator. Civil law also conceived of the king as a ruler-in-majesty—in other words, as a *semideus*, a ruler of almost priest-like character. On the basis of the civilian conceptions a powerful new image of the king was fashioned. In the 'Coronation' portrait Richard was shown crowned and with the orb and sceptre, the symbols of sovereignty, staring out frontally like an iconic close-up of the face of Christ. In the Wilton Diptych he was shown in the company of saintly sponsors and receiving a banner from the Virgin Mary and Child. As portrayed in these works Richard seemed on a different plane from his subjects. The impression was given that he was in a world unknown to mere mortals. This was a perception reinforced by the encouragement of the new vocabulary of address—that is, to forms like 'your highness' and 'your majesty', which replaced the more traditional 'my lord'. People

[45] J. J. N. Palmer, 'The Impeachment of Michael de la Pole in 1386', *BIHR* 42 (1969), 96–101; id., 'The Parliament of 1385 and the Constitutional Crisis of 1386', *Speculum*, 46 (1971), 477–90.
[46] Knighton, 404.

were encouraged to think of Richard as somehow above them, and to direct towards him the kind of responses that previously they had reserved for God. These image-building measures played a major role in the revamping of Richard's kingship in the 1390s but, of course, by themselves they were inadequate. They could do little to address the underlying issue highlighted by the Appellant triumph, namely the king's lack of coercive power. When it had come to a confrontation with the Appellants Richard had simply been outgunned. He had no ready army and his supporters were too few. Thus it was necessary for the image-building to be complemented by more concrete measures to strengthen and broaden the royal power-base. Richard's first, and most vital, initiative was to create a new courtier nobility to replace the one destroyed by the Appellants. John of Gaunt was welcomed back to the royal camp after his return from Spain in 1389, and for the next decade his support was crucial to Richard's success. Other magnates of royal blood, like Edward of Rutland, the duke of York's son, and the Hollands, Richard's half-brothers, were built up in power and esteem to compensate for the king's lack of immediate kin; at the same time, at a lower level, noble scions like William Scrope and Thomas Percy were drawn into the royal orbit by their employment at court.[47] Secondly, and in what constituted a break with earlier practice, Richard sought to strengthen his power-base among the gentry. He did this by building up an affinity. In the years after 1390 he took on no fewer than eighty-two 'king's knights', where earlier there had been only seven. Many of these knights were men of considerable importance in their shires. Indeed, it seems to have been Richard's deliberate policy to recruit at what Dr Given-Wilson calls 'the top end of the market'.[48] Thus in 1387, at the height of the Appellant crisis, Richard took on the major Worcestershire landowner Sir John Russell of Strensham who was already a retainer of the earl of Warwick; and two years later he recruited Sir Edward Dallingridge of Bodiam, a retainer of another Appellant lord, the earl of Arundel, and himself a leading patronage broker in east Sussex.[49] Other active and important knights were attracted to royal service in the years that followed, among them the ill-famed Bushy, Bagot, and Green who figured so prominently as councillors

---

[47] R. A. Griffiths, 'The Crown and the Royal Family in Later Medieval England', in id. and J. Sherborne (edd.), *Kings and Nobles in the Later Middle Ages* (Gloucester, 1986), 19; J. A. Tuck, *Richard II and the English Nobility* (London, 1973), 138, 143, 180–1.

[48] *Royal Household and King's Affinity*, 214.

[49] *CPR 1385–1389*, 273; *CPR 1388–1392*, 80, 102. For Dallingridge's earlier connections with Arundel see S. K. Walker, *The Lancastrian Affinity 1361–1399* (Oxford, 1990), 127–41.

after 1397.[50] Esquires were initially retained in smaller numbers, but later on the imbalance was redressed and by the end of the reign there were as many as 125 of them.[51] It is evident that by the later 1390s Richard had taken into his pay a large and dependable corps of retainers through whom he was able to reach out to the much greater number of 'substantial and influential' gentry in the shires. As a result of his recruiting there would clearly be little danger that in a future confrontation he would again find himself devoid of support. Thus, it was secure in the knowledge of widespread gentry and magnate backing that he embarked on the final phase of his political programme: the destruction of the former Appellants.

Why Richard chose to take this dramatic initiative at the time that he did—in July 1397—is unclear. A number of possibilities have been mooted. One is that the king was motivated by an appetite for revenge. This was the view of the Kirkstall Chronicler, who wrote that Richard 'recollected and recalled to mind the injuries which had been done to him' in the year 1388, and resolved to avenge them.[52] The second—and this was the explanation that Richard himself put forward—is that a plot against the king had been unearthed. Counting against the king's claim, however, is the fact that when the former Appellants were put on trial in September no evidence of such a plot was produced. Given the exiguous nature of the source-material it is possible that the truth about the episode will never be known[53] but of the general character of Richard's thinking at the time there can be little doubt. Two ideas were of particular importance in influencing him. The first was the subject's obligation of obedience to the king and the second the notion of 'peace' as the expression of a united realm.

The notion that the subjects of a king had a binding obligation to obey him was one that had been circulating at Richard's court for some time by the 1390s. The origins of the idea, as of so many others that Richard espoused, were to be found in Giles of Rome's *De Regimine Principum*.[54] Giles had stressed the obligation which the subjects of a ruler were under to obey him. Obedience, he said, was the source from which the values of the commonwealth were derived, and honour, safety, and an abundance of prosperity were the rewards that obedient subjects might expect. These

[50] Given-Wilson, *Royal Household and King's Affinity*, 186–7.   [51] Ibid. 215.

[52] *The Kirkstall Abbey Chronicles*, ed. J. Taylor (Thoresby Soc. 42, Leeds, 1952), 118; C. Given-Wilson (ed. and trans.), *Chronicles of the Revolution, 1397–1400: The Reign of Richard II* (Manchester, 1993), 94.

[53] The latest review of the evidence is offered by R. Mott, 'Richard II and the Crisis of 1397', in I. Wood and G. A. Loud (edd.), *Church and Chronicle: Essays presented to John Taylor* (London, 1991), 165–77.

[54] See above, pp. 44–5.

were arguments that appear to have appealed to the Black Prince and his servants, chief among them Burley, who owned a copy of the treatise, and Michael de la Pole. Significantly it was the latter—Richard's chancellor between 1383 and 1386—who provided the first, and the clearest, statement of the meaning of 'obedience' when, addressing Parliament in 1383, he said that proper obedience to the king was 'the sole foundation of all peace and quiet in the realm'.[55] De la Pole's speech was made less than two years after the Peasants' Revolt and with the events of that upheaval in mind; and a decade later, in the aftermath of another crisis— the Appellants' coup—other officers spoke in a similar vein. Archbishop Arundel, addressing Parliament as chancellor in 1395, declared that subjects had a binding obligation 'to honour, cherish and obey the king, and to employ all their power in his service'.[56] Two years later, in the Parliament of September 1397 at which Richard's *coup d'état* was ratified, Arundel's successor Bishop Stafford declared that in a well-governed realm 'every subject should be duly obedient to the king and his laws'.[57] An interesting parallel to these ideas is to be found in a contemporary tract, the *De Quadripartita Regis Specie* which was probably written by John Thorpe and presented to Richard in 1391 or 1392. Though the greater part of the tract is unoriginal, there is a striking passage in which the writer says that nothing was more likely to force a king to impose penalties on his subjects than an act of disobedience.[58] This was a view that corresponded very closely to Richard's own. Richard, brought up to have a high sense of his regality, saw disobedience as tantamount to an act of rebellion. In a letter to Manuel Paleologus, the Byzantine emperor, in 1398, he vented his hatred of what he called the 'wantonness and rebellion' of his enemies among the magnates: their behaviour had led him, he said, to stretch forth his arm, tread on the offenders' necks, and grind them down, even to the root.[59] What he was doing here was using Old Testament language to describe Old Testament vengeance. The former Appellants were cast in the role of his hapless victims.

The second factor which weighed with the king in punishing the Appellants was the need to establish what he called 'peace' in the realm. This is a point which emerges clearly from the letters that he wrote to foreign rulers in the wake of the coup. To Albert duke of Bavaria, for example, he wrote that, having punished the malice of those treacherous

---

[55] *RP* iii. 150.   [56] Ibid. 329.   [57] Ibid. 347.

[58] J.-P. Genet (ed.), *Four English Political Tracts of the Later Middle Ages* (Camden Soc., 4th ser. 18, London, 1977), 35–6.

[59] A. R. Myers (ed.), *English Historical Documents*, iv. *1327–1485* (London, 1969), 174–5.

nobles whom he had raised to the highest peaks of honour and having adjudged them to a natural or civil death, he had brought to his subjects a 'peace' which, by the grace of God, would last for ever.[60] To Manuel Paleologus, in the letter already quoted, he wrote in a similar vein. Being unable, he said, to endure any longer the 'wantonness and rebellion' of his enemies among the magnates, he had stretched forth his arm and had trodden on the necks of the proud and the haughty, so restoring to his subjects the 'peace' for which they craved and which by God's blessing should last for ever.[61] By 'peace' in these letters Richard did not mean an end to external hostilities. Hostilities with both Scotland and France had effectively been ended by the truce agreed at Leulinghen eight years earlier. What he had in mind was rather the establishment of internal unity. It was in this sense that 'peace' was understood by contemporary academics. Jean Gerson, the chancellor of the University of Paris, enjoined peace on the competing factions at the French court in a sermon in November 1408 in which he stressed the danger to the realm of the evils of internal discord and dissent. Peace, he said, was the guarantee of internal unity; it should exist between those of the same blood, even those of the same royal blood; if it did not, the realm would never be able to resist its enemies.[62] This was a doctrine of unexceptional character; indeed, it ranked as one of the commonplaces of the age. In 1433 it was to be enjoined upon the competing factions at another court—that of Henry VI—in a sermon delivered by the chancellor, John Stafford.[63] However, in Richard's hands it was turned into a doctrine almost absolutist in tone. 'Peace' in this sense, the sense of unity, was identified with obedience and submission to the king's will. Chancellor Stafford made this point clear in his address to Parliament in September 1397. Taking as his text, 'There shall be one king over all' (Ezekiel, 37 : 22), he said that if the realm were to be well governed three things were needed: first, the king should be powerful enough to govern; secondly, his laws ought be well kept and justly executed; and thirdly, his subjects should be duly obedient to him and his laws.[64] Unity —peace, that is—was incompatible with dissent. What the king required was unquestioning acceptance of his rule and submission to his will.

To secure these two ends Richard took a variety of measures over the next two years. County sheriffs were required to take new forms of oath

---

[60] J. Harvey, 'The Wilton Diptych: A Re-examination', *Archaeologia*, 98 (1961), app. 2.
[61] Myers (ed.), *English Historical Documents*, iv. 174–5.
[62] C. M. D. Crowder, 'Peace and Justice around 1400: A Sketch', in J. G. Rowe (ed.), *Aspects of Late Medieval Government and Society* (Toronto, 1986), 59.
[63] Ibid. 53–4.   [64] *RP* iii. 347; and see above, p. 52.

on assuming office. Charters were exacted giving the king *carte blanche* over the lives and goods of his subjects, and oaths were demanded from the leaders of the local communities to ensure the upholding of the acts of the Revenge Parliament.[65] Overall the effect of these and the other measures taken between 1397 and 1399 was almost the precise opposite of that intended. Instead of confirming and strengthening the king's subjects in their love and respect for him they brought about their alienation. Many who had once borne the king goodwill now felt repelled and estranged. Typical of their number was the writer John Gower, whom Richard only a few years before had commissioned to write the *Confessio Amantis*.[66] In his poem *O Deus Immense* Gower appealed to the king to realize the error of his ways. The people were suffering, he said, because of the wrongs that Richard had committed. Instead of initiating purges and imposing censorship, he should hasten into the highways and byways and listen to what his subjects had to say to him. He should let them speak openly, for to suppress their talk was to store up danger. Above all, he should avoid avarice, for the treasure to be collected in peoples' hearts was more valuable by far than any amount of treasure he could collect in coin.[67] Gower's words, however, for all their eloquence, fell on stony ground. Richard was not to be swayed by these or any other words of wisdom.[68] The affection of his people meant less to him than his desire to secure 'peace' and obedience. The fact that the reality of that 'peace' bore little relation to the ideal was a paradox that bothered him but little.

Yet it was a paradox the fruits of which were everywhere visible. Discord took the place of unity, and enmity that of goodwill. Nowhere in the realm was there evidence of the spirit of reconciliation which alone would have made the king's actions acceptable to his people and closed the wounds that he had opened. Richard showed himself apparently unable to understand the feelings and aspirations of his subjects. Instead of reaching out and offering them a vision with which they could identify and to which

---

[65] C. M. Barron, 'The Tyranny of Richard II', *BIHR* 41 (1968), 1–18.

[66] G. B. Stow, 'Richard II in John Gower's *Confessio Amantis*: Some Historical Perspectives', *Mediaevalia*, 16 (1993), 3–31.

[67] John Gower, *The Major Latin Works*, ed. and trans. E. W. Stockton (Seattle, 1962), 290–326. For a discussion of the poem see J. H. Fisher, *John Gower: Moral Philosopher and Friend of Chaucer* (London, 1965), 130–1.

[68] Chaucer's *Lak of Stedfastnesse*, which ends with a plea to Richard to 'hate extorcioun', was probably written in the final two years of the reign. For the textual problems raised by the poem, see J. Norton-Smith, 'Textual Tradition, Monarchy and Chaucer's *Lak of Stedfastnesse*', *Reading Medieval Studies*, 8 (1982), 3–11.

they could direct their own endeavours, he merely retreated inwards and became ever more immersed in a myopic preoccupation with the symbols of regality. To judge from the surviving evidence, the imagery of power appears to have interested him more than its substance. He decked himself out in the most splendid of robes.[69] He made lavish use of badges and livery.[70] He displayed the sunburst on his banners and standards.[71] He laid special stress on the properties of anointing.[72] Yet in the moment of the realization of his power he appears not to have known what to do with it. His programme of renewal consisted of no more than restless journeyings around the central and western parts of his realm.[73] At the heart of Richard's personality there was a barren emptiness, an area of desolation which left him incapable of offering the leadership for which his people craved.

When the challenge from Bolingbroke came, then, there were relatively few who were willing to champion his cause. Dr C. M. Barron has argued that the position would have been different if Richard had been physically present in the realm and able to offer leadership in person.[74] However, it is difficult to believe that this would have been the case. From the summer of 1397 Richard had taken a host of measures to safeguard his position, yet in the end these all proved unavailing. The courtier nobility and the hand-picked sheriffs, even when they stirred themselves into action, encountered at best indifference, and at worst resentment, from the king's

---

[69] According to the Evesham writer, Richard once purchased a robe costing £20,000 (*Vita*, 156). For more general comments on Richard's desire for splendour see *Eulogium*, iii. 384. See below, pp. 139–40, for Richard's costly tastes.

[70] Richard employed two badges. The first was the crown, which had long been in use and which, according to the Westminster writer, his serjeants distributed in East Anglia in 1387 (*Westm. Chron.* 186). The other was the white hart, first distributed at the Smithfield tournament of 1390. For a discussion see M. V. Clarke, 'The Wilton Diptych', *Burlington Magazine*, 58 (1931); repr. in id. *Fourteenth Century Studies* ed. L. S. Sutherland and M. McKisack (Oxford, 1937), 276–7. Though the white hart gained the greater notoriety, it was the crown badge which was probably distributed in greater number: J. Gillespie, 'Richard II's Cheshire Archers', *Trans. of the Historic Soc. of Lancashire and Cheshire*, 125 (1974), 5–6. See also below, pp. 124–6.

[71] Kantorowicz, *King's Two Bodies*, 32–3.

[72] T. A. Sandquist, 'The Holy Oil of St Thomas of Canterbury', in id. and M. R. Powicke (edd.), *Essays in Medieval History presented to Bertie Wilkinson* (Toronto, 1969), 330–44. Richard probably wanted to see the English monarchy invested with a mystique comparable to the French: the French kings were anointed with a holy oil brought from heaven by a dove at Clovis's baptism. See also above, p. 31, and below, pp. 86–7, 202.

[73] For the king's itinerary in the final years of his reign see T. F. Tout, *Chapters in the Administrative History of Mediaeval England*, 6 vols. (Manchester, 1920–33), iv. 33–5.

[74] C. M. Barron, 'The Deposition of Richard II', in *Politics and Crisis*, 132–49.

subjects. Richard's rule had generated an unhappy condition of faction and feud. Magnate had been set against magnate, and even courtier against courtier.[75] Uncertainty had been bred by the demands for 'blank charters' and by the other devices of the tyranny. Fear and suspicion had been aroused by the manipulation to which local office-holding had been subjected; antipathy and distaste were felt towards those thought to have profited excessively from royal favour.[76] Alienation from the court was running at a higher level than at any time since the 1320s.[77] The idea of taking up arms on behalf of Richard and his friends was one that clearly appealed to few.

More damaging still to the king's cause was a deep-seated weakness at the heart of his political design. As had become apparent since 1397, the end that he strove for was incompatible with the means that he employed to achieve it. The end was the creation of a universal kingship, a kingship all-embracing in its appeal; but the means to that end was the anything but universal one of the exercise of private lordship. In late fourteenth-century conditions the two could not easily coexist. Appeal to lordship through the medium of affinity-building tarnished the very regality that it was supposed to uphold.[78] The king's governance was seen to be factional and partisan in character, as Henry IV was to find when he placed similar reliance on his own affinity after 1399.[79] Those who were excluded from favour found it difficult to identify with their ruler: they felt left out and strayed down the path to rebellion. Richard's kingship fell victim

---

[75] Richard's policy of building up the power of court-based magnates inevitably had the effect of eating into the power of existing territorial lords. In the north, for example, the Percies and the Nevilles resented the intrusion of the dukes of Aumale and Exeter, and in Gloucestershire Lord Berkeley was unhappy with the growing eminence of Thomas Despenser. Within the court there was friction between those who favoured the seizure of the Lancastrian inheritance and those, connected with John of Gaunt, who did not: see C. Given-Wilson, 'Richard II, Edward II and the Lancastrian Inheritance', *EHR* 109 (1994), 553–71.

[76] Antipathy for the courtiers is strongly suggested by e.g. the attacks on the Gloucestershire property of Sir Andrew Hake, one of Richard's knights and a newcomer to the county (PRO SC8/212/10568 and SC8/221/11045).

[77] Dr Barron argues that Richard's rule was not unpopular. It is difficult to accept this in the light of the evidence of the uprising at Bampton (Oxon.) in 1398, when the insurgents called for the destruction of the king and the magnates and attempted to seek out the king at Bristol and Gloucester E. G. Kimball (ed.), *Oxfordshire Sessions of the Peace in the Reign of Richard II* (Oxford Record Soc. 53, London, 1983), 83–9.

[78] Gillespie, 'Richard II's Cheshire Archers', 32–3.

[79] A. L. Brown, 'The Reign of Henry IV: The Establishment of the Lancastrian Dynasty', in S. B. Chrimes, C. D. Ross, and R. A. Griffiths (edd.), *Fifteenth Century England, 1399–1509* (Manchester, 1972), 1–28; N. E. Saul, 'The Commons and the Abolition of Badges', *Parliamentary History*, 9 (1990), 302–15.

to this deep inner contradiction. Founded on the premisses that it was, it stood little chance of survival in the longer term. Resort to force and a clampdown on dissent could only delay the day of its demise and never completely avert it. Stability in the long run could only be assured by the bringing of a genuine peace to the realm, not Richard's perverted distortion of it.

4

Richard II's Councils

Anthony Goodman

I The King's Council

In the fourteenth century the king sought counsel from magnates, leading royal officers, 'official' councillors, and others who happened to be staying with him, and from certain members of his Household. More formally, magnates gave advice when summoned as Lords of Parliament, or to Great Councils meeting the king at one of his residences. Coincidentally, there developed a formal group of official councillors, the King's Council. This met in regular sessions, and was often, but not exclusively, concerned with devising ways of executing policy decisions referred to it by the king, and with making decisions on minor or routine matters. Under Edward III, Professor Ormrod has remarked, 'it is difficult to find any aspect of administration in which it [the King's Council] was not involved'.[1]

Key bureaucratic features of the Council became fixed by or in the early fourteenth century. It was customary for councillors to be retained as such, for them to take an oath of office, and to receive fees or wages for conciliar service. The Council was composed chiefly but not exclusively of royal officials. The chancellor and the treasurer were ex officio councillors, but justices were summoned to sit at the Council board when legal issues were on the agenda, or when the Council was sitting as a court. Councillors consulted frequently, particularly during legal terms. The Clerk of

I am heavily indebted to the criticisms of Prof. A. L. Brown of the University of Glasgow.

[1] W. M. Ormrod, *The Reign of Edward III: Crown and Political Society in England 1327–1377* (London, 1990), 75. Further points about Edward's Council are indebted to this work. See also A. L. Brown, *The Governance of Late Medieval England 1272–1461* (London, 1989), ch. 2, and J. F. Baldwin, *The King's Council in England during the Middle Ages* (Oxford, 1913), ch. 4.

the Council John Prophete's 'Journal of the Council' recorded fifteen meetings in February 1392 and a total of forty-one for the period covered (20 January 1392–21 February 1393). One councillor, Sir Edward Dallingridge, attended thirty-three of these sessions, but his account for conciliar service covering an almost identical period shows him to have been working for two hundred and seven days. On many of these he was travelling on business as directed by the king or Council, but on some he was residing with the king, and, it is to be assumed, was being consulted by him in person, or considering issues as directed by him, in the company of fellow 'official' councillors, and of unofficial ones.[2]

'Official' councillors naturally gravitated to court: it was proper and convenient for their sessions to proceed in close consultation with the king. An example is to be found in a Council minute of October 1389.[3] Richard II remitted an important matter to the councillors: they discussed it at two sessions, after each of which they reported back to him (the second time at Kennington), the chancellor acting as their spokesman. The sessions were presumably both held at Westminster: since the business of other royal offices which the councillors occupied often took them there and information relevant to conciliar matters was to hand there, there was a long-standing tendency for the Council to meet in Westminster palace or in one of the principal London friaries, even though the king might be distant. The Star Chamber, a new chamber in the palace, was put at the Council's disposal in the 1340s, and became the Council's regular meeting-place— it was there that one of the sessions cited in 1389 was held.

Communication between an itinerating king, when he was making important decisions in consultation with those around him, and councillors in session at Westminster, might not be easy and smooth. In these circumstances the liaising role of men such as Sir Edward Dallingridge, who was both an officer of the king's Chamber and a councillor, was important. The lot of a councillor was physically as well as mentally strenuous, as can be seen from the travels recorded in Dallingridge's account. Between early January and early March 1392 he spent fifty-seven days on the Council's business in London. In March he was in Kent and Sussex for a fortnight, at Leeds, Dover, and Battle abbey. Five days after Easter (14 April), he was back at work, packing in twenty-eight days in London in that month and May, before travelling northwards to serve for forty-two days at Stamford and Nottingham (where the king held Great Councils). Dallingridge's conciliar commitments slackened in the summer, but the king sent him

[2] Baldwin, *King's Council*, 489–504; PRO E101/96/1.   [3] *POPC* i. 12[b–d].

to London for business with the controller of the Household in July (five days), and in August he was there again for the settlement of the dispute between the king and the citizens of London. His conciliar duties remained light for the rest of the year: a week at Woodstock for a Council meeting (27 September–5 October, presumably, a Great Council), and ten days' work in December in London on the chancellor's business. Soon after Epiphany, Dallingridge was back in harness attending Parliament at Winchester, and Council sessions in London.[4]

The bureaucratic form which the Council had assumed evolved as a convenient habit: the parts it played in government were not rigidly fixed. It was a flexible instrument of royal policy, the evolution of which was a response to the needs of the king and officers of state. The composition of the Council and the ways in which it was employed were above all matters for the king's decision: it was up to him as to how much he sought the advice and assent of his appointed councillors, either individually or collectively, as to what sort of business he remitted for their consideration, and as to what degree of responsibility for decision-making he accorded to them.

This particular evolution of the Council was acceptable to informed public opinion in the fourteenth century, partly because it had correspondences with the evolution of the private councils which magnates relied on to assist in the management of their affairs. Moreover, the clearer bureaucratic profile of the Council enabled subjects to focus on it and exploit it as a vehicle for the reform of government, framing measures to redefine its composition; to make it more efficient and responsive to their concepts of the common good; and to entrust it with important and exclusive responsibilities. By Richard's reign there existed notional panaceas for the revival of a sick polity by the reform of the Council, even the extension of its powers to give it certain exclusive responsibilities. In the period 1376–90, Lords and Commons in Parliament, and those summoned to Great Councils were often busy framing devices for the Council. Richard came to view such parliamentary initiatives with suspicion, fearing that they would curtail his freedom to choose and control his own chief officers, to seek the advice of whom he wanted, and be unconstrained by the necessity of having the advice and assent of his official councillors for certain types of business. However, it would be mistaken to conclude that the reign witnessed the emergence of fixedly opposed views about the role of the Council, particularly about who should have a say in making and approving the appointment

[4] PRO E101/96/1.

of councillors, and about the degree of autonomous power they should collectively exercise. Rather, in a period when confidence in government tended to be low, Lords and Commons in Parliament displayed an unusually lively, even presumptuous, interest in devising practical measures designed to secure a curative 'ideal Council'. In so doing they were guided by two different, and not always easily reconcilable, sets of precepts about monarchical power. On the one hand, there were the prescriptions of philosophy, which Richard could have generally endorsed with heartfelt enthusiasm. On the other hand, there were precedents from movements to reform the government of his royal ancestors, which he doubtless regarded unfavourably.

The most influential works of political theory in fourteenth-century England which contained reflections on the role of counsel emanated from, or were based on, the views of Aristotelian schoolmen of the thirteenth and early fourteenth centuries. They had been concerned to define the role of councillors in upholding and promoting the monarchy as an institution ordained for the public good, and to specify their necessary qualifications and qualities. An influential treatise was the *Secretum Secretorum*, Arabic in origin, and believed to be advice given by Aristotle to Alexander. The *Secretum* insisted on the necessity of counsel for a ruler. The counsel of those who were young or lowborn was not to be despised. To control and test the worthiness of his councillors, the king ought to consult them singly as well as collectively. He should reject their unanimous advice if he considered it to be *inutile*. The necessity of informed wisdom was emphasized: councillors should possess *sciencia* and *sapiencia* as well as *virtutes*, so that they could give *consilium philosophicum*. If Richard read the *Secretum*, much of what it said would have been music to his ears: if he wished to emulate Alexander, he had *carte blanche* to raise up the young and obscure as councillors and to use their counsel as he thought fit.[5]

Another key work, equally strongly in favour of royal authority, was Giles of Rome's *De Regimine Principum* (1277–9), which its author had presented to his former pupil Philip IV of France. Edward III owned a copy, and John Trevisa translated *De Regimine* into English for his patron Lord Berkeley, *c.*1390. In 1387 Sir Simon Burley, Richard's former governor, owned 'a book of government of kings and princes' in French. In 1397 the duke of Gloucester had a Latin copy in his library at Pleshey castle, and in 1399 his widow the Duchess Eleanor bequeathed a copy in French to

---

[5] A. H. Gilbert, 'Notes on the Influence of the *Secretum Secretorum*', *Speculum*, 3 (1928), 95–8; M. A. Manzalaoui (ed.), *Secretum Secretorum*, i. *Nine English Versions* (EETS, 1977), 74–80. For the subject of counsel in general, A. Black, *Political Thought in Europe 1250–1450* (Cambridge, 1992), ch. 5.

their son Humphrey. Thomas Hoccleve, in *The Regement of Princes* (1411–
12), expressed his belief that Henry prince of Wales, to whom he presented
his work, was familiar with both the *Secretum* and the *De Regimine*.[6] Giles
emphasized the necessity of having several councillors to consider important matters, and defined the qualities and qualifications that councillors
should possess. Their deliberations (to quote an early translation) should
be 'mult secré' and they should be 'preudons et de bone vie, et amis as
rois et as princes, et sages et avisez'. Giles of Rome went on to distinguish
the principal matters on which councillors were to give advice. The first
of these was royal revenue and taxation. Here they were to keep in mind
two objectives: that the people were not oppressed by unreasonable taxes,
and that the king was not cheated of his due revenues.[7]

These standard works of political education in the fourteenth century
inculcated the king's right to seek the counsel of whom he wished, and
the desirability of elevating councillors whose distinction lay in qualities
of character, mind, and training. However, their models of ideal monarchy also provided a critique by which the king's choice of councillors,
the extent to which he relied on their judgement, and the worth of their
performance of their duties could be judged. Moreover, for the critical
there was a much more authoritative source which encouraged a severe
judgemental attitude towards kings and their councillors—the Old Testament. Archbishop Stratford, in his celebrated letter to Edward criticizing
his government (1 January 1341) held up the examples of Solomon and
Rehoboam. Israel had flourished under Solomon, who took as his councillors 'lez plus aunciens et plus sagez de la terre', but Rehoboam lost the
allegiance of most of the tribes of Israel because he dismissed his father's
councillors, 'et fist apres le consail de jeune gentz qe luyt voleient pleare'.[8]
The equation of mature age with the requisite conciliar virtues was a lesson
which Gower wished to impress on Richard II and Henry of Lancaster
in the 1390s. In the seventh book of *Confessio Amantis*, he cited the same
exemplary tale as Stratford, concentrating on how 'Roboas' (Rehoboam)
rejected the good council of 'the wise knyghtes olde', preferring that of
foolish young men who despises these elders. Gower concluded:

[6] N. Orme, *From Childhood to Chivalry* (London, 1984), 90–7. Prof. Charles F. Briggs
read an instructive paper at Kalamazoo, May 1992 on 'Princely Mirrors and Diverse
Readers: The Late Medieval English Audience of Giles of Rome's *De regimine principum*';
cf. Brigg's Ph.D. thesis, 'The English Manuscripts of Giles of Rome's *De Regimine
Principum* and their Audience, 1300–1500' (Chapel Hill, NC, 1993).

[7] *Li Livres du Gouvernement*, ed. S. P. Molenaer (New York, 1899), 330–5.

[8] Printed in S. B. Chrimes and A. L. Brown (edd.), *Select Documents of English Constitutional History 1307–1485* (London, 1961), 58–60.

> That young conseil, which is to warm,
> Er men be war doth ofte harm.
> Old age for the conseil serveth,
> And lusti youthe his thonk deserveth
> Upon the travail which he doth . . .

Though the poet followed a format similar to the *Secretum*, the instruction of a pupil, he may well have thought that the advice about young councillors in the *Secretum* was too heady for young princes: they required Old Testament admonition.[9]

The authors of 'mirrors of princes' had not suggested ways in which subjects could intervene to assist in procuring and checking on model councillors. In England, however, there were notable precedents going back to the thirteenth century for action by the 'community of the realm' to replace 'evil' councillors, and to ensure that government was conducted by worthy ones. Past struggles of leading tenants-in-chief, to ensure that kings sought their advice and assent on matters which touched them all, had helped to mould a political culture in which lords, when times were bad, nobly turned away from the business of their private administrations and from their sports, and professed their willingness to shoulder even the burdens of being official councillors. This did not appear as an unnatural role to them, as it might have done to older generations of continental Aristotelian schoolmen, who saw such tasks as more fitting for their own kind, the clerical *legisperiti*. In fourteenth-century England a trinitarian hierarchy of nobles was one conciliar model which came to be much admired. In an age when dukes and earls might well be learned, and barons and bannerets might have careers as royal officials, opinion accepted that many of those trained primarily to practise chivalry could make as adept bureaucrats as any canonist.

Examples of attempts in the fourteenth century before Richard's reign to impose conciliar devices on kings are well known. In 1311 Edward II had been compelled to accept the ordinances, in order to correct government carried on 'par mauveis consail et deceivant'. He gave assent for the Lords and Commons to select prelates, earls, and barons who appeared 'suffisauntz' to them. These should have 'plein poer de ordiner lestat de nostre Hostiel et de nostre roiaume', so that the ordinances be maintained.[10]

---

[9] John Gower, *The Complete Works*, ed. G. C. Macaulay, iii (EETS, Oxford, 1901), 348–51. Views congenial to Richard on the attitudes and qualities he sought in councillors, and how they might be tested in candidates, may be reflected in 'De quadripartita regis specie', in J.-P. Genet (ed.), *Four English Political Tracts of the Later Middle Ages* (Camden Soc., 4th ser. 18, London, 1977), 38–9.

[10] *RP* i. 281–6.

In 1316 Edward was forced to accept the appointment during Parliament of certain prelates, earls, and barons to be his councillors.[11] In 1340 the Commons petitioned Edward III to agree to the appointment of councillors who were dedicated and diligent, loyal and of good character, and subjects of the realm. They requested that these be elected in Parliament, and from Parliament to Parliament, to which they would be answerable— similar provisions were to be made in Richard's reign.[12] The system of conciliar government in his minority was to be closely modelled on the most recent and elaborate of these reform schemes: that put forward by the Commons in the Good Parliament of 1376. The assurance with which this scheme addressed conciliar organization suggests that it was drafted with the aid of men who had sat at the Council board. The Commons asked for ten or twelve temporal lords, prelates, and others to be added to the Council. They should rotate their service so that six were continually involved. Important business was to be settled with the advice and assent of all; other matters required a quorum of six or four. Reports to the king of the Council's decisions, for his advice and assent, should be made only by councillors (for example, by two of them so deputed).[13]

Conciliar government in the minority was based on the scheme set out in the Commons petition of October 1377. This scheme proposed how the Council was to be 'enlarged', and how it was to conduct its business, on lines similar to those adumbrated in 1376. Then the objective had been to create a politically formidable Council which could outweigh the influence of John of Gaunt and members of the Household over the ailing Edward III. In 1377 the Commons wanted to create a counterweight to Gaunt and his brothers. Their petition was more emphatic about the qualifications and qualities which the eight councillors appointed to assist the king's officers should possess. They were to be 'sufficient persons of various estates and degrees', drawn from the most knowledgeable in dealing with abuses and emergencies. The Commons requested that they be told the names of the councillors, and that councillors should normally be elected in Parliament. In fact the names of nine councillors (bishops, earls, barons, and bannerets) were announced in Parliament, appointed with the advice of the Lords. It was laid down that they and their successors were

[11] *RP* i. 351.
[12] Text in B. Wilkinson, *Constitutional History of Medieval England 1216–1399*, ii (London, 1952), 194–7; cf. G. L. Harriss, 'The Commons' Petition of 1340', *EHR* 78 (1963), 625–54.
[13] *RP* ii. 322. The councillors were not to accept substantial gifts, and were to swear to keep the ordinance. In giving assent, Edward III made the practical proviso that the chief officers should be able to dispatch their departmental business without the presence of these additional councillors.

to hold office for one year only, and were not to be reappointed for two years.[14] This system of conciliar government, involving magnates in day-to-day business, was to be adjudged a qualified success: it was terminated in the Parliament which met in January 1380.[15] Magnates were probably weary of discharging conciliar responsibilities, and suspicion of Gaunt's intentions had lessened. The Commons then requested that the Council should henceforth be composed of the chief royal officers, among whom they included the chamberlain and treasurer of the Household.[16] They wished to prolong features of the recent parliamentary scrutiny of the Council, asking that they be told the names of councillors, and that the latter should remain in office till the next Parliament. They seem to have accepted with some apprehension that a king nearing adulthood would increasingly rely for counsel on those in his company.

For the period 1380–6 the absence of records of appointments of councillors, and of payments to them of fees and wages—contrasting with their relative abundance for the early years of the reign—hampers reconstruction of the personnel and work of the Council.[17] Presumably the 'core' official councillors, as laid down in Parliament in 1380, were the five principal royal officers. However, it is likely that important decisions, especially over the distribution of patronage, were made by the king on receipt of petitions, on the advice of individual 'official' councillors who happened to be in his company, and/or of unofficial ones, denizens of the Household. Such methods lay within his prerogative, but they undermined the code of 'conciliar good practice' which the estates had striven to establish. Yet this change was not the burden of complaint: concern was voiced about the quality of advice which Richard was receiving. In 1381 the Commons asked that bad officers and councillors should be ousted, and that better ones who were more virtuous and sufficient should replace them. They wanted

---

[14] *RP* iii. 5–6; T. F. Tout, *Chapters in the Administrative History of Mediaeval England*, iii (Manchester, 1928), 333–6. The arrangement made in 1376 for liaison between the council and the king was dropped. Perhaps this was not good for Richard's *amour propre*. It is not clear whether the unhappy precedent of the arrangements for Edward III's minority government was considered. Then fourteen magnates (four bishops, four earls, six barons) were appointed to remain with the king to counsel him (Baldwin, *King's Council*, 98). Sir John Gildsburgh, Speaker of the Commons in 1380, asserted that Edward III at the start of his reign had had no other councillors apart from the five principal officers (*RP* iii. 73).

[15] *RP* iii. 35–6, 55. For the composition and functioning of these 'continual' councils, N. B. Lewis, 'The "Continual Council" in the Early Years of Richard II, 1377–1380', *EHR* 41 (1926).

[16] *RP* iii. 71–3.

[17] For the Council in 1381, J. A. Tuck, *Richard II and the English Nobility* (London, 1973), 48.

Richard to have in his company and as his councillors the most sufficient and discreet bachelors who could be found in the realm. The earl of Arundel and Sir Michael de la Pole were appointed to reside in the Household, and 'to council and govern' the king.[18] An episode the following year, which Walsingham recounts, suggests that public opinion remained disquieted about the advice which Richard was accepting, and that the measures for good counsel taken in the 1381 Parliament were ineffective. The chronicler says that the chancellor, Richard lord Scrope, refused to seal grants of the late earl of March's lands, which the king had made in response to the petitions of ambitious knights and esquires of low degree.[19] Anthony Tuck has shown that many of the recipients of these grants of wardship were members of the Household or close associates of the court.[20] Scrope was conscientiously trying to protect the interests of the heir, Roger Mortimer, against piecemeal exploitation sanctioned by a young king who cared more about being lavish to his servants than protecting the interests of an eminent kinsman.

Continuing public concern about royal decision-making was reflected in the measures proposed somewhat half-heartedly in both 1383 Parliaments to set up mechanisms to influence the process. Richard's firm rejection of these was facilitated by divisions in the élites over a variety of policies—both between Lords and Commons, and between the ecclesiastical and secular peers. In the first 1383 Parliament, the Commons tried to revive the 1381 scheme to influence counsel, petitioning that certain lords be assigned to stay with the king and counsel him, according to the advice of the Lords. Richard refused, asserting his right to choose members of his Household.[21] In the second Parliament, according to the Westminster Chronicler, unnamed peers opined that the king 'followed insane council, and on account of this he was not supported by good rule about him'. The chronicler (perhaps with tongue in cheek) recounts how lords called to mind a golden age in England, when the king's most illustrious predecessors had been ruled by the advice of their lords. Whatever sort of appointments and sanctions the Lords were proposing, they cut no ice with Richard or the Commons—or with the monk chronicler. With constitutional propriety and historical impeccability, and to the satisfaction of the Commons,

---

[18] *RP* iii. 100–1, 104. The access to court of the king's confessor Thomas Russhook was restricted.

[19] *Hist. Angl.* ii. 69–70. This episode is discussed at length below, pp. 120–1.

[20] *Richard II and the English Nobility*, 88–90. Pressure from the kinsmen of the heir, Roger Mortimer, led to the cancellation of the grants.

[21] *RP* iii. 147.

Richard argued against his being ruled or led exclusively by the Lords' advice, but said that he was willing to accept with all deference the advice of those whom he described, in the politically correct fashion, as 'viros electos et probatos'.[22]

Though these fine and demure words impressed the chronicler, he was to show disillusion with the king's attitudes, decisions, and policies over the next two years. So was Walsingham, who asserted that in 1384 the king's accustomed councillors were two clerks of the royal household chapel—possibly he was reporting a jibe made by a high-placed visitor to his abbey.[23] A flood of light on informed perceptions of Richard's use of his Council in these years is provided by the document known as the 'Advice', which John Palmer has identified as a draft made in the Lords in the 1385 Parliament.[24] Its authors were imbued with the tendency abroad since 1376 to construct rules to enlarge the powers of the Council. Besides being concerned to remedy what they considered as Richard's cavalier and disorderly approach to business, they recognized that there were long-term conciliar problems, notably the difficulty of co-ordinating policy between peripatetic kings and councillors who were often physically separated from them, whose business was more conveniently conducted at Westminster. The 'Advice' urges that the king should give authority to the Council to determine matters concerning the law and the realm, and should not countermand them by message or letter. If anyone sought an audience with the king to raise such matters, he should be denied, but should be sent to the Council for examination. The king should hold regular audiences with the Council to discuss important business. This would make him better informed, and the issues would be more efficiently and speedily dealt with. The problem of misinformation, especially acute when king and Council were in separate places, was met by the suggestion that the chamberlain, steward, and keeper of the Privy Seal (ex-officio councillors) should be his sole intermediaries. One of the most important recommendations, accepted by a committee of the Lords set up to consider the 'Advice', was that any grants to individuals affecting the disposal of revenue should be made with the full advice and assent of the Council.

The recommendations of the 'Advice' were not embodied in an ordinance. Lords and Commons were reluctant to press the king hard: he had, after all, recently led an impressive army which had devastated his Scottish enemies, and he was in the process of conferring signal honours

---

[22] *Westm. Chron.* 54–5.   [23] *Hist. Angl.* ii. 113.
[24] Printed in Chrimes and Brown (edd.), *Select Documents*, 160–2.

and favours on his uncles. The conciliar scheme of 1377–80 was not revived: the Commons more circumspectly petitioned that they might be told which lords would be appointed to the Council, and that these councillors be empowered to institute a search for debts owed to the king. This was assented to: the venerable and distinguished bishops Wykeham and Brantingham were nominated, and it was promised that two bannerets would be too.

Dr Palmer has shown how the agitation in the 1386 Parliament, which inaugurated the central crisis of the reign, was crucially related to the failure of government to implement aspects of the reform programme agreed on in the 1385 Parliament.[25] The mode of attack favoured by the Commons in 1386—the impeachment of de la Pole for his conduct as chancellor—did not focus directly on the role of the Council, but that too was important in the Commons' eyes. As part of his defence, de la Pole argued that responsibility for the alleged failure to implement the ordinance for financial reform did not lie solely with him, but also with the other chief officers and the Council. Since he said that they were prepared to join him in replying, they too were manifestly ready to uphold a principle of collective conciliar responsibility. However, the Commons treated this as a diversionary tactic, though according a degree of agreement with de la Pole's premiss: they declared that they found the others culpable too, in this matter and concerning two other articles, but him above all, as the principal royal officer.[26]

Deep disillusion with Richard's handling of his Council, as well as with the failure and divisiveness of his policies, led the estates in 1386 to impose a form of conciliar government modelled on that of 1377–80. The Commons petitioned for the appointment in Parliament of the chancellor, treasurer, keeper of the Privy Seal, steward of the Household, 'and also other lords of your great and continual council', and for the grant to them of a sweeping commission to reform and oversee government. Most of the points in the petition were accepted: the Council was given statutory authority, to last for a year. With the king's hostility in mind, the Council's responsibilities and duties were spelled out elaborately, and it was given a more eminent component in its membership than the Councils of 1377–80. A recommendation in the 1385 'Advice' was formulated with sharp teeth: none 'of whatsoever dignity, estate, nation or condition he might be, should be so bold, either in private nor openly, to council or

---

[25] J. J. N. Palmer, 'The Parliament of 1385 and the Constitutional Crisis of 1386', *Speculum*, 46 (1971); id., 'The Impeachment of Michael de la Pole in 1386', *BIHR* 42 (1969).
[26] *RP* iii. 216–18.

procure anything contrary to what the said lords and officers wish to council, and this on grievous penalty'. Recognition was given to what had been implied in the 'Advice'—that the business of the Council was customarily discharged chiefly in London. The chief officers and councillors were enjoined to reside there continually, so that they might more easily consult the records, and the justices and officers, of Chancery, Exchequer, and other departments. The Council was composed, besides the chief officers, of the customary hierarchical trinity, but with slightly larger numbers than hitherto (five ecclesiastics, three lay magnates, and three barons), and with more eminent members—the two archbishops and the two available royal uncles.[27]

In view of the stringency of the 1386 commission, and the sensitivity that Richard had displayed in previous years over his freedom to seek counsel, it is not surprising that he was bitterly opposed to aspects of this Council's authority, as well as to the manner of its appointment. The bizarre situation in 1387, when he was attempting to undermine the authority of his own Council, was to some extent facilitated by the stipulated concentration of its business in London, encouraging his spoiling tactic of absenting himself from customary royal haunts. With the court itinerating in unusual and sometimes obscure places, courtiers were emboldened to place restrictions on councillors' access to the king, and to tender advice contrary to that proffered by the Council, in complete defiance of its commission. Yet, despite the king's obstructiveness, and the emergence of a definable court party opposed to the Council, the latter, it has been demonstrated, fulfilled the terms of its commission with some *éclat*. It effected economies in the Household and administration, and launched a campaign against the French and their allies, which had some showy success. As Professor Tuck has pointed out, there is evidence for the Council dutifully seeking the king's will. He transmitted instructions under the signet to the chancellor and keeper of the Privy Seal.[28] However, at the same time he plotted to criminalize the commission and its procurers.[29]

Consequently, conciliar authority became a central issue in a revolt. The Appeal of Treason accused the favourites of having abused royal authority in the king's youth, by proffering bad counsel, and excluding others from influence. They had diminished prerogative, as the king 'was sworn to be governed, counselled and guided by them'. A number of clauses in the Appeal more specifically outlined the ways in which they had flouted

[27] Ibid. 221, 224.   [28] *Richard II and the English Nobility*, 109–10.
[29] *RP* iii. 233–4.

the authority of the 1386 commission, and also instigated attempts to seek punishment for those who had procured it.[30] The success of the Appeal in the Merciless Parliament of 1388 and of the Commons impeachments related to it, powerfully underscored the primacy and powers of the Council as an instrument of government. The problem of keeping king and courtiers in step with the Council was met, according to the Westminster Chronicler, by another parliamentary measure, similar to the one rejected by Richard in 1383—the appointment of a group of lords who were to attend continually on the king, without whose consent he should do nothing. Five were appointed, all mature men who had been prominent in royal service—Bishops Wykeham and Braybrooke, the earl of Warwick, and Lords Scrope and Cobham.[31] It does not appear, however, that the Council was backed by a renewal of the 1386 commission. It may be that Richard was thought to be sufficiently cowed and docile, and the hostile court party thoroughly broken up. Also, Richard's campaign against the terms of the commission in 1387 may have raised sufficient doubts to induce caution about renewing them. The commission was to remain the high watermark in the reign of attempts to define an exclusive authority for a highly aristocratic Council.

Within a year of the end of the Merciless Parliament, Richard's declaration to his lords that (in Walsingham's words), 'I will call whom I will to the Council', and his dismissal of the duke of Gloucester and the earl of Arundel as councillors, represented a remarkable reversal in his fortunes (8 May 1389).[32] Measures taken over the next few years suggest that one factor in the revival of his fortunes was his willingness to embrace (however much as a marriage of convenience) aspects of the conciliar reform programme which he had tried to evade. He encouraged leading courtiers to co-operate with the Council, especially in implementing reform measures. He agreed to ordinances defining the Council's powers and responsibilities, and attempting to bring orderliness to its proceedings. He sought parliamentary approval for its conduct. In all these matters he may have been following seriously for the first time the advice of eminent servants of his grandfather (notably Bishop Wykeham), who had been heavily involved in conciliar reform programmes since 1376, and who now

---

[30] Ibid. 229–45.
[31] *Westm. Chron.* 332–3. For this group, see Tuck, *Richard II and the English Nobility*, 127. A statute enacted on a Commons petition laid down severe penalties for anyone who concerned themselves with government, unless by order of the Council and with the king's assent (RP iii. 246).
[32] *Hist. Angl.* ii. 181.

saw the implementation of parts of them as the foundation for restoring the king's battered personal authority.

It is noteworthy that the Great Council held at Windsor on 20 August 1389 was attended by six mature and long-serving Chamber knights who had managed to avoid obloquy in the recent controversies—John Clanvowe, William Neville, Nicholas Sharnsfield, Lewis Clifford, Richard Stury, and Edward Dallingridge.[33] They were all to be appointed, if they had not been already, as councillors, and were to be prominent in attendance at Council sessions in London in the early 1390s. They inaugurated the leading roles which officers of the Chamber were to play for the rest of the reign, as members of the Council operating both in the Household and away from it, rather than acting as unofficial councillors in palace closets.[34]

The accountability of the chief officers and the Council to the community of the realm was demonstrated in the Parliament of January 1390, when the chancellor (Wykeham), the treasurer (Houghton, bishop of St Davids), and 'all the lords of the Great Council except the clerk of the privy seal' were, on their own petition, formally discharged. They asked anyone to declare to the king in Parliament defaults which they had committed in office. The estates professed themselves to be fully satisfied with their conduct, and the king reappointed them, with the addition, as in 1386, of two of his uncles (Lancaster and Gloucester). When the officers and councillors appeared in order to take their oaths of office in the presence of Parliament, Richard made it clear that he did not wish the discharge and reappointment of his officers there to be a precedent. Reiterating the statement of prerogative which he had declared to the Great Council of May 1389, he said that 'he wished to be free and able to remove and choose his councillors entirely at his own will, and whenever it pleased him'.[35] Nevertheless, the ordinance made at a Council meeting in his presence in March 1390 'sur le gouvernement a tenir par le Conseil du Roi' shows that he considered it prudent to subscribe to measures which channelled the exercise of some of his prerogatives through the Council.[36] It was agreed that no grant or gift which might reduce the king's revenue was to be

[33] *POPC* i. 6–11. Sir John Devereux, steward of the Household, also attended the Windsor meeting and the Great Council at Clarendon on 13 Sept., as did the chamberlain Sir Peter Courtenay, Sharnsfield, Sir Richard Abberbury, Clifford, Neville, and Dallingridge (ibid. 11). Some of the ordinances regarding patronage and financial administration passed at the Windsor meeting touched on the role of the King's Council (ibid. 9–11).

[34] For an example of Dallingridge and Clifford acting in 1389 as intermediaries on behalf of their fellow councillors with the king, ibid. 14[b–c].

[35] *RP* iii. 258.   [36] *POPC* i. 18[a–b].

made without the advice and assent of a quorum of two of the three royal uncles, together with the chancellor. Apart from this, the 1390 Ordinance is remarkable for its codification of the Council's responsibilities and procedures. In some respects, this was probably a summary of customary business practices which had evolved in the course of regular meetings in Westminster and London, and in response to the need to give priority to the weightiest business, in face of the large numbers of petitions remitted for the Council's consideration or addressed directly to it. The lords of the Council were to attend between eight and nine o'clock at the latest. They were to give priority to the affairs of the king and realm. As appropriate, business was to be passed on to the justices, to the chancellor (in Chancery), and to the Exchequer. All other matters which could not be decided without the king's advice were to be referred to him to know his will. Once an item was brought before the Council, a response should be given before the next item was raised. The *bachilers* (in this context, the Chamber knights) were to have reasonable wages for their Council work, and the lords an expense allowance as determined by king and Council. The existence of different sorts of Council sessions was acknowledged: ones which discussed the most important matters required the presence of the chief officers. Consideration and determination of less important petitions required the presence only of one of them, the keeper of the Privy Seal.

In the 1390s Richard came to appreciate better that a Council with a high and prestigious profile, clearly defined responsibilities, good business practices, and close, harmonious relations with the Chamber, added to the lustre and effectiveness of his authority. The system of conciliar government principally by the chief officers and Chamber knights continued till the end of the reign. In the mid-1390s, the older generation of chief officers and councillors, many of whom had been involved in the conciliar reforming schemes of 1376–90, were giving way to others who, though not insufficiently qualified by status, age, learning, and experience, were more compliant to the king's rigid views on prerogative and bolder in seeking rewards for their services.[37] Differences in attitude are illustrated by the contrasting careers in royal service of Richard lord Scrope; a supporter of reforms in the 1370s and 1380s, and his son William (chamberlain 1395, earl of Wiltshire 1397, treasurer 1398), who was executed by the rebels in 1399. William Scrope, and the Chamber knights John Bussy, Henry Grene (both appointed as councillors 1 August 1397), and William Bagot, were

---

[37] For the changes in personnel, C. Given-Wilson, *The Royal Household and the King's Affinity* (New Haven, 1986), 185–7.

to be prominent in the rogues' gallery of pro–Lancastrian chroniclers.[38] Professor Tuck has analysed the important part which the Council played in implementing the 'tyranny' of 1397–9.[39] A great deal of conciliar business was generated by the 1397 forfeitures. Bussy was a conspicuously trusted and busy administrator: he earned Walsingham's hatred for his highly charged and partisan role as Speaker of the Commons in the 1397–8 Parliament. The chronicler acknowledged Bussy's administrative and political talents, and pictured him as often in contact and conversation with Richard.[40] His name frequently appears in the lists of councillors present at a session, together with a note of the decision and the action to be taken which were often written on the dorse of petitions in these final years of the reign. Some examples of endorsements follow. At a Council meeting on 19 October 1397, Bussy and Sir Henry Grene reported the king's will concerning the duke of Exeter's petition about forfeited Arundel lands.[41] On 20 March 1398 Bussy and Grene were in the king's presence at Bristol when he granted a remission to the prior and convent of Canons Ashby.[42] Bussy was frequently in session when small groups of councillors settled less important petitions. On 26 April 1398 he was one of four who agreed to the petition, addressed directly to the Council by the royal esquire William Assh, concerning the terms on which he should hold forfeited estates.[43] On 2 May following, the chancellor, treasurer, and keeper of the Privy Seal, together with Bussy and Sir John Russell, agreed to the tenor of a petition from the lieges of Lancashire, who wanted exemption from new customs impositions.[44] The following day the same group, with the exception of the chancellor, concerted measures in response to a petition from the burgesses and community of Great Yarmouth.[45] On 2 December Bussy was present at a fuller meeting, with the chancellor, treasurer, the bishops of London and St Davids, Grene, Russell, Ralph Selby, and Lawrence Dru, at which a petition from a citizen of Bayonne was dealt with.[46]

---

[38] Walsingham bracketed them as 'evil councillors' with the dukes of Aumale, Norfolk, and Exeter (*Annales*, 225).

[39] Tuck, *Richard II and the English Nobility*, 196–200.

[40] *Annales*, 209–12, 214–15.   [41] PRO SC8/269/13406.

[42] PRO SC8/226/11253.

[43] PRO E28/4/61. The others were the keeper of the Privy Seal, Grene, and Russell.

[44] PRO SC8/221/11021.

[45] PRO E28/4/46. On 11 May 1398 the chancellor, treasurer, keeper of the Privy Seal, Selby, Bussy, Grene, Russell, and Dru considered a petition from Florens Montendre (PRO E28/4/63), and on 23 May the same three officers, Russell, Dru and one other (illegible), considered one addressed by William Wollaston to the Council (PRO E28/4/65).

[46] PRO SC8/221/11010. The petition has an endorsement on the front in another hand stating the king's will (faded).

This kind of evidence shows how effectively Richard used the Council during the 'tyranny', and why some of its members became unpopular, as conspicuous and eager executors of the 'tyranny'. Nevertheless, as regards policy-making, it is probable that even Bussy, Grene, and Bagot were small fry, and that Richard took crucial and controversial decisions in 1397–8 closeted with nobles who were to be their principal beneficiaries, such as those who were to plot desperately for Richard's speedy restoration in 1399. The Articles of Deposition only deplore by implication the behaviour of Richard's most partisan and influential councillors: William Scrope, Bussy, and Grene had already conveniently suffered as scapegoats for the regime. The Articles did not take Richard to task for ignoring the rules framed in the years 1377–90 to enhance the role of the Council in decision-making, and the precedents of influence exercised then in Parliaments over the personnel and responsibilities of the Council. Doubtless Henry of Lancaster was as eager as Richard to preserve his freedom in seeking counsel. Yet the years of conciliar reform did have lasting effects on the role of the Council. The 'community of the realm' had on occasion immersed themselves in the methods and problems of the Council, and by so doing had reinforced its authority, helping to mould a conciliar culture in which priority was given at its sessions to the discharge of the business of the king and realm, according to practised administrative guidelines. At the end of Richard's reign the Council remained, in the community's eyes, the king's concern, to be used by him in ways which he thought fit. Yet, if he did not run an effective Council, he courted political trouble. Informed public opinion regarded the Council as a touchstone of good government, and had acquired, especially in Richard's reign, a sharp agenda about its form and uses. Henry IV, to his chagrin, found that the composition and competence of his Council were issues on which reform-minded knights of the shire felt free to pronounce in Parliament. However, by the end of the fifteenth century public opinion unambiguously accepted Richard II's view that full royal control of the Council was an important part of royal prerogative. Why did this opinion prevail? The long-simmering dynastic issue had provided a respectable means of bypassing parliamentary agitation—the drastic solution of deposing the king. The precedent of 1399 thus eventually worked in favour of Richard's views of kingship. Moreover, it worked more positively than I have suggested. The abasements endured by kings during the Wars of the Roses led to their emphasis on majesty and its attributes, whose implications were more readily accepted by early Tudor subjects than they had been by Richard's. The latter had no experience or folk-memory of the toils and travails of civil war. It seems that under Edward IV and Henry VII there developed a widespread perception that dynastically insecure kings could not restore or maintain stability if their control of the Council was in any way compromised. Richard II did not have the benefit of such a consensus.

II Great Councils

In Richard II's reign the term 'Great Council' was applied to the enlarged 'continual' councils set up in the first years of the reign and in 1386. However, in Professor A. L. Brown's words, from *c*.1350 the expression was used as 'a technical term for assemblies varying in size from thirty to forty to several hundred men summoned by writs under the privy seal'.[47] These assemblies had become distinctive from Parliaments: they usually consisted of the King's Council in session for one or a few days with some peers. Great Councils discussed and gave advice on the important affairs of the king and realm. Though they had no power to make a statute or to grant a subsidy, they could promote either of them, as well as formulating conclusions about military and diplomatic policies and appointments, and the settlement of domestic tensions. Great Councils were essentially extended meetings of the King's Council. Minutes made by the Clerk of the Council in the reign fail to distinguish between Great Councils and routine meetings of the King's Council.

The political circumstances of Richard's early years stimulated recourse to Great Councils. It was at a Great Council held in June 1377, the day after the coronation, that prelates, earls, barons, and others present settled on an interim form of government, which functioned until Parliament met in October. They decided that ten persons should be appointed to assist the chancellor and treasurer—two bishops, two earls, two barons, two bannerets, and two bachelors, and they proceeded to elect them.[48] In the following years the king's 'tender age' made the chief officers and councillors appointed in Parliament acutely aware of the need to secure the support of the higher nobility for policies, not least as a means of reassuring and persuading the Commons in Parliament. The summons of a Great Council, before Parliament met, provided a means of hopefully presenting a solid noble front. For instance, in the first Parliament of 1379, the chancellor, Richard Scrope, explained that, in a recent Great Council, in response to official expositions of the foreign threat and the lack of funds

---

[47] Brown, *Governance*, 35, 174–5; cf. P. J. Holmes, 'The Great Council in the Reign of Henry VII', *EHR* 101 (1986), 840–2.

[48] Tout, *Chapters*, iii. 326–9; Tuck, *Richard II and the English Nobility*, 36–7.

to finance the war, those present concluded that a parliamentary subsidy needed to be raised. In the mean time, they decided, naval forces would be organized for the defence of the coast: the lords present offered loans towards the cost of this and royal requests to the Londoners and others for further loans were approved.[49] Richard was to show that he appreciated the importance of Great Councils as a means of consolidating and gaining support among the higher nobility. Though support in a Great Council could not be guaranteed, unless summonses were very selective and partisan, and though the support of a Great Council did not ensure the acceptance of a policy, he continued to summon Great Councils frequently after he asserted his majority in that of May 1389, in which he made a public demonstration of his prerogative by dismissing officers and councillors, and by appointing new ones.

The form of summons to a Great Council, issued by the authority of either the Privy Seal or signet, was fairly standard. Essential elements in it included the place at which the session was to be held, and the date at which it was to start, and the statement that its agenda concerned the affairs of king and realm.[50] For instance, certain bishops and barons were summoned to attend a Council at Reading in August 1381 'to counsel there concerning the state of the king and the realm'.[51] Sometimes it was said that the agenda would be revealed at the Council.[52] Summonses were normally sent out to a selection of spiritual and secular peers.[53] Signet letters requesting attendance at the Great Council which met at Berkhamsted in October 1381 were sent at least to the duke of Lancaster,

[49] *RP* iii. 55. Scrope also said that this Great Council had been summoned because the Gloucester Parliament had failed to take meaures for the war. In the first Parliament of 1382 Bishop Braybrooke reported that Great Councils (held respectively at Windsor and Westminster) had advised the king to lead an overseas expedition (ibid. 122, 144).

[50] The Register of Thomas Appleby, bishop of Carlisle, 1363–95, has several transcripts of Privy Seal summonses to Great Councils, with no year given; e.g. a summons to London to discuss Scottish negotiations. 'Et ce en nul manere ne lesse sur la foy ques nous vous deuetz' (Cumbria Record Office, DRC1/2, fo. 12ʳ). I owe thanks to Dr Richard Rose for allowing me to use his transcript of the register.

[51] PRO E403/485, 23 July (signet); cf. PRO E403/468, 4 June (letters sent for attendance at Great Council, London, 1378). All the leading men were summoned to Reading (*Westm. Chron.* 18–21).

[52] Implicit in a summons to the Stamford Council in 1392 (PRO E28/6/34; Privy Seal, Westminster, 24 Apr.). Cf. summons to a Council at Windsor castle, Privy Seal, Westminster, 3 May (BL MS Harley 3988, fo. 38ᵈ). The Westminster Chronicler, habitually well informed about proceedings in Great Councils, notes that in that of Jan. 1389 at Westminster, 'several matters were raised and discussed that were not disclosed' (*Westm. Chron.* 376–7).

[53] The Lords were nominally a body of *c.*100, of whom less than half of those summoned probably attended (A. L. Brown, 'Parliament, *c.*1377–1422', in R. G. Davies and J. H. Denton (edd.), *The English Parliament in the Middle Ages* (Manchester, 1981), 116).

the earls of Northumberland and Warwick, and the bishops of Lincoln and Salisbury.[54] The Great Council which met at Clarendon on 13 September 1389 was attended by the duke of York, six earls, the prior of the Hospitallers, and a baron, who sat together with members of the King's Council.[55]

The year 1389 (a politically fraught period) was a notable year for Great Councils. Besides the Clarendon Council, ones met at Westminster (January and May), Sheen and Windsor (August), Westminster (September), and Reading (December).[56] Venues reflected the royal itinerary. Such Councils were convenient and flexible instruments of policy, which could be often summoned at short notice, and generally accommodated with ease within the Household, and which dispatched their limited remit with merciful brevity.[57] Great Councils were particularly useful in emergencies, such as the prolonged crisis which arose from the Scottish victory at Otterburn in 1388. When crucial matters were at stake, summonses sometimes went out more widely to peers—and, indeed, on a few occasions to a selection of commoners as well. The Great Council which met at Westminster on 20 January 1379 was attended by 'almost all the prelates and abbots and dukes, earls, barons and bannerets and other *Sages* in the realm'.[58] In 1383, at Westminster, there were present 'a great part of the Lords Spiritual and Temporal . . . and great numbers of *pluis suffisantz* bachelors'.[59] Richard summoned to the controversial Nottingham Council in 1387 many Londoners, the sheriffs, and all the justices.[60] The Council at Westminster in January 1389 was attended by 'most of the great from all over England, together with other worthies drawn from the commons', and at the one the following May there were present, besides lords, 'many of the most worthy men in the kingdom'.[61] The 1392 Council at Stamford, which considered peace proposals from the French, was 'as well attended as a parliament, for from every county there came to it those knights and *viri pericores* in the whole of England'.[62]

Nevertheless, Great Councils were often ill-attended, because lords found it inconvenient or impolitic to do so. Frequent Councils, the Westminster

---

[54] PRO E403/485, 3 Sept.   [55] *POPC* i. 11.

[56] *Westm. Chron.* 376–9, 390–3, 402–3, 402 n. 2, 406–9.

[57] The summons copied into BL MS Harley 3988, fo. 38ᵈ, was for the following Saturday. A summons of 24 Apr. 1392 to Stamford was for 24 May (PRO E28/6/34).

[58] *RP* iii. 55. Monastic representation was high in the Council held at Westminster in Mar. 1382, to which the abbot of Westminster and certain London priors were summoned (*Westm. Chron.* 24–5).

[59] *RP* iii. 144.   [60] *Vita*, 105; *Westm. Chron.* 376–7.   [61] *Vita*, 121.

[62] *Westm. Chron.* 489–93.

Chronicler implied, exhausted them.[63] At Nottingham in 1383 Lancaster and Cambridge were the only magnates present, since 'the nobles from the remoter districts declined to make the journey'.[64] Lancaster excused himself from attending the Reading Council in May 1385 on the grounds that a French force had landed in Scotland.[65] The effects of absenteeism depended on circumstances. At Reading the Council made important decisions about the proposed expedition to Scotland, whereas, at the Council held there two years later, de la Pole's petition for the reversal of the recent parliamentary judgement against him was turned down, because of the absence of the duke of Gloucester and other nobles.[66] Reading again proved a disappointing venue for the king in 1390: the nobles present refused to comment on the proposal that Richard should meet Charles VI. Since the archbishop of Canterbury and other lords were not there as they should have been, they declined until a meeting of all the interested parties.[67]

In a summons to a bishop dated 1398–9, it was stipulated that if he could not attend in person, he was to send from two or four of his own council, 'qualified and discreet'.[68] Summonses customarily enjoined attendance with greater firmness. One summons to Windsor castle charged the addressee to come 'sans nulle deffaute . . . Et ce en nulle manere ne laissez sur la foy ques vous nous devez'.[69] Evidence from chronicles suggests that in tense political circumstances Richard may have made attendance a real test of loyalty. In January 1385, it was alleged, when the duke of Lancaster wrote to him asking to be excused from appearing at a Great Council summoned to meet at Waltham, the latter insisted that his uncle should attend on his allegiance. The duke, on the advice of his own council, complied.[70] The chronicler who recounted this considered a plausible explanation for the arrests of Gloucester and the earl of Arundel in 1397 to be that Richard was angry with them, because they had excused themselves from going to a Council on the grounds of illnesses.[71]

There is evidence for Richard's attendance at some Great Councils: it is likely that the king customarily presided. In December 1387 assembled lords expected him to come, and were disconcerted by his refusal. Business

[63] Ibid. 186–7.
[64] Ibid. 42–5. The Council went ahead, with the participation of three ex-officio councillors: the chancellor, treasurer, and keeper of the Privy Seal.
[65] Ibid. 120–1 and 120 n.   [66] Ibid. 186–7.
[67] Ibid. 456–7. The meeting was adjourned to Westminster.
[68] PRO E28/4/81.   [69] BL MS Harley 3988, fo. 38ᵈ.
[70] *Vita*, 85–6. Lancaster went to the Council with an armed retinue, for which he obtained a pardon.
[71] Ibid. 137.

was held up until he sent word that they were to proceed with the agenda in his absence.[72] The Monk of Evesham gives details about his arrival at the one held at Westminster on 8 May 1389. He surprised the large array of lords who stood waiting for him by entering the council chamber suddenly and unceremoniously. He sat down casually, and put a leading question to them about his authority. This account suggests that the lords may have expected a solemn royal entry and enthronement; perhaps, too, the rehearsal of the cause of summons by the chancellor or treasurer.[73] In May his subject-matter was certainly exceptional: he led a discussion about his right to personal rule and himself announced dismissals and appointments of leading officials. His participation was, indeed, significant on other occasions. At Windsor the following August he pronounced his assent to reforming ordinances, and ordered that his signet seal be attached to the bill.[74] The promises which he made to the lords on 15 February 1392 appear to have been uttered in person.[75]

As in the King's Council, the chancellor or another of the principal royal officers may have sometimes conducted proceedings.[76] At Stamford in 1392 the duke of Lancaster, leader of the recent delegation to negotiate with the French Crown, expounded the peace proposals. Councillors sat and probably spoke in order of precedence. In March 1386 Richard, 'in token of the duke's (Lancaster's) royal dignity (his claim to the Castilian Crown), caused him to be seated at the council table above the archbishops and next to himself'.[77] At a Great Council the previous year, the archbishop of Canterbury had addressed the king on behalf of the assembled lords.[78] Lancaster's report to the Stamford Council, and the responses to it illustrate how Great Councils might have roles in the diplomatic process. On occasion they were addressed by foreign dignitaries and envoys. In 1391 a papal envoy, the abbot of Nonantola, made a speech to one Council, and another was terminated by Richard because Charles VI's envoys failed to attend.[79]

Though many measures brought by the king or one of his chief officers before Great Councils were given assent without demur and, perhaps, on

---

[72] *Westm. Chron.* 216–19. The king's presence was minuted at Windsor 20 Aug., Clarendon 13 Sept., and Reading 10 Dec. 1389, and on 12–16 Feb. 1392 (Baldwin, *King's Council*, 493–6; *POPC* i. 11, 17).

[73] *Vita*, 121–2.   [74] *POPC* i. 10–11.   [75] Baldwin, *King's Council*, 494–5.

[76] For a discussion of proceedings in the Lords, and analogies between them and proceedings in Great Councils, see Brown, 'Parliament, *c.*1377–1422', 123 and n. 48.

[77] *Westm. Chron.* 164–5.   [78] Ibid. 116–17.

[79] Ibid. 458–9, 478–9. In 1385/6 the king of Armenia had addressed king and Council (ibid. 154–5).

occasion without debate, they could not always be relied on to 'rubber-stamp' royal proposals or reach a consensus about an issue. Hostility to Richard's policies surfaced in the Council held prior to the parliamentary confrontation of 1386.[80] The Council of February 1392 was contentious. The Clerk of the Council recorded the solemn promises which the king and lords made to each other at the session on 15 February. Richard assured them that it was not his intention to restore or recall any of those who had forfeited for treason.[81] The Clerk's record fails to reveal that this was the outcome of a tense confrontation with him, ending with his humiliation. The Westminster Chronicler makes clear that Richard's assurance was a response to the 'vehement demand' that he should not pardon Alexander Neville and Robert de Vere.[82] At Stamford the following year, the Commons forcefully rejected the peace proposals favoured by the king. Though he did not feel bound to accept their advice, their attitude probably had some effect on the course of negotiations. The king's will was not always so clear as at Stamford: he is likely to have been more ambivalent over the Gascon appeals against the legality of the grant of Aquitaine to the duke of Lancaster, which came before the Council held at Eltham on 22 July 1395.

Proceedings in this Council are particularly well documented, as there is an official minute about the appeal from Bordeaux and Froissart's more general and circumstantial account of the proceedings.[83] The chronicler was then staying at Eltham and says that he derived his information about the Council from the royal councillor Sir Richard Stury (whom the minute lists as among those present at this weightily composed Council).[84] The minute is concerned primarily with the presentation of evidences by the emissaries from Bordeaux and by Lancaster's counsel, and the expert legal opinion given in favour of the city's privileges. All the lords who were asked their opinions, it says, agreed with the clerks, but the duke of Gloucester and the earl of Derby made provisos for further examination, clearly acting in Lancaster's interest.

Froissart is concerned to project the atmosphere of the Council, and to explain its political significance: in painterly fashion he gives us, besides set speeches, the informal reactions of the lords—their silences, caballing, and attempts to attract the king's attention. They gathered in his presence

[80] In 1386 at Oxford nobles refused to back a plan for a royal expedition to France (*RP* iii. 215).

[81] Baldwin, *King's Council*, 495.

[82] *Westm. Chron.* 484–7: 'domini . . . vehementer insteterunt'.

[83] Baldwin, *King's Council*, 504–5; Froissart, xv. 156–67.

[84] Froissart's list of those present is not so full.

in the King's Chamber at eight o'clock in the morning: the session lasted more than four hours. After the parties had presented their evidences concerning the grant to Lancaster of the duchy of Aquitaine, the king first formally asked the prelates for their opinions. They deferred to the king's uncles, who at first excused themselves, on the grounds that the matter should be deliberated 'par commun conseil', rather than according to nearness of blood to the king and to favour. Nevertheless, Gloucester proceeded to argue firmly on his brother's side and was seconded by Derby. Gloucester's stance displeased many lords but they were cautious in their opposition, because of his overbearing nature, and out of deference to Derby's presence. The Council broke up into small groups: Gloucester haughtily withdrew, with Derby in his company, to have dinner in hall, where they were joined by the duke of York. Faced with a lack of consensus, Richard did not express a clear opinion and the Council did not come to a clear conclusion.[85]

At the Eltham Council conflict and personal antagonisms seem to have been muted, to the frustration of many present. This contrasted with the more robust opinions expressed by lords in some previous Great Councils in the reign. Lords considered that, when summoned, they had a right to express their opinions on the agenda, though there were doubtless other occasions besides 1395 when treacherous political cross-currents constrained them. The importance of Great Councils in their eyes is shown by clause twenty-three of the Articles of Deposition, which concerned the rights of lords, justices, and others summoned to them: the accusation against Richard was that, 'when offering their advice according to their discretion, [they] were often so sharply rebuked and reproved by the king that they dared not speak the truth concerning his welfare and that of the kingdom'.[86] This may reflect his increasing intolerance in recent years. Nevertheless, overall Richard has a good record of consulting magnates and others in Great Councils. He was not a king who habitually refused his nobles the opportunity to give advice. It is likely that he sought this widely too when magnates attended him at court, at the times revealed by their witnessing of his charters.[87]

[85] Froissart says that Gloucester left after dinner, before the conclusion of the Council, which reconvened in the afternoon to discuss proposals for the king's marriage. The king asked the archbishop of Canterbury to open the debate on these proposals.

[86] Trans. from C. Given-Wilson (ed. and trans.), *Chronicles of the Revolution 1397–1400: The Reign of Richard II* (Manchester, 1993), 179.

[87] I owe thanks to Prof. A. L. Brown for letting me see his tabulations of witnesses to royal charters in the reign enrolled on the Charter Rolls (PRO C.53/155–167), whose detailed analysis would shed welcome light on attendances at court.

5

Richard II and the Church

Richard G. Davies

The reign of Richard II coincided externally with the Great Schism of the west and internally with John Wycliffe and the emergence of the Lollard sect.[1] These alone have seemed enough to some historians to presume that the king had to wrack his mind over religion. By identifying the Church as an integral, but complacent and out-of-condition, part of an old European order under challenge, other historians have portrayed it as in general crisis, its authority as noisily under threat in England as anywhere. What disappointment, then, if Richard could ride impervious through such uproar. Some have refused to believe it. Biographers of the king himself have also found it hard to suppose that Richard II could have been ordinary in his piety. Even in some more temperate works the king's piety is often given an originality and uniqueness it did not have.[2] Thus, on the

[1] J. H. Dahmus, 'Richard II and the Church', *Catholic Hist. Rev.* 39 (1953), 408–33; P. Heath, 'Richard II, 1377–1399: The Clergy under Attack', in id., *Church and Realm, 1272–1461* (London, 1988), ch. 7. N. E. Saul, *Richard II* (New Haven, 1997), including ch. 13 'Piety and Orthodoxy', appeared after this chapter was written.

[2] See e.g. A. B. Steel, *Richard II* (Cambridge, 1941), 7–8, 174–5; R. H. Jones, *The Royal Policy of Richard II: Absolutism in the Later Middle Ages* (Oxford, 1968), 167–9, 172, 175; G. Mathew, *The Court of Richard II* (London, 1968), 7, 15 for the king's 'febrile piety'; much more sober, J. H. Harvey, 'Richard II and York', in *Reign of Richard II*, esp. 203, and J. Taylor, 'Richard II's Views on Kingship', *Proceedings of the Leeds Philosophical and Literary Soc.* 14 (1970–2), 189–205. See, however, J. I. Catto, 'Religious Change under Henry V', in G. L. Harriss (ed.), *Henry V: The Practice of Kingship* (Oxford, 1985), 106, who refers to Henry V as 'the first king since Henry III to have shown more than conventional piety': see also Harriss's important introd. (esp. 2–6, 10) on contemporary literary efforts to urge God-given authority—and responsibility—on Richard. See also the important discussion of religious attributes of kingship at this time by R. N. Swanson, *Church and Society in Late Medieval England* (Oxford, 1989) 95–9, but cf. W. Ullmann, *Principles of Government and Politics in the Middle Ages* (4th edn., London, 1978) 181–6, for the view that Richard championed a theocratic kingship rendered impotent by developments over the last 200 years.

one side the earth was moving, on the other a strange giant was walking the land. When two such fantasies meet, the truth can seem very dull. Richard's relationship with the Church was in fact a setpiece in conventionality. From personal piety to public policy, Richard rarely strayed from this path. At times this is even remarkable. This does not mean he was blasé. Indeed, it provides insight into his person and rule.

Within his Household, for example, Richard practised devotion and charity on very traditional lines.[3] An annual total in almsgiving of between £350 and £700 was respectable but not likely to win fame or sanctity. The way it was doled out suggests that Richard was unmoved by the sharp contemporary debate about the identity of the true poor, the morality of poverty, and the role of almsgiving generally, sparked off by the demographic decline and consequent opportunity, or even obligation, for anyone able to work.[4] Whatever the puritan, crypto-Wyclifite views of some of those around him at court, the king edged, if anything, into an even older-fashioned stance. What little we know of Richard's personal choice of literature suggests that religion hardly came into it, especially when compared with the likes of his uncle, Thomas of Woodstock, or others of his court and nobility, amongst whom some highly charged sensitivity and personal piety have been detected.[5] Richard's lack of literature does not mean uninterest: it means conservatism. There was nothing unusual about the mood and culture of his court as he himself ordered it.[6] Some efforts to suggest

[3] C. Given-Wilson, *The Royal Household and the King's Affinity: Service, Politics and Finance in England, 1360–1413* (New Haven, 1986), 69–70, for an excellent analysis, prudently allowing for the survival of only four detailed household accounts. Like Edward III, Richard doled out 4s. 0d. a day *pro forma* in alms and 6d. each to 100 paupers on Maundy Thursday. He kept 24 paupers on regular commons of 2d. a day (plus leftovers?), far more than Edward III had done. On the other hand, whereas Edward III made offerings of £25 on each of the four major festivals, Richard substituted a more spectacular handout on Good Friday: 4d. each to 1,598 paupers, and 1d. each to 3,120 (£89. 12s. 0d.), e.g. in 1384. At Easter 1396 when he was in York, he excelled himself with doles 'with his own hands' of 4d. each to 12,040 paupers (£200 13s. 4d.). As Harvey ('Richard II and York') remarked, the problem is not so much how and whether Richard could find the energy for such a marathon, but where and whether so many paupers could be rounded up. At daily morning mass Richard (a dutiful attender) gave 7d., at the four great feasts 6s. 8d. The scheduled pilgrimage to Becket's shrine at Canterbury each May cost 6s. 0d. in offertory, a bargain considering the large-scale hospitality beholden upon the archbishop, cathedral, and citizens.

[4] C. Dyer, *Standards of Living in the Later Middle Ages: Social Change in England, c. 1200–1520* (Cambridge, 1989), ch. 9, 'Poverty and Charity', and refs. cited there.

[5] See e.g. the superb essay by J. I. Catto, 'Religion and the English Nobility in the Later Fourteenth Century', in H. Lloyd-Jones *et al.* (edd.), *History and Imagination* (London, 1981), esp. 44–5, 48–50, although subsequent work by scholars of literature would tone down his emphasis on an identifiable court culture, and he, like others, tends to equate literary and artistic with religious patronage too readily.

[6] V. J. Scattergood, 'Literary Culture at the Court of Richard II', in *English Court Culture*, 30–41; but cf. A. I. Doyle, 'English Books In and Out of Court from Edward III to Henry

levity, lasciviousness, and too many bishops at court attracted half-hearted attention at the time, most notably in 1397 when Thomas Haxey's petition roused the king himself to a furious reaction. This might suggest an uneasy conscience, but more probably, as it seemed when it happened, Richard was simply outraged by what was at least impertinence, arguably a constitutional offence, most alarmingly a possible portent of a repeat of the hostile 1386–8 purges of his court.[7] There was widespread consternation at the time that he should take it so badly. Since then, even the more basic accusations of Household extravagance have been passed off as little more than the common currency of the politically alienated. On the other hand, there was neither a heavy smell of ornate sanctity at Richard's court nor that of damply fashionable puritan gloom. From his chapel Nicholas Slake, Richard Medford, Richard Clifford, and John Lincoln emerged to become close and trusted secular officers: this is scarcely sufficient, though, to see them or it as a prime instrument in some 'striving towards autocracy'.[8]

Richard took a cool view of the supernatural. If he did possess a handsomely wrought work on the role of astrology in politics, he did not dog-ear it.[9] If he touched for the King's Evil, he did it very unobtrusively.[10] On 15 June 1381 he consulted John Murimuth, the anchorite at Westminster, prior to his confrontation with the rebels in London, an incident not well authenticated but frequently recalled by historians despite the king's tender years and the fact that he is not known to have made another such appointment in his whole life.[11] In the summer of 1383, when Sir James Berners was blinded by lightning during a royal shrine-crawl, the king chivvied the Ely clergy into securing a swift remedy from the local patron

---

VII', in *English Court Culture*, 168: 'in Richard II's reign and court, however, there is no doubt that English religious prose of pronouncedly serious character did become fashionable, not least in the form of Lollard scriptural translations'. Several chapters of this book recycle the same anecdotal and specific pieces of evidence—not always to convincing effect but a common habit amongst those musing on Richard's attitudes of mind.

   [7] *RP* iii. 339, 341. See now A. K. McHardy, 'Haxey's Case, 1397: The Petition and its Presenter Reconsidered', in J. L. Gillespie (ed.), *The Age of Richard II* (Stroud, 1997), 93–114, which narrates his career but to no convincing conclusion.

   [8] Quotation from T. F. Tout, *Chapters in the Administrative History of Mediaeval England*, 6 vols. (Manchester, 1920–33), v. 216. For Richard and his Household clerks, see Given-Wilson, *Regal Household*, 175–83.

   [9] Copied for him a second time into Oxford, Bodley MS 581, as discussed by Mathew, *Court of Richard II*, 40–1; J.-P. Genet (ed.), *Four English Political Tracts of the Later Middle Ages* (Camden Soc., 4th ser. 18, London, 1977), 22–3.

   [10] M. Bloch, *The Royal Touch*, trans. J. E. Anderson (London, 1973), 248–9.

   [11] The earliest source seems to be John Stow; R. M. Clay, *The Hermits and Anchorites of England* (London, 1914), 153–5. Cf. M. D. Knowles, *The Religious Orders in England*, 3 vols., (Cambridge, 1948–59), 2, 220, for identification.

saints.[12] In 1390 he did travel to Gloucester to participate in the official examination of the miracles he had submitted to Rome in the cause of Edward II's canonization: such personal interest was, of course, political, not credulous.[13] According to monastic gossip, Richard found the freshly beheaded earl of Arundel haunting his dreams in September 1397.[14] More to the point, the king had heard of popular rumours that the earl's head and torso had miraculously grown back together. Not unwisely, he had a weighty delegation exhume the ten-day-old corpse. They scotched the rumours: at most, some stitched repairs were found; by other accounts, nothing. Richard nevertheless had the grave stripped of identity and paved over. He knew all about political cults and rightly took no chances. Would that Henry IV had been so nimble-footed with Archbishop Scrope's tomb in 1405.[15] In 1399 one William Norham, hermit, prophesied doom to the king's face. He declined the king's challenge to walk on water to prove his credentials. Richard placed him in custody. In 1403, free and no doubt buoyed up by his remarkable earlier success, Norham turned up again to give Henry IV a similar black spot. Henry had him beheaded.[16] Various other prophecies of Richard's fall found their way into the chronicles, several actually pinpointing Henry Bolingbroke as the catalyst. These would be more compelling had they been recorded before, rather than after, the event.[17] As for the discovery in the Tower of an ampulla containing oil originally provided by the Blessed Virgin Mary to Becket for the anointing of kings, with the promise of great times ahead, Richard was not its first finder or the inspiration behind the idea.[18] It hardly smacks of eccentric

---

[12] *Westm. Chron.* 43.

[13] Ibid. 437–9. For the canonization suit initiated between 1385 and 1387, see J. Bray, 'Concepts of Sainthood in Fourteenth-Century England', *BJRL* 66 (1984), 46–58; E. Perroy, *L'Angleterre et le grand schisme d'occident* (Paris, 1933), 301, 330, 341–2; S. Walker, 'Political Saints in Later Medieval England', in R. H. Britnell and A. J. Pollard (edd.), *Political Saints in Later Medieval England* (Stroud, 1995), 83–4. Richard's attempt to have Edward II canonized is often cited as evidence of a concern for the sanctity of kingship that bordered on the bizarre. Was it really so improbable that a king faced with serious internal criticism should seek to make such a point? Edward was no less plausible a candidate than some of those cult figures promoted in opposition to the Crown, such as Thomas of Lancaster and Richard earl of Arundel (see n. 15, below).

[14] L. D. Duls, *Richard II in the Early Chronicles* (The Hague, 1975), 79–80.

[15] J. W. McKenna, 'Popular Canonization as Political Propaganda: The Cult of Archbishop Scrope', *Speculum*, 45 (1970), 608–23; Bray, 'Concepts of Sainthood', 46–58; J. M. Theilmann, 'Political Canonization and Political Symbolism in Medieval England', *JBS* 29 (1990), 253–64; Walker, *Political Saints*, 84–5.

[16] Catto, 'Religion and English Nobility', 158–9, tells the story.

[17] Duls, *Early Chronicles*, 79–80, 109, 115–16, 140, 192. See notably Adam of Usk, 200–2 for the numerous portents at Richard's coronation, but cf. *Westm. Chron.* 415–17 for a far more prosaic explanation of the same.

[18] T. A. Sandquist, 'The Holy Oil of St Thomas of Canterbury', in id. and M. R. Powicke (edd.), *Essays in Medieval History Presented to Bertie Wilkinson* (Toronto, 1969), 330–44.

credulity if (as some sources say) he was keen to be the first to enjoy the unction. If the archbishop of Canterbury did deny him, Richard accepted the decision without demur. At most he adopted the relic as a talisman. However, if Richard took a dispassionate view of some of the traditional mysteries, he was no more zealous for new fashions. The Carthusian Order enjoyed a flurry of high fashion at this time, especially in the king's own circle. Yet, Richard himself took no personal initiative in the foundation of new houses, and was benevolent but business-like in his dealings with them.[19] He laid the foundation stone of the house by Coventry in 1385 and accepted the formal title of founder, but was actually only seeing through the project of the late William lord Zouche of Harringworth. Without belittling his contribution, his grants of estates to the house, generally from the forfeitures of alien priories, were not rent-free. His grants to Mount Grace, the Yorkshire house favoured by his half-nephew, Thomas Holand, duke of Surrey, were more generous; for example, for £1,000 he quit an annual rent of £245 on the alien priory of Ware. This, however, was in 1398 when, with the war with France in long-term truce, alien mother houses might well have sued for restitution. Richard was also a confrater of the London house, having granted it an advowson, and from 1391 secured a promise of soul-masses from the Hull foundation very cheaply by handing back some items of property it had held before the forfeiture of its founder and his loyal friend Michael de la Pole. True he made festive gifts to one house or another (like his grandfather), but it all adds up to not much more than polite goodwill towards the enthusiasm of some close friends.

More famous is Richard's affection for the Dominican Order of friars. Though far from mythical, it should not be exaggerated. In February 1400 his corpse was displayed in the habit of the Order. In the circumstances, this was probably not his own idea, and it was far from what he had had in mind when he made his will ten months earlier.[20] Even his burial in the Langley convent (located within a royal park and thus prudently immune from becoming a cult centre) was said, if only by the embittered John Gower, to have been indicative of nothing more than the fact that nowhere else would take him.[21] Founded by none other than Edward II (who buried Piers Gaveston there) and much favoured by Edward III, the house

---

[19] J. M. Thompson, *The Carthusian-Order* (London, 1930), 192 n. 3, 203, 209–11, 230–1 for what follows. T. Wright (ed.), *Political Poems and Songs relating to English History* 2 vols. (RS, London, 1859), i. 433 for Richard's snatching of John lord Cobham out of Carthusian monasticism to face trial for treason.

[20] Duls, *Early Chronicles*, 183–4 collects the references to Richard's funeral.

[21] John Gower, 'Tripartita Chronica', in id., *The Complete Works*, ed. G. C. Macaulay (Oxford, 1902), iv. 341: 'corpus . . . quod mundus habere negavit'; Gower, *The Major Latin Works*, ed. and trans. E. W. Stockton (Seattle, 1962), 325: 'which the world at large refused to accept', but was the phrase really meant quite so literally?

was closely dependent for its good health upon the royal family's long-term liking for the royal manor in which it stood. Richard too liked the manor, but the house itself (where his brother was buried) had not featured in his will (or the Order generally) and it had actually had a very difficult time during his reign, directly because until April 1399 Richard had perverted his grandfather's settlement of secure estates upon it.[22] Certainly Richard did have three Dominicans in turn as his personal confessor. In this he was simply following the unfailing custom of his grandfather. The provincial prior Thomas Rushook (who was prior of Hereford) was appointed at the accession of the boy-king.[23] If not a personal choice, he became the youngster's close friend and mentor. As early as November 1381 there were unsuccessful calls in Parliament for him to come to court only on the four great feast-days. John Gower thought him a belligerent, two-faced troublemaker. In the Merciless Parliament of 1388 (unlike others under attack, he had not fled) he was impeached, specifically for threatening the king's judges the year before, but as much for his general ill fame—voiced again by the Commons rather than those closer to the centre. Eventually he was banished to Ireland, the pope helpfully glossing this with his episcopal translation to Kilmore. When Richard recovered some of his authority he quickly awarded him £40 a year (his old salary), but could not recall him. There is really no evidence that Rushook had played a large part in the making of royal policy or even taught the boy-king anything unusual about kingship. Like several of his successors, Rushook suffered from the convention that an unpopular king must have an unpopular confessor.

His successor in 1388, Alexander Bache, also came from the Hereford convent, but presumably the king had little say in his appointment either.[24] Politically, Bache may have been more widely acceptable than Rushook, but personally he proved frail. The Westminster Chronicle snarled that he had begun as a showy ascetic, even trailing the royal entourage on foot, yet swiftly became arrogant and avaricious.[25] After his death in 1395,

---

[22] W. Page (ed.), *The Victoria History of the Counties of England: Hertfordshire*, iv (London, 1923), 447–8.

[23] For Rushook, see R. G. Davies, 'The Episcopate and the Political Crisis in England of 1386–1388', *Speculum*, 51 (1976), 674–5; generally C. F. R. Palmer, 'The King's Confessors', *Antiquary*, 22 (1890), 265–6. Gower, *Complete Works*, iv. 317 and cf. 319 (*Major Latin Works*, trans. Stockton, 294, 297), which broadens the attack on to the friars' influence with the king generally.

[24] For Bache, C. F. R. Palmer, 'King's Confessors', 24–6; R. G. Davies, 'The Episcopate in England and Wales, 1375–1443', Ph.D. thesis, (Manchester, 1974), vol. iii, pp. xviii–xix.

[25] *Westm. Chron.* 435.

the king eagerly called up Rushook's old chaplain and companion at court John Burghill, whom he had been quietly caring for at Hereford.[26] His reinstatement at court was a clear signal by the king that the old days were back. Very quickly he became a bishop, and in 1398 secured the see of Coventry and Lichfield, much the greatest promotion of any royal confessor thus far.[27] Burghill was profiting from Richard's determination to promote intimates, but he had no political weight himself. He was obviously one of those several bishops whose residence at court was attracting ill fame. After Richard's fall he and Tideman of Winchcombe, the king's controversial doctor, retreated hastily to their dioceses. Burghill never again came to Parliament or played any public role.[28] Richard's preference for Dominicans could come down to loyalty to the confessor he had been given as a boy and a characteristic demonstration of that loyalty in his later years to friends who had suffered for him in 1388. However, he did have Dominican preachers at court on important feast-days and used the Order's daily rite. Even if these practices were likely at his confessor's suggestion, they are fair evidence of his taste. They should just be held at that. There is no call to postulate some peculiar fixation with the Order.

Richard took a pragmatic attitude to the monastic orders. They were a part of the social fabric, dignified enough to stage acts of (genuine) royal devotion and very useful as virtually free lodgings when the royal household was on the road. On the other hand, he included monks amongst his notoriously close friends in his last years, for example Tideman of Winchcombe and Thomas Merk, and was starting to nominate religious to bishoprics, rather against recent fashion. Unlike Henry V, however, he did not take an active interest in the health of their orders. In August 1385 he fired Melrose, Newbattle, and Holyrood abbeys readily enough, although, of course, they were schismatic and centres of Scottish resistance to his army.[29] Thomas Walsingham was especially incensed about the king and queen's leisurely tour of abbeys in the summer of 1383, '*non offerre sed auferre*' (one of his few better jokes), with an excessive

---

[26] Davies, 'Episcopate in England and Wales', vol. iii, pp. lxxi–iv.

[27] R. G. Davies, 'Richard II and the Church in the Years of "Tyranny"', *JMH* 1 (1975), esp. 353–4. Edward III had tried to promote his veteran confessor John Woodrow to Ely in 1372 but had been frustrated by intrigue within his own court. Indicative of Richard's empathy with Burghill, he attended the bishop's installation and spent Christmas with him.

[28] For Winchcombe's relationship with the king, see *Vita*, 165. Burghill did travel to Langley for the king's funeral in Feb. 1400.

[29] *Westm. Chron.* 129.

entourage—especially the rapacious Bohemian element in it.[30] By this account, the king greedily extorted gifts from all and sundry and insisted that his wife have presents of equal value. Earlier, in July 1381, the abbot of St Albans had been appalled at the idea of the king's entourage descending to deal with local rebels, for fear of the inherent cost and upheaval to the district, and tried in vain to pre-empt it.[31] All in all, Walsingham had little to complain about regarding the king's involvement in Church affairs. He found him irresolute on two particular matters (the notorious disputed abbatial election at Bury St Edmunds and the rescue of Bishop Despenser from his ill-fated crusade in Flanders), at fault in the expense of burying Queen Anne in 1394 and still more in assaulting the earl of Arundel at that funeral, and deplorable (writing after the revolution) in exiling Archbishop Arundel. On the other hand, Walsingham found nothing to complain about regarding the king's attitude to the Great Schism, and Richard was remarkably sound on the subject of heresy; perhaps for these reasons especially, Walsingham felt obliged to target his virulence against secular aspects of the king's rule.[32]

Richard was not a great benefactor of churchbuilding, although he contributed appropriately to the major projects at York and Canterbury. It is facile to say he was too busy or burdened, because he found the time and cash to upgrade royal residences that were not in bad condition.[33] True, he was only 32 when he fell, and maybe the welfare of his soul would have come to matter more in later life. Westminster abbey stands apart. It needed fundamental restoration, and Richard led the way eagerly in the renewal of this Plantagenet Saint-Denis and the stamping of his own presence upon it. He found a good friend there in Thomas Merk, and Abbot William Colchester was to make it a base for the Epiphany Plot of 1400. Here Richard intended his first queen and himself to lie in truly regal state, within the foundation of one of his major patronal saints, Edward the Confessor. The two tombs were to be of the grandest, and Richard intended

---

[30] *Hist. Angl.* ii. 96–7, 103, and cf. 119; *Westm. Chron.* 43, more sympathetically saw this as a pilgrimage to Walsingham. See *Vita*, 148 for Richard's tour of West Midlands houses in 1398.

[31] *Hist. Angl.* ii. 22, 29, 31, 38.

[32] *Ibid.* 68, 97 (Bury St Edmund's), 88, 109, 141 (Despenser), 215 (the queen's funeral), 224 (Arundel's exile), and cf. 216–17, 219.

[33] See J. W. Sherborne, 'Aspects of English Culture in the Later Fourteenth Century', in V. J. Scattergood and J. W. Sherborne (edd.), *English Court Culture in the Later Middle Ages* (London, 1983), 1–27, esp. 24–5; Mathew, *Court of Richard II*, ch. 4, which also notes his inclusion of a substantial chapel in Windsor manor, to be decorated with white harts. Harvey, 'Richard II and York', 208–9 comments usefully on Richard's benefactions, but perhaps exaggerates their effect.

statuary and painting as further memorials. He attended services in the abbey, at least on those feast-days which had a point for him (the Confessor and St Edmund the Martyr usually), knelt at Edward's shrine to sanctify important occasions, and even made well-publicized barefoot processions out of the precinct.[34] The two monk-chroniclers of the abbey found him an acceptable neighbour, but despite his benefactions they only really became enthusiastic over his defence of their right of sanctuary. This would be more impressive were it not that Richard's concern arose entirely out of the abduction from the sanctuary (and subsequent judicial murder) of his loyal officer Sir Robert Tresilian in February 1388.[35] The king was appalled, both generally because the abbey's privilege came from his own Anglo-Saxon predecessors and specifically because of the victim's identity. According to the monks, his affirmation of the house's rights on this occasion typified many other defences he made of church liberties in his realm. Although the example given is unconvincing, this sentiment is echoed by even hostile monastic sources.[36] At least they were thankful that he did not respond to the current tide of lay criticism, which they feared would drown them. The Tresilian affair moved the chronicler to emotion: 'in what awe and reverence this king of ours holds God's church! . . . there is not a bishop so jealous as he is for the rights of the church, so that on many occasions but for him and him alone she might have lost her privileges'. Richard did little else to move his Westminster neighbours so deeply. Probably wisely, he even allowed a feud over jurisdiction between St Stephen's chapel and Westminster to grind on for nearly twenty years without getting enmeshed in it himself, as he was being sorely tempted to do.[37] Here, as in other respects, Richard deserves some credit for keeping well out of the way of ecclesiastical politics. There were all too many factions urging him to his royal duty to support their corner. Richard's record is a sure-footed one.

This comes out particularly clearly in the matter of heresy. Richard II's response to the spread of Wyclifite ideas and evolution of a distinct dissenting movement was firmly orthodox. Whatever else was cast at him, especially after 1399, of this no one had any doubt. Some historians have

---

[34] e.g. *Westm. Chron.* 9–11, 131–3, 181, 207–9, 451, 507, 509; Wright (ed.), *Political Poems*, i. 282–300, on the pageant of reconciliation between Richard and London on 29 Sept. 1393. Richard's acts of friendship towards Westminster Abbey are surveyed briefly by B. F. Harvey, 'The Monks of Westminster and the University of Oxford', in *Reign of Richard II*, 108–9, and ead., *Westminster Abbey and its Estates in the Middle Ages* (Oxford, 1977), 397 and n. 2, 403. See also above, p. 42, and Saul, *Richard II*, 312–16.

[35] *Westm. Chron.* 311–13, 325–9, 337–41, 343.   [36] e.g. *Vita*, 167.

[37] *Westm. Chron.* 39, 379–83.

shown surprise. His court contained the nucleus of those knights and magnates reckoned to be actively sympathetic to early Wyclifite ideas, several of them formerly in his parents' retinues and likely to have his ear.[38] Furthermore, recent work on Wyclifite thinking has highlighted its social conservatism and its emphasis upon the role of the lay hierarchy, especially of the king, in reforming the state of the Church and the morals of the people. In this context, it might be thought that a king like Richard, supposedly predisposed to high royalism, would respond all too eagerly to such proposed extensions of his authority in his own realm, not to mention the baser temptations of disendowment of the Church to one whose serious political difficulties were basically financial in origin. It has even been argued ingeniously that Wyclifitism was by intent a royalist theology, at least as expounded by its friends at court.[39] Similarly, it has been proposed that the Lollards chose to confront the Parliament of January 1395 with their *Twelve Conclusions* whilst Richard was away in Ireland precisely because they did not want to embarrass a sympathetic ruler to his face.[40] This is the exact reverse of Walsingham's view, but whilst the chronicler's assertion, that the king raced back from Ireland specifically to put down this Lollard effrontery, does lack credibility, so does such sharp revisionism.[41] Walsingham was very willing to attack the late king and was a particular hard-liner on the treatment of Lollards, but on this topic he found no fault in him.

Nevertheless, the question is often asked why capital punishment for obstinate dissent was not introduced late in Richard's reign, even though the prelates and clergy petitioned for it in 1397, with the pope adding his voice and the king anxious to have clerical support for his political coups of 1397–8. There had even been broad expectation for some years that such a measure was only a matter of time.[42] Various explanations have been

---

[38] K. B. McFarlane, *Lancastrian Kings and Lollard Knights* (Oxford, 1972), pt. 2, esp. pp. 177–92; P. McNiven, *Heresy and Politics in the Reign of Henry IV* (Woodbridge, 1987), esp. pp. 45–8. For Richard's responses to heresy, see also below, pp. 246–8 and 248, n. 53.

[39] M. Wilks, 'Royal Priesthood: The Origins of Lollardy', in id., *The Church in a Changing Society* (Uppsala, 1978), 63–70.

[40] McNiven, *Heresy and Politics*, 56–61. Text in A. Hudson (ed.), *Selections from English Wycliffite Writings* (Cambridge, 1978) 24–9, 150–5.

[41] *Hist. Angl.* ii. 216. Dr McNiven is a nimble advocate, but in equating Richard's failure to thunder anathema at the Lollards with some privy sympathy for them, he out-Walsinghams Walsingham. The Church hierarchy knew—and spent thirty years labouring over it—that to get the lay authorities to move they had to show Lollards' sedition, not doctrinal deviation; hence Walsingham's wild gloss that they threatened as much if the Conclusions were not accepted.

[42] H. G. Richardson, 'Heresy and Lay Power under Richard II', *EHR* 51 (1936), 20–2; McNiven, *Heresy and Politics*, 59–62, 79–92.

offered: that Richard was not by nature a blood-letter; that he was not ill-disposed to many of the Wyclifite ideas which the Church wanted to exterminate so ruthlessly and not at all convinced that they were seditious or heretical; that he had too much else on his mind; or that he knew that he was already trying his lay subjects with such controversial measures that he would do well to avoid adding to them with such a draconian extension of ecclesiastical power. Lords and Commons were always very uneasy about any such extension, and it has rightly been observed that such concessions were usually made only in a time of difficulty for the government, as in 1382 in the aftermath of the popular revolts or in 1388 when the Lords Appellant urgently needed the prelates' moral support.[43] It is hindsight to construe from this any deliberate advance of royal authority over the definition of faith. By the same token, in 1401 when Henry IV, a usurper, was unsteady on the throne, he had to concede capital punishment to the Church because he needed legitimacy, manpower, and money in return. Apart from which, there were now preachers attacking him rather than the Church: *De Heretico Comburendo* in this light was something other than the altruistic response of a dutiful Christian king.[44]

Such ideas have obvious merit but do not add up to an entirely convincing account. It should be borne in mind that, even after the statute had been brought in and William Sawtry made the showcase victim, it was only used once more (and that again for political show) in Henry IV's reign.[45] Thus, Richard's 'failure' to introduce the death penalty is not at all evidence in itself of a private weakness for Wyclifitism or that his permission would have been the signal for a pogrom. Rather like the so-called 'anti-papal legislation' of his reign, such a deterrent appears much less ultimate close to. Seeing how the Church authorities felt their own way so uneasily towards defining their quarry, it is no wonder that the king moved slowly too and behind them. The Church had to break up any incipient alliance between malcontents within the political establishment (to whom some private freedom of religious thought might safely be allowed) and lower-born freethinkers who might overturn the order of Church and society. Richard was well placed to see both sides of the equation: the need to bolster the Church in its role of conservator of social norms; the interesting reformist and puritan thinking going on amongst some of his own

---

[43] Richardson, 'Heresy and Lay Power', 10; see also M. E. Aston, 'Lollardy and Sedition, 1381–1431', in ead., *Lollards and Reformers* (London, 1984), 38–43.

[44] I discuss the reconciliation of social and political conformity with deviant belief in 'Lollardy and Locality', *TRHS*, 5th ser. 41 (1991), 191–212.

[45] For the trial of John Badby, see McNiven, *Heresy and Practice*, ch. 12.

closest associates. As with other religious enthusiasms, Richard does not seem to have been at the cutting edge, even when those close to him were. Quite probably, he did keep a mainly benign eye on those of his courtiers who were interested in Wyclifite ideas—and thus made it even more difficult for the prelates to set out their preferred, implacable opposition to any such thinking—and yet slapped them down, as reputedly he did Sir Richard Stury, if their interest seemed to be spilling over from personal self-improvement to active patronage of dissenting preachers at large. Perhaps it is significant that several of these so-called 'Lollard knights' had drifted away from the court by 1399.[46] Richard prided himself as a hammer of heretics, and Archbishop Arundel (before they fell out) congratulated him as such.[47] There is a danger of implicitly adopting Walsingham's criterion that anything short of violent extermination of dissent was treachery. In Richard's time, a more discerning stance could still seem quite severe enough. To someone with an eye firmly on social and political upheaval, there was little to fear in Lollardy. Still, if Richard's orthodoxy was not violent, it was in his blood.

The same could be said of his attitude to the Great Schism. The English decision to remain loyal to Pope Urban VI in 1378 had been taken on the best ecclesiastical advice. Whilst the adhesion of the French to the rival line of popes did add a political dimension, fundamentally it did no more than fortify existing sentiment, in effect a moral affirmation that the English had got it right.[48] Despite the deep rifts in English religious life in the years that followed, there was a remarkable unity of attitude amongst clergy, politicians, and ordinary layfolk that Urban and his successor, Boniface IX, were the true line. This was not something to be lightly tossed aside whenever the politics of the Hundred Years War so required. When Richard first took much direct interest in such matters around 1389, Urban VI had just responded all too easily to the Lords Appellants' request for an unprecedented and expensive reshuffle of the episcopate, to the disgrace and demotion of the king's strongest supporters.[49] A grumbling confrontation between England and the papacy over revenues, provisions, and jurisdictional rights was starting to develop, provoked by the uncertainties

[46] *Hist. Angl.* ii. 217 for Stury. On Sir John Cheyne's expulsion from the realm, see J. S. Roskell's biographical essay in his *Parliament and Politics in Late Medieval England*, 3 vols. (London, 1981–3), esp. 75–81.

[47] Richardson, 'Heresy and Lay Power', 23 and n. 2.

[48] Perroy, *Grand Schisme*, esp. 51–95, remains the classic, if somewhat anglophobic, account, but see J. J. N. Palmer, *England, France and Christendom, 1377–1399* (London, 1972) for important reappraisal.

[49] Davies, 'Episcopate and Political Crisis', 659–93.

of 1388 when the Commons had had their chance to explode over sores old and new.[50] Richard was saddled with this. In 1389 Henry Percy, earl of Northumberland, did suggest in council that recognition of the new pope (Boniface IX) be delayed to give time for further discussion. Although the king agreed not to communicate with the Curia in the mean time, this incident was not intended as an initiative towards ending the schism.[51] For all the difficulties that followed, neither public opinion (critical as it was) nor Richard's own principles would permit any idea of abandoning Rome, even as a diplomatic ploy.

It has been argued that Richard could and did contemplate exactly this, once he had his eyes on peace with France, and that he even saw resolution of the schism as part and parcel of that settlement and as a vehicle for the restoration of his personal prestige and that of kingship generally.[52] Less dramatically, others have agreed that Richard may have wavered under French blandishments and been ready for joint action against both rival popes, to the extent that he was annoyed when the English universities and leading canon lawyers could not or would not provide him with the ideological case for such a desertion of Rome.[53] Most recently, however, a good case has been made that Richard was in complete control of the debate in England and obtained answers from his intellectuals in 1399 that suited both his policies and his conscience.[54] If he had become more alive to the stain on Christian society of two popes, he was no more inclined than before to disbelieve what had always been an article of faith: the legitimacy and authority of Rome. Peace with France had been obtained without any resolution of this difference of opinion, and if some of the French (whose unanimity was never secure) appeared to be moving towards a renunciation of their man in Avignon, that was a welcome step in the right direction. Just at this time Richard secured both papal

---

[50] Perroy, *Grand Schisme*, 306–8, 331–7; Heath, 'Richard II', 213–17; W. E. Lunt, *Financial Relations of the Papacy with England, 1327–1534* (Cambridge, Mass., 1962), 389–95. See also W. T. Waugh, 'The Great Statute of Praemunire, 1393', *EHR* 37 (1922), esp. 173–85.

[51] *POPC* i. 14ᵇ; Perroy, *Grand Schisme*, 308–11.

[52] Palmer, *England, France and Christendom*, esp. 220–2; id., 'England and the Great Western Schism, 1388–1399', *EHR* 83 (1968), 516–22.

[53] Perroy, *Grand Schisme*, 336–51, 365–86; W. Ullmann, 'The University of Cambridge and the Great Schism', *Journal of Theological Studies*, NS 9 (1958), 53–77.

[54] M. M. Harvey, 'The Letter of Oxford University on the Schism, 5 February 1399', *Annuarium Historiae Conciliorum*, 6 (1974), 121–34; ead., 'The Power of the Crown in the English Church during the Great Schism', in S. Mews (ed.), *Religion and National Identity* (Oxford, 1982), 229–41: 'the evidence suggests that the real decisions about church policy between 1394 and 1399 were made by him and that the church in England accepted this' (pp. 238–9). Cf. also Davies, 'Richard II and the Church', 354–5.

ratification of his coups in Parliament in 1397–8 and a personal concordat by which to guarantee his control of principal Church appointments in the future.[55] This has sometimes been seen as Richard putting naked self-interest over any concern for the shame of the schism. More likely, he saw no such conflict. Boniface's spiritual authority would not be invalidated, however the schism was resolved.

Richard's conservatism, just as it was the basis of his kingship, led him straight into full recognition of the spiritual authority of the pope and, as chroniclers said, a reluctance to encroach into traditional preserves of the English Church as a whole. In that sense, he was indeed a respecter, even defender, of Church liberties and Church property. Although there were boundary disputes between royal and Church courts, there is no sign that Richard encouraged his justices into aggressive constructions of Crown rights.[56] When the so-called 'anti-papal statutes' of Provisors (1390) and Praemunire (1393) were re-enacted, there was actually inherent in them a fraught recognition of the pope's authority. These were, in any case, clumsy manœuvres in a row with Pope Boniface IX which was based as much on mutual misunderstanding and nervous posturing as on any real hostility or basic problem of principle. The king took immediate evasive action to avoid having actually to enforce Provisors, whilst the pope used the same envoys he sent to protest about the statutes to pursue the more urgent task of persuading Richard that the English realm and the Roman papacy would stand or fall together in the face of French malevolence.[57] The pope, like the French in their turn in 1395, put up the idea of a crusade to the Holy Land as the ultimate seal of any settlement in the west. Certainly Richard did have quite serious aspirations to the imperial title in his last years, which might have seemed to some to raise the obligation to lead Christendom against the infidel; in truth, however, Richard was always, and as emperor would have been, politely sympathetic and personally inactive in this respect as in so many others.[58] Others eagerly took the crusading vow: Wilton Diptych permitting, Richard was at least

[55] Printed by Perroy, *Grand Schisme*, 419–20; see Davies, 'Richard II and the Church', 355–6.

[56] For perspective, see the important and undervalued article by F. Cheyette, 'Kings, Courts, Cures and Sinecures: The Statute of Provisors and the Common Law', *Traditio*, 19 (1965), 295–349.

[57] *Hist. Angl.* ii. 200–1; *Westm. Chron.* 463–9.

[58] Philippe de Mézières, *Letter to King Richard II: A Plea Made in 1395 for Peace between England and France*, ed. and trans. G. W. Coopland (Liverpool, 1975), pp. xxiii–xxv, for one deluded veteran's hopes being raised by a second-hand report. Palmer, *England, France and Christendom*, esp. 192–207, believes the Anglo-French project to have been a serious one, although he offers little evidence that Richard intended to participate in person.

honest enough with himself not to. More prosaically, even though Bishop Henry Despenser claimed crusading rights to fight in Flanders in 1383 and John of Gaunt the same in Castile in 1386, Richard did not seek similar bulls of approval for his comparable expedition to Scotland in 1385.[59] In this, Richard passed up a chance to bleed the clergy for money. He never did oppress them, although often pressed to do so by the laity and always a taskmaster. Although clergy and laity in practice paid direct taxation to the Crown in more or less consistent proportions, the laity felt they shouldered too big a share. Not surprisingly, the clergy were sensitive to any attempt by the Commons to realign the ratio or even any presumption that the clergy would follow the laity's lead automatically. In 1380 (when the Commons laid down that the clergy must raise no less than one-third of the poll-tax) and in December 1384 (when Archbishop Courtenay objected formally to a Commons' stipulation that their grant must be matched in the usual way by the clergy) they reacted furiously.[60] Richard was quick to soothe them on the latter occasion: point made, he made sure of the money. In spring 1388 the southern Convocation and Commons were agreed for once, when both made grants only if the Convocation of York not only reversed its outright refusal of 1386 (when Archbishop Neville was not there to chivvy them) but also matched the new subsidies.[61] Direct refusal was rare, although twice in 1388 (to the discomfort of Richard's opponents, not himself, of course) the southern clergy demanded a year's moratorium. What Richard did face—from 1383, interestingly—was a series of grants wherein half or more was to be conditional upon his personal leadership of a military expedition abroad. In the 1390s he sought less direct taxation, and there was commensurately less bickering all round. In 1395 the clergy's grant was supposedly a reflection of their gratitude for the king's stand against heresy, but it only matched the lay subsidy as usual and, in fact, reintroduced conditionality.[62] Overall, Richard received roughly the equivalent of a half-tenth per year from the

[59] Lunt, *Financial Relations*, 536–50; M. E. Aston, 'The Impeachment of Bishop Despenser', *BIHR* 38 (1965), 127–48 (and see N. Housley, 'The Bishop of Norwich's Crusade', *History Today*, 33 (1983), 15–20); P. E. Russell, *The English Intervention in Spain and Portugal in the Time of Edward III and Richard II* (Oxford, 1955), 348, 409.

[60] D. Weske, *Convocation of the Clergy* (London, 1937), 166, 209 n. 58; J. H. Dahmus, *William Courtenay, Archbishop of Canterbury, 1381–1396* (Philadelphia, 1966); *Hist. Angl.* ii. 140. On the other hand, in 1377 the Convocation of Canterbury itself only granted two-tenths on condition that the Commons (who usually went first) came up with the laity's customary share.

[61] Weske, *Convocation*, 166.   [62] Ibid. 178.

clergy, just about the exact average amongst later medieval kings.[63] He turned a deaf ear to controversial ideas about disendowment. Conscious of the suspicion between Commons and Convocation, he did well to support the status quo. No one could seriously attack him for that. A policy that shut the door completely on direct taxes to the papacy and restricted crusading taxes solely to expeditions devoted to English interests in Flanders and Castile naturally attracted no domestic criticism at all.[64]

Richard's personal relations with the Church hierarchy were correct rather than close. At Canterbury Archbishop William Courtenay (1381–96) was sensitive to the rights of the Church in general and to his own in particular, but disinclined to become involved in politics and government if he could avoid it. His one attempt (under persuasion), in 1385, to play the heavy father-figure threw the young king into a violent rage.[65] Although placed ex officio at the head of the reform commission of 1386, he played a limited part in the subsequent crisis. He formally protested the rights of the Church in 1384, 1388, and 1391 and meant it, and worried about Wyclifitism, but he aged quickly. The king had a warm respect for him, accorded him his place in council, but really they went their separate ways. At York Richard had inherited Alexander Neville, a quite unsuitable younger son of a leading local magnate family, who had been intruded by them and the pope when the Crown was weak. He conducted feuds with his suffragans, religious houses, and a good many other people and rarely left his diocese until, picking up with Richard during the Scottish expedition of 1385, he suddenly became a fixture at the royal court. There he lent neither talent nor good repute, just when the king needed both. What the king saw in him is a mystery. His flight into exile in 1388 was a rare sensible decision.[66]

Into Neville's place at York stepped Thomas Arundel, bishop of Ely at 21 through his father the earl of Arundel, and now elevated by his brother Earl Richard, the Lord Appellant and the king's most personally detested opponent. The new archbishop was no cipher and had himself played a leading part in the current crisis. None the less, as chancellor of the realm

    [63] For discussions: ibid. 166–79, 260–70, 288–95; Heath, 'Richard II', 197–200; A. K. McHardy, 'The English Clergy and the Hundred Years War', in W. J. Shields (ed.), *Studies in Church History*, xx (Oxford, 1983), 171–2; Swanson, *Church and Society*, 111–15, and literature cited there.
    [64] Lunt, *Financial Relations*, 114–22, 536–50; cf. Perroy, *Grand Schisme, pièces justificatives* no. 6, cl. 7 (p. 403).
    [65] Dahmus, *Courtenay*, 161–86; *Hist. Angl.* ii. 128; *Westm. Chron.* 117, 139.
    [66] R. G. Davies, 'Alexander Neville, Archbishop of York, 1374–1388', *Yorkshire Archaeological Journal*, 47 (1975), 87–101.

from 1391 to 1396 he became quite hopeful that time was a healer and that he and the king were collaborating well. Recently, Arundel has become something of a cult figure amongst historians as one who, for all the political mire through which he walked for the rest of his life, had a first love for the Church, which he expressed through endearingly unsubtle pugilism on her behalf against all deriders, imagined or real.[67] However exaggerated this enthusiasm, there is no doubt that he was delighted to be proposed by the king to succeed Courtenay at Canterbury in 1396 and had no intention of staying on as chancellor as well. He was not being 'kicked upstairs'. Richard's vicious coup against his brother, himself, and other Lords Appellant in 1397 took him more than anyone by surprise. Not for the only time he showed more trust in human nature than one would expect from someone of such tough experience.[68] His bitterness showed through in 1399.[69]

With Arundel removed from Canterbury, Richard put in his treasurer Roger Walden, a decent man personally (with Westminster abbey bloodties, most obviously) but with neither the blood nor the background to overcome such a controversial beginning.[70] He was not even a bishop at the time. Only Richard knows what he hoped for in Walden as archbishop and why he did not disarm controversy either by persuading the most active elder statesman on the bench, his distant kinsman Robert Braybrooke of London, to step up or by advancing the attractive (if actually lightweight) Richard Scrope of Coventry and Lichfield. Meanwhile, the king had promoted Robert Waldby to fill Arundel's place at York in 1396. A Yorkshireman, an Augustinian friar, theologian, and physician, Waldby confuses the prosopographer by filling high administrative posts in Aquitaine and Ireland.[71] By dying as soon as December 1397, he left little evidence of what the king wanted from him. Ostensibly, it was the pope who then put in Richard Scrope, but it is hard to be sure. At first sight, the king

---

[67] M. E. Aston, *Thomas Arundel* (Oxford, 1967), esp. chs. 9–12; Davies, 'Thomas Arundel as Archbishop of Canterbury, 1396–1414', *Journal of Ecclesiastical History*, 24 (1973), 1–14; McNiven, *Heresy and Politics*, esp. ch. 4.

[68] Three other very different incidents—Henry IV's deception of him over the execution of Archbishop Richard Scrope in 1405; his considerate treatment of the eccentric Margery Kempe, and his expressed distaste to William Thorpe of Wyclifites' self-righteous condemnation of the frailties of common folk—all hint at a trusting, charitable nature.

[69] See J. W. Sherborne, 'Perjury and the Lancastrian Revolution of 1399', *Welsh History Review*, 14 (1988), esp. 218, 240–1.

[70] Davies, 'Richard II and the Church', 337–43; for Walden's background, id., 'The Episcopate in England and Wales', vol. iii, pp. ccc–ccciii.

[71] Id. 'The Episcopate in England and Wales', i. 160–1, 166–7; vol. iii, pp. ccxcvii–ix; E. A. Foran, 'Robert de Waldeby, O.S.A.', *Irish Ecclesiastical Record*, 5th ser. 16 (1921), 356–64.

should have been delighted.[72] Well born, Yorkshire-born, well qualified academically (unlike most aristocratic churchmen), experienced in both episcopal administration and the papal Curia, the king's personal proctor in the canonization cause of Edward II, and closely related to Sir Richard Scrope and his son, the king's trustee William Scrope (newly created earl of Wiltshire), the new archbishop seemed to have it all. Unfortunately —something Richard perhaps spotted—Scrope's niceness and honest endeavour stopped at that. He went along wide-eyed with the revolution of 1399; and then equally so to his death as a stooge, leading a naïve, belated attempt at righteous rebellion in 1405.[73]

Richard II had an episcopal bench filled with heavyweights, many of whom were not his appointees, nor personally close to him, and yet with whom he had few problems. He did much better in this respect than those who tried to rule in his grandfather's last years. For example, the most famous 'proud prelate' of them all, the admirable William Wykeham, saw Richard in and out.[74] The civil-servant bishop *par excellence*, twice disgraced politically (by anti-court and court forces in turn within just five years, 1373–7), Wykeham now had his affection set on his relatives, estates, cathedral, school (Winchester), and college (New, Oxford); and his mind on his diocese. He came to Parliaments dutifully, as did his episcopal colleagues with experience in government. The rest of the bishops only turned up in numbers in a crisis.[75] Wykeham came out of retirement to act as chancellor, 1389–91, when it seemed that his country needed him, but he would rather go home. Most bishops were like him. They were not politicians, even if some had once been government servants, and others filled the great offices of state as usual. If most were not close to Richard II, they were not against him. He had his job; they had theirs. In 1388 and 1397 they protested their right to sit in the Lords in Parliament but to abstain from judgements of blood; and gave spiritual sanction to those assemblies at their conclusion.[76] Otherwise, they did little in concert in political life, save to deliberate in Convocation. Large-scale episcopal absenteeism from dioceses for secular reasons and close partisanship for or against the

---

[72] Davies, 'Richard II and the Church', 346–8.

[73] P. McNiven, 'The Betrayal of Archbishop Scrope', *BJRL* 54 (1971–2), 173–213.

[74] Remarkably, there is no modern biography of Wykeham. See, however, P. Partner, 'William of Wykeham and the Historians', in R. Custance (ed.), *Winchester College: Sixth-centenary Essays* (Oxford, 1982), 1–36.

[75] R. G. Davies, 'The Attendance of the Episcopate in English Parliaments, 1376–1461', *Proceedings of the American Philosophical Society*, 129/1 (1985), esp. 45–6, 55–9.

[76] Id., 'Episcopate and Political Crisis', 669–72; id., 'Richard II and the Church', 338–40, for full discussions and references.

ruler of the day are amongst the most dubious myths of English medieval history.[77] On the other hand, there are signs that, if Richard had survived much longer, he might have given reality to both these charges. The composition of the episcopate interested him. There were relatively few appointments to bishoprics in the first half of his reign, partly a chronological quirk but also because of the elevation of several young aristocrats in Edward III's last years. Although Richard's government was reasonably successful in controlling appointments, there is evidence of unease about the freedom of individual candidates, however meritorious, to aspire to bishoprics in competition with the Crown's own nominees and that it was having trouble satisfying even all its own hopefuls, with so settled a bench. Yet it worked for a settlement rather than a confrontation with the pope, trying to resuscitate the Concordat of 1375, particularly the procedures for nomination. What the pope did against royal wishes, rather in error than defiance, the Crown accepted with surprisingly good grace.[78] In 1388 the Appellants, unsurprisingly, made no attempt to break from this convention of enhancing the senior administrators of the day.[79] None the less, if unexceptional in personnel, the appointments they secured were unprecedented in their flexibility, and the possibilities of demotion or exile (by fictitious translation to schismatic parts) opened up possibilities which cannot have been ignored. In the event, no further use of such contrivances was actually made, except to inflict an analogous revenge on Archbishop Arundel in 1397 and (when he proved obdurate) Thomas Merk in 1400.[80] Yet Bishop John Buckingham's involuntary removal from the see of

[77] Id., 'Episcopate in England and Wales', ii. 543[a–b], provides a tabular record of residence by diocese in this period. After much needful revision, overall suggestions of 70% residence in England and (tentatively) 40% in Wales during Richard II's reign may not be too inexact.

[78] Even leaving aside the appointments made in 1388 at the behest of the Lords Appellant, about one-third of the provisions/translations in the reign may have been independent of the wishes of the Crown, although several of these cases arose from competition within the ranks of royal servants. In the absence of much inside information about intrigue after promotion, and yet clear signs that a good deal went on, no exact measurement can be taken. An independent election by a cathedral chapter never succeeded, although at St Asaph John Trevor was appointed with royal approval at a second attempt. With the one possible exception of William Bottlesham (Llandaff and Rochester), the papacy does not seem to have made any appointment of a candidate lacking substantial support in England. In 1386 and 1398 Richard had domestic competition in mind when seeking to get assurances from the papacy that it would conform to his nominations.

[79] Davies, 'Episcopate and Political Crisis', 675–90.

[80] Aston, *Thomas Arundel*, 365–73; Davies, 'Episcopate in England and Wales', i. 197–202 (Merk).

Lincoln to that of Lichfield (which he refused, preferring retirement) and Ralph Erghum's fear of a similar fate may be significant signs of underlying nervousness.[81]

In the immediate aftermath of the crisis of 1388, one is most struck by the king's lack of recrimination against the pliancy of the pope towards his opponents, and by his apparent anxiety, greater indeed than that of the pope, to restore the former harmony of their relationship. In smaller sees the pope in both 1389 (when he was being somewhat aggressive in such matters) and the decade following had his share of patronage. For his part, Boniface IX made no attempt to infiltrate his 'own men' into the greater sees, or even to influence the placing of those who were sponsored by the Crown. More significantly, he found himself still not infrequently with rival candidates claiming the Crown's support. For all the efforts of the Crown to arrange a smooth flow of nominations—in 1375, 1386, and 1398 specifically—it seems to have recognized its own inability to dominate appointments. Its greater problems lay not with the pope but with cathedral chapters, whose occasional independence seems still to have been regarded as a considerable nuisance, and still more with its own candidates, who evidently felt able, or even obliged, to work for themselves against one another. Richard may have paid the price for tolerating this when John of Gaunt achieved the displacement of Buckingham at Lincoln in favour of his own son, Henry Beaufort in 1398 and in the process disturbed the king's own plans for dealing with the vacancy at York. Rivalry for promotion was one thing; the displacement of established bishops was another. Admittedly there was only one Gaunt, with only one son in holy orders, but Richard clearly felt he had to draw the line and not let false signals be given to other would-be patrons. If the Convocation of Canterbury gave him the only answer it could, as he knew well, that the pope's powers to translate were beyond challenge, none the less his display of irritation was both genuine and a clear warning to all concerned. It was logical that he should turn at once to the pope for a formal agreement that he should have at least a general right to approve provisors to bishoprics, even if he could not name the precise person.[82]

Specifically, in the last years of his reign he did start to promote his own particular protégés, men who were not unworthy of such favour as

---

[81] Davies, 'Richard II and the Church', 348–9; BL MS Arundel 68 fo. 19ᵛ (Buckingham); Oxford, Bodleian Library MS 859, fos. 22ᵛ–27ᵛ, 30–40 (Erghum). There is also some possibility that William of Wykeham once feared a like fate.

[82] PRO C.147/14/32, printed by Perroy *Grand Schisme*, (*pièces justificatives* no. 16 (pp. 419–20)); Davies, 'Richard II and the Church', 355–6.

such, but too obviously the personal associates of an unpopular king.[83] The translation of Robert Waldby to York (1396), the immediate promotion of Roger Walden to Canterbury (1397), and places for the king's physician (Tideman of Winchcombe) at Worcester (1395) and confessor (John Burghill) at Coventry and Lichfield (1398) all suggest that Richard had in mind to move such personal associates to the very top as vacancies occurred. Such portents, and the fact that, at least whilst in their lesser sees, such men were inclined to absenteeism and residence with the king, may help explain the hostile comments they attracted.[84] It could be argued that his choices, at least as they looked in 1399, were often promising and imaginative, remaining broadly within the understood framework of criteria for promotion, but introducing a breadth of talent and intellect to the bench which did not exclude, but went wider than, the conventional mix of civil servant and aristocrat. None the less, it is clear that personal association with himself was the common factor that provided variety.[85] Meanwhile, leading officials were still well rewarded. If by the end of his reign this meant that there were far fewer non-graduates on the bench and more doctors of civil and canon law, in detail this reflects what was to be a long-term trend regarding recruitment to high office of state rather than anything more personal to the king.

Richard made his final will on 16 April 1399, before he left for Ireland.[86] Its well-turned preamble is only a variation on the well-worn theme of the certainty of death and the uncertainty of its hour. It is as predictable as the rest of the document. To find in it the mind of a megolomaniac or theocrat is to betray an ignorance of convention amongst medieval rulers. Certainly, he spends time in detailing the 'kingly way' in which he must be borne to his prepared tomb in Westminster abbey or, if he dies irrecoverably abroad or at sea, the way in which the rites should proceed none the less. Certainly too, he had already spent heavily and carefully on his tomb. He was to be buried with crown and sceptre, but with no jewels save one ring. An impressive sum of £4,000 was reserved for the rites.

[83] It should not be ignored that Arundel's own supplanter, Roger Walden, was restored to the bench as bishop of London in 1405; that Thomas Merk was twice rescued from himself and yet was still given considerable comfort and public favour after 1399; and that leading royal administrators in Richard's last years, such as Edmund Stafford and Richard Clifford, survived and prospered with scarcely a tremor.

[84] Most famously, *Vita*, 165–6; and Thomas Haxey's petition in Feb. 1397 (Aston, *Thomas Arundel*, 363–5).

[85] 'The episcopacy must almost have come to resemble an extension of the household'; Given-Wilson, *Royal Household*, 182, getting just a little too excited.

[86] J. Nichols (ed.), *A Collection of the Wills of the Kings and Queens of England* (London, 1780), 191–200.

Still, Richard was disposing of over £65,000 in the will as a whole, and especially after John of Gaunt's recent spectacular last journey home across England, as specified in his will, the king's choice of rites was well in order.[87] The rest of the will is practical: the remuneration of servants, the transfer of regalia and other jewels to his successor, the rich endowment of the Holands, his cousin Edward of Aumale, and his new creation, the earl of Wiltshire, and the preservation of the Acts in the 1397–8 Parliaments by financial inducements (Richard's one real call from the grave, and perhaps the time-bomb that exploded in the Epiphany Plot of 1400).

Then there is the so-called Wilton Diptych. Despite much ingenious scholarship, its mystery remains.[88] If, as some sort of present consensus suggests, it was commissioned by the king himself around 1395–6, it is prime evidence. If it is post-1399 (at least in its present form), its place becomes more doubtful. Either way, it need not unhinge our view of Richard as king or man. Many fantasies have been woven around its impressively allegorical tableau. Yet, remembering 'how God became an Englishman' during the Hundred Years War and how Wyclifite pamphleteers toiled so heavily in 1395 itself to create ponderous, oleaginous puns between Richard's white hart badge (which the angels bear in the painting) and God's own emblems, the diptych can be seen as a plain statement of the achievement and standing of a king coming into his prime.[89] Although Richard worked for peace with France, he never saw it in terms of surrender. If the diptych is full of subtlety, it is not full of eccentricity.

Although the bishops, Merk and (to a lesser extent) Despenser apart, went along with the revolution in 1399, there is little sign that many were militants.[90] Arundel thundered in Convocation about the perils to the Church in the late reign, but found it hard to be specific. 'Offences' by Richard against the Church were not easy to muster, even in this open

---

[87] F. Devon (ed.), *Issues of the Exchequer* (London, 1837), 258; J. B. Post, 'The Obsequies of John of Gaunt', *Guildhall Studies in London History*, 5 (1981), 1–12.

[88] C. T. Wood, 'Richard II and the Wilton Diptych', in id. *Joan of Arc and Richard III* (Oxford, 1988), 75–90, and literature cited there; cf. Palmer, *England, France and Christendom*, 242–4.

[89] J. W. McKenna, 'How God became an Englishman', in id. and D. J. Guth (edd.), *Tudor Rule and Revolution* (Cambridge, 1982), esp. 30–2 (although he does not see Richard promoting this theme). See Harvey, 'Richard II and York' 207; Mathew, *Court of Richard II* ch. 4 for the king's use of the white hart motif at York and Windsor.

[90] R. L. Storey, 'Episcopal Kingmakers in the Fifteenth Century', in R. B. Dobson (ed.), *The Church, Politics and Patronage in the Fifteenth Century* (Gloucester, 1984), 82–98, argues that Arundel and the other bishops had their eyes firmly on the Church's chance to take advantage of the deposition, but this only emphasizes (treatment of heretics apart) how relatively marginal their demands were.

season.[91] To John Gower, as to the deposition assembly, God presided over Richard's fall and Henry IV's accession in a rather indeterminate and approximate way, although the recourse to canon law as a mode of deposition was fundamental, and frequent reference was made to the king's coronation oath.[92] Arundel's banishment and removal from Canterbury were played for all they were worth, although Pope Boniface IX's implication in the affair was unhelpful, and it was awkward to overlook the way that Richard's opponents (including Arundel himself) had done exactly the same to Archbishop Neville and Bishop Rushook in 1388. The enforced supply of waggon trains for Richard II's Irish expeditions came up in both the Articles of Deposition and the clerical *gravamina* in Convocation.[93] Whilst evidently a particular grievance with the religious on several occasions, it is hard to believe that even the secular clergy, still less the laity, felt very moved by this particular outrage. The fact that Richard had sought out papal anathema against anyone opposing the parliamentary Acts of 1397–8 was pulled into the Deposition Articles as evidence of his willingness to alienate the sovereign integrity of the realm, an unconvincing deviation from the main tenor of the charges that here was someone with a quite outrageous belief in that sovereignty.

The clerical *gravamina* were the first since Richard's own accession. The lower clergy were worried about heretical calls for Church disendowment, about certain rights of incumbents as affected by the writ *quare impedit*, and the need for corporeal penance for grave sins such as adultery. The prelates, slightly more concerned about the judicial bounds of lay and Church courts, noted the seizure of tithes and spiritualities during wardships, neglect by lay judges of the accustomed consultation processes in certain cases, abuse of the Marshal's jurisdiction, arrest of clergy in holy places, and—an old favourite—extortion by local lay officials. Although enumerated at length, the complaints hardly drew up a picture of a Church

[91] See R. L. Storey, 'Clergy and Common Law in the Reign of Henry IV', in R. F. Hunnisett and J. B. Post (edd.), *Medieval Legal Records in Memory of C. A. F. Meekings* (London, 1978), esp. 342; W. R. Jones, 'Bishops, Politics and the Two Laws: The *Gravamina of the English Clergy*, 1237–1399', *Speculum*, 41 (1966), esp. 236–7.

[92] G. E. Caspary, 'The Deposition of Richard II and the Canon Law', in S. Kuttner and J. J. Ryan (edd.), *Proceedings of the Second International Congress of Medieval Canon Law* (Vatican, 1965), 189–201; Adam of Usk, 29–30, 181–2, for meetings of canon lawyers and others. It is striking that Gower, fully alive to the issue, still could not rise to the occasion for sustained violent rhetoric and managed little more than dull cliché; Wright (ed.), *Political Poems*, i. 434; Gower, *Complete Works*, iv. 448–51. See also J. B. Gillingham, 'Crisis or Continuity? The Structure of Royal Authority in England 1369–1422', 59–80.

[93] *RP* iii. 420; D. Wilkins (ed.), *Concilia Magnae Britanniae et Hiberniae*, 4 vols. (London, 1737), iii. 245; cf. *Hist. Angl.* ii. 199.

emerging from an era of tyranny. There is no evidence that Henry IV felt the need to respond formally to any of the complaints. Nor is there much here to suggest a Church leadership confident and eager to exploit the weakness of a usurper. Rather, Archbishop Arundel was deeply fearful that the clergy would be more vulnerable to criticism themselves under the new regime: he urged immediate attention to such questions as non-residence in order to pre-empt any moral posturings by the Commons in Parliament as a vehicle for more explicit dangers such as the perennial idea of disendowment.[94] The king had been the impenetrable conservative. Sometimes this had inclined him to leave the Church to sort out its own problems when he might usefully have helped. In matters like taxation and Church appointments it had inclined him to make sure he got his customary share. Above all, though, it had rendered him immune to the siren calls of the Church's critics. Personally, and as an Englishman, Thomas Arundel rejoiced in Richard's demise. As primate of all England, he was much less sure.

[94] Walsingham, *Annales*, 290–1, 301–2.

6

Richard II and the Higher Nobility

Chris Given-Wilson

The nobles who exercised the greatest individual influence on the politics of Richard II's reign were his uncles—especially John of Gaunt, duke of Lancaster and Thomas of Woodstock, duke of Gloucester: it is worth noting, for example, that when a 'continual' council was established at the 10-year-old king's coronation in July 1377, the three royal uncles were empowered to 'surveye and correcte the defautes of them that were appointed for to be of the kingis counseil'.[1] Kinship ties remained crucial. It was Gaunt's relationship with his nephew which above all wrought division in political circles during the first nine years of the reign, and Gloucester's during the next eleven. Richard never fully trusted either of them.[2] (His third uncle, Edmund of Langley duke of York, may have been trustworthy, but he was a political lightweight.) This may be why Richard strove to augment the power and status of other kinsmen such as his half-brother John Holand, his nephew Thomas Holand, and his cousin Edward earl of Rutland. One consequence of this, and of the king's childlessness, was a factious undercurrent of rivalry for the succession, surfacing at moments of tension such as 1387 and 1398.[3] Moreover, Richard's character was a destabilizing factor: emotional, over-impressionable, and

---

[1] See Humphrey duke of Gloucester's memorandum of 1422 in S. B. Chrimes and A. L. Brown (edd.), *Select Documents of English Constitutional History 1307–1485* (London, 1961), 249.

[2] For Richard's relations with Gaunt see S. K. Walker, 'Lordship and Lawlessness in the Palatinate of Lancaster, 1370–1400', *JBS* 28 (1989), 344–8; A. Goodman, *John of Gaunt: The Exercise of Princely Power in Europe* (London, 1992), *passim*.

[3] For 1387 see M. V. Clarke and V. H. Galbraith, 'The Deposition of Richard II', *BJRL* 14 (1930), 157–61 and *Westm. Chron.* 194–5. For 1398 see *Annales*, 304, and C. Given-Wilson (ed. and trans.), *Chronicles of the Revolution 1397–1400: The Reign of Richard II* (Manchester, 1993), 17–18.

prone to violence, the king's well-publicized personal quarrels with his magnates are one of the chief reasons why the Parliaments and politics of the 1380s and 1390s often seem to have such a destructively subjective edge to them. The natural leaders of the nobility were the earls and dukes, of whom there were between ten and twenty. The king's kinsmen excepted, the most politically significant of the earls during Richard's reign were Richard Fitzalan, earl of Arundel; Thomas Mowbray, earl of Nottingham; Robert de Vere, earl of Oxford; Michael de la Pole, earl of Suffolk; Henry Percy, earl of Northumberland; and Thomas Beauchamp, earl of Warwick. Their roles, standpoints, and fates are well documented. In the crises of 1386–8 and 1397–9, they are the ones to whom, along with a handful of great ecclesiastics such as Thomas Arundel and Alexander Neville, both contemporary chroniclers and later historians have devoted their attention.[4] Their pre-eminence also allowed them to colour the history of their times. Substantial sections of the most detailed account for the years 1387–8—that of the Westminster Chronicle—emanate from the circle of Richard's opponents, the Lords Appellant.[5] The most influential accounts of the years 1397–9—those of Thomas Walsingham's *Annales Ricardi Secundi* and the Monk of Evesham's *Historia Vitae et Regni Ricardi Secundi*—also owe much to the propaganda put about by the victors of 1399.[6] Thus the king is often seen as an isolated and unpopular monarch, achieving what he did in 1397 only through force, fear, and the compliance of a narrow and self-interested cabal of favourites, while the overwhelming drift of noble and popular sympathy lay with his enemies.

Going beyond the standard accounts, support for at least some of the king's followers and actions appears stronger than we are expected to credit. Richard's dominance of the 1397–8 Revenge Parliament was almost complete. For example, the king was granted the wool subsidy for life. Walsingham *et al.* would have us believe that this was achieved through bully-boy tactics, and many historians have accepted this, seeing in it a method whereby Richard might extend his tyranny to non-parliamentary government. Yet when Henry V was granted the wool subsidy for life some twenty years later, this was, we are usually told, a mark of respect, of the

---

[4] See e.g. A. Goodman, *The Loyal Conspiracy* (London, 1971); J. S. Roskell, *The Impeachment of Michael de la Pole Earl of Suffolk in 1386* (Manchester, 1984); J. A. Tuck, *Richard II and the English Nobility* (London, 1973); M. E. Aston, *Thomas Arundel* (Oxford, 1967).
[5] *Westm. Chron.* p. lxv.
[6] The most recent discussion of this is in C. M. Barron, 'The Deposition of Richard II', in *Politics and Crisis*, 132–45.

confidence which the Commons placed in their king, a reward for his achievements. Why must we accept such different interpretations of these grants? Is it simply that this was the construction placed on them by the chroniclers of the day, to whom (in both cases) propaganda was of greater concern than objectivity? The only chronicle dealing with the 1397-8 Parliament to be written before 1400, and thus without either knowledge of Richard's fate or the yoke of Lancastrian misinformation, was the Kirkstall Chronicle. Its account of the 1397 Parliament is so different from the others that it is worth quoting in detail:

In the year of grace 1397, and the twenty-first year of his reign, King Richard, remembering and again recalling to mind the injustices which had been inflicted upon himself and his kingdom by a number of English lords in the year of Christ 1388, determined to right those injustices, and set out to bring the kingdom of England under his control. . . . On the second day, in full and open parliament, Lord Thomas Arundel was publicly proclaimed a traitor to king and kingdom, and sentenced by judgement of parliament to be exiled from England within forty days following. It was alleged against him that, at the time when he had first been appointed as the king's chief councillor, he had consistently revealed all the king's secret deliberations to someone who was opposed to the king, namely his brother the earl of Arundel; and it was because of this, as well as other things imputed to him, that he was exiled from England. Next day the aforesaid lords, namely the duke of Gloucester and the earls of Arundel and Warwick, were called to stand trial. When the earls had been brought in—the duke of Gloucester appeared in a higher court, before the Supreme Judge—and when the charges against them, so grave as to comprise treason towards the king, had been read out, they were condemned to death, and all their goods were judicially declared to be forfeited to the lord king. At length, however, heeding the pleas for mercy of Lady Isabelle, queen of England, the king relented and granted Lord Thomas earl of Warwick his life; thus, tempering the wine of justice with the oil of clemency, he banished him to the Isle of Man, granting him also a fixed annuity for the term of his life. The earl of Arundel, however, was beheaded that same day—that is Friday, the feast of St Matthew the Apostle [21 September]—on the same spot hard by the Tower of London where Lord Simon de Burley had been executed. How admirable and long-suffering is the king's forbearance! Previously the sun was hidden behind a cloud —in other words, the royal majesty was obscured by a hostile force—but now, soaring in arms above the mountains, and bounding over the hills with his might, he has dispersed the clouds with his sun, whose light shines ever more brightly.[7]

What are we to make of the Kirkstall Chronicler? Is his picture of a 'long-suffering' king firmly yet mercifully reasserting the rights of the Crown

---

[7] *The Kirkstall Abbey Chronicles*, ed. J. Taylor (Thoresby Soc. 42, Leeds, 1952), 117; Given-Wilson (ed. and trans.), *Chronicles of the Revolution*, 94–6.

against a treacherous band of awkward customers simply a lone voice, or does he represent widely held opinions in England in the summer of 1397? There is little contemporary evidence for Richard's unpopularity in the mid-1390s, indeed quite the opposite. The Westminster Chronicler, as Barbara Harvey noted in her edition of the chronicle, took a distinctly more favourable view of Richard at this time than he had in the 1380s. This, she speculated, might have been evidence that the king was better at dissembling by now: the chronicler might have been 'deceived' by the king's 'new ways', so that he became 'a little naive in judgment'.[8] But was not Richard truly a much more reputable king by this time? His relations with Parliaments between 1390 and 1395 were singularly easy. His extensive retaining of knights and esquires at this time had broadened the basis of his support and seems to have raised no objections.[9] Gloucester and Arundel, the two leading Appellants of 1387–8, lost much ground politically during these years, their growing isolation reflected in the Monk of Evesham's story that they alone refused to come to the council of February 1397.[10] Perhaps what we see in 1397 is a relatively popular king taking measures which were widely supported, in an attempt to reassert the traditional authority of the Crown against a group of public nuisances who had, through a succession of political own goals, failed entirely to capitalize on the advantage they had gained in 1387–8. The later lionizing of Richard's victims in 1397 is largely propaganda.

Why then was Richard deposed in 1399? Not, it would seem, for what he had done between 1389 and 1397. The crux of Richard's failure was his tendency to overreact. His designs on the Lancastrian inheritance and his treatment of Bolingbroke and Mowbray in 1398–9, as well as his growing financial embarrassment and political proscription from the early months of 1398, were the actions of a man who did not know when to stop.[11] Yet the king could (indeed did) cite a precedent here, that of 1388. The government was certainly more discredited in 1388 than it was in 1397 (the questions to the judges, in particular, were a catastrophic miscalculation), but not so universally reviled as the king's opponents would have us believe. The Westminster Chronicler's account of the Merciless Parliament is revealing here, for he has in fact two accounts of the proceedings,

---

[8] *Westm. Chron.*, pp. lxxiv–lxxv. Cf. the discussion of the Westminster Chronicler's views of Richard above, pp. 25–6.

[9] C. Given-Wilson, *The Royal Household and the King's Affinity: Service, Politics and Finance in England 1360–1413* (New Haven, 1986), 212–26.

[10] *Vita*, 137. See also *Westm. Chron.* 516–18 and *RP* iii. 313.

[11] C. M. Barron, 'The Tyranny of Richard II', *BIHR* 41 (1968), 1–18 and Tuck, *Richard II and the English Nobility*, 194–209.

one 'official'—that is, the Appellants' version of events—the other 'un-official'—his own narrative. In the first, the emphasis is on the guilt of the king's supporters and the unanimity of the verdicts. In the second, the picture is more complex. The trials of Nicholas Brembre and Simon Burley were especially controversial. A committee of twelve 'great lords', including York, Northumberland, Kent, and Salisbury, declared that they found no cause for death in Brembre's actions. The Appellants 'were con-sequently moved to indignation against them'. The chronicler's account of his execution—'his contrition and piety moved almost all the bystanders to tears'—leaves little doubt as to where he thought most sympathies lay. Burley's trial occasioned still greater acrimony. The Appellants, the chronicler tells us,

anxious to press their appeals to a conclusion, worked for a fortnight or more on means to have execution done upon those who had formerly surrounded the king and at that time exerted an evil influence on him, but owing to the strength enlisted for the opposition they were unable to realize their fervently cherished desire. Thus on 27 April, the duke of York rose in full parliament on behalf of Sir Simon Burley who, he declared, had been in all his dealings loyal to the king and the realm; and to anybody who wished to deny or gainsay this, he would himself give the lie and prove his point in personal combat. In reply the duke of Gloucester said that Burley had been false to his allegiance, and this he offered to prove, if need were, with his own sword-arm and without multiplying arguments. At this the duke of York turned white with anger and told his brother to his face that he was a liar, only to receive a prompt retort in kind from the duke of Gloucester; and after this exchange they would have hurled themselves upon each other had not the king, with his characteristic mildness and good will, been quick to calm them down.[12]

York and John Cobham continued to appeal for Burley's life, as did the king and queen in person. Even the Appellant Bolingbroke, according to the Monk of Evesham, 'tried by every means' to secure Burley's pardon, which pleased Gloucester not at all.[13] However, Gloucester and Arundel were out for blood, and on 5 May Burley went to his death on Tower Hill. The Commons—who spoke, although they may not have thought, as one —were also apparently out for blood, but the Lords were less sure. It was 'certain of the lords', according to the Westminster Chronicle, whose entreaties, together with those of the clergy, saved the king's judges and his confessor Thomas Rushook from a similar fate.[14] Like Richard after 1397, the Appellants (or at least some of them) were driven by personal antagonisms into actions which sullied their name and forfeited their

---

[12] *Westm. Chron.* 329.   [13] *Vita*, 118.   [14] *Westm. Chron.* 317.

support. It was a lesson not lost on Henry Bolingbroke, whose desire to bury the hatchet in and after 1399 did much to preserve his throne. However, moderate voices found it hard to be heard during Richard's reign. Yet moderate voices there were. York was one, and the Westminster Chronicler's remarks imply that there were others to be found among the barons. Lords from about eighty families received personal summonses to Parliament during Richard's reign. For the majority of these, it is only possible to speculate as to their political allegiance. A few much-quoted incidents—such as Ralph lord Basset's famous remark, reported by Knighton in 1387, that although he counted himself a loyal subject to the king he had no intention of getting his head broken for the duke of Ireland— usually have to stand in the place of detailed analysis of the motivation and allegiance of the baronage.[15] Yet in a few cases it is possible to go further than this. Two of the wisest heads in England at this time were those belonging to Richard Scrope, lord of Bolton-in-Wensleydale, and John lord Cobham of Kent. Both born in the 1320s, they were experienced in war and administration, widely respected by their fellows, involved to the hilt in the events of 1386–9, and suffered personal tragedy during Richard's last years.

Cobham—described by Walsingham as 'vir grandaevus simplex et rectus'—was appointed by the Lords to be Richard's guardian in 1379, to the parliamentary commissions of 1385 and 1386, and to the committee of five set up at the end of the Merciless Parliament 'to be in constant attendance upon the king'. During the following year he acted as the chief intermediary between king and council.[16] Arrested by the king on 8 September 1397, he was tried on 28 January 1398 at Shrewsbury on two counts: that he had been a member of the 1386 commission and that he had sat in judgement on Simon Burley and James Berners in 1388.[17] Both were true, but there was much about Cobham's part in the events of 1386–8 that the king chose to overlook. Richard himself had chosen Cobham to mediate between him and the Appellants in November 1387, and when the king asked Cobham to intercede with the Commons for Burley's life in April 1388, it was a task which, although ultimately fruitless, he undertook with vigour and compassion.[18] Nevertheless he was convicted of treason and sentenced to perpetual imprisonment on Jersey, whence he was

---

[15] Knighton, ii. 244.
[16] *Westm. Chron.* 333; Tuck, *Richard II and the English Nobility*, 44, 137; *CP* xii, *sub* 'Cobham'.
[17] *CCR 1396–1399*, 157; *CPR 1396–1399*, 244; *RP* iii. 381.
[18] *Westm. Chron.* 331. Goodman, *Loyal Conspiracy*, 26, 46.

recalled by Bolingbroke in October 1399. According to Walsingham, it was his speech which set the tone for the debate on the fate of Richard's supporters in the October 1399 Parliament—a measure of the respect in which Cobham was held.[19]

Richard Scrope was successively treasurer of England, steward of the royal household, and chancellor between 1371 and 1382, until in the latter year he was dismissed by the king over the affair of the March inheritance, as a result of which, Walsingham tells us, 'he refused to accept any office under the king again'.[20] However, responsibilities in plenty continued to be thrust upon him. Like Cobham he was a member of the 1385 and 1386 commissions, and of the committee to oversee the king in 1388. Like Cobham, he was chosen by the king to mediate with the Appellants in November 1387, and tried to defend Burley and the other Chamber knights from the full wrath of Gloucester and Arundel. He also tried to defend Michael de la Pole (his brother-in-law) when the latter was impeached in 1386.[21] Yet he too was to be ground down by Richard. Although probably saved from John Cobham's fate by the fact that his eldest son William was one of the most resolute supporters of the king during the last years of the reign, he was nevertheless forced on 29 November 1397 to make a public admission of his treason in having adhered to Gloucester and Arundel.[22] However, if the son had saved the father, the father was unable to save his son. William Scrope was executed by Bolingbroke at Bristol in July 1399. When this was followed by William's posthumous attainder in October 1399, Scrope implored the new king in Parliament not to disinherit him or any of his other children as a consequence. Bolingbroke asked him whether he approved of the executions at Bristol. Scrope supposed that he did, but since one of them was his own son, 'il fuist trop dolent'. This Bolingbroke accepted, for, he added, he had always deemed Scrope to be a loyal knight. He continued to enjoy his lands and title until his death in 1403.[23]

Richard Scrope and John Cobham were both 'loyal knights', impelled to the forefront of affairs at times of difficulty on account of their wisdom and moderation. Richard's decision to humiliate them in 1397 and after is symptomatic of his desire to be rid not only of his known enemies, but also of those whose loyalty he merely had reason to suspect. It may be significant that no other barons were hounded by the king through these

---

[19] *Annales*, 306–7.   [20] *CP* xi, *sup* 'Scrope', and see below, pp. 120–1.
[21] Tuck, *Richard II and the English Nobility*, 77; Goodman, *Loyal Conspiracy*, 26; *Westm. Chron.* 169 and n.
[22] *CPR 1396–1399*, 272; *Vita*, 159.   [23] *RP* iii. 453.

years. Come 1399, there were plenty of barons ready to join Bolingbroke's army, raise their fists for the revolution, and denounce the rule of Richard and his followers over the past two years: among the first to join Henry in July (in addition to the earls of Northumberland and Westmorland) were Lords Greystoke, Willoughby, and Roos, soon followed by Berkeley and Seymour.[24] Those most vociferous in condemning the old regime in October 1399 were Lords Morley, FitzWalter, and Bergavenny, who accused Rutland and Salisbury of complicity in the duke of Gloucester's death.[25] Roos, Willoughby, Berkeley, and Bergavenny were also among the lords (as was Richard Scrope) deputed to hear Richard's resignation in the Tower on 30 September 1399. These names are unsurprising. Greystoke, Roos, and Willoughby all had significant connections with the House of Lancaster. Thomas Lord Morley and Walter Lord FitzWalter had been close associates of Gloucester's (both were knighted by him on his French campaign of 1380),[26] while William Beauchamp, Lord Bergavenny, the brother of the earl of Warwick, openly defied the king in 1387 and was briefly arrested for his temerity.[27] He was evidently trusted by Boling-broke: Usk tells us that it was Bergavenny who took him to visit Richard in the Tower on 21 September 1399.[28]

The witness lists of royal charters from 1377 to 1399 also afford some information on the barons. These are not easy to interpret, for while earls who witnessed charters are regularly recorded on the lists, barons appear only occasionally unless they held office under the king and thus witnessed ex officio. However, this creates a strong presumption that when barons (excluding office-holders) were listed as witnesses, this was either because they were sufficiently active in government to merit inclusion, or because their personal influence was being recognized.[29] The three barons whose names feature most frequently on the lists are Cobham, Scrope, and John Lovell. Cobham and Scrope witnessed charters between 1386 and 1394, but not thereafter—an indication, perhaps, of their growing alienation from the court. Lovell's name is recorded occasionally between 1385 and 1396,

---

[24] *Vita*, 154; Adam of Usk, 174.   [25] *Annales*, 310–14; Adam of Usk, 206.
[26] Goodman, *Loyal Conspiracy*, 96, 124.
[27] J. J. N. Palmer, *England, France and Christendom 1377–1399* (London, 1972), 109–15, disputes Knighton's story that William Beauchamp sent the fugitive Michael de la Pole from Calais back to England in 1387, and thus argues that Beauchamp remained loyal to the king, but he ignores the important evidence from Knighton that Beauchamp refused to surrender Calais to the king, and sent the king's letters to that effect straight back to the duke of Gloucester, for which the king imprisoned him; Knighton, ii. 243–4, 251.
[28] Adam of Usk, 182.
[29] C. Given-Wilson, 'Royal Charter Witness Lists 1327–1399', *Medieval Prosopography*, 11 (1991). 35–93.

then more frequently in 1397–8. He was a man much involved in government, and evidently a royalist. Despite being arrested and dismissed from court as an undesirable by the Appellants in 1388, he was a regular member of the council in the early 1390s, was retained for life by the king in February 1395, and accompanied Richard to Ireland in 1399.[30] The only other baron who began to witness charters after 1397 was Reginald lord Grey of Ruthin, in whom Richard had sufficient confidence to entrust the custody of the duke of Gloucester's heir during the Irish campaign of 1399.[31] Yet neither Lovell nor Grey attempted to resist Bolingbroke,[32] and the only baron to join the 'earls' rising' of January 1400 (apart from Thomas Despenser, newly demoted from his earldom of Gloucester) was the otherwise rather obscure Ralph lord Lumley. It certainly does not seem to have been a barons' rising.

Yet Richard clearly found some support from the baronial class. In addition to Lovell, four other lords—John Beaumont, Thomas Camoys, Hugh Burnell, and William la Zouche of Harringworth—were also expelled from court by the Appellants in 1388, presumably because it was thought that they were supporters of the royalist cause. Beaumont and Camoys were certainly close to the king, although Burnell came from a Shropshire family which traditionally served the earls of Arundel, and he rapidly established his Lancastrian credentials after 1399.[33] Zouche may have been regarded as more of a troublemaker than a royalist. John Latimer, the Carmelite friar who created such a stir at the Salisbury Parliament of 1384 with his accusations against Gaunt, accused Zouche of concocting the charges in the first place, and in 1387 he was apparently meddling in London affairs in an attempt to secure the release of John of Northampton.[34] These were dangerous matters, and Zouche may have been well advised to take a sabbatical from politics.

In 1399 too, there were one or two barons prepared to stand up and be counted for Richard—Robert lord Ferrers of Chartley, for example[35]—but no widespread movement in support of the king. The years of strife had bred discretion; loyalties had become incompatible. Thomas Morley, bitter critic of Richard and his regime in the Parliament of October 1399,

---

[30] Id., *Royal Household*, 184–5, 215.   [31] *Annales*, 321.

[32] *Vita*, 155, says that Lovell came to join Henry at Chester with Aumale, Surrey, Worcester, and John Stanley—good royalist company.

[33] *Annales*, 252–4; Adam of Usk, 184. For Camoys and Beaumont see Given-Wilson, *Royal Household*, 62, 164, 169–71, 213, 247.

[34] *Westm. Chron.* 69–79, 184 n.; *Vita*, 81; *Hist. Angl.* ii. 114, which provides a less guarded account than that in *Westm. Chron.*

[35] PRO E.403/562, 12 July (payment of wages to the duke of York's forces in 1399).

was the same man who had led the earl of Arundel to his death in September 1397.[36] John Lovell and Hugh Burnell were both to become influential councillors under Henry IV who in 1388 had demanded their dismissal from court. Taking the reign as a whole, it is possible to point to only a handful of barons who made any real political impact. John Cobham and Richard Scrope did: although in 1397 the king chose to regard them as seditious, in fact they were two of the most level-headed of contemporary nobles. So did John Lovell who, despite his close associations with the court, was well enough trusted by the Appellants to be chosen to mediate on their behalf with the king in November 1387.[37] So did William Beauchamp, lord Bergavenny: a former chamberlain of the royal household, his interest in the Hastings inheritance gave him every incentive to retain the king's favour, but, despite defying Richard in 1387, he managed to avoid sharing his brother the earl of Warwick's fate in 1397 and soon found favour with the new regime.[38] Most barons, however, maintained a lower profile. In groups, they were perhaps capable of exerting a moderating influence—as they tried to do during the trials of Brembre and Burley in 1388—but most of them were more concerned to avoid trouble than to take a stand, and both the evidence of charter witness lists and the reticence of chroniclers and official records suggests that few of them were about the court or government with any frequency.

With a few notable exceptions, therefore, it was to the earls and dukes that political leadership fell during Richard's reign. What then were the issues at stake between the king and his magnates, and between individual magnates? Foreign policy was certainly one. In any discussion of the late fourteenth-century nobility it needs to be emphasized that the conduct of the war was a prime cause of dissension among the higher nobility.[39] So were questions of rank and influence. They were closely linked, but rank could be (and increasingly was) more precisely measured than influence, and with it the king's judgement. Fourteenth-century English kings were more willing than their predecessors to create earldoms (and later dukedoms and marquisates) for men who were not of royal blood.[40] At the same time, as the peerage became more exclusive and hereditary, the issuing of a personal summons to Parliament came increasingly to

---

[36] *CP* ix, *sub* 'Morley'.   [37] Knighton, ii. 243.

[38] For the case of the Hastings inheritance see R. I. Jack, 'Entail and Descent: The Hastings Inheritance 1370–1406', *BIHR* 38 (1965).

[39] See Palmer, *England, France and Christendom* and J. A. Tuck, 'Richard II and the Hundred Years War', in *Politics and Crisis.*

[40] C. Given-Wilson, *The English Nobility in the Late Middle Ages: The Fourteenth Century Political Community* (London, 1987), 29–54.

be seen as a conscious act of promotion by the king. Edward III had bestowed honours to good effect. His aims were unsurprising: to provide incentive, to ensure a higher nobility that was both loyal and useful, and to place his own family at the summit of English society. His grandson tried to follow in his footsteps. Why then did Richard's promotions fail to gain approval? To judge from contemporary reactions, much has to be put down to personalities, but there were other factors too. As notions of hereditary nobility hardened, the king had less scope to fashion his own nobility in the way that Edward III had done. Moreover, Edward's creations had enjoyed the reflected glory of English victories against France and Scotland. Richard's merely became the scapegoats for English failure, both at home and abroad.

Was there also perhaps a more conscious flouting by Richard of the conventions by which (some at least might have thought) he ought to have been guided? His promotions of 1385–7 provide an example. Promotions needed consent. They should also conform to the accepted values and social perceptions of the nobility. The obvious place to obtain consent was in Parliament. Edward III had always created new earls or dukes in Parliament. In 1385, however, Richard broke with precedent.[41] The Westminster Chronicler says that on 6 August, the day that he entered Scotland, the king 'created knights, earls and dukes: advancing the earl of Cambridge (Edmund of Langley) to duke of Canterbury and the earl of Buckingham (Thomas of Woodstock) to duke of Aumale; while Sir Michael de la Pole was raised to earl of Suffolk and Lord Nevill to earl of Cumberland'.[42] Later, in his narrative of the October 1385 Parliament, the chronicler gives us the true story: in fact Langley was made duke of York, Woodstock duke of Gloucester, and de la Pole earl of Suffolk (John Neville never received an earldom). In addition, Robert de Vere was promoted from earl of Oxford to marquis of Dublin, the first marquisate created in England.[43] Knighton's account raises further problems, for although he gives Langley, Woodstock, de Vere, and de la Pole their (ultimately) correct titles, he adds that Simon Burley was made earl of Huntingdon. In fact Burley never became an earl either.[44] Walsingham reports the promotions correctly, adding what he claimed to be the contemporary reaction:

In this parliament a new dignity was created, previously unknown in England: Lord Robert de Vere, who as everyone knows was earl of Oxford, was created and

---

[41] The five new earldoms of 16 July 1377 were not of course created in Parliament, but at Richard's coronation, where the extent of noble consent available was doubtless even greater than in Parliament.
[42] *Westm. Chron.* 127.   [43] Ibid. 141, 145.   [44] Knighton, ii. 205.

styled marquis of Dublin in Ireland, an honour of which the other earls considered him unworthy, for they realized that he would thus enjoy a superior rank to them, for no other reason than that the king wished to dignify him thus; yet in no way did they think of him as worthier than them, either in sagacity or in feats of arms. New dukes were also created, despite the fact that the titles had already been bestowed by the king when he was in the field on his Scottish campaign.

The promotion and endowment of Gloucester and York is then recorded:

At this time also Lord Michael de la Pole, who was then chancellor of the realm, was made earl of Suffolk and granted a thousand marks yearly out of the royal purse. He was a man more fitted to the business of the merchant than that of the knight. What he knew about was not the bearing of arms in time of war, but the conduct of the counting-house in time of peace.[45]

which, in Walsingham's opinion, should not have put him in the running for an earldom.

There was clearly both confusion and anger over the promotions of 1385. It is highly probable that Burley and Neville were created earls by Richard as he marched into Scotland, but that their elevation met with objections and had to be countermanded. It is also probable that the original title granted to Thomas of Woodstock was duke of Aumale, for it was by this title that he was summoned to Parliament on 3 September 1385,[46]—and if the Westminster Chronicle is right about this, he may well be right too in saying that Edmund of Langley was initially made duke of Canterbury. There also seems to have been some debate about de Vere's marquisate, for this new title was only finally ratified on 1 December, three weeks after the 'official' promotions of Woodstock, Langley, and de la Pole. These objections were on a number of counts: partly personal, partly social, partly perhaps motivated by concern that the higher ranks of the nobility —traditionally a warrior class—were being infiltrated by men with little expertise in warfare.[47] There was also concern that the promotions had not been carried through with proper consent from fellow peers, and the desire to single out de Vere by creating a new title for him must also have raised

---

[45] *Hist. Angl.* ii. 140–1. For the projected 1385 promotions, see also below, n. 48.

[46] *Westm. Chron.* 126 n.; see also J. J. N. Palmer, 'The Parliament of 1385 and the Constitutional Crisis of 1386', *Speculum*, 46 (1971), 477–90.

[47] Walsingham's comment was in part a reference to the fact that Michael de la Pole's father had started life as a merchant from Hull—though in fact Michael was far from short on military experience. On this theme see also the speech—made, ironically, by de la Pole himself—against Henry Despenser, bishop of Norwich at the Parliament of November 1383, accusing him of acting too much like a temporal lord (*Westm. Chron.* 53).

some eyebrows: novelty was unwelcome in so delicate a matter. Finally, there were financial objections. The endowment of Richard's new creations was undoubtedly going to cost money, and money was in critically short supply at this time. This was probably what swung the Commons against the king's promotions.[48]

Given these objections, Richard's promotions over the next two years—Robert de Vere was made duke of Ireland in 1386, and John Beauchamp of Holt became baron of Kidderminster in 1387—can only be seen as political folly. Walsingham, alert as ever to a hint of foible, proclaimed that de Vere's dukedom stemmed from 'familiaritatis obscenae' between him and the king.[49] The well-known creation of a 'barony by patent' for John Beauchamp in October 1387 was equally controversial, being the first time that the status of baron (as opposed to banneret) had been treated as a dignity not arising from the holding of lands by barony.[50] The Lords' attitude was made clear a few months later when, on trial for his life in the Merciless Parliament, Beauchamp was refused the right to be judged by his peers—the implication being that he was not one of their peers. He was referred to throughout simply as 'John Beauchamp, knight', and it was as John Beauchamp, knight, that he followed Burley to his death on Tower Hill on 12 May.

York and Gloucester excepted, Richard's creations of 1385–7 were entirely undone by the end of the Merciless Parliament, and for the next decade he avoided promotions which might be regarded as controversial. Having regained the fullness of his power in the autumn of 1397, however, he was impatient to reward his supporters in full measure. On 29 September 1397 Richard created five dukes, one duchess, one marquis, and four earls. Once again he was demonstrating his indifference to precedent: given de Vere's fate, John Beaufort's marquisate was a calculated gamble, while Margaret Marshal became the first woman to hold the title of duchess in her own right. Early in 1398 he even revived the barony

---

[48] Palmer, 'Parliament of 1385'; *Westm. Chron.* 147. The curious alteration of Thomas of Woodstock's title from Aumale to Gloucester might possibly have been at the behest of Gaunt: the last person to hold the title of Aumale had been Edmund of Lancaster (d. 1296), and in 1412 it would be held again by Gaunt's grandson Thomas of Lancaster, so it is possible that he thought of it as an honour which should by rights belong to the House of Lancaster (although he evidently raised no objection to the earl of Rutland's promotion to duke of Aumale in 1397). Edmund of Langley's alleged dukedom of 'Canterbury' may well be a slip on the chronicler's part for 'Cambridge', of which Langley already held an earldom. See *Westm. Chron.* 126 n.

[49] *Hist. Angl.* ii. 147.

[50] J. E. Powell and K. Wallis, *The House of Lords in the Middle Ages* (London, 1968), 403–4. *Westm. Chron.* 179, simply remarked that 'the king subsequently made him a baron'.

of Kidderminster for John Beauchamp's son, again by letters patent.[51] Walsingham was characteristically caustic about the five new dukes: 'the common people', he declared, 'contemptuously called them, not "dukes", but "dukettes" [*duketti*]'.[52] But he was writing many years later, after Richard's deposition, and after four of them had been demoted (in the Parliament of October 1399) from the titles which they had acquired in 1397. In fact four out of the five were very closely related to the king (a half-brother, two cousins, and a nephew), and although there may have been some feeling that the title was being cheapened, Walsingham probably exaggerated the degree of public censure. The proceedings of October 1399 indicate that they were demoted not because of the irregularity of their promotion but for crimes committed since then.

The necessary link between status and land meant that promotions had to be properly endowed, and Richard's attempts to manipulate the property market on his followers' behalf provide a further reason for suspicion between king and magnates. Ultimately, it was to be the king's disregard for Bolingbroke's claims over his father Gaunt's inheritance which led to the revolution of 1399, but criticism of Richard's attitude to the property rights of his nobles dates from early in the reign. The case of the March inheritance in 1382 provides an example. Edmund Mortimer, earl of March, one of the three or four greatest landholders in England, died in December 1381 leaving a son Roger who was aged only 7. There was thus the prospect of a long, and potentially for the Crown very lucrative, minority. Richard promised these revenues to some of his knights and esquires—'familiars of inferior status', Walsingham calls them—and consequently sent orders to his chancellor, Richard Scrope, to draw up the necessary charters awarding custody of the lands. A hundred, perhaps even fifty, years earlier, there probably would have been few objections to the notion that the king was free to distribute these lands during the minority according to his wishes, but the problem for Richard was that ideas on wardship were changing during the fourteenth century. Statutes passed in the Parliaments of 1339 and 1376 had endorsed a different view of wardship as a family matter in which the prime concern was the safeguarding of the heir's and the family's rights rather than the exploitation of the inheritance for the profit of the lord (i.e. in this case, the king).[53] Although there were still plenty of occasions on which the Crown took full advantage of

[51] *CP* ii, *sub* 'Beauchamp of Kidderminster'; he was demoted again after the Acts of the 'Merciless' Parliament were confirmed in 1399, and died in 1420 without having regained his baronial status.

[52] *Annales*, 223.   [53] *RP* ii. 104, 341.

its feudal rights, Edward III had in practice often been prepared to be lenient with his nobles on the question of wardship.[54] However, Richard II showed little perception of this, and his promises placed Scrope in a quandary. Walsingham shows Scrope as adopting the moral high ground: 'ardently desiring to act for the profit of the realm and the good of the king', he declared that such grants were contrary to 'the custom of the realm' and 'absolutely refused' to seal the charters, whereupon Richard demanded, and received, his resignation. Eventually, during the winter of 1383–4 the entire March inheritance was entrusted to a consortium of lords headed by the earl of Arundel (who had close familial and territorial links with the Mortimers), in return for £4,000 a year to be paid to the Exchequer, and so conscientiously did they do their job, according to the Mortimer family chronicler, that by the time the young heir came of age in 1394 no less than 40,000 marks had been accumulated from the estate revenues and set aside as a reserve fund for him.[55]

According to Walsingham, not only Scrope but many other lords, as well as lesser men, were indignant at Richard's behaviour over the March inheritance—which is far from surprising, since it concerned matters close to their hearts. Similar issues were raised by the case of Edward III's will.[56] Shortly before his death, Edward enfeoffed very substantial lands which he had acquired during his lifetime, amounting to about £1,000 worth of annual income, to a high-ranking group of trustees including Gaunt and the archbishop of Canterbury. The object of the grant was that after the king's death the lands should be used to endow three of his favourite religious houses. To ensure this, Edward employed an enfeoffment-to-use, a relatively novel form of trust which, although not yet protected at law, was by this time becoming a popular and accepted device by which landlords could circumvent the rigour of feudal inheritance law.[57] Richard and his ministers, ever mindful of the needs of the Crown, were unhappy about the grant, and tried every possible means to regain the lands. The validity of the grant was extensively discussed in Parliament and the King's Council, and pressure was put on both the trustees and the king's law officers, but they could not get round the fact that the grant itself was legal, so eventually, once he reached his majority in 1383, Richard simply used the power of the Crown to overcome the law. He took the lands back and

[54] J. M. W. Bean, *The Decline of English Feudalism 1215–1540* (Manchester, 1968).
[55] *Chron. Angl.* 353; Tuck, *Richard II and the English Nobility*, 88–9. R. R. Davies, *Lordship and Society in the March of Wales 1282–1400* (Oxford, 1978), 44.
[56] C. Given-Wilson, 'Richard II and his Grandfather's Will', *EHR* 93 (1978), 320–37.
[57] Bean, *Decline of English Feudalism 1215–1540*, 126.

between 1383 and 1385 granted them to Simon Burley, John Holand, and Robert de Vere. They were to form the territorial basis of Burley's proposed earldom of Huntingdon,[58] de Vere's elevation to a marquisate, and an earldom for John Holand. Such behaviour aroused deep resentment, and once Richard's fortunes had been reversed in 1386–8 the Appellants revoked his grants and returned the lands (or at least most of them) to Edward III's intended beneficiaries, the three religious houses.

In these two cases, the themes are almost identical: Richard's insistent desire for lands with which to reward his supporters; the attempt by the king to exploit uncertainties which had arisen during a period of change in the laws and customs of real property, followed by more arbitrary action when the initial attempt was frustrated; and strong resistance to the king's designs from some members of the nobility, leading ultimately to defeat for Richard. There was nothing inherently wrong in the king's desire to acquire property—few nobles acted differently, and few would have expected the king to do so—and it is difficult not to feel some sympathy for Richard, for suitable estates with which to reward his supporters (as was expected of a king) were hard to come by in the 1380s, and he must have felt keenly that this detracted from the quality of his kingship. Moreover, manipulation of the property market in their own interests was characteristic of medieval kings. Edward I's chicanery is almost legendary, and even Edward III, usually thought of as a friend to the nobility, was not completely blameless on this score.[59] Part of Richard's problem was that he lived in an age of tenurial change and, while he did not attempt actually to reverse the direction of change, he did try, when it suited him, to pretend that it was not happening. The nobility, however, had grown accustomed to its new-found freedoms.

Yet this was only a part of Richard's problem. During the 1390s resources were much more freely available to the king than they had been in the 1380s, but Richard squandered them on courtly splendour, so that, in order to boost his revenues and reward his followers in the style which he considered appropriate, he was led to commit excesses comparable with those of Edward II and the Despensers in the 1320s. Richard's conduct in 1397–9 aroused the profoundest misgivings among his nobles: in 1397 he seized the entailed and enfeoffed lands of the Appellants; hardly was the ink dry on these acts when he began scheming to recover (as he saw it) the lands

---

[58] Above, p. 117.
[59] For Edward I see K. B. McFarlane, *The Nobility of Later Medieval England* (Oxford, 1973), 248–67 and M. Prestwich, *Edward I* (London, 1988), 103–5. For Edward III, see Given-Wilson, *English Nobility*, 39–40.

of the duchy of Lancaster for the Crown, a process which culminated in his confiscation of the Lancastrian and Norfolk inheritances in the spring of 1399. It was these actions which, because they challenged the very basis of property-holding in England, gave legitimacy to Bolingbroke's invasion —and there were well-founded suspicions that the king planned to go much further than this.[60] The lands thus acquired were divided between the Crown and a few select followers such as John and Thomas Holand, William Scrope, and Edward earl of Rutland: as many as possible of the major financial and territorial resources of his kingdom were to be under the control of the king's dutiful coterie.

Yet territorial and financial resources were ultimately only a means to an end. One of the reasons why Richard was so keen to acquire them, especially after the débâcle of 1386–8, was in order to buy and maintain the support of a following sufficiently powerful to ensure that his opponents would be unable to humiliate him a second time. Fourteenth-century kings and lords secured the allegiance of their social inferiors through grants of land, office, or money; through support in times of difficulty (e.g. lawsuits); or through the more nebulous but similarly attractive exercise of 'good lordship'. Loyalties were frequently reinforced by long tradition: most magnate affinities were stable in composition, sometimes over several generations. Upon this stability depended the maintenance of law and order in their 'countries'. No one at this time objected to the idea of retaining: that is, the formal attachment to a lord (or king) of lesser persons through indentures of retainer. On the contrary, it was regarded as part of the natural order of things. However, novelties which masqueraded as permutations of the retaining system, but which in practice undermined traditional loyalties, caused much misapprehension. It was these fears which gave rise to one of the most protracted controversies of Richard's reign, that concerning the distribution of livery badges.

Livery badges (*signes*, or *signa*), which were also described as collars, and might be worn on the chest, the sleeve, or around the neck, were small, cheap, and easy to assume or discard.[61] Herein lay their danger: they were easier and quicker to distribute than the other two principal types of livery: hoods or suits. Yet they were evidently a potent symbol of status and authority. Walsingham has a revealing passage on livery badges during his

---

[60] For the Appellant forfeitures in 1397 see C. D. Ross, 'Forfeitures for Treason in the Reign of Richard II', *EHR* 71 (1956), 560–75; for Richard and the Lancastrian inheritance see Given-Wilson (ed. and trans.), *Chronicles of the Revolution*, 17–24.

[61] Many of them were probably like the white hart badges in the Wilton Diptych. For further references see Given-Wilson, *Royal Household*, 236–42. See also above, p. 55, n. 70.

description of the London riots against John of Gaunt on 19 February 1377. One of the duke's knights, Sir John Swinton, foolishly decided to demonstrate his contempt for the rioters by parading through the city with a badge of the duke's livery hanging from his neck; spotted by the mob, he was dragged from his horse, had the badge ripped from his neck, and only escaped with his life through the intervention of the mayor. 'Following this episode,' the chronicler goes on,

it was a wonderful sight to witness how fortunes changed: for those to whom the duke had given these badges, whose pride the land could scarcely contain, were now so abased that they removed the collars which the duke had given them from their necks and made haste to conceal them in their pockets or their sleeves. Those badges, through which previously they had thought themselves capable of gaining possession of both heaven and earth, which had up until that time made them both famous and powerful, now by contrast rendered them, to the same degree, objects of suspicion and contempt.[62]

According to the Westminster Chronicler, the Commons were equally concerned about the symbolic potency of the livery badge and the sort of collective mentality which it inspired. At the Salisbury Parliament of 1384 they complained about 'the tyranny of certain locally powerful persons' whose lordly connections enabled them to ignore the laws of the land, only to be silenced by Gaunt's retort that 'every lord was competent and well able to punish his own dependants for such outrages'.[63] As Gaunt must have known, the problem went deeper than this. It was not the formal, long-standing retainer—the true 'dependant'—at whom this complaint was directed. The Lords were unwilling to abandon their use of livery badges because it afforded them a method by which floating voters and malcontents could be rapidly recruited, and, in an age which put great store by the open display of allegiance, by which their power could be visibly demonstrated. The popularity of the livery badge introduced a heightened competitive edge to retaining in the last quarter of the fourteenth century. Richard II, unable to beat his enemies, decided to join them. In the summer of 1387, at a time when he was desperate to build up support as rapidly as possible, the Westminster Chronicler tells us that he

continually took into his personal service men of the country through which he travelled. Besides this he sent into Essex, Cambridgeshire, Norfolk and Suffolk a sergeant at mace, who was commissioned to cause the more substantial and influential inhabitants of those counties to swear that to the exclusion of all other lords

---

[62] *Chron. Angl.* 125–6. Walsingham erroneously calls him Sir Thomas Swinton.
[63] *Westm. Chron.* 81–3.

whatsoever they would hold with him as their true king, and they were to be given badges, consisting of silver and gilt crowns, with the intention that whenever they were called upon to do so they should join the king, armed and ready. This serjeant was eventually arrested in those parts, not far from Cambridge, and committed to prison.[64]

Richard's conduct is substantiated in the proceedings of the Merciless Parliament, where de Vere and the other 'traitors' were accused of having 'caused the king to have of late a great retinue of sundry people and to give them sundry badges, otherwise than was wont to be done of ancient time by any kings his progenitors, to the end that they might have power to perform their false treasons aforesaid'.[65]

The events of 1387–8 brought the question of livery badges and competitive retaining to the forefront of national politics, and gave rise to the legislation of 1388–90. In the Cambridge Parliament of September 1388 the Commons demanded that the use of badges should be abolished entirely, for

those who wear them are, by reason of the power of their masters, flown with such insolent arrogance that they do not shrink from practising with reckless effrontery various forms of extortion in the surrounding countryside . . . and it is certainly the boldness inspired by their badges that makes them unafraid to do these things and more besides.

Once again the Lords tried to evade the issue by insisting that the Commons cite specific cases, but 'so far from being satisfied with this undertaking, the commons were firm in their demand that if the lords wanted to have peace and quiet in the kingdom they must drop the use of badges altogether'. It was at this point that the king, 'to set an example to others', offered to discard his own badges, 'an offer which gave the utmost satisfaction to the commons', but the Lords refused to do the same, and eventually, after much 'abuse and vituperation', the matter was postponed until the next Parliament.[66]

These episodes help to identify the nature and extent of the problem. The Lords, many of whom remained suspicious of Richard, were fearful that the abolition of livery badges would give the Crown, with its greater resources, too much of an advantage when it came to recruiting followers —the point about badges being that their affordability minimized the gap in resources between king and lords. The Commons, many of whom were

---

[64] Ibid. 187. See also T. Favent, *Historia Mirabilis Parliamenti*, ed. M. McKisack *Camden Miscellany*, xiv (London, 1926), 4.
[65] *Westm. Chron.* 257.   [66] Ibid. 355–7.

suspicious of both king and lords, were concerned about the threat to law and order in the shires. The Ordinance of May 1390 represented a compromise: livery badges were not abolished but in future they were only to be worn as part of a formal and properly constituted life contract. Thus, rather than undermining lord–retainer relationships, they were intended to reinforce them. Richard, who was prepared to put substantial resources into the retaining of men in the 1390s, benefited most from these arrangements. According to the Monk of Evesham, it was at the Smithfield tournament of October 1390 that, 'for the first time, that remarkable badge or mark [*signum vel stigma*] of the white hart with a crown and a chain of gold, was given out' by the king.[67] During the 1390s the king, making generous use of life-retaining contracts, continued to build up his retinue steadily, and there seems to have been little criticism of his behaviour.[68] After 1397, however, he and, with his sanction, his followers used their livery badges to recruit freebooters who became not the chief guarantee of justice and stability in the realm but a serious threat to that stability. The chronicles are full of stories of the depradations of Richard's Cheshire archers: Adam of Usk described them as the chief cause of the king's ruin.[69] His principal supporters among the lords were accused, in the Parliament of 1399, of having committed numerous oppressions 'under colour of their lordships', and were forbidden ever to distribute 'liveries of signs' again. So determined were both Lords and Commons that this should not be allowed to happen again that a statute was now passed forbidding any lord from the use of livery badges in future; only the king was to be allowed the use of badges and he could not give them to anyone below the rank of esquire. Nor could those who received them from the king wear them anywhere except in the king's presence; in particular, they were forbidden to wear them in their localities.[70]

The controversy over livery badges during Richard's reign was, of course, a symptom not a cause of the troubles of the times. It was because relationships between the magnates, and between them and the king, were fraught that it was important to control the means whereby those lords who either felt threatened, or wished to threaten others, sought to attract followers to their cause. One might think that the campaign against livery badges was rather pointless: surely, if this avenue was closed to them, lords could find other ways of buying support? Perhaps they did, but the visible display of a follower's allegiance was clearly of more than symbolic

---

[67] *Vita*, 132; see the Wilton Diptych badges.
[68] Given-Wilson, *Royal Household*, 214–15.   [69] Adam of Usk, 169–70.
[70] *RP* iii. 428, 477–8, 523–4.

importance to both lords and their retainers, and it is probably this which explains the tenacity with which the campaign was pursued. Livery badges seem to have induced precisely that sort of 'gang culture' which was seen as such a threat to stability in the shires. They worked against, rather than supplemented, the accepted forms of retaining, which were seen as upholding public peace. Their prevalence, and the fear they aroused, are indicative of the tensions which dislocated political life under Richard II.

The epithets which cling to Richard's reign—'Merciless Parliament', 'Revenge Parliament', and so forth—proclaim it as an age of invidious personal conflict between king and nobility. Was this Richard's fault? K. B. McFarlane, in a famous essay, argued that it was:

The root trouble about most late-medieval constitutional history is its assumption that the interests of king and nobility were opposed, that conflict could not be avoided. This assumption seems to me false. The only thing that can be said for it is that conflicts sometimes occurred; that they did so was almost always the fault of the king; which is as much as to say that it depended how often the hereditary succession brought those unfit to rule to the throne. Edward II, Richard II, and Henry VI were the penalties that monarchy paid for its dependence upon the chances of heredity. It would be a mistake to judge the institution solely by its failures. The fact that neither Edward II nor Richard II could get on with their magnates and that Henry VI was totally incapable of government may be allowed to bulk too large, though the consequences were serious for them. In fact the area of possible conflict was extraordinarily small and any competent king had no difficulty in avoiding it.[71]

Such sentiments, written over forty years ago, now seem somewhat overindulgent to a baronage that has (largely thanks to McFarlane) been studied by the present generation of historians like none before it. It is too easy simply to cry foul at England's 'bad kings', just as it was too easy, before McFarlane began the serious study of their records, to ascribe the troubles of late medieval England to the ogre of the 'overmighty subject'.[72] There was, surely, potential for conflict at every turn. What nation can fight a war—let alone an unsuccessful war, and England's war had turned sour long before Richard came to the throne—without disagreements over policy? The great ideological debates of later eras—Catholic versus Protestant, labour versus capital—may have been largely absent from the medieval council chamber,[73] but disputes over status, and over

---

[71] *Nobility*, 120–1.   [72] Ibid. 283–4.

[73] However, the 1381 rising and the Lollard disturbances of the time were far from negligible factors in the high politics of Richard's reign.

landed, financial, and human resources, were endemic among the medieval political classes, to say nothing of financial or mercantile or ecclesiastical policy. Richard II failed to contain conflict. That he did so was undeniably to some extent his own fault; that historians have been led to argue that it was almost entirely his fault is a measure of the success of his opponents' propaganda.

7

Richard II and London

Caroline M. Barron

Froissart, writing in the years immediately following the deposition of
Richard, attributed a leading role in the king's downfall to the Londoners
who, 'being rich from their trade, are enabled to live in state, and by whom
the other parts of England are generally governed . . . said to one another
privately . . . "if this wicked king Richard be suffered to rule according to
his pleasure, we must all be ruined and the country destroyed. Ever since
he began his reign, the kingdom has not prospered to the degree in which
it did before".'[1] Froissart's analysis is neither particularly subtle, not particularly accurate. In fact, Richard probably disliked the Londoners rather
more than they disliked him, and their role in his deposition was minor
compared with that played by the retinues of the disaffected nobility.[2] However, Richard could not ignore the men of London, even if he found their
company uncongenial, and it is clear that at times he took trouble to cultivate their loyalty and to curb their lawlessness. It has been customary to
consider the relationship between the Crown and the city from the point
of view of the Londoners and to chart their struggles to win, and then to
defend, their privileges and freedoms.[3] In this chapter the focus will shift
from the Londoners to the Crown. What did Richard require, or desire,

I am very grateful to Professor Nigel Saul and Prof. Paul Strohm for reading a draft of this
chapter and for making a number of helpful suggestions for improvement.

[1] Sir John Froissart, *Chronicles of England, France and Spain*, ed. and trans. T. Johnes, ii.
(London, 1857), 683.

[2] For the further development of this argument, see C. M. Barron, 'The Deposition of
Richard II', in *Politics and Crisis*, 132–49, esp. 139–40.

[3] R. Bird, *The Turbulent London of Richard II* (London, 1949); P. Nightingale, 'Capitalists, Crafts and Constitutional Change in Late Fourteenth-Century London', *Past and Present*,
124(1989), 3–35.

from his 'capital city'? How far did the Londoners meet his needs and
expectations, and what could the king do to elicit a better response?

When Richard became king on the death of his grandfather in June 1377,
his inheritance was a reasonable one: the monarchy was popular and both
Edward III and the Black Prince had been respected and admired. Richard's three surviving uncles were committed to loyalty to their brother's
son. Richard was 11 when he became king; four years later he married Anne
of Bohemia and might have been expected to become actively engaged
in the business of ruling his kingdom. However, he seems, rather, to have
chosen to prolong his minority and to have been content with the trappings, rather than the realities, of royal power. He was happy to govern
by fits and starts and to leave the routine work to others. How long this
state of affairs might have continued is difficult to say, but the death of
his mother, Joan of Kent, in 1385, the mounting aristocratic opposition
in Parliament and the imposition of the Commission of 1386, jolted Richard
into action. In 1387, when he was 21, Richard began to take his kingship
seriously but this was too late to save him from the ignominy of the
Merciless Parliament of February 1388. From this nadir of royal authority Richard developed his 'will to power' and in 1389 he formally declared
his minority to be at an end.[4] The Londoners were not the only ones to
be caught out by this change of mood and style. What Richard had tolerated in the 1380s would be tolerated no longer, and the lightning attack
on the city's liberties in 1392 was a vigorous manifestation of this new
'hands-on' style of royal government.

Richard did not spend much time in London, which is neither unusual
nor surprising. Edward III had spent more time at Eltham and Sheen
than he did at Westminster or the Tower.[5] Indeed Richard's personal ex-
periences of the Tower in June 1381 and in December 1387 cannot have
engendered in him warm feelings for the place. However, unlike his grandfather, Richard spent a great deal of time travelling around his kingdom.
The chronicler Thomas Walsingham attributed his travels to a desire to
live at the expense of others.[6] In the 1380s he probably travelled in search
of pleasure and entertainment, but in the 1390s he demonstrated a desire
to be king throughout his realm. Whatever Richard may have felt about
London, it is clear that he favoured Westminster, and in this he resembled
Henry III, whose patronage of Westminster was in marked contrast to his

---

[4] *Westm. Chron.* 391–3.
[5] C. Given-Wilson, *The Royal Household and the King's Affinity: Service, Politics and Finance
in England 1360–1413* (New Haven, 1986), 33–4.
[6] *Hist. Angl.* ii. 96–7.

contentious relations with the Londoners.[7] Perhaps both kings sought in Westminster the 'perfect capital city' which London seemed so conspicuously unable to provide.

What did Richard require from London? Financial wealth and expertise was increasingly concentrated among the merchants who traded in and out of London and the king needed their financial support. He needed the large sums raised there by direct taxation, and the even larger sums raised by the indirect taxation of the customs. More crucially, the king needed a buoyant money market where he could raise cash loans quickly and efficiently to maintain the business of government while waiting for the parliamentary taxes to lumber slowly into the Exchequer. The king expected gifts, as well as loans, in celebration of coronations, weddings, or victories, and as bribes, or, occasionally, to ward off a dire threat to the security of the realm. The Londoners themselves, when they greeted their new monarch in 1377, acknowledged that the city was 'camera vestra', a phrase which may have fallen on receptive young ears.[8] Later kings hoped and expected to be able to exercise a certain amount of patronage in the city in the giving of the freedom, or civic offices. However, this kind of urban patronage does not seem to have been as important a means of stretching the royal revenue in the fourteenth century as it became later under the Lancastrians and Tudors.[9]

When England was at war, the king expected that the most populous city in his realm would provide men to fight and ships to transport them across the Channel to foreign fields. It was also in London that the king might look to acquire the large numbers of bows and bowstrings, armour, harness, food supplies, and all the accoutrements of war without which large numbers of men could not be converted into armies. However, Richard also hoped, misguidedly as it turned out, that the city would provide men to fight not only against foreign enemies but also against noble enemies from within the realm. In the autumn of 1387 Richard believed that with the help of the current mayor of London, the fishmonger Nicholas Exton, and the influential ex-mayor, the grocer Nicholas Brembre, he would be able to raise an army in London to use in his planned moves against Gloucester, Arundel, and Warwick. However, this attempt to use

---

[7] G. Rosser, *Medieval Westminster 1200–1540* (Oxford, 1989), 97–100: N. E. Saul, 'Richard II and Westminster Abbey', in W. J. Blair and B. Golding (edd.), *The Cloister and the World: Essays in Medieval History presented to Barbara Harvey* (Oxford, 1995), 196–218.

[8] *Hist. Angl.* i. 329.

[9] For examples of civic offices requested by Richard II for his servants, see *LBH* 208, 282–3, 316–17, 338; *CPMR 1381–1412*, 104.

Londoners to form an army for 'internal' use was a dismal failure. When the king sent for the mayor and aldermen to ask how many men-at-arms they could supply, they replied that the inhabitants of the city were craftsmen and merchants who had no military experience, and they could only be used to fight to defend the city. The wardens of the city crafts, whom Richard summoned the following day, gave him the same answer.[10] The Londoners were not willing to fight for the king against the retinues of lords with whom he was at variance. That Richard thought that they would do so demonstrates how far, at that point, his finger was from the pulse of his kingdom.

It was in the City of London that the king expected to find the skilled craftsmen and the luxury goods which would grace and elevate his court. It was in the workshops of London that tailors, goldsmiths, skinners, jewellers, embroiderers, weavers, painters, and saddlers could be found to create the trappings of majesty. It was on the wharves and in the warehouses of London merchants that the officers of the Wardrobe would hope to find the silks, velvets, furs, and gold wire out of which to fashion the visible grandeur of the monarch. The role of foreign merchants—in particular the Italians—as importers and suppliers of these expensive goods who traded in England under royal protection, but in a state of constant rivalry with denizen, or native, merchants, provided a source of fruitful conflict between the king and the Londoners. The king encouraged the presence of alien merchants in London as an alternative source of revenue, to provide luxury goods, and as a sword of Damocles to hold over the heads of the English merchants who were not always eager to dance to the royal tune.

But the City of London was, for the Crown, more than simply an urban conglomeration of people and buildings. It was the capital of England. It was here that royal visitors were brought, such as the king of Armenia at Christmas 1385,[11] and where jousts and tournaments were held. Here royal 'triumphs' and processions were played out. The appearance of the city was a matter of concern to the king: he wanted his capital city, his processional city, perhaps even his New Jerusalem, to be clean and impressive. The king needed also a peaceful and orderly city. The Westminster Chronicler notes that disturbances in London were particularly troubling to the king since the city was 'cameram suam'.[12] It was London's failure to be orderly that provoked Richard's sharp action against the city

[10] *Westm. Chron.* 207–8, 217; H. T. Riley (ed. and trans.), *Memorials of London and London Life in the XIIIth, XIVth and XVth Centuries 1276–1419* (London, 1868), 499; *LBH* 321.
[11] *Westm. Chron.* 155–7.   [12] Ibid. 62.

in 1392.[13] If members of the King's Household, and nobles and their retinues, could not walk safely in city streets, then the king himself felt insecure, and if city government had degenerated into a mass of squabbling factions and street fights, then London was failing to provide an appropriate ambience for the king's regality.

Finally, Richard wanted, and perhaps politically he needed, to be popular in the City of London. Here he required to feel loved and secure, to be greeted by cheering crowds, and to be ushered through the streets by deferential aldermen. He wanted their love and their loyalty, and to feel that they would stand with him against all comers. When love and loyalty failed to come spontaneously from the Londoners, Richard tried to bludgeon such popularity out of the city.[14] However, in the event he acquired the appearance, but not the reality. Certainly he had his supporters among the London élite—and possibly also lower down the economic scale—but widespread popularity eluded him. Richard's failure in his relations with London is a microcosm of his failure as a king: a tendency to mistake the appearance for the reality, and to rely upon the part rather than the whole. The ends which he was pursuing were not unreasonable ones, but he chose inappropriate means to secure them.

The strengths and weaknesses of the monarchy on the death of Edward III have been recently characterized,[15] but what was the state of the City of London in 1377 when Richard came to the throne? There is no doubt that it was in the midst of a constitutional crisis, immediately provoked by the events of the Good Parliament of 1376 but with roots that went much deeper.[16] London in the reign of Richard II has been characterized as 'turbulent', but students of London history will know that for most of its history London had been turbulent.[17] It was only in the reign of Edward III that London had enjoyed a measure of stability. The turbulence of Richard's reign was a reversion to the norm, but the causes of that turbulence had shifted. When men and women live together in closely packed, but not necessarily closely knit, communities, the opportunities for dispute, and for the verbal and physical expressions of disagreement, are manifold.

[13] For a discussion of the causes and course of this quarrel, see C. M. Barron, 'The Quarrel of Richard II with London, 1392–1397', in *Reign of Richard II*, 173–201.

[14] *Westm. Chron.* 207–8, 215–19; Riley (ed. and trans.), *Memorials of London*, 500.

[15] W. M. Ormrod, *The Reign of Edward III: Crown and Political Society in England 1327–1377* (London, 1990); A. Goodman, *John of Gaunt: The Exercise of Princely Power in Fourteenth-Century Europe* (London, 1992), ch. 1.

[16] G. Holmes, *The Good Parliament of 1376* (Oxford, 1975); C. M. Barron, *Revolt in London: 11th to 15th June 1381* (London, 1981), esp. 12–20; Nightingale, 'Capitalists'.

[17] G. A. Williams, *Medieval London from Commune to Capital* (London, 1963).

London was not immune from the wide-ranging results of the catastrophic mortality of the Black Death in 1348–9. The crisis mortality ratio
in London seems to have been 18 per cent, almost three times more acute
than the worst plague epidemics of the sixteenth century. Keene has estimated that the city, which may have had a population of 70,000–100,000
in 1300, dropped to nearer 40,000 by the 1380s.[18] In London the loss of
population seems to have been largely beneficial for the survivors: there
was more space and better living conditions. Labour was scarce and so
the wage-worker was able, in spite of the Statute of Labourers and the
restrictive practices of the employers, to push up his wages and his standard of living. Women were allowed, indeed encouraged, to play a part in
the industrial and mercantile life of the city.[19] Apprentices, of both sexes,
were in short supply and so their conditions of service improved. As wages
rose, so there was increased demand for consumer goods, clothes, household wares, shoes, jewellery, armour, and for a widening range of food-
stuffs. As standards of living rose, so the urban proletariat became more
prosperous, more skilled, more educated, and more vociferous. The
'small people'[20] were on the march, and they began to look critically at the
way in which the city was governed and to form themselves into groups
to resist the controlling authority, whether of the masters of their craft or
of those who ran the government of the city.

Since the inauguration of the commune in 1189, the City of London
had been governed by a mayor and twenty-four aldermen who were drawn,
almost exclusively, from mercantile trades, i.e. men who traded in wine,
or wool, or spices, or cloth or furs. Others who took part in governing the
city were jewellers and goldsmiths, who were skilled craftsmen rather than
merchants, but wealthy because they worked on such expensive materials.
The fishmongers also governed the city because they not only monopolized the sale of fish, but owned most of the ships which were the sinews
of overseas trade. It was these wealthy merchants who dominated the government of London. Moreover, the importance of such men had been
enhanced by the notorious bankruptcies of the Italian firms of the Bardi
and the Peruzzi in the 1350s. Native Englishmen now moved into royal

---

[18] D. Keene, 'A New Study of London before the Great Fire', *Urban History Yearbook
1984* (Leicester), 11–21, esp. 20.

[19] C. M. Barron, 'The "Golden Age" of Women in Medieval London', in K. Bate *et al.*
(edd.), *Medieval Women in Southern England* (Reading, 1989), 35–58.

[20] This phrase is used by Thomas Usk, the 'secretary' to John of Northampton's party,
in his Appeal in which he gives evidence against his former master, R. W. Chambers and
M. Daunt (edd.), *A Book of London English 1384–1425* (Oxford, 1931), 18–31; P. Strohm,
Hochon's Arrow (Princeton, 1992), ch. 7 and app. 1 by A. J. Prescott.

finance, an area which had previously been monopolized first by the Jews, and then by the Italians. Now it was Englishmen who acted as bankers to the Crown and not all of them were Londoners. The Hull merchant William de la Pole and Richard earl of Arundel played important roles in financing Edward III's wars against the French.[21] However, London merchants were also drawn into royal finance: Adam Fraunceys, John Pyel, Richard Lyons, Adam Bury, and John Pecche. None of these men was born in London: they were all rich and successful immigrants.[22] They had bought up manors which had belonged to families wiped out by the Plague, or ruined by their expenses in France. They traded overseas in wool and cloth, collected the royal customs, lent money to the Crown (or organized such loans), owned houses and shops in London and manors in the country, and held office in the city by virtue of their wealth. They were clever, successful, ruthless, and opportunist. Within this élite mercantile class there were acute rivalries, for example between the Grocers and the Drapers.[23] There were conflicts between these men as employers of labour and sellers of goods, and those whom they employed, often the poorer members of the same craft. The mercantile trades often did not see eye to eye with the artisan crafts in the city, and they were frequently in conflict among themselves. The interests of those who produced and sold food were different from those of the consumer. Most craft organizations wanted to exercise a monopoly of their own craft while encouraging a free market elsewhere in the interests of lower prices. These economic rivalries were not novel but, since the community had shrunk in size and acute poverty no longer curbed protest and enterprise, the conflicts were overt and articulated. Golden opportunities beckoned and seemed to be within reach. So the base on which the government of London rested in the late fourteenth century was particularly unstable as rival groups gained and lost control of civic government. There was a high rate of immigration and only a slowly developing sense of communal responsibility. The causes of turbulence were many and varied, and it is not surprising that neither Richard, nor his counsellors, understood the issues which were tearing London apart, nor could they control the contending factions. In the end Richard imitated the strong-arm tactics of Edward I and successfully brought the Londoners to heel. However, in the earlier part of his reign he had tried, as did his uncle John of Gaunt, to harness one faction to his

---

[21] Holmes, *Good Parliament*, 69–79.

[22] Barron, *Revolt*, 13–14; S. O'Connor (ed.), *The Cartularies of Adam Fraunceys and John Pyel* (London, 1994).

[23] Nightingale, 'Capitalists', 17–20.

cause. The failure of this policy was apparent when Nicholas Brembre was executed in 1388, and Richard came to realize that he must stand above civic faction. This was a lesson that he might, with profit, have applied to his kingdom as a whole. It would be difficult to argue that London failed Richard in its role as royal banker. The Londoners, like other Englishmen, contributed to the three poll-taxes of 1377, 1379, and 1380,[24] and to the thirteen direct parliamentary taxes granted during Richard's reign: these taxes amounted, for the Londoners, to seventeen fifteenths, i.e. a total of about £12,750.[25] On seven occasions, moreover, between October 1377 and March 1388, the Londoners corporately provided seven substantial loans ranging in amount from £2,000 to £5,000.[26] These loans were usually advanced on the security of the customs or parliamentary taxation, and on four occasions royal jewels or plate was handed over as additional security. In September 1380, when the mayor and commonalty lent £2,000, they were given as security a coronet decorated with gold, diamonds, sapphires, and pearls. However, in January 1382 the king was obliged to ask for the coronet back, so that it could be used at his wedding.[27]

The bulk of the parliamentary taxation and all the London loans fall in the period before 1388. It might be thought that this decline in financial support was the result of Richard's 'personal rule' which began in 1389. However, it is probably of more significance that in July 1389 the first of a series of truces with France was proclaimed in England.[28] In these circumstances neither Parliament nor the Londoners felt the king's needs to be so pressing. Richard may not, however, have experienced a diminished need for money and it is clear from the Receipt Rolls of the Exchequer that the king now turned to Italians to provide the resources which the Londoners were unable, or unwilling, to offer him.[29] Whereas

[24] See C. Oman, *The Great Revolt of 1381*, ed. E. B. Fryde (new edn., Oxford, 1969), ed.'s introd., pp. xii–xxii.

[25] For a list of the taxes granted to Richard II, see J. H. Ramsay, *A History of the Revenues of the Kings of England*, 2 vols. (Oxford, 1925), ii. 433. For the relative weight of direct and indirect taxation, see below, Fig. 8.8.

[26] 5 Oct. 1377, £5,000, *LBH* 79–80, 87–8; Riley (ed. and trans.), *Memorials of London*, 410–12; PRO E.401/528; 16 Mar. 1379, £5,000, *LBH* 119–21, 122–3, 149; Riley (ed. and trans.), *Memorials of London*, 429–30; PRO E.401/535; 16 Sept. 1380, £2,000, *LBH* 156, 159, 160; PRO E.401/539; 22 Sept. 1383, £2,666. 13s. 4d., *LBH* 218–19; PRO E.401/550; 26 June 1385, £5,000, *LBH* 267–8; 29 Nov. 1386, £4,000, *LBH* 293–4; 25 Mar. 1388, £5,000, *LBH* 323.

[27] *LBH* 156, 159, 160; Riley (ed. and trans.), *Memorials of London*, 443–4. This may have been the same crown that was given as security in Sept. 1383 and borrowed back again for Christmas, *LBH* 219.

[28] July 1389, May 1392, May 1396 (*LBH* 342, 377, 414, 450).

[29] H. Bradley, 'Italian Merchants in London', Ph.D. thesis (London, 1992), 213–15, 456.

the Londoners were prepared to acknowledge themselves to be the king's chamber in time of war, they were less willing to offer financial help in peace (or truce) time. The king, on the other hand, required temporary funding to maintain his household and to live like a king. Corporately the city did not lend to the Crown after 1388, but some individual Londoners were prepared to finance the Crown, and in 1397 Richard Whittington appears to have taken over where Nicholas Brembre had left off.[30]

While England was at war with France, the king expected the city to forward the war effort in a number of tangible ways which extended well beyond the simple provision of finance. The extent to which Londoners joined the English armies—the Pistols and Bardolfs of the Cheapside taverns—is hard to say. Some must have joined the various expeditionary forces, but they did so as individuals retained by particular lords.[31] There is no evidence that the city, in Richard's reign, raised a contingent of its own to send as it did in 1436 and 1449.[32] However, it was in the London workshops that armour, harness, and bows were fashioned to equip those who did cross the Channel.[33] It may have been London shipping which was most important to the war effort (finance apart) and it was because fishmongers owned ships that they played such an important role within the mercantile community of London. In 1373 the city had provided the king with a fully equipped barge, *The Paul of London*, which was captained by William Martlesham, 'mariner of London'.[34] It is not clear what role it played, but the barge was refurbished, and sent back to the fray in 1376.[35] Seven years later, however, the barge was lying derelict in the Thames, fit for neither war nor commerce, and so the chamberlain was instructed to sell it as profitably as he could.[36] There was continual pressure on London shipping to transport armies or make attacks on enemy shipping.[37] Just as the English preyed on French shipping, so the enemy fleets seized English

---

[30] J. A. Tuck, *Richard II and the English Nobility* (London, 1973), esp. ch. 4; C. M. Barron, 'Richard Whittington: The Man Behind the Myth', in A. E. J. Hollander and W. Kellaway (edd.), *Studies in London History presented to Philip Edmund Jones* (London, 1969), 197–248.

[31] For examples of writs of protection issued to individuals to travel abroad on military service in the retinues of particular lords, see *CPMR, 1364–1381*, 268, 270, 287; *CPMR 1381–1412*, 23, 39, 40, 43, 81, 161, 261; see J. W. Sherborne, 'Indentured Retinues and English Expeditions to France 1369–1380', *EHR* 79 (1964), 718–46.

[32] C. M. Barron, 'The Government of London and its Relations with the Crown', Ph.D. thesis (London, 1970), 457–61.

[33] e.g. the royal writs of May 1376, Feb. 1381, Oct. 1386 (*LBH* 27, 160, 288–9).

[34] Riley (ed. and trans.), *Memorials of London*, 368–71.   [35] *LBH* 20.

[36] *LBH* 215–16, 236; in Oct. 1380 the city provided armed barges for the defence of the realm, *LBH* 155.

[37] Apr. 1385, Aug. 1387 (*LBH* 263, 311).

goods when they could.[38] These were not the conditions in which cross-Channel trade could flourish.

On occasion the war came nearer home. It was feared that the French would seize the opportunity provided by the death of Edward III to attack not only the south coast but also to sail up the Thames to London. In preparation for this attack, the city gates were chained, the quays downstream of London Bridge were 'bretasched' (i.e. fortified against attack), elaborate measures were taken to guard the city's walls and river frontage, and the inhabitants of the wards were compelled either to join the 'home guard', or to contribute cash, or to provide a day's labour, all this in the city's defence. The fear of attack, judging by the detailed measures worked out to repulse it, seems to have been real enough.[39] Further steps were taken in 1380: a fifteenth was levied to pay for armed barges, and a further tax of 6*d*. in the pound on rents to provide enough money to build a stone tower to match that already built by the munificent John Philpot, one on each bank of the Thames, 60 feet high and linked by an iron chain which could be drawn across the river to protect the city, and the English fleet, from attack.[40] While Richard was away on campaign in Scotland in the summer of 1385, there was a further fear of French invasion and men were rushed to the coast. The large sum of two fifteenths (about £1,500) was raised in the wards to be used to safeguard the city.[41] The size of the sum suggests genuine anxiety. The usual midsummer festivities of wrestling matches at Smithfield and plays at Skinnerswell were banned: at the approach of the enemy, in true Homeric fashion, women and children were to stay indoors while the men at arms, and the archers, were to go forth to fight.[42] The acute fear of a French attack continued into the next year, when a sales tax was imposed in the city to pay for the cost of repairing the walls 'especially in this time of war'.[43] However, the 1389 truce with France brought these military efforts to an end and the Londoners ceased to hold either themselves or their purses ready for the defence of the city.

---

[38] June, Aug. 1376 (*LBH* 31, 33); for piracy at sea in 1387, see *Westm. Chron.* 181–5; for a discussion of the effects of the French wars on shipping, see Nightingale, 'Capitalists', 28.

[39] *LBH* 64–6.

[40] 2 Oct. 1380, Riley (ed. and trans.), *Memorials of London*, 444–5. It seems unlikely that the tower was ever, in fact, built.

[41] *LBH* 269–71; *Westm. Chron.* 125.   [42] *LBH* 272.

[43] *LBH* 297–9; there had been earlier efforts to repair the city's walls in 1378, 1379, 1384, and 1385 (*LBH* 116, 137, 236; *CPMR 1381–1412*, 56). The fear of enemy attack was such that in Sept. 1386 the city prepared for a siege (*LBH* 285–6; Knighton, ii. 211–13). To deal with the emergency the city had to borrow from Biernes Chest (£500) (*LBH* 342–3).

There seems to be little doubt that London was able and willing to provide the royal court and household with the trappings of majesty. In the course of Edward III's reign the royal household had appeared increasingly extravagant particularly after 1360, as more was spent on luxury goods and less on war. Both the Black Prince and the king himself had established Wardrobes in the city which served as purchasing centres, storehouses, centres of household administration, and, occasionally, for residence.[44] Many great lords (e.g. Henry of Bolingbroke) likewise established town houses which also served as purchasing offices for their households.[45] London merchants and craftsmen responded eagerly to this challenge and Richard, like his grandfather and his contemporaries, was able to find among the workshops and warehouses of the city, craftsmen and luxury goods of a quality well suited to decorating his court: painters like Gilbert Prince and Thomas Lytlington, goldsmiths like Nicholas Twyford and Christopher Tildesley, saddlers like Henry Pountfreyt, skinners like William Wiltshire, and silkwomen like Mathilda Bailly.[46] The quality of the craftsmanship of these London workshops is apparent from the surviving examples brought together in the Age of Chivalry exhibition.[47] There was a boom in the development of luxury crafts in London, fuelled by royal extravagance, and the cessation of the war with France. Edward III's expenditure in the Great Wardrobe in the last ten years of his reign averaged just over £3,000 per annum, and in the first ten years of Richard's reign the expenditure was much the same at £3,170 per annum. However, in the period of Richard's personal rule, from 1390, the average spending rose to nearly £10,000 per annum.[48] Royal expenditure now shifted

---

[44] For the various royal Wardrobes in the city, see M. D. Lobel (ed.), *The City of London from Prehistoric Times to c.1520* (Oxford, 1989), 78, 84.

[45] Henry of Derby's London Wardrobe, like his London residence, seems to have been remarkably peripatetic: in 1381–2 it was in Coleman Street; in 1387–8 it was near Baynard's Castle possibly in the building later known as the Duke's Wardrobe (PRO D.L.28/1/1 and 2).

[46] Between 1378 and 1384 Nicholas Twyford, a London goldsmith, was paid over £70 for various silver gilt cups bought from him, usually as gifts for visiting envoys (PRO E.401/530, 533, 535, 537, 556); for skinners see E. M. Veale, *The English Fur Trade in the Later Middle Ages* (Oxford, 1966), 85, 134–5; for silkwomen, see K. Lacey, 'The Production of "Narrow Ware" by Silkwomen in Fourteenth and Fifteenth Century England', *Textile History*, 18 (1987), 187–204; for the London painters see J. Mitchell, 'The Painters of London', MA thesis (Royal Holloway, Univ. of London, 1989); and for the goldsmiths see T. F. Reddaway and L. M. Walker, *The Early History of the Goldsmith's Company 1327–1509* (London, 1976), esp. 311–12, and C. M. Barron, 'The Deposition of Richard II', in *Politics and Crisis*, 139–40.

[47] J. Alexander and P. Binski (edd.), *Age of Chivalry: Art in Plantagenet England, 1200–1400* (London, 1987).

[48] Given-Wilson, *Royal Household*, 80–5, and table p. 82.

from armourers and bowyers to painters and goldsmiths. In both cases, however, the suppliers were Londoners. Richard's developing taste for royal magnificence, the outward and visible signs of royal power, worked to the advantage of the Londoners. The king certainly wanted gifts and loans to finance his court and household, but his officers usually spent this money in London warehouses.

The Londoners were not, however, the exclusive partners in this symbiotic relationship. Some of the larger Italian banking houses, the Bardi and the Peruzzi, had been bankrupted by Edward III in the 1340s, but there is no doubt that the Italians remained active in the city both as royal financiers and as suppliers of luxury goods to the Wardrobe.[49] In 1389 the king needed to present gifts to Waleran count of St Pol and his companions when they left for France, having sworn to observe the truce. He purchased two cloths, one red and one violet, from the London draper John Hende at a cost of £22, but eleven lengths of cloth of gold and four pieces of silk at a total cost of £74, from the the Italian Bett Lombard.[50]

From the king's point of view it was advantageous not to allow the citizens of London to monopolize his custom. There were two groups of outsiders who challenged the Londoners' control of the trading and craft activities that went on in the city: foreigners, i.e. Englishmen who were not citizens of London, and strangers or aliens, i.e. those born outside the allegiance of the king of England. On the whole the Londoners were united with each other, and against the king, in their desire to restrict the activities of aliens and strangers in the city. They were, however, much less united about the extent to which they wished to curtail the activities of foreigners in London and, in particular, the activities of foreign fishmongers. Quite clearly different groups within the city had very different economic interests and these interests were neither consistent nor coherent.

By long tradition the king protected alien merchants who traded within his realm. These men brought into England goods which could not otherwise be obtained: silk thread and cloth, velvet, spices, wax, gold wire, furs, and they could be made to pay for the privilege of access to this market by providing cash loans when required, and by paying customs dues at a higher rate than denizen merchants.[51] Alien artisans could also be encouraged to introduce into England skills which were unknown or inexpertly

---

[49] Bradley, 'Italian Merchants', 255, 257–8.
[50] PRO E.403/524. I am grateful to Professor Nigel Saul for this reference.
[51] E. Carus-Wilson and O. Coleman, *England's Export Trade, 1275–1547* (Oxford, 1963), 11–13.

practised. In London groups of Flemish and Brabant weavers had been organized into craft guilds[52] and in 1377 these clothworkers were specifically taken under the king's protection.[53] This did not, however, prevent sixty of them from being massacred in June 1381.[54] Alien craftsmen were rarely welcome in the city, and royal protection was crucial, but not always effective. Alien merchants were, likewise, regarded with suspicion. The king had good reasons, as we have seen, to encourage them to come to England, to import rare goods, and to export English wool and cloth paying a high rate of custom. The most contentious aspect of the alien merchants' operations was their constant infringement of the citizens' exclusive right to buy and sell retail in London. Alien merchants were free to sell wholesale to London merchants, who would then be responsible for their retail distribution. The Londoners fought bitterly to maintain the exclusive right of citizens to trade retail in the city which had been established by the Statute of York in 1335. This privilege, known as the 'franchise' was, on occasions, suspended by both Edward III and Richard II: it was in the king's interest to encourage alien merchants and to remove the citizens' monopoly over retail sales of alien imports, since this brought down the prices at which those goods were sold. An astute king could play off one interest group against another, but this was a difficult and, sometimes, dangerous game.[55]

However, the city's franchise also curtailed the activities of foreigners (i.e. non-citizens) in the London markets. How far were foreigners able to buy and sell freely in the city? When the Londoners succeeded in 1376 in securing the restoration of the franchise after a period of twenty-five years, this reinstated, among other monopolistic controls, the London fishmongers' monopoly over the retail sale of fish in the city. This became an important issue in the civic disputes of the 1380s. Most Londoners, apart from the fishmongers and their supporters, wanted to see this particular monopoly abolished so that fish would be available more cheaply in the city. This was the popular cause championed by John of Northampton. Those who supported the franchise, and thereby the fishmongers' monopoly, could

---

[52] In 1375, 1376 (*LBH* 17, 50).

[53] *CPMR 1364–1381*, 251; for examples of hostility to alien craftsmen in London see *LBH* 95, 135.

[54] *Westm. Chron.* 5–7; Riley (ed. and trans.), *Memorials of London*, 450.

[55] Nightingale, 'Capitalists', 9–16. For a discussion of the privileges of the Hanse merchants see H. Palais, 'England's First Attempt to Break the Commercial Monopoly of the Hanseatic League, 1377–1380', *American Hist. Rev.*, 64 (1959), 852–65; and M. M. Postan, 'The Economic and Political Relations of England and the Hanse from 1400–1475', in id. and E. Power (edd.), *Studies in English Trade in the Fifteenth Century* (London, 1933).

argue that since the mayor and aldermen already controlled the prices at which many victuals were sold in the city (e.g. bread, wine, beer, poultry, and fish), the prices could not be kept artificially high by the fishmongers' monopoly. The fishmongers, moreover, did not see why the city franchise which protected the monopolistic interests of all London crafts and trades, should be removed only in their case.[56]

The interests of the king were not clear-cut in this debate. Whether a free market in the retail sale of food or a series of monopolies mitigated by price control was 'better', i.e. produced cheaper food, was not clear. What harvest could the Crown reap out of this contentious field? It appears that Richard II attempted to use the divisive issue as a means of developing a party of supporters in the city. Whereas John of Gaunt seems to have supported the draper John of Northampton and the anti-monopolists, Richard II cultivated the grocer Nicholas Brembre and his successor in the mayoralty, the fishmonger Nicholas Exton. Both of these men, and their supporters, wanted to maintain the city's franchise and the monopolies enjoyed by all citizen retailers, including the fishmongers.[57] What the king wanted was that alien craftsmen and merchants should be able to live and work peacefully in London, whether they were Flemish clothworkers or Italian or Hanseatic merchants, and that these men should be able to create, import, and sell high quality goods, while paying the Crown for the privilege of so doing. By and large the king achieved this objective. However, Richard had great difficulty in deciding how to handle the divisive civic struggles over the retail food monopolies. His partisan interventions in the 1380s aggravated the armed disputes which it was in his best interests to contain. The autocratic policies which the king adopted in the 1390s at least had the advantage of raising the Crown above civic faction. Whereas he might have thought in the 1380s that his best policy was to divide and rule, he came to realize that the Crown was best served by a peaceful and united city.

It was important to the king that London, his capital city, should be clean, healthy, and safe. It has been argued that the ravages of the Black

---

[56] See the protests voiced by the fishmonger and late mayor Nicholas Exton as a Member in the Parliament of 1382 (*RP* iii. 143).

[57] In the Merciless Parliament of 1388 the city lost its 'franchise', i.e. the right of the citizens to monopolize the retail sale of goods in the city. This meant that aliens and foreigners could buy and sell freely in the city notwithstanding the city's privileges, *Westm. Chron.* 323; O. Ruffhead (ed.), *Statutes at Large* (London 1769), vol i, 11 Richard II, cap. 7, pp. 375–7. The Westminster Chronicler believed that the Londoners deserved this loss of their privileges, because they were behaving in such a factious way, although he makes it clear that in his view the protests against the monopoly of the victuallers were 'wrong-headed' (*Westm. Chron.* 335).

Death and the subsequent outbreaks of plague made the city governors more aware of the need to keep London clean.[58] In this the interests of the city and the Crown coincided, but it was the Londoners who had to pay for improved urban hygiene. There is considerable evidence that the mayor and aldermen were taking much more trouble to see to the cleaning of the city than they had done in the earlier part of the century. Each year the men of the wards were reminded of their responsibility for keeping the streets clean and civic rubbish tips were provided.[59] There was particular concern about the state of the quays downstream from London Bridge[60] and about the Walbrook which flowed through the centre of the city as an open sewer.[61] In 1385 the city appointed its first sanitary officer, known as the serjeant of the Channel, and his task was to ensure that the city's streets and lanes were kept free of rubbish.[62]

However, there was a particular aspect of city hygiene which was of concern to the king and that was butchering. It appears that more fresh meat was consumed in the later fourteenth century than had been the case earlier; in part because of the greater availability of pasture land, and in part because of the rise in real wages and the increased standard of living.[63] The Black Death not only encouraged the growth of the butchering industry, but also made people more conscious of the health risks from blood, offal, and carcasses left rotting in public places.[64] In 1369 Edward III sent a fierce writ to the mayor and aldermen complaining about the 'grievous corruption and filth' which arose in the lanes and streets of the city from the blood and offal which the butchers left on the road from the Shambles to Newgate, and on the banks of the Fleet river where they washed their carcasses. Slaughtering was, in future, to be done away from the city, either in Knightsbridge to the west or in Stratford in the east.[65] It was the butchers who worked in the western part of the city who caused the trouble, for it was in the western suburbs that most of the town houses of

---

[58] E. Sabine, 'City Cleaning in Medieval London', *Speculum* 12 (1937), 19–43.

[59] e.g. 1375, 1378, 1379, 1382, 1385 (*LBH* 3, 108, 111, 137, 183, 255–6).

[60] Years 1377, 1379, 1385 (*LBH* 63, 137, 152, 255, 256).

[61] Year 1383 (*LBH* 216).

[62] In 26 Oct. 1385 (*LBH* 275); in 1390 Nicholas Foche was appointed as 'Surveyor of streets and lanes within the liberty of the City' (*LBH* 355).

[63] On the increased urban consumption of meat, see C. Dyer, *Standards of Living in the Later Middle Ages: Social Change in England* c.*1200–1520* (Cambridge, 1989), 196–202.

[64] E. Sabine, 'Butchering in Medieval London', *Speculum* 8 (1933), 335–53. The Cambridge Parliament of 1388 was also concerned about the unhealthy squalor of towns (Ruffhead (ed.), *Statutes at Large*, vol. i, 12 Ric. II, cap. 13, p. 382).

[65] Years 1369, 1370 (Riley (ed. and trans.), *Memorials of London*, 339, 356–8). In 1380 the prohibition was confirmed in Parliament (*LBH* 301).

the aristocracy were situated. When the king himself had to come from Westminster, he would ride along Fleet Street and have to pick his way through the discarded entrails around Fleet Bridge. It was, clearly, much more difficult for the butchers to slaughter beasts further away from the markets in which they sold the meat, and it looks as if little was done to meet the royal and aristocratic complaints in spite of reminders. On this issue it is clear that the interests of the butchers were in direct conflict with the interests of the aristocratic inhabitants of the city. In 1391 the leading inhabitants of the great houses lying to the north-west of the city got together to petition the king about the slaughtering of animals at Holborn Bridge, led by the duke of Lancaster and including the bishops of Lincoln and Ely whose houses were in Holborn, the heads of the religious houses of St John of Jerusalem, St Bartholomew's, and Clerkenwell, and the abbot of Leicester and the prior of Sempringham whose town houses lay east of Holborn Bridge, outside the city walls. The king insisted that slaughtering at Holborn Bridge was to stop within three months on the threat of a £1,000 fine.[66] The mayor and aldermen secured two extensions, and then the city was swept into the king's hand.[67] In 1393, when the dust of the great quarrel between the Crown and the city had settled, it appears that a partial compromise on the matter of the butchers was worked out, whereby they cut up their offal and deposited it from boats in the Thames in mid-stream.[68] Richard, and his aristocracy, wanted London to be clean and wholesome: a city of which they could be proud and where they could move about their business with ease. The city governors appeared to be indifferent to this concern, or unable to enforce the royal will. London had failed to look the part.

But if the dirt and offal in the London streets were unpleasant, the lawlessness and violence were dangerous. Many English towns in the later four-teenth century were turbulent, but London was turbulent on a greater scale and its disorders impinged more upon the king and the court. There were points in the yearly cycle when the rulers of London anticipated misrule and violence, and took measures to control it. The legitimated disorder at Christmas, and at Midsummer, posed particular problems for the mayor, and the aldermen were instructed to be particularly vigilant and visible at these times.[69] Some of the lawlessness in the city was imported by the

---

[66] 6 Dec. 1391, *LBH* 372.   [67] *LBH* 375–6; Barron, 'Quarrel', 175–6 and nn. 9–11.

[68] *LBH* 392; in the wardmotes held in June 1393 enquiries were to be carried out into butchers' nuisances (*LBH* 394).

[69] Mayoral writs at Christmas 1376, 1378, 1380, 1383, 1384, 1387, 1388, 1390, 1391, 1393 (*LBH* 54, 111, 157, 224, 254, 321–2, 337–8, 361, 373, 405); in 1393 the king reinforced the mayor's writ with his own (*LBH* 405); for mayoral writs at Midsummer, see 1378, 1381, 1384, 1385, 1386, 1387 (*LBH* 92, 165, 232, 266, 283, 308; Riley (ed. and trans.), *Memorials*

household retainers of the great lords who enjoyed provoking the local inhabitants while their masters were lodging in London.[70] With this in mind the mayor and aldermen tried to ensure that great lords and their households lodged outside the city in the suburbs.[71] However, there is no doubt that the constitutional and economic conflicts of the 1370s and 1380s were home-grown, and the issues were often fought out with fists in the streets of London.[72] There were times during the later fourteenth century when the mayor was unable to keep the city 'surely and safely' for the Crown as he promised to do when he took up office, and then the king had to intervene as Edward III did in July 1376, in the wake of the disputes over the method of electing the Common Council. On this occasion the citizens were quick to deny that there had been any tumult and to assure the king that the matter was now under control.[73] When the new mayor, elected in the following October, failed to ensure good order in the city, the king removed him and ordered the mayor and commonalty to elect someone else.[74] In March 1378 there was further rioting, between the goldsmiths and the pepperers, and in August a fight broke out near Ludgate when a fishmonger and his family were turned out of their house by a gang of men led by William Leek, a tailor.[75] Two months later the king's uncle, Thomas of Woodstock, and his servant were attacked by a gang of Londoners led by John Maynard, a waxchandler.[76] A month later groups of craftsmen, in particular cordwainers and glovers, created disturbances which were sufficiently serious for the king to send a writ of enquiry.[77] The rebels, therefore, from the countryside around London did not fall upon a peaceful and united city in June 1381: their numbers were swelled by the inhabitants of the city itself, anxious to find violent expression for their own rivalries and grievances.

The events of June 1381 did not bring peace to the city in their wake. The faction fighting intensified and two broadly based parties emerged:

---

of London, 488). The earlier writs simply instructed the aldermen to ensure that measures were taken against fire, and that proper watch and ward was kept. In 1384, however, the writ specified the eves of St John (24 June) and Sts Peter and Paul (29 June), and instructed the aldermen to come arrayed 'according to ancient custom' (*LBH* 232). The reference to 'ancient custom' usually suggests an innovation, and may have misled John Stow into believing that the Midsummer watch processions were older than they, in fact were (J. Stow, *A Survey of London*, ed. C. L. Kingsford 2 vols. (Oxford, 1908), i. 101–4).

[70] Barron, 'Revolt', 16–18.   [71] e.g. *Westm. Chron.* 225–7.
[72] See Strohm, *Hochon's Arrow*, 11–31.   [73] *LBH* 35–7.
[74] The incompetence of the mayor, Adam Stable, is suggested by the royal writs addressed to him in Feb. and Mar. 1377 (*LBH* 57, 60).
[75] *LBH* 98–9, 113–14; Riley (ed. and trans.), *Memorials of London*, 415–17.
[76] *LBH* 104, 111; Riley (ed. and trans.), *Memorials of London*, 424, 427–8.
[77] *CPMR 1364–1381*, 275–6, 279.

one led by the grocer Nicholas Brembre and the other by the draper John of Northampton, who was elected mayor in October 1381. It appears to have been Northampton's policy to widen participation in civic government, and to try to run the city in the interests of the 'small people', the less affluent craftsmen and shopkeepers who were not engaged in overseas trade. By abolishing monopolies Northampton hoped to keep down food prices, and by ensuring that there was an adequate supply of small change, to ensure that food and other necessaries could be bought piecemeal by the poor.[78] Of course these policies did not command universal support, but at first they seem to have been welcomed by the king. In October 1382 Richard wrote twice to the Londoners urging them to re-elect John of Northampton as mayor. This was the first time that a king had overtly tried to influence the city in its choice of mayor.[79] Richard may have been moved to this course of action by Northampton's ability, as it seemed, to keep London under control. He was duly re-elected but his second mayoralty was much stormier than the first and Richard seems to have lost confidence in him and in his policies for in the following October Nicholas Brembre was elected mayor 'rege favente'.[80] The election was virtually a riot and Northampton's refusal to accept the outcome led to his imprisonment, trial by the king, and banishment from the city for the next seven years.[81]

The lawlessness in London had become so bad by the beginning of 1384 that the king was forced to intervene in order to remove Northampton and his principal allies from the scene, and also to support Brembre in making an example of one of Northampton's supporters from among the 'small people', and thereby frighten the citizens into order. John Constantine, a cordwainer who was convicted of having urged the citizens to close their shops and rise in support of the arrested Northampton, was executed and his head displayed above Newgate. This summary, and unprecedented, execution was not accepted without protest, and the Westminster Chronicler noted that he had been a man of godly life who attended church

[78] *LBH* 183.

[79] *LBH* 200–1. At this time Robert Braybrooke, bishop of London, was chancellor of England; Professor Saul has suggested to me that Braybrooke may have influenced Richard in favour of Northampton.

[80] *Westm. Chron.* 59–63. No royal letter sent in support of Brembre is recorded in the city's own letter-books. For the hostility which Northampton's policies aroused, especially among the fishmongers, see *LBH* 203–5; Riley (ed. and trans.), *Memorials of London*, 473–4; *CPMR 1381–1412*, 36.

[81] For an account of the riot at the mayoral election in Oct. 1383, see Thomas of Usk's appeal, Chambers and Daunt (edd.), *Book of London English*, 18–31; *CPMR 1381–1412*, 53–7.

regularly.[82] Early in April Richard sent a writ ratifying the actions of the mayor and aldermen in condemning Constantine. He sent the writ to strengthen the government of the city, to repress and check conspirators and those who broke the peace, and to prevent riot and insurrection.[83] The execution, which seems to have served as a warning to others, was successful in that the more extreme rioting was brought under control. However, the mayor was clearly unable to keep control of the city without royal help and the king cannot have been pleased with the perpetual rioting which disfigured civic life.

In the following October the king went further in his intervention in the mayoral election. He forbade the carrying of arms in the city[84] and he sent three members of his Household, John lord Neville of Raby, Lord Fitzwalter, and Sir Thomas Morieux, a Chamber knight, to act as 'observers' and to ensure that the election was conducted peacefully and 'according to custom'.[85] Although over 300 citizens were duly summoned,[86] other 'persons of the middle sort' turned up uninvited, and protested vigorously when Brembre was re-elected.[87] The king favoured Brembre's re-election but the the protesters wanted the goldsmith, Nicholas Twyford. Both sides probably tried to use strong-arm tactics and the presence of the courtiers seems not to have had any effect. However, from this time on it became usual for the mayor to try to restrict participation in the mayor's election to the 'better sort' who had been summoned.[88] The involvement of the

---

[82] *Westm. Chron.* 65; for the details of the Constantine case, see *LBH* 231; Riley (ed. and trans.), *Memorials of London*, 482–3; *CPMR 1381–1412*, 50–1. John Constantine had joined Bishop Despenser's crusade to Flanders in 1383, PRO C76/6/67 n. 8 (I am grateful to Colin Paine for this reference.)

[83] *CPR 1381–1385*, 391; in sending this writ, Richard was responding to a petition from the mayor, Nicholas Brembre (PRO S.C.8/183/9147). (I am grateful to Professor Nigel Saul for this reference.)

[84] Writ sent from the manor of Sheen (*LBH* 250); 12 Oct. 1385, royal proclamation to restrict those attending mayoral election to the 'good folk' elected from the wards for Common Council, and others especially summoned (*LBH* 251). The mayor also issued writs to prevent 'conventicles and gatherings', July 1384, 21 Sept. 1384, 18 Oct. 1385 (*LBH* 241, 249, 274).

[85] *LBH* 250; *CPMR 1381–1412*, 62–3.

[86] Ninety-four Common Councilmen and 237 other 'good men', *CPMR 1381–1412*, 84–9.

[87] The protests against Brembre's re-election were led by armourers (17), goldsmiths (14), tailors (8), and mercers (7), with a sprinkling of pinners, cutlers, cordwainers, broiders, fullers, skinners, and haberdashers (*LBH* 63–9). The disaffected electors wanted Nicholas Twyford, a goldsmith, in preference to Brembre who was, however, elected with the king's approval (*Westm. Chron.* 101–3); later there were protests to Parliament about the 'gang warfare' surrounding Brembre's re-election, see 'A Petition of the Folk of the Mercerye', in Chambers and Daunt (edd.), *Book of London English*, 33–7; PRO S.C.8/199/9925.

[88] Years 1385, 1386 (*LBH* 274, 289).

Crown also became the norm: in October 1385 Brembre was re-elected for a third term 'rege annuente'.[89] Two years later Richard wrote to the mayor, aldermen, and commons of the city, threatening them that if they did not choose a mayor 'who could govern the city well', he would refuse to allow the barons of the Exchequer to take his oath. The Westminster Chronicler records that Nicholas Exton was re-elected 'rege volente'.[90] In the aftermath of the Merciless Parliament of February 1388, the king warned the mayor and commonalty to ensure the peaceful election of a 'trusty and loyal mayor'. Their choice of Nicholas Twyford, the rejected candidate of 1384, may well not have found favour with the king.[91] The king's seizure of the city's liberties in 1392 and the appointment of a warden to govern the city was the most extreme form of royal intervention. However, even after the restoration of the city's liberties, the king continued to keep an eye on the mayoralty and, when Adam Bamme died in office in May 1397, the king did not allow the citizens to elect his replacement, but simply himself chose Richard Whittington and imposed him upon the city.[92]

Richard did not rely solely upon the mayor to impose order in the city; he tried to make contact more directly with the citizens by demanding oaths of fealty. Such oaths, in various different forms, were to become one of the hallmarks of Richard's government. The use of oaths was not unique to the king. In 1377 all the members of fifty of the more powerful misteries, whether masters, servants, or apprentices had been sworn to keep the peace, obey mayoral summonses, put down conspiracies, keep the city's secrets, and only come to Guildhall if summoned.[93] Similar oaths were demanded of all the 'good men' of the city in March 1382, February 1384, and May 1385.[94] Presumably it was hoped that by these means the city would be fashioned into a giant fraternity bound together by mutual oaths. It was therefore no novelty for the Londoners to find themselves expected to swear to 'live and die' with King Richard against all rebels in the autumn of 1387.[95] It was Brembre's role in collecting these oaths which formed the basis of some of the charges against him in the Merciless

---

[89] *Westm. Chron.* 136.   [90] Ibid. 206; *LBH* 317.

[91] *LBH* 334–5; *Westm. Chron.* 371. The mayoral elections in London continued to be contentious: in Oct. 1389, when William Venour, a grocer, was elected, the goldsmiths, drapers, and mercers shouted for Adam Bamme, a goldsmith. The Westminster Chronicler thought that this demonstrated how serious were the divisions which had torn the city apart since the early 1380s (*Westm. Chron.* 405; *LBH* 348).

[92] On 8 June 1397 (*LBH* 436; Riley (ed. and trans.), *Memorials of London*, 544–5; Barron, 'Quarrel', 198–9).

[93] On 12 Mar. 1377 (*LBH* 59).   [94] *LBH* 178, 228, 264.   [95] *LBH* 314–15.

Parliament.[96] The archbishop of Canterbury, Thomas Arundel, in January 1388 absolved the Londoners from these oaths, but at the end of the Merciless Parliament the aldermen and chief men of the city were required to bind themselves once again: this time to uphold the Acts of the recent Parliament.[97] With a touching faith, those in authority continued to use the sanctity of oaths as a means of imposing order and extracting loyalty.[98] Richard's incessant, and ultimately useless, demands for oaths during the last years of his reign found their way into the Articles of Deposition.[99] What the king, and others in authority wanted, was for men to take 'vertical' oaths, i.e. to masters, or lords, or city rulers, or to the king, but not to take 'horizontal' oaths among themselves.[100] Ultimately the king's use of oaths to try to ensure a peaceful and loyal city was a failure: perhaps because those who took the oaths were not those who broke the peace, or perhaps because the sanction of the Church was not sufficiently feared.

What Richard wanted from London during his reign was a clean, beautiful, and peaceful city. He did not get it. It may be that more systematic efforts were made during his reign to keep the city clean and to deal with the problems of butchers' offal in the western suburbs. However, the city was exposed to almost continuous rioting during the 1370s and 1380s. Richard's policy at first was strongly to back a favoured mayor, like Brembre, and to use the 'king's party' thus created to impose order, and to build up support for royal policies in the city. The fate of Brembre demonstrates both how this policy had failed and also how it was resented. In 1392 the king declared a 'plague on both your houses' and simply suspended the city's freedoms and ruled London directly. This policy may not have made Richard more popular but it seems to have made London more peaceful. The deaths of some of the charismatic ringleaders may also have helped: Brembre in 1388, Twyford in 1391, Exton in 1393, and, finally, John of Northampton himself in 1398. The Londoners seem to have grown tired of their persistent form of mercantile 'bastard feudalism', and the rampant economic opportunism of the 1370s settled down into comfortable,

---

[96] *Westm. Chron.* 264.

[97] Ibid. 233; *LBH* 328; *RP* iii. 251–2. The return to the writ lists 490 citizens and 93 clerics who had taken the oath (*CPMR 1381–1412*, 144–5).

[98] e.g. *LBH* 375.

[99] C. M. Barron, 'The Tyranny of Richard II', *BIHR* 41(1968), 1–18.

[100] The fear of 'horizontal' oaths is apparent in the terms of the enquiry into guilds and fraternities initiated by the Cambridge Parliament of 1388, see L. Toulmin Smith and L. Brentano (edd.), *English Guilds: The Original Ordinances of More than One Hundred Early English Guilds* (EETS, London, 1870), 127–31.

but reasonably benign, oligarchy. Paradoxically Richard's strong-arm tactics contributed to the creation of peace in London, but similar measures deployed against the nobility created enmities which the king could not contain, and which led, ultimately, to his own deposition.

Above all, perhaps, Richard wanted entertainment from London: pageantry and a stage and cast for dramatic events in which he would be the star performer. It may be that Richard's youthful accession to the throne gave him an exaggerated taste for such 'shows', for he was only 11 when he was crowned. The city was specially cleaned and decorated for the procession and the Great Conduit in Cheapside was transformed into the Heavenly City, where four virgins stood scattering gold leaves and coins. These virgins offered the king a cup of wine from the conduit, which normally flowed only with water. From the centre of the Heavenly City a mechanical angel bowed down and offered the king a golden crown. The chronicler Thomas Walsingham does not record whether the king spoke or not, but there is no doubt that Richard was the most important spectator and participant, the focus of the pageant.[101] Doubtless he enjoyed this. The following Christmas 130 London citizens rode through the city to entertain the young king at Kennington where he was staying with his mother and his uncles. The group passed through the city from Newgate, along Cheapside and over London Bridge to Southwark, accompanied by a large company of musicians. When the Londoners reached Kennington they donned masks and dressed up as knights and esquires escorting an emperor and a pope and twenty-four cardinals. They brought with them loaded dice and offered to play with Richard: three times he threw the dice and three times he won: a gold bowl, a gold cup and a gold ring. The lords also won rings and then there was dancing and feasting.[102] Such festivities were clearly enjoyable and Richard may have begun to develop a taste for such things. It may not have been helpful to him to have begun to believe that the dice were always loaded in his favour. There seems to have been some celebration for Anne of Bohemia when she arrived to marry Richard, for she was certainly led in procession through the city and the Great Conduit was once again decorated.[103] But once Richard and his queen were crowned, there were no more triumphs provided by the City of London. He was now expected to turn his attention to the serious

---

[101] *Chron. Angl.* 153–6; arrangements for the coronation, *LBH* 69.

[102] The Londoners came to visit the king on the Sunday before Candlemas (Stow, *Survey of London*, i. 96–7).

[103] *Westm. Chron.* 23–5; *CPMR 1381–1412*, 3; see petition presented to the new queen by the Londoners (*CPMR 1381–1412*, 7–8; Reddaway and Walker, *Goldsmith's Company*, 44–5).

business of governing his realm and leading English troops in foreign conquests. But in the 1380s Richard showed little sustained interest in either or these tasks. His taste for pageantry and spectacle had to be satisfied by the tournaments which were a regular feature of courtly life.[104]

The dramatic and humiliating events of 1388 left their mark upon Richard's kingship. At the end of the Merciless Parliament, all the lords renewed their coronation oaths and the reign began again. Richard decided to take his kingship seriously and to put away childish things. In 1389 he declared himself to be of age,[105] and he reasserted royal authority by controlling the localities, building up noble alliances, and making a truce with France. However, the desire for pageantry appears not to have left him and at the end of 1389 he learnt about the magnificent 'triumph' provided for Isabella of Bavaria, the young queen of Charles VI, by the citizens of Paris. Froissart's description of this sumptuous spectacle is such as to make any king envious. When Richard heard of the Parisian pageant he decided 'in imitation of this' to hold a series of grand tournaments and feasts in London.[106] In fact 1390 was a bumper year for tournaments: Richard held a tournament at Smithfield and then immediately afterwards the famous jousts were held at St Ingelvert near Calais. But the tournaments which Richard organized at Smithfield early in October were particularly magnificent, and considerable time and effort went into their preparation. Sir William, son of the count of Hainault, and Waleran count of St Pol were among the foreign knights who came to take part. In all sixty knights and their ladies rode mounted through the city from the Tower to Smithfield, and Richard's knights 'had their armour and apparell garnished with white harts and crowns of gold about the harts' necks'. Richard and Anne lodged in the bishop of London's palace lying just to the north of St Paul's cathedral and every night the guests were entertained there with dinners and dancing. Clearly for the Londoners the presence of so many lords and their retinues in the city posed a peace-keeping problem, and must have inconvenienced the normal business of the city. On the other hand such an influx of wealthy young aristocrats must have been good for business, as Froissart shrewdly notes.[107]

[104] *Westm. Chron.* 111, 165; for the Smithfield tournament of 1386, see Stow, *Survey of London*, ii. 30; R. V. Barber, *The Tournament in England 1100–1400* (Woodbridge, 1986), 100, 185.
[105] *Westm. Chron.* 391–3.
[106] Froissart was an eyewitness to the Parisian reception: Froissart, xiv. 253.
[107] Ibid. 257; J. S. Davies (ed.), *An English Chronicle of the Reigns of Richard II, Henry IV, Henry V, and Henry VI (1377–1461)* (London, 1856), 6; Riley (ed. and trans.), *Memorials of London*, 521–2; S. Lindenbaum, 'The Smithfield Tournament of 1390', *Journal of Medieval and Renaissance Studies* 20 (1990), 1–20.

In spite of the magnificence of these jousts and festivities, it seems clear that Richard still yearned for a second coronation procession, such as he remembered from his youth and such as the citizens of Paris had provided for Isabella. Two years later he seized the opportunity presented by his quarrel and reconciliation with the City of London to extract a 'triumph' from the citizens. To argue that Richard quarrelled with the Londoners in order to achieve a magnificent reception would be to stretch the evidence, and it is clear that he was primarily concerned about the endemic disorder in the city, but he was not slow to seize the opportunity that had been created. There is no doubt that Richard was anxious to extract a useful fine from the Londoners, and to curb their arrogant lawlessness, but the form of his reconciliation was probably just as important to him. The importance of the civic triumph of 1392 may be reflected in the fact that two accounts of it survive: a Latin poem written by Richard of Maidstone and a letter written in French which describes the same occasion.[108] Was it the Londoners or the king who commissioned these accounts?

It seems likely that the Londoners had some shrewd advice as to what themes and pageants would be acceptable to the king. It may be that the agent in these difficult negotiations was the royäl warden Sir Baldwin Raddington or, more likely, his predecessor, Sir Edward Dallingridge. The procession on August 21 was well rehearsed and well prepared: the warden offered the king the keys of the city and the civic sword, and begged him to enter his chamber. Richard took the sword and keys and agreed to enter London to see 'whether my people have learned to recognize their king'. The queen, who accompanied the king throughout the pageant, suggested to the warden and aldermen that there was hope. If Richard had pardoned the citizens at this point, he might not have been offered the pageants: it was necessary to keep the Londoners on tenterhooks. Also, he wanted to see the quality of their gifts.[109] At the conduit in Cheapside,

---

[108] Maidstone's poem is printed in T. Wright (ed.), *Political Poems and Songs relating to English History*, 2 vols. (RS, London, 1859), i. 282–300; part of the poem is trans. in E. Rickert, *Chaucer's World* (New York, 1948), 35–9. See also below, pp. 244–6. For Maidstone see A. B. Emden, *A Biographical Register of the University of Oxford to A.D. 1500*, 3 vols. (Oxford, 1957–9), ii. 1204; *Westm. Chron.* 503–9. Suggett suggests that both the Westminster Chronicler and the author of the letter in French may have been dependent upon a newsletter (H. Suggett, 'A Letter describing Richard II's Reconciliation with the City of London, 1392', *EHR* 62 (1947), 209–13).

[109] All the sources record that both the king and the queen were given fine horses, as well as the rich inanimate gifts. The author of the letter in French records that on the day following the procession, the king was given a silver-enamelled altarpiece, and the queen a crystal hanaper and gold-mounted ewer (Suggett, 'Reconciliation', 212).

groups of singing angels scattered golden leaves, very much as they had done for Richard's coronation pageant. Further west along Cheapside, Richard and Anne encountered a much more ambitious pageant, a castle suspended by ropes in the air and inhabited by a youth and a girl who miraculously descended and presented the king and queen with two crowns, symbolizing both earthly rule and eternal rule in heaven. At the west end of Cheapside, at the little conduit, God Almighty sat enthroned and surrounded by three circles of singing angels. The royal party then went into St Paul's before riding westwards over Fleet Bridge to Temple Bar where the city had staged the most elaborate of the pageants. John the Baptist, Richard's particularly favoured saint, stood surrounded by savage beasts snapping and snarling. John pointed to the Lamb of God while an angel descended to the street bearing two gold altarpieces, one for Richard and one for Anne, and each bearing an image of the Crucifixion to remind the king of the suffering and the forgiveness of Christ. Richard then turned and spoke to the citizens, and in the sight of Christ, his Mother, and St John, he declared 'I freely forgive all the crimes of my people'.[110] The rituals of festive reconciliation continued into the evening, and probably even into the next day.[111]

If we are right in assuming that these pageants reflected an agreed agenda between Richard and the citizens, then the events of 21 August 1392 can reveal something about Richard's image of the appropriate relations between a king and his capital city.[112] The choice of images in the pageants is religious and not military: the king comes to his city, as Christ comes to the Heavenly Jerusalem, or as a bridegroom to the bridal chamber.[113] The city is cleaned and decorated and beautified as the citizens await the coming of their king. The throngs of Londoners are respectful, orderly, and pleasing to the eye since they are dressed up in their liveries. Through the warden the citizens offer the king not only rich and well-chosen gifts but also humility and loyalty. The king, magnificently dressed can, at the same time, be both impressive and magnanimous. By means of these

[110] The author of the letter in French places the reconciliation in Westminster hall where the queen, the archbishop of Canterbury (William Courtenay), and the bishop of London (Robert Braybrooke) pleaded on their knees for the city. The steward (Sir John Devereux) then, on the king's behalf, forgave the citizens and largely restored their liberties (Ibid.). On the role of Queen Anne as intercessor, see Strohm, *Hochon's Arrow*, 105–11.

[111] Suggett, 'Reconciliation', 212–13.

[112] See G. Kipling, 'Richard II's "Sumptuous Pageants" and the Idea of the Civic Triumph', in D. M. Bergeron (ed.), *Pageantry and the Shakespearean Theatre* (Athens, Ga., 1985), 83–103.

[113] For an interpretation of the symbolism of these events rather different from that of Kipling, see Strohm, *Hochon's Arrow*, 105–11.

orchestrated pageants it might well have seemed that Richard and his people were bound together in a shared ideal of the harmonious Christian polity. However, it was, of course, drama and not life.

Although Richard forgave the Londoners, he did not remit their fine, nor did he restore their liberties completely. The citizens had no choice but to continue to play their penitent role. Just as they had visited Richard at Kennington at Christmas following his coronation, so at Christmas 1392 the Londoners sought out the king at Eltham and presented Richard and his queen with extraordinary and expensive gifts: for Richard a golden dromedary ridden by a boy, and for the queen a pelican, to remind her of the self-sacrificing role that she was expected to play. The king 'ad instanciam domine regine' pardoned the Londoners and remitted £20,000 of the £30,000 fine which they owed him.[114] For the Londoners the expensive and humiliating drama had finally come to an end.

Richard's style of government, and there is much that can be admired about it, was not in harmony with the nobility nor with the London merchants and artisans. In spite of the shared festivities of August 1392, he was not at ease with them, nor they with him. Whereas Richard in the pageants played a role which was as real to him off the stage as on it, the role played by the Londoners did not come naturally to them. They continued to find Richard baffling and inscrutable. The king never really trusted the Londoners and the scar tissue left by the wound inflicted by the Appellants four years earlier never properly healed. So the elaborate pageants of 1392 remained as symbols only, and in reality the relations between the king and the Londoners continued on an uneven and uncertain course. Once again Richard had mistaken the trappings of royalty for the reality of royal power. The Londoners could, when sufficiently goaded, supply the trappings, but only the king could make royal power a reality.

---

[114] *Westm. Chron.* 510; the next year 1393 the Londoners again visited the king at Christmas, bringing with them a ship crammed with spices and gifts to be distributed to the king and queen and others at court (ibid. 517).

8

Finance and Trade under Richard II

W. M. Ormrod

I

The kingdom of England was probably more dependent on the revenue derived from the taxation of international trade than any other monarchical state in later medieval Europe. The intimate connection between the financial (and therefore also the political) fortunes of the Crown on the one hand and the volume and value of overseas trade (above all, of English wool exports) on the other had its origins in the thirteenth and early fourteenth centuries, when the Crown first established a permanent system for raising customs duties on exports and imports. It was not until the opening of Edward III's wars with France, however, that the taxation of overseas trade became a major, indeed after 1350 the principal, element in the finances of the state as a result of the long series of supplementary subsidies on wool exports which the Crown negotiated first with the merchant community and later with Parliament. It has long been appreciated that there was a fundamental flaw, not to mention a certain irony, in the Crown's use of the customs and subsidies as a means of raising the financial resources it needed to fight the Hundred Years War, for while the rhetoric of strategy often presented the war as a necessary means by which to maintain England's trading interests, the subordination of economic policy to financial exigency had the effect of creating structures and conditions that were fundamentally hostile to the English trading economy as a whole. Those structures—the wool staple, the bullion ordinances, and the wide range of punitive measures taken against alien merchants operating within England—were the inevitable compromises the Crown had to make with the native merchant community in order to conceal the still greater flaw that existed in a fiscal system that depended primarily on the exploitation of the export, rather than the import, trade.

These complicated conflicts of interest have, not surprisingly, been the subject of much analysis by both economic and political historians. Notable among such contributions are two works that provide the historiographical background to this chapter: the pioneering collection of essays edited by George Unwin, *Finance and Trade under Edward III* and, more recently, Dr Wendy Childs's article on 'Finance and Trade under Edward II'.[1] The present contribution seeks, as it were, to complete the set of fourteenth-century reigns by exploring the relationship between foreign trade, royal finance, and domestic politics under Richard II. It needs to be stressed at the outset, however, that the subject is approached here not so much from an economic as from a fiscal perspective: in other words, it is concerned less with a discussion of the general state of overseas trade or even with the long-term effects of the Crown's attempts to exploit this sector of the economy and much more with measuring the ability, or inability, of the Crown in the later fourteenth century to adapt to changes within the structure and balance of international commerce and turn those changes to its own financial advantage. By making a new and more precisely statistical analysis of the customs accounts of the reign of Richard II, this study aims to demonstrate both the vigour with which the Ricardian administration pursued its fiscal rights and the enormous problems that the late medieval Crown faced in its attempts to ensure the continued profitability of indirect taxation.[2]

---

[1] G. Unwin (ed.), *Finance and Trade under Edward III*, (Manchester, 1918); W. Childs, 'Finance and Trade Under Edward II', in *Politics and Crisis*, 19–37. The most important contributions to Unwin's volume were F. R. Barnes, 'The Taxation of Wool 1327–1348', 137–77, and G. Unwin, 'The Estate of Merchants, 1336–1365', 179–255. They have been subject to much scrutiny and revision, e.g. by B. Wilkinson, *Studies in the Constitutional History of the Thirteenth and Fourteenth Centuries* (2nd edn., Manchester, 1952), 55–81; G. L. Harriss, *King, Parliament and Public Finance in Medieval England to 1369* (Oxford, 1975), 420–49; T. H. Lloyd, *The English Wool Trade in the Middle Ages* (Cambridge, 1977), 144–92. Dr Childs's article should be read in conjunction with the new data and evidence presented in W. M. Ormrod, 'The Crown and the English Economy, 1290–1348', in B. M. S. Campbell (ed.), *Before the Black Death: Studies in the 'Crisis' of the Early Fourteenth Century* (Manchester, 1991), 167–75; id., 'Political Theory in Practice: The Forced Loan on English Overseas Trade of 1317–1318', *Historical Research*, 64 (1991), 204–15.

[2] The statistical material on which this chapter is based is stored in electronic form in ESFDB, deposited in the Economic and Social Research Council Date Archive at the University of Essex. It may be consulted via JANET (e-mail: archive@uk.ac.essex). The author is deeply indebted to Dr M. M. Bonney for her assistance in compiling and processing the data and constructing the graphs that accompany this chapter.

II

The development of the English customs system is one of the wonders of medieval institutional and financial history.[3] The general move away from administrative history since the 1930s, however, means that the long series of medieval customs accounts still surviving in the Public Record Office has been used principally to establish economic data on the commodities and values of goods subject to customs duties rather than on the revenue thus provided for the Crown.[4] Without giving a full breakdown of the system, it is clearly necessary at the outset to appreciate the basic structure of indirect taxation as it existed at the start of Richard II's reign. For present purposes, there are two important points to be made. The first concerns the distinction between customs and subsidies. The customs proper consisted of three elements: the ancient custom of 1275, levied on exports of wool, wool-fells, and hides; the new custom of 1303 paid only by aliens and consisting of an additional duty on wool exports as well as charges on imports of wine and imports and exports of general merchandise; and the cloth custom of 1347 paid by denizens and aliens on cloth carried out of the country. Although they were originally negotiated with assemblies of merchants and magnates, by the second half of the fourteenth century these customs were collected permanently, as of right, and were considered part of the ordinary revenue of the Crown. By contrast, the subsidies were

[3] N. S. B. Gras, *The Early English Customs System* (Cambridge, Mass., 1918). For studies of the customs administration in the first three-quarters of the fourteenth century see R. L. Baker, *The English Customs Service 1307–1343: A Study of Medieval Administration* (Philadelphia, 1961); M. Mills, 'The Collectors of Customs', in J. F. Willard *et al.* (edd.), *The English Government at Work, 1327–1336* (Cambridge, Mass., 1940–50), ii. 168–200; E. B. Fryde, 'Edward III's War Finance, 1337–1341: Transactions in Wool and Credit Operations', D.Phil. thesis (Oxford, 1947); id., 'The English Farmers of the Customs', *TRHS*, 5th ser. 9 (1959), 1–17; W. M. Ormrod, 'The English Crown and the Customs, 1349–1363', *EcHR*, 2nd ser. 40 (1987), 27–40; id., *The Reign of Edward III: Crown and Political Society in England 1327–1377* (London, 1990), 181–94.

[4] Full-length studies on a national rather than a local scale include, in order of appearance: A. Beardwood, *Alien Merchants in England, 1350–1377* (Cambridge, Mass., 1931); M. M. Postan and E. E. Power (edd.), *Studies in English Trade in the Fifteenth Century* (London, 1933); E. M. Carus-Wilson and O. Coleman, *England's Export Trade, 1275–1547* (Oxford, 1963); E. M. Veale, *The English Fur Trade in the Later Middle Ages* (Oxford, 1966); E. M. Carus-Wilson, *Medieval Merchant Venturers* (2nd edn., London, 1967); J. L. Bolton, 'Alien Merchants in England in the Reign of Henry VI', B.Litt. thesis (Oxford, 1971); M. K. James, *Studies in the Medieval Wine Trade* (Oxford, 1971); J. Hatcher, *English Tin Production and Trade before 1550* (Oxford, 1973); Lloyd, *Wool Trade*; A. R. Bridbury, *Medieval English Clothmaking* (London, 1982); T. H. Lloyd, *Alien Merchants in England in the High Middle Ages* (Brighton, 1982); id., *England and the German Hanse, 1157–1611* (Cambridge, 1991).

extraordinary levies validated only by some form of consent. There were two subsidies known in England at the beginning of Richard II's reign: the levy on alien and denizen imports of wine and imports and exports of general merchandise, known as tonnage and poundage, which was still very much in its infancy; and the wool subsidy, often known to historians by the pejorative nickname of the 'maltolt' which it earned when first imposed in 1294–7. To draw a sharp distinction between customs and subsidies at the end of the fourteenth century may seem unrealistic, for the maltolt was collected almost continuously from 1342 and, unlike direct taxation, was not restricted to periods of active warfare. Nevertheless, the three brief intervals which Parliament imposed in the series of wool subsidies during the 1380s provided a powerful symbol of the distinction between customs and subsidies which was not entirely eliminated even after the precedents of 1398 and 1415 persuaded Parliament to make life grants to fifteenth-century monarchs both of the maltolt and, from the latter date, of tonnage and poundage.[5]

The second preliminary point to be made about the customs system in the later fourteenth century concerns the commodities that were, and were not, taxed. All native and foreign merchants were subject to duties on exports of wool and cloth, albeit at differential rates. Aliens were also permanently liable to pay taxes on exports and imports of a wide range of other goods. Prior to 1370, however, when tonnage and poundage was a highly exceptional levy still in the experimental phase, denizen merchants paid no taxes on exports other than wool and cloth and, with the exception of the ancient prise of wine, no duties at all on imports. This helps to illustrate three very important points. First, the English customs system differed fundamentally from those of most other western European monarchies in that it was intended as a means of profit rather than of protectionism. Secondly, and consequently, the Crown was not fundamentally concerned with the economic impact of the very heavy taxes applied particularly to the export of home-grown wool. Thirdly, there were significant, though by their very nature largely unquantifiable, elements in both the export and the import trades which still in 1370 were not liable to royal taxation.

Although fiscal historians have shown a keen interest in what might be called the 'first century of the English customs service' after 1275, there has been very little adequate work done on developments within the

<hr />

[5] Lloyd, *Wool Trade*, 235–8; J. G. Edwards, *The Second Century of the English Parliament* (Oxford, 1975), 18–23; J. A. F. Thomson, *The Transformation of Medieval England 1370–1529* (Harlow, 1983), 257–9.

system during the late fourteenth and fifteenth centuries. This neglect arises from an assumption that the various elements that went to make up the taxation of overseas trade were all more or less in place by the middle of the fourteenth century and that the late medieval customs administration, like the system of direct taxation, became ossified, a victim of its own earlier success, preserving an increasingly antiquated structure that signally failed to exploit the marked changes in overseas trade during the century and a half following the Black Death.[6] This picture of decline has received powerful endorsement from the existing published data on the export trade. Fig. 8.1 shows Carus-Wilson and Coleman's figures for exports of wool and cloth, cloth being expressed as sacks of wool according to the rate of conversion suggested by A. R. Bridbury.[7] On this scale, it is evident that the well-known increase in cloth exports during the last decades of the fourteenth century was of relatively little significance in comparison with the sharp falling-off of wool exports after about 1370: indeed, using this converter, the combined volume of wool and cloth exports never achieved the levels of the 1350s either in the period surveyed here or, indeed, in the century following 1450.[8] The point shows through with even greater clarity if wool and cloth are expressed in their domestic market prices according to the data supplied by T. H. Lloyd and J. L. Bolton (Fig. 8.2).[9] As a result of a marked downturn in wool prices during the last decades of the fourteenth century, the wool line takes an even sharper tumble, particularly in the 1370s, against which the rise in the value of exported cloth again seems relatively insignificant. Since the duties on wool represented a much larger proportion of the commodity's total value than did those on cloth, it is not surprising that, when Carus-Wilson and Coleman's data are expressed in revenue using multipliers for the various duties falling on these items, we find the most dramatic picture of all (Fig. 8.3): a seemingly disastrous drop in the revenue from taxation of wool against which the almost imperceptible rise in the estimated customs on cloth carries

[6] For comment on the long-term decline of the customs see A. L. Brown, *The Governance of Late Medieval England, 1272–1461* (London, 1989), 69.

[7] ESFDB \orm\engg034. Carus-Wilson and Coleman, *England's Export Trade*; A. R. Bridbury, *Economic Growth: England in the Later Middle Ages* (2nd edn., Brighton, 1975), 31–3.

[8] For the period down to 1547 see M. M. Bonney, 'The English Medieval Wool and Cloth Trade: New Approaches for the Local Historian', *Local Historian*, 22 (1992), 25, graph 1.

[9] ESFDB \orm\engg035. T. H. Lloyd, *The Movement of Wool Prices in Medieval England* (*EcHR* suppl., 6 Cambridge, 1973); J. L. Bolton, *The Medieval English Economy 1150–1500* (London, 1980), 292. It must be stressed that this graph underrates the real domestic market value of exported wool since it uses not the highest but the mean average data in Lloyd's series.

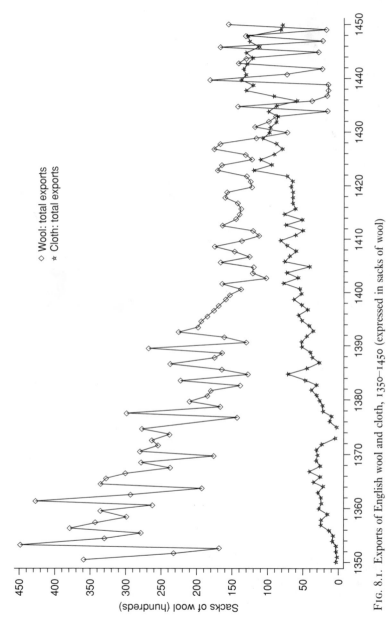

Fig. 8.1. Exports of English wool and cloth, 1350–1450 (expressed in sacks of wool)

Source: ESFDB \orm\enggo34

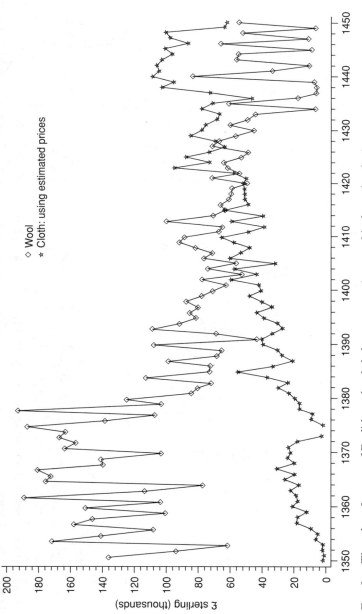

Fig. 8.2. The value of exports of English wool and cloth, 1350–1450 (expressed in domestic prices)

Source: ESFDB \orm\enggo35

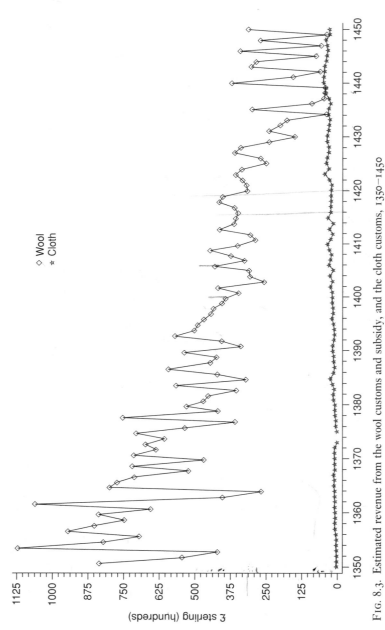

◇ Wool
⋆ Cloth

£ sterling (hundreds)

FIG. 8.3. Estimated revenue from the wool customs and subsidy, and the cloth customs, 1350–1450

Source: ESFDB \orm\engg036

virtually no significance.[10] Finally, the emergent picture of fiscal paralysis appears to be supported by the customs accounts themselves. The totals worked out by Sir James Ramsay, shown in Fig. 8.4, on which most historians of Richard II still rely, suggest that after the admittedly very high peaks of the 1350s and 1360s, the profits of overseas trade took a serious fall during the second half of the 1370s and then stabilized at little more than half their previous value in the last decades of the fourteenth century.[11]

Taken together, then, the available published data appear to provide incontrovertible evidence in support of two enduring assumptions about the policies of Richard II's government. First, it is argued that many of the economic strategies of the English Crown in the late fourteenth century were directly injurious to overseas trade. Although the exact link between high taxation and the decline of wool exports is still contested, most historians are persuaded that the wool trade was directly impeded by the restrictive practices associated with the continental staple and that at least some imports were adversely affected by the bullion policies of the 1390s.[12] Secondly, the Crown's slavish attachment to the wool subsidy and the considerable political problems experienced by the Ricardian regime in securing grants of the tax during the 1380s prevented the government from identifying and exploiting other potential sources of indirect taxation and thereby set the Crown on the road if not to immediate then at least to long-term financial ruin. In both economic and fiscal terms, then, the late fourteenth century appears to provide a foretaste of the greater disasters that befell English trade, and English royal revenues, in the reign of Henry VI.

---

[10] ESFDB \orm\enggo36. It must be stressed that this graph omits poundage on cloth in order to reflect the arguments of Carus-Wilson and Coleman, *England's Export Trade*, 22–3, 194–5.

[11] ESFDB \orm\enggo38. Ramsay published his data twice: J. H. Ramsay, *The Genesis of Lancaster 1307–1399*, 2 vols. (Oxford, 1913), ii. 101, 390; id., *A History of the Revenues of the Kings of England*, 2 vols. (Oxford, 1925), ii. 292, 431.

[12] The arguments of E. E. Power, *The Wool Trade in English Medieval History* (Oxford, 1941), 88–103, have had a particularly enduring influence on attitudes to the staple. For detailed studies of trade and the bullion regulations see J. H. A. Munro, *Wool, Cloth, and Gold: The Struggle for Bullion in Anglo-Burgundian Trade, 1340–1478* (Toronto, 1972), 11–63; Lloyd, *Wool Trade*, 225–56; id., 'Overseas Trade and the English Money Supply in the Fourteenth Century', in N. J. Mayhew (ed.), *Edwardian Monetary Affairs (1279–1344)* (Oxford; British Archaeological Reports, 36; 1977), 117–21. More recently, id., *England and Hanse*, 96–107, has pointed out that although they reduced alien imports of general merchandise, the bullion laws may well have been advantageous to the export trade in cloth.

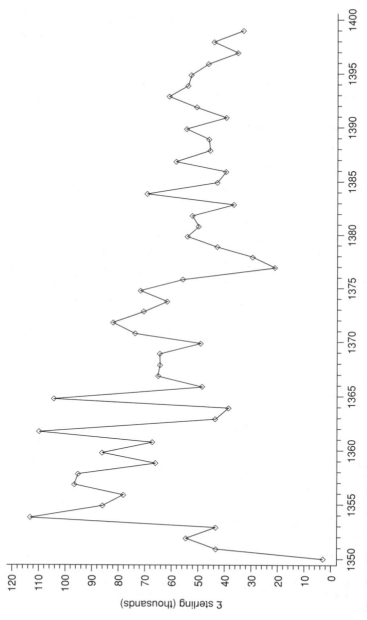

FIG. 8.4. Total receipts from customs and subsidies on overseas trade, 1350–1399, as calculated by Sir James Ramsay

Source: ESFDB \orm\enggo38

III

To what extent are these rather dismal conclusions justified? While not implying that Richard II's financial policies were anything like as innovative or successful as those of Edward I and Edward III, the analysis that follows does seek to challenge some of the assumptions about the inertia of the Crown's fiscal administration in the late fourteenth century and to stress that, at least until the time of the Lancastrian revolution, the customs system was still evolving to accommodate the financial demands of the State. It should be emphasized that arguments which connect the decline of the customs under Henry VI with longer-term structural problems supposedly emerging during the late fourteenth century not only demonstrate the dubious value of hindsight but also ignore the very considerable differences that developed both in the pattern of overseas trade and in the fiscal policies of Crown and Parliament between the 1390s and the 1440s.[13] Wool was, and remained, the single most important commodity in English trade at least until the 1420s, and was not decisively overtaken by cloth until the 1450s; to rely so heavily on the taxation of wool therefore made much better fiscal sense in the late fourteenth century than it was to do by the mid-fifteenth.[14] While it is undeniable that the high rates of taxation obtaining from the 1330s and the development of the Calais staple after the 1360s did little to stimulate and much, ultimately, to destroy the wool trade, there is in fact remarkably little correlation between fluctuations in the maltolt and the state of the domestic wool market, suggesting that other more fundamental economic influences may also have to be taken into account.[15] There is also much to be said for the suggestion that the downturn in English wool exports during the late fourteenth century arose from political factors outside the control of the English government, in particular the internal conflicts in Florence and in the Flemish towns which severely disrupted the traditional markets for English wool during the 1370s and 1380s.[16]

[13] For more optimistic interpretations of the state of indirect taxation in this period see J. B. Gillingham, 'Crisis or Continuity? The Structure of Royal Authority in England 1369–1422', *Vorträge und Forschungen*, 32 (1987), 62–4; G. L. Harriss, 'Political Society and the Growth of Government in Late Medieval England', *Past and Present*, 138 (1993), 42.

[14] Compare the data in Fig. 8.1 with the slightly different calculations (based on standard figures for wool as well as cloth) given in Bolton, *Medieval English Economy*, 292–3.

[15] Lloyd, *Movement of Wool Prices*, 13–24.

[16] G. Holmes, *The Good Parliament of 1376* (Oxford, 1975), 81–5, 125–6; D. Nicholas, 'The English Trade at Bruges in the Last Years of Edward III', *JMH* 5 (1979), 23–61; Lloyd, *Wool Trade*, 225–6. The crusade of Bishop Despenser in 1383 was partly intended to reestablish trade links with Flanders: M. E. Aston, 'The Impeachment of Bishop Despenser', *BIHR* 38 (1965), 134–40.

Furthermore, it is important to notice that some of the additional inhibiting factors which did so much to reduce wool exports in the fifteenth century were either not present at all or only in their very early stages of development while Richard II sat on the throne of England. In this respect, the Crown's attitude to alien merchants and its policy on the import of bullion are of particular relevance. One of the principal reasons for the decline of wool exports in the fifteenth century was the withdrawal of foreign traders, forced out not simply by the restrictive practices of the Calais staple but also by Parliament's decision to set the wool subsidy at higher rates for aliens than for denizens.[17] This meant that the differential between export costs incurred by the two groups increased rapidly from the basic additional premium of 3s. 4d. paid by foreigners under the terms of the *Carta mercatoria* of 1303 to £1. 3s. 4d. for most of the period between 1422 and 1453 and to a punitive £1.16s. 8d. by the later fifteenth century.[18] It is interesting to note, then, that despite hints of a desire on the part of the Commons to introduce such a system in the late fourteenth century, the practice was virtually unknown before 1399: apart from a token reduction of 1s. for denizens in 1385–8, the native and alien rates of the wool subsidy remained the same until, in the lifetime grant of the maltolt extracted by Richard II in 1398, they were fixed at £2. 3s. 4d. for English exporters and £2. 10s. for foreigners.[19] For almost all of Richard's reign, therefore, the government maintained a fundamentally traditional policy towards the relative tax burden incurred by denizen and alien merchants.

The bullion policy pursued by Richard's ministers was almost equally as conservative. Since the 1340s spasmodic attempts had been made to guarantee that a proportion of the profit made from the sale of English wool on foreign markets found its way back into the internal economy and thus maintained the otherwise rapidly dwindling stock of specie within the kingdom. In 1391 the traditional mechanism was revived and all merchants, denizen and alien, were required to deposit at the royal mint one ounce of gold in foreign currency for every sack of wool exported. Apart from the confusion caused to denizens and aliens alike about whether this deposit should be made at the mints in London or Calais, there is no particular evidence to suggest that this type of bullion regulation had any

---

[17] This point is stressed by Lloyd, *Wool Trade*, 284.

[18] The rates set out in graphic form by Carus-Wilson and Coleman, *England's Export Trade*, 196, demonstrate this point, though it should be noted that their data are not always completely accurate.

[19] *RP* iii. 204; *CFR 1383–1391*, 163; *RP* iii. 368.

notably adverse effects on overseas trade.[20] More ominous in the long term were the so-called 'Employment Acts' which required alien merchants bringing goods into England to spend some or all of the value of their imports on the purchase of English goods for export and to pay for the latter not with letters of exchange but in ready cash. The first of these measures was in fact adopted under Richard II in 1390. However, unlike later Employment Acts, this cannot be said to have been intended deliberately to victimize foreign merchants since it was part of a larger experiment that actually gave aliens a notable advantage by awarding them a temporary monopoly over the export of English wool.[21] Certainly there is nothing in the pattern of overseas trade during the 1390s to compare with the devastating slump brought about by the bullion and partition ordinances of 1429–30.[22] While it is true that overseas trade showed comparatively little sign of buoyancy in the last decades of the fourteenth century, it is therefore not at all clear that its fluctuations were directly or solely dictated by government policies.

IV

The ability of international commerce to accommodate such policies and withstand at least some of their more ominous implications is of particular importance to the central section of this chapter. Contrary to the widespread assumption that the basic framework of the late medieval customs system was more or less in place by 1350, it appears that the English Crown retained an active interest in extending the range of indirect taxation for the rest of the fourteenth century and that Richard II's reign actually witnessed some interesting efforts to ensure that the State derived financial advantage from some of these changes. That this sensitivity and flexibility was lost after 1399, when the customs system really did become static, also serves to emphasize the particular determination that may be said to have characterized Richard's financial machine.

It is necessary to begin with purely administrative considerations. There are strong indications that the period after 1388 was one of interesting and sometimes useful experimentation in royal government, and the reform of

[20] Munro, *Wool, Cloth, and Gold*, 36, 40, 46, 54; Lloyd, *Wool Trade*, 239–48. These authors differ in their interpretations of the permanence of the bullion regulations of the 1390s and on certain other details.

[21] Munro, *Wool, Cloth, and Gold*, 46; Lloyd, *Wool Trade*, 243. See also the arguments of Lloyd cited above, n. 12.

[22] E. E. Power, 'The Wool Trade in the Fifteenth Century', in Postan and Power (edd.), *Studies in English Trade*, 79–90; Lloyd, *Wool Trade*, 257–87; Bolton, *Medieval English Economy*, 299–300.

the customs administration in the early 1390s has a natural place in that larger story.[23] It is only quite recently, however, that S. H. Rigby has demonstrated the specific reason for the novel policy of introducing royal clerks into the collectorships of customs in 1390–1 by associating the reform with the implementation of the new bullion regulations.[24] Whether this policy was also intended to improve the productivity of the customs system now seems somewhat doubtful. For present purposes, however, the principal significance of the reform lies in the greater degree of central control that was implied by associating officials of the Westminster administration with the local merchants who normally acted as collectors of customs in the head ports.

The greater emphasis on using the centre as a check on the localities is also demonstrated by a notable change in the administration of the one internal sales tax collected by the English Crown in the later Middle Ages, namely the alnage, an excise duty of 4*d.* levied on every cloth of assize or equivalent exposed for sale in domestic markets. Under pressure from Parliament in 1394, the Crown abandoned the farm of the alnage that had operated since the later 1350s and made the local collectors account directly to the Exchequer for the proceeds of this tax. Again, it is improbable that the Crown saw this specifically as a means of making money, since the yield of the alnage during the years of direct management from 1394 to 1398 was well under £1,000 per annum.[25] Nevertheless, the short experiments in more direct methods of management both of the customs and of this excise duty bore a striking parallel with an earlier period of administrative reform in the 1350s, when Edward III's government had

---

[23] J. A. Tuck. 'The Cambridge Parliament, 1388', *EHR* 84 (1969), 225–43; R. L. Storey, 'Liveries and Commissions of the Peace, 1388–1390', in *Reign of Richard II*, 131–52; A. B. Steel, 'The Collectors of Customs at Newcastle upon Tyne in the Reign of Richard II', in J. Conway Davies (ed.), *Studies presented to Sir Hilary Jenkinson* (London, 1957), 380–413; O. Coleman, 'The Collectors of Customs in London under Richard II', in A. E. J. Hollaender and W. Kellaway (edd.), *Studies in London History* (London, 1969), 181–94; A. Steel, 'The Collectors of the Customs in the Reign of Richard II', in H. Hearder and H. R. Loyn (edd.), *British Government and Administration* (Cardiff, 1974), 27–39.

[24] S. H. Rigby, 'The Customs Administration at Boston in the Reign of Richard II', *BIHR* 58 (1985), 12–24.

[25] For the history of this subsidy see E. Lipson, *The Economic History of England, i. The Middle Ages* (12th edn., London, 1959), 461–3; H. L. Gray, 'The Production and Exportation of English Woollens in the Fourteenth Century', *EHR* 39 (1924), 13–35. Gray estimated that *c.*50,000 cloths were produced per year in the 1390s; at 4*d.* per cloth of assize, this would yield £833. The farm of the alnage was fixed at about the same levels. G. L. Harriss, 'Financial Policy', in id. (ed.), *Henry V: The Practice of Kingship* (Oxford, 1985), 171 and n. 15 notes that Henry V raised the farm from £758 to £958. By 1433, however, it had fallen to an estimated £721: J. L. Kirby, 'The Issues of the Lancastrian Exchequer and Lord Cromwell's Estimates of 1433', *BIHR* 24 (1951), 132.

placed particular emphasis on the close supervision of the structure of indirect taxation as the best means of guaranteeing maximum profit to the Crown.[26] That similar concerns were at least partly in the minds of Richard II's financial administrators during the 1390s becomes more likely when we turn to the specifically fiscal novelties introduced into the customs system in the last decades of the fourteenth century.

The first of those novelties was the extension of the cloth custom of 1347 to incorporate a wider range of English cloth exports. The duties imposed in 1347 had been chiefly designed to exploit the top end of the market, by imposing differentiated sliding scales on dyed and undyed cloths of assize exported by natives and aliens. The only other cloths subject to the 1347 custom were worsteds, which were rated at 1*d.* each for denizens and 1½*d.* for aliens as against 14*d.* and 17*d.* respectively for cloths of assize without grain. Carus-Wilson and Coleman argued that this differential in taxation represented the relative values of broadcloths and worsteds and decided to omit the latter from their published data on cloth exports on the grounds that worsteds were of negligible importance to the overall balance of trade.[27] T. H. Lloyd has pointed out, however, that the real market value of worsteds was considerably higher than the 1347 duties suggest.[28] Fig. 8.5 works back from material published by Carus-Wilson and Coleman and uses the revised converter supplied by Lloyd to demonstrate that worsteds formed a much more considerable proportion of the total value of cloth exports in the 1350s than has previously been appreciated.[29] At the same time, however, since worsteds were undertaxed in relation to broadcloths, it becomes evident that any computation for the potential revenue from that trade would fail to alter the picture already presented in Fig. 8.3. In other words, despite its declared intention to benefit as much from cloth exports as from wool,[30] the government of Edward III had made a serious error in its assessments which deprived it of potentially significant amounts of tax revenue in the 1350s.

The situation changed significantly under Richard II. By the 1390s exports of worsteds had fallen, both in proportion to the rapidly expanding trade in broadcloths and in direct relation to the figures for the 1350s (Fig. 8.5).

[26] W. M. Ormrod, 'The English Crown and the Customs, 1349–1363', *EcHR*, 2nd ser. 40 (1987), 29–32. The internal duty of 4*d.* on cloth sales was also subject to direct management from its institution in 1353 until 1358: Gray, 'English Woollens', 19.

[27] Carus-Wilson and Coleman, *England's Export Trade*, 199–200. See also J. H. Munro, 'Industrial Transformations in the North-West European Textile Trades, *c.*1290–*c.*1340: Economic Progress or Economic Crisis?', in Campbell (ed.), *Before the Black Death*, 134 and n. 86.

[28] 'Overseas Trade', 114.   [29] ESFDB \orm\engbo18.

[30] *CFR 1347–1356*, 28.

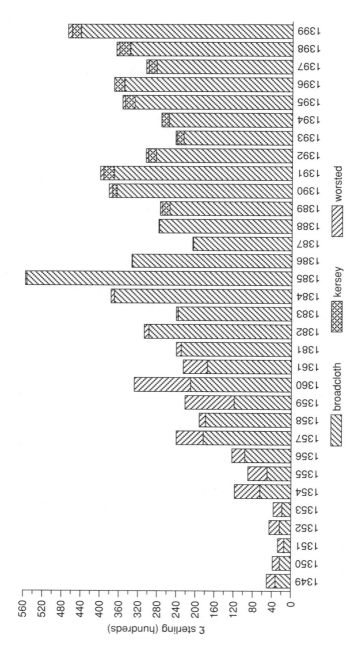

FIG. 8.5. Revised values of English cloth exports subject to the customs, 1349–1399

Source: ESFDB \orm\engbo18

Any incentive that the government may have had to increase the duties on worsteds had therefore already evaporated. On the other hand, the export of another cheap range of cloths, kerseys, had now become appreciable enough for the Crown to attempt that extension of the cloth custom so notably missing in the 1350s. Temporarily from 1388 and permanently after 1390, kerseys and straits became subject to the cloth custom. This was not all gain: although denizens had previously paid nothing on these cloths, kerseys had been liable to the *ad valorem* duty of 3*d.* in the pound paid by aliens under the terms of the new custom of 1303, and in order to off-set the opposition to the new duties of 1388 the Crown found it necessary to exempt kerseys from the new custom.[31] The most important point, however, is that in sharp contrast to the situation in 1347, the Crown now significantly overvalued kerseys in relation to broadcloths: using T. H. Lloyd's calculations again, the total duty on kerseys may have represented as much as 10 per cent of their domestic market value if exported by denizens and up to 23 per cent if carried out by non-Hanseatic aliens, as against 3 per cent and 7 per cent respectively for cloths of assize without grain.[32] The effect seems to have been to increase approximately sixfold the duties paid by aliens on exports of kerseys.[33] The overall impact on the revenue derived from the taxation of cloth cannot be calculated precisely because of uncertainty about the numbers of kerseys being exported in this period, but if the fairly conservative estimate used in constructing Fig. 8.5 (which expresses kerseys as 15 per cent of the total volume of broadcloth exports) is employed, the revenue from the cloth customs rises from approximately 3 per cent of the revised valuations in the 1350s to approximately 4 per cent of those for the 1390s (see Table 8.1).[34] Finally, it is worth noting that the new arrangements made for the direct administration

[31] Gray, 'English Woollens', 27–8; Carus-Wilson, *Medieval Merchant Venturers*, 263; Lloyd, *England and Hanse*, 77–8.

[32] Lloyd, *England and Hanse*, 77–8, giving a value ratio of 10 : 1 as against a tax ratio of 3 : 1, and taking a cloth of assize to be worth £2. Note, however, that Gray, 'English Woollens', 27 n. 6, found considerable variations in the market value of kerseys, and some flexibility in the converters used to assess them for taxation at the ports. See also the valuations supplied by Munro, 'Industrial Transformations', 134 n. 87.

[33] Using the figures cited by Lloyd, *England and Hanse*, 77.

[34] The estimate that kerseys comprised 15% of the total trade is taken from the figures cited by Gray, 'English Woollens', 28. It should be noted that the calculations in ESFDB \orm\engmo19 exclude the revenue which the Crown would have derived prior to 1388 from the 3*d.* in the pound payable by aliens, since it is impossible to establish what proportion of the undifferentiated total valuations of imports and exports of merchandise subject to this duty (as printed by Lloyd, *England and Hanse*, 98–9) was made up by cheap ranges of cloth exports. It is assumed, however, that this trade was of no significant size and of negligible value.

TABLE 8.1. *Estimated annual average figures for the cloth customs, 1350–1359 and 1390–1399*

Period	Value of cloth (£)	Revenue from cloth customs (£)	Revenue as percentage of value
1350–9	11,388	344	3.02
1390–9	35,018	1,416	4.04

Source: ESFDB \orm\engmo19

of the alnage in 1394 also, for the first time, made kerseys subject to this internal sales tax.[35] Although it may therefore be said that the combined yield of the customs and excise duties was probably increasing faster than the overall value of the cloth trade, the proportion of that total value effected in income for the Crown remained very modest and in no way compared with the corresponding figures for wool. Nevertheless, the fact that Richard II's government had apparently identified and successfully exploited a growth market within the larger scheme of English cloth production says at least something about the ability of his financial regime to adapt and survive.

This very modest extension of the customs duties on cloth becomes rather more impressive when it is set alongside a much more significant advance in indirect taxation during the late fourteenth century: namely, the adoption of tonnage and poundage as a regular element within the wider customs system. The origins of tonnage and poundage lie in special subsidies imposed in the mid-fourteenth century to support naval forces for the protection of the wine fleet and other English trading vessels threatened by attacks both from pirates and, more particularly, from enemy shipping.[36] For a number of reasons, however, it may be argued that it was Richard II's government rather than Edward III's that first identified and exploited these subsidies as a source of royal income. Before 1369 subsidies for arming ships were highly exceptional and short-lived, and although they ran more frequently in the 1370s, they did not in fact form a regular and continuous sequence until after 1388. Furthermore, the collection and/or the expenditure of all such levies until 1384 (and once thereafter, in 1390)

[35] H. Heaton, *The Yorkshire Woollen and Worsted Industries* (2nd edn., Oxford, 1965), 69; Carus-Wilson, *Medieval Merchant Venturers*, 279. Kerseys were charged 1*d*. per cloth as against 4*d*. on a cloth of assize.

[36] This paragraph represents a summary of a more detailed forthcoming study on the political significance of the subsidy of tonnage and poundage.

was carefully separated from the administration of the other customs and subsidies and normally put in the hands of agents who were empowered to raise the necessary ships, arms, and men at the local level: in other words, the duties were earmarked for specific needs and were not available for the general expenditure of the Crown. Finally, the rates at which tonnage and poundage were set once again suggest a significant change in function after 1386. Prior to that date, with one brief exception, the rates never rose above 2s. on a ton of wine and 6d. in the pound on general merchandise.[37] From 1386 to 1399 they stood almost continuously at 3s. per ton and 1s. in the pound.[38] When all these points are taken into consideration, it is possible to identify 1386 as the crucial year in which tonnage and poundage was symbolically upgraded from a modest tax in aid of local defence to a national subsidy paid into the royal treasury and available for the general expenses of the Crown. It is apparently no coincidence that the generous and trend-setting grant of 1386 should have been offered in the Wonderful Parliament and made dependent on the king's willingness to honour the powers delegated to the extraordinary commission appointed in this assembly for the reform of the realm.[39] Nevertheless, Richard's success in securing a virtually continuous series of such subsidies from the inception of his personal rule in 1389 (the first time, it may be noted, that tonnage and poundage had been granted during a formal truce with France) and his ability to avoid the various restrictions and conditions that Parliament still occasionally placed on the tax represents a considerable fiscal and political achievement which provides interesting parallels with Edward III's earlier management of the wool subsidy.

To assess the full financial benefits offered by tonnage and poundage is a particularly difficult task, given the complicated systems of local expenditure and separate accounting normally employed until the 1380s. In order to compensate for such lacunae, a preliminary attempt has been made to reconstruct the potential revenue from the subsidy on the basis of known and estimated totals for the various commodities liable to tonnage and poundage between 1350 and 1399 (Fig. 8.6).[40] This material must be treated with great caution and is intended to demonstrate general trends rather than provide detailed annual statistics. Indeed, apart from helping to validate

---

[37] The exception is 1350, when the wine rate rose to 3s. 4d. per ton: M. K. James, *Studies in the Medieval Wine Trade* (Oxford, 1971), 25; Harriss, *King, Parliament and Public Finance*, 462.

[38] The exception is the period from Mar. to Christmas 1390: *RP*, iii. 262; *CFR 1383–1391*, 316–18.

[39] *RP* iii. 220–1; *CFR 1383–1391*, 169–70.   [40] ESFDB \orm\engbo23.

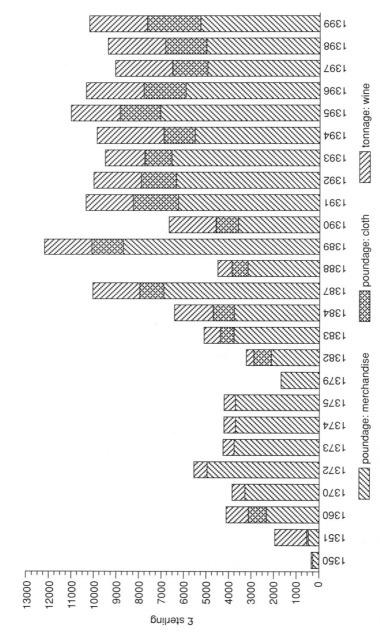

FIG. 8.6. Potential revenue to the Crown from tonnage and poundage, 1350–1399

Source: ESFDB \orm\engbo23

a thesis already implied (namely, that there was an appreciable increase in the profitability of the subsidy after 1386), the principal interest of the graph lies in the information it provides on the various commodities liable to tonnage and poundage in the later fourteenth century. Two new and quite significant elements in overseas trade previously untouched by the national customs system now enter the picture: imports of wine brought in by English shippers, and both imports and exports of general merchandise carried by denizens. Given that English merchants were responsible for about 50 per cent of general imports and up to 80 per cent of wine imports, and given that there was a substantial increase in imports of luxury goods to feed the well-known explosion of consumerism in the later fourteenth century, it is indeed intriguing to speculate on the extent to which the Crown's determination properly to institutionalize the subsidy of tonnage and poundage was itself spurred on by an awareness that a significant proportion of the total value of overseas trade would otherwise remain untaxed.[41]

Even more important, however, is the appearance of exported cloth among the commodities liable to poundage as represented in Fig. 8.6. There has been much misunderstanding about the particular groups that were required to pay poundage on cloth, arising from the false assumption that the immunity enjoyed by native and Hanseatic merchants in the mid-fifteenth century applied also in the earlier stages of the tax.[42] It cannot be stressed too strongly that no such general exemptions in fact existed before 1422.[43] This means that the total charge made on cloth exports was significantly higher than that included in the customs duties as represented either in Fig. 8.3 or in the revised calculations in Table 8.1. After 1386 the combined customs and subsidies payable on each broadcloth carried out of the country would have been 2s. 11d. in the case of denizen merchants, 2s. 9d. for Hansards, and 4s. 9d. for other aliens. If these figures are expressed

---

[41] For consumerism see C. Dyer, *Standards of Living in the Later Middle Ages: Social Change in England c.1200–1520* (Cambridge, 1989). It is significant in this respect that the English Parliament considered the idea of a comprehensive internal sales tax in 1380: *RP* iii. 89–90.

[42] The source of the misinformation appears to be H. L. Gray, 'English Foreign Trade from 1446 to 1482' and 'Tables of Enrolled Customs and Subsidy Accounts: 1399 to 1482', in Power and Postan (edd.), *Studies in English Trade*, 6, 328–9. Carus-Wilson and Coleman, *England's Export Trade*, 194–5 projected Gray's findings back into the 14th cent. Their conclusions are corrected, *inter alia*, by S. H. Rigby, 'Boston and Grimsby in the Middle Ages', Ph.D. thesis (London, 1982), 478, but the ambiguity still remains: see e.g. W. R. Childs (ed.), *The Customs Accounts of Hull 1453–1490* (Yorkshire Archaeological Society Record Series, 144, Leeds, 1984), p. xii; Munro, 'Industrial Transformations', 135 n. 89.

[43] The point was first demonstrated by Gras, *Early English Customs System*, 82–3; for a recent detailed analysis see Lloyd, *England and Hanse*, 109–72, *passim*.

TABLE 8.2. *Estimated annual average figures for the total taxation of overseas trade in cloth, 1350–1359 and 1390–1399*

Period	Value of cloth (£)	Revenue from cloth customs (£)	Revenue from poundage (£)	Total revenue as percentage of value
1350–9	11,388	344	11	3.10
1390–9	35,018	1,416	1,655	8.76

Source: ESFDB \orm\engm019

as a proportion of the conventional values attached to English cloths of assize (namely £1. 15s. for denizen and Hanseatic merchants and £2 for those carried by other aliens), then the total duties levied on cloth after 1386 represent *ad valorem* charges of 8–12 per cent, a significant advance on the 3–7 per cent accounted for by the cloth customs alone.[44] Furthermore, when poundage is taken into account, the overall value of cloth taken in royal taxation rises considerably more steeply than was suggested by the revised data in Table 8.1, from a base of 3 per cent in the 1350s to a rather more impressive 8.75 per cent in the 1390s (see Table 8.2).[45] If these figures are indeed reliable, then tonnage and poundage can be said to have done more than anything else to protect the Crown from the adverse financial implications resulting from the changing pattern of overseas trade in the later fourteenth century. They also, incidentally, throw into much sharper focus the serious fiscal implications of the decision to exempt denizen and Hanseatic merchants from poundage on cloth in the reign of Henry VI.

How, then, did the considerable fiscal potential offered by the new subsidy actually work out in practice? Fig. 8.7 represents the present author's calculations from the Exchequer accounts for all customs and subsidies on overseas trade between 1350 and 1399 set against the figures from the same sources as published by Sir James Ramsay.[46] Given the complexity of the accounts, some margin of error is only to be expected, and apart from two notable discrepancies in the mid-1360s and the mid-1370s, the figures run in reasonably compatible series until the 1380s. Thereafter, however,

---

[44] It should be noted that the latter calculation uses a standard of £2 for all *broadcloths*: see above, n. 32. Carus-Wilson and Coleman, *England's Export Trade*, 22–3, calculated that the cloth customs represented an *ad valorem* duty of 2–6%.

[45] The very low figure for poundage in the 1350s is explained by the fact that the subsidy was applied only briefly in that period.

[46] ESFDB \orm\engg039.

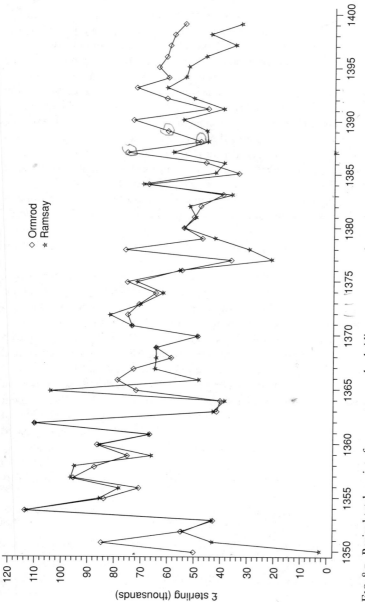

Fig. 8.7. Revised total receipts from customs and subsidies on overseas trade, 1350–1399

Source: ESFDB \orm\enggo39

they diverge significantly, with the new calculations consistently standing some £10,000–£15,000 per annum in excess of Ramsay's. The only satisfactory explanation that can be found for this discrepancy is that Ramsay was apparently unaware of the separate series of accounts recording the profits of tonnage and poundage: in other words, that the gap between the two sets of data represents, very roughly, the profits of those subsidies of tonnage and poundage that were accounted for by special collectors directly answerable to the Exchequer.[47] This discovery is of signal importance, for it demonstrates that tonnage and poundage very largely offset the decline that has otherwise been assumed to have taken place in the profits of indirect taxation during the last decades of the fourteenth century, and even effected a modest rise in the grand total during the last decade of Richard II's reign. In short, the new taxes developed since the 1370s and so effectively exploited in the 1390s appear to have made a significant contribution to the financial stability of Richard's personal regime during the last decade of the reign.

V

To substantiate the latter point it is necessary to move beyond the history of indirect taxation alone and to place the customs and subsidies into their more general fiscal, political, and economic context. It has long been appreciated that in financial terms, as in so many other ways, the reign of Richard II divides naturally at 1389.[48] Up to that date, the king was often in deep difficulties, as high military expenditure on a series of controversial and unproductive military campaigns coupled with the notable reluctance of successive Parliaments in the early 1380s to concede direct taxes produced a serious gulf between the Crown's financial commitments on the one hand and its financial capacity on the other.[49] After the Anglo-French truce of 1389, however, things improved significantly. The Exchequer was able to meet most of the demands on royal resources and to increase considerably the proportion of revenue received in cash rather than assigned away in advance of collection.[50] The very considerable increase in the expenditure

[47] These accounts are found in PRO E356/5. For the separation of tonnage and poundage from the main customs system in this period see e.g. Rigby, 'Customs Administration at Boston', 24.
[48] T. F. Tout, *Chapters in the Administrative History of Mediaeval England*, 6 vols. (Manchester, 1920–33), iv. 206; A. Steel, *The Receipt of the Exchequer, 1377–1485* (Cambridge, 1954), 103–48.
[49] J. Sherborne, 'The Defence of the Realm and the Impeachment of Michael de la Pole in 1386', in *Politics and Crisis*, 97–116.
[50] Steel, *Receipt*, 111–12.

of the Royal Household during the later 1390s was itself, at least in part, a sign of this new security and prosperity.[51] In several ways, then, the pattern of royal income and royal spending during the 1390s echoed that of the last significant period of peace during the nine years following the treaty of Brétigny of 1360. As Fig. 8.8 demonstrates, the balance between direct and indirect taxation during the 1390s was a good deal closer to that of the period 1355–69 than to that of the 1370s and 1380s.[52] The same pattern is discernible in Fig. 8.9, which expresses the new data for the profits of indirect taxation as a percentage of the total revenue accounted for in the receipt rolls of the Exchequer: again, if slightly less obviously, a reversion to the practices of the 1350s and 1360s is evident, with the early 1390s showing a particularly striking increase in the relative importance of the taxes on overseas trade.[53] The analogy with the years of peace under Edward III cannot be taken too far, for Richard II still had active military commitments during the last decade of his reign. Nevertheless, in the proportionate terms measured in Figs. 8.8 and 8.9, Richard's use of the customs and subsidies as the basis of peacetime finance does indeed appear to have been as judicious and successful as that of his grandfather.

In political terms, too, the management of royal taxation in the 1390s represented a rather greater achievement than has often been suggested. During the 1380s Richard II was faced with successive refusals of direct taxation and with a series of short interruptions in the collection of the wool subsidy—interruptions which not only signified the tense relationship between Crown and Parliament in these years but also served to remind the Crown of the extraordinary nature of this vital form of revenue.[54] The reservation of both direct and indirect subsidies for particular forms of expenditure and their administration by a series of war treasurers was perhaps even more ominous, for it deprived Richard of the right, so vigorously defended by Edward III, to organize the expenditure of taxation as the king and his ministers thought fit.[55] During the 1390s, however, Parliament proved notably more co-operative and Richard II enjoyed

---

[51] C. Given-Wilson, *The Royal Household and the King's Affinity: Service, Politics and Finance in England 1360–1413* (London, 1986), 94.

[52] ESFDB \orm\engbo21.

[53] ESFDB \orm\engbo22. It should be noted that the totals up to 1376, extracted by Mr R. Axworthy and stored in ESFDB \orm\engdo25, are as given in the receipt rolls, whereas those for the period 1377–99, taken from Steel, *Receipt*, 426–7, are corrected to compensate for bookkeeping entries and mathematical errors.

[54] See the refs. cited above, n. 5.

[55] Given-Wilson, *Royal Household*, 121–7. For the situation under Edward III, see Ormrod, *Reign of Edward III*, 49.

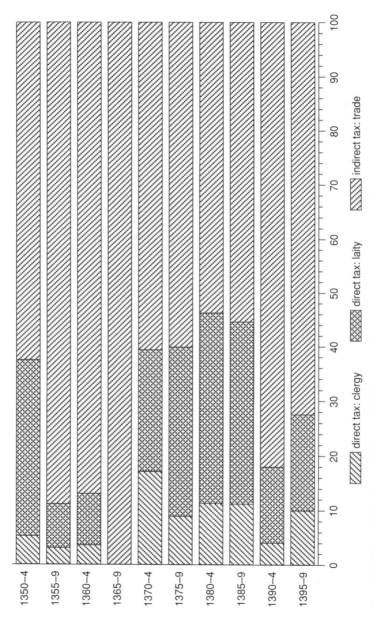

Fig. 8.8. The relative values of direct and indirect taxation, 1350–1399

Source: ESFDB \orm\engbo21

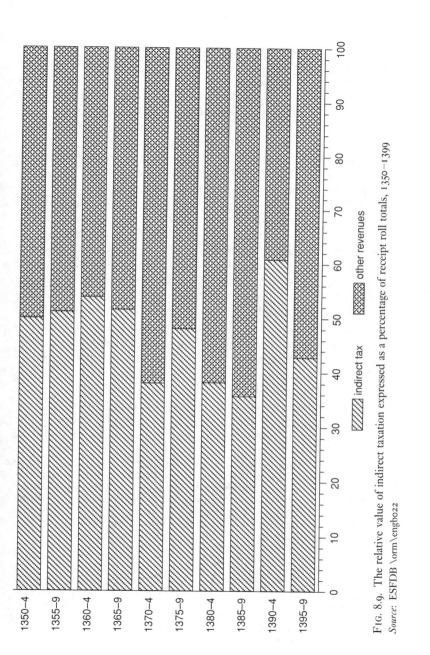

Fig. 8.9. The relative value of indirect taxation expressed as a percentage of receipt roll totals, 1350–1399

Source: ESFDB \orm\engb022

a new freedom in the management of his extraordinary revenues. The Crown achieved some success in persuading the Commons to sanction direct taxes outside periods of active war and faced no further demands for the appointment of separate treasurers to administer them.[56] Perhaps most notable of all, however, was the king's success in winning an uninterrupted series of indirect taxes in the form of the wool subsidy and of tonnage and poundage. The traditional preoccupation with Richard II's despotic tendencies as demonstrated in the undue pressure he brought to bear on Parliament in 1398 to secure a life grant of the wool subsidy has tended to overshadow the real achievement of his regime during the 1390s in persuading the Commons of the need to extend indirect taxation into a period of peace. This chapter has already drawn attention to the unprecedented continuation of tonnage and poundage after the truce of 1389; Richard's success in this respect is further emphasized by the abandonment of the subsidy during the early years of Henry IV's reign and its partial remission on the accession of Henry VI to the throne of France in 1422.[57] Almost equally as impressive, and certainly of the greatest financial importance, was Richard's ability to secure an unbroken series of grants of the wool subsidy at wartime rates after 1389. Although both Crown and Parliament were coming more and more to treat the maltolt as a permanent element in the king's finances, it was still fundamentally regarded as an extraordinary levy intended for special needs and which might therefore be reduced, if not remitted, once the necessity had passed: witness in this respect the 50 per cent cut made in the rate between 1362 and 1365 and the 23 per cent reduction in the denizen duty effected in 1422.[58] Given that Richard managed, through open negotiation, to overcome any arguments that may have been put forward in favour of such reductions not only after the

---

[56] G. L. Harriss, 'Theory and Practice in Royal Taxation: Some Observations', *EHR* 97 (1982), 813–14; Given-Wilson, *Royal Household*, 126–7. It is worth pointing out that Richard was rather more scrupulous in honouring the conditions set on parliamentary subsidies in this period than has often been assumed. He honoured the terms set down both for the grant of the wool subsidy and tonnage and poundage in 1390, and those for the 1½ fifteenths and tenths granted in 1391: Steel, *Receipt*, 63; *Second Report of the Deputy Keeper of the Public Records* (London, 1841), app. II, 178.

[57] The subsidy was not collected between 1399 and 1401: see *CFR 1399–1405*, 95–6, 121; *RP* iii. 455. In 1422–5 it was temporarily restricted to aliens only: *RP* iv. 173, 200, 276; *CFR 1422–1430*, 24–5, 27, 60–1, 89–90, 107–8, 117–18.

[58] *RP* ii. 273, 285; iv. 173; Carus-Wilson and Coleman, *England's Export Trade*, 196. It must be noted that since 1369 the collectors of customs, under the guidance of the Exchequer, had treated the wool subsidy as an integral part of the system of indirect taxation and accounted for it along with the ancient and new customs on wool. As Beardwood, *Alien Merchants*, 136–8, notes, this was an important stage in the transformation of an extraordinary into a customary levy.

temporary truce of 1389 but also following the twenty-eight-year Anglo-French truce of 1396,[59] it is indeed something of a puzzle as to why he should have brought such pressure to bear to secure the life grant of the subsidy in 1398. Presumably it was increasing public comment and criticism (most obviously, though by no means solely, from Thomas Haxey in 1397) about the use of such extraordinary taxes to subsidize the king's domestic extravagances that provoked this controversial demand.[60] Certainly, it would seem that it was the necessity brought on by very obvious financial need, rather than some grand scheme to free the Crown from parliamentary control, that led Richard to attempt such a bold leap forward in the constitutional structure of public finance.

This mention of financial need inevitably raises important questions about the overall success of the fiscal policy analysed in this chapter. The researches on Richard II's later finances undertaken by Caroline Barron, Anthony Tuck, Chris Given-Wilson, and others have indicated that for all the notable structural and political achievements noted above, Richard II was not, in the end, a wealthy king.[61] The financial expedients adopted in the years of tyranny and the evidence of serious overspending in the Household at the end of the reign indicate that the system was becoming severely strained and could certainly not sustain either the king's military commitments in Ireland or even his escalating expenditure on diplomacy without injections of extraordinary direct taxation. In this sense the 1390s provide a notable contrast with the years of peace under Edward III. During the 1360s Edward seems to have drawn freely on the proceeds of the wool subsidy not only to cover the many war debts left over from the 1350s but also to support one of the most lavish and expensive displays of courtly magnificence yet witnessed in medieval England.[62] That this caused so little political concern owed much not only to the extraordinary popularity of a warrior king and his careful management of Parliament but also to the fact that Edward was prepared to allow a substantial proportion of the £200,000 received between 1357 and 1364 from the ransoms of Charles of Blois, David II of Scotland, the duchy of Burgundy, and John

---

[59] In 1397 Richard was granted the wool subsidy at standard rates for five years effective from a retrospective starting date of Nov. 1396: *RP* iii. 340.

[60] *Hist. Angl.* ii. 196, discussed by Given-Wilson, *Royal Household*, 127; *Mum and the Soothsegger*, ed. M. Day and R. Steele (EETS, orig. ser. 194; 1936), 23–4, cited by Harriss, 'Theory and Practice', 818. For Haxey's petition, see Given-Wilson, *Royal Household*, 113.

[61] C. M. Barron, 'The Tyranny of Richard II', *BIHR* 41 (1968), 1–18; A. J. Tuck, *Richard II and the English Nobility* (London, 1973), 143–5, 197–8; id., 'Richard II and the Hundred Years War', in *Politics and Crisis*, 126; Given-Wilson, *Royal Household*, 76–141, *passim*.

[62] Harriss, *King, Parliament and Public Finance*, 466–87.

II of France to be used for the Crown's continuing commitments in France
—above all, for the maintenance of the Calais garrison and the establishment of the Black Prince's new regime in Bordeaux.[63] Richard II's income
from indirect taxation may have been more substantial than has previously been thought, and rather more impressive in comparison with that
of Edward III, but the balance between domestic and military expenditure had altered decisively by the 1390s and even those without access to
Exchequer records were quite clear that 'public' funds were being squandered, as never before, on the 'private' extravagances of the court. Richard
II's marked reluctance to follow his grandfather's lead and allow any of
the personal income received from the one major windfall of his last years
—the dowry of Queen Isabella—to be deployed by the Exchequer in support of the expenses even of the Household, let alone of the State, may
well have added to this sense of grievance.[64] That Richard's ministers realized the importance of the customs and subsidies and sought to maximize
the revenue from this source certainly provides an important new slant on
the financial history of the reign. In the final analysis, however, their over-
reliance on this one source proved a point of weakness and manifestly failed
to revolutionize royal finances. It is perhaps not so surprising that, in its
efforts to restore the financial credibility and stability of the monarchy,
the early Lancastrian regime should have directed its attention away from
the customs and subsidies and back to the structure of direct taxation.[65]

VI

The most fundamental of the flaws in the Ricardian fiscal policy discussed here, however, lay in the relationship between the potential and

[63] Ibid. 490–6.

[64] For the dowry see J. J. N. Palmer, *England, France and Christendom 1377–1399*
(London, 1972), 173–4, 212; Given-Wilson, *Royal Household*, 300 n. 32. The only dowry
money released to the Exchequer was the £6,666 made over as a loan from the Chamber in
Mar. 1397: Steel, *Receipt*, 75. Loans from the Chamber to the Exchequer had not been
unknown in the 1360s, but were much smaller in value than the free transfers of cash: Harriss,
King, Parliament and Public Finance, 500; Given-Wilson, *Royal Household*, 88. For both
Richard's private wealth and his insistence on Exchequer funding to the Chamber in the
1390s see Given-Wilson, *Royal Household*, 86–90. It is noticeable, however, that he was not
as systematic as some of his predecessors in reserving *all* prerogative windfalls for private
use: Steel, *Receipt*, 118.

[65] A. Rogers, 'Henry IV, the Commons, and Taxation', *Mediaeval Studies*, 31 (1969),
44–70; K. B. McFarlane, *Lancastrian Kings and Lollard Knights* (Oxford, 1972), 97–9; Given-
Wilson, *Royal Household*, 128–38; G. L. Harriss, *Cardinal Beaufort: A Study of Lancastrian
Ascendancy and Decline* (Oxford, 1988), 18–67. See also the suggestion of id., 'The Management of Parliament', in id. (ed.), *Henry V*, 149–51, that Henry V attempted in 1421 to
establish the principle of peacetime direct taxation.

the operating tax bases. The main lesson offered by the royal management of indirect taxation in the later fourteenth century seems to lie not so much in the supposed incompatibility between the fiscal interests of the Crown and the size and value of overseas trade but in the constant challenge of ensuring that new elements within that trade were identified and adequately exploited. Despite the notable extension in the taxation of cloth exports and the increase in the revenue from imports of wine and luxury goods to which this chapter has drawn attention, the government of Richard II appears ultimately to have been less successful than that of Edward III in the proportion of the value of overseas trade that it was able to realize through the customs and subsidies levied in the ports.

To calculate such proportions is inevitably a complicated, hazardous, and ultimately rather subjective task, depending as it does on very notional and sometimes no doubt artificial estimates for the total value of the principal commodities exported and imported during this period. The computations are not helped by a notable ambiguity between 'value' in the sense of the price paid to the producer and 'value' in the sense of the price paid at the other end of the market chain by either the buyer or the final customer.[66] Nevertheless, the crude figures are interesting and instructive.

[66] Despite his intensive work published in *Movement of Wool Prices*, T. H. Lloyd has preferred to use a notional figure of £8 a sack (representing the domestic market price plus the customs and subsidies: i.e. the price 'for the overseas buyer') in his computations on the balance of trade in the second half of the 14th cent. (id., 'Overseas Trade', 113–15; id., *England and Hanse*, 104, 106). By contrast, in his work on the fifteenth-century balance of trade, Bolton, *Medieval English Economy*, 292–3, 306–7, uses only the domestic market prices. (The problem here is that, as Lloyd, *Movement of Wool Prices*, 4, points out, the available data on the domestic market is skewed towards the middle and cheaper ranges of English wool, so that his index fails to reflect the higher, if still probably declining, amounts paid for those top-quality wools that were most in demand in foreign markets: see also above, n. 9.) In the following calculations I have attempted to give the value of exports in terms of a figure representing the cost 'for the overseas buyer', and have tried to compensate for the discrepancy between Lloyd and Bolton on wool by taking Bolton's earlier, and higher, valuations of the domestic market price (Bolton, 'Alien Merchants', 43–8), and rounding up both his original and revised calculations for the total value of overseas trade in the period 1442–52 ('Alien Merchants', 61 = £2,980,110; *Medieval English Economy*, 307 = £2,964,100) to £3,000,000. The prices paid by consumers of English wool on the continent are largely unknown, though the figures discovered by Nicholas, 'English Trade at Bruges', 32, suggest that exporters could still expect a very high profit margin in the later 14th cent. In this respect, see also N. J. M. Kerling, *Commercial Relations of Holland and Zeeland with England from the Late 13th Century to the Close of the Middle Ages* (Leiden, 1954), 63. So far as cloth is concerned, the valuations cited above, worked out by Bolton in reference to the first half of the 15th cent. ('Alien Merchants', 32–3, 38–9; *Medieval English Economy*, 292), and now widely used for the whole of the later Middle Ages (e.g. by Lloyd, *England and Hanse*, 104, 106), are also those paid on the domestic market. They inevitably obscure the very wide range of prices commanded by different ranges of English broadcloth: see *inter alia* J. H. Munro, 'Monetary Contraction and Industrial Change in the Late-Medieval Low Countries, 1335–1500', in N. J. Mayhew

During the period 1353–62, royal revenue from the customs represented 18.5 per cent of the total estimated value of exports and imports and a significant 23.5 per cent of the value of those commodities actually subject to taxation. By the 1390s, when the adoption of tonnage and poundage meant that almost all materials and goods had effectively been brought within the scope of the customs system, the Crown was only managing to raise 15 per cent of their total value.[67] The drop is significant, for it demonstrates that the interesting fiscal initiatives undertaken by Richard II's government ultimately failed to compensate for an excessive dependence on the taxation of wool. Had those initiatives been followed up by the Lancastrian regime and an effective means of taxing the export of English cloth been found, the decline might yet have been halted or at least slowed down. However, by the middle of the fifteenth century such efforts had long since been abandoned, and the customs and subsidies seem to have shrunk still further to under 12 per cent of the total value of exports and imports.[68]

In the end, then, the chief interest and importance of the Ricardian experiments in indirect taxation lie in their structural rather than their purely financial implications, representing as they did the last attempts before Tudor times to reform the actual base on which indirect taxation was assessed. In conclusion, the late fourteenth century should be seen as a period in which the English Crown fought a hard, significant, but ultimately somewhat unsatisfactory campaign against the apparently inexorable tendency, demonstrated in so many medieval and early modern examples, for fiscal systems to outlive their periods of productivity and come to serve the interests not of the State but of its subjects.

(ed.), *Coinage in the Low Countries (880–1500)* (Oxford; British Archaeological Reports, International Series, 54; 1979), 97. However, since English cloth was taxed at a low rate in comparison with wool, and since the chief attraction to the foreign buyer and consumer in this period seems to have been its cheapness (P. Chorley, 'English Cloth Exports during the Thirteenth and Early Fourteenth Centuries: The Continental Evidence', *Historical Research*, 61 (1988), 1–10), the problem of a wide profit margin does not seem to apply: see also Nicholas, 'English Trade at Bruges', 28.

[67] Michaelmas 1352–Michaelmas 1362: value of overseas trade, Lloyd, 'Overseas Trade', 113–15; tax revenue, Ormrod, *Reign of Edward III*, 207. Michaelmas 1391–Michaelmas 1399: value of overseas trade, Lloyd, *England and Hanse*, 104, 106; tax revenue, ESFDB \orm\ engdoo6.

[68] Michaelmas 1442–Michaelmas 1452: value of overseas trade £3,000,000 (see above, n. 66); tax revenue £351,377 (ESFDB \orm\engmoo9). See also W. M. Ormrod, 'The Domestic Response to the Hundred Years War', in A. Curry and M. Hughes (edd.), *Arms, Armies and Fortifications in the Hundred Years War* (Woodbridge, 1995), 93–4 and n. 16.

9

Richard II and the Wider Realm

Michael J. Bennett

I

In the spring of 1399 Richard II set in train his second expedition to Ireland. Though not as large a force as he had taken five years earlier, it was still a right royal expedition. His host included about a dozen English peers, no less than six English bishops, and the abbot of Westminster.[1] Foreign visitors joined the expedition, anticipating great deeds and merriment.[2] From the outset the undertaking was made to appear portentous. While provisions and men were being assembled at Milford Haven, the king held court at Windsor, where he made his will, 'very prejudicial to the realm', on 16 April, held the traditional feast for the Order of the Garter on St George's Day, and bade fond farewell to his child-bride, kissing her forty times and offering her the curious consolation that she would eventually follow him to Ireland.[3] There were other signs that the king intended more than a brief show of arms in the lordship. He took with him not only the accoutrements of his splendid household, but also his crown jewels.[4] According to Thomas Walsingham, there was a general feeling that Richard was repudiating England, that he would never view it

---

[1] The peers included the dukes of Aumale, Exeter, and Surrey, the earls of Salisbury, Gloucester and Worcester, Lords Bardolf, Beauchamp, Grey of Ruthin, and Morley, as well as the heirs of the late duke of Gloucester and the exiled duke of Hereford: T. F. Tout, *Chapters in the Administrative History of Medieval England*, 6 vols. (Manchester, 1923–35), iv. 53–5; *CPR 1396–1399*, 524–69.

[2] Deposition of Richard II, Webb, J. (ed. and trans.), *Archaeologia*, 20 (1824), 314. Foreign lords included Pontius lord of Castillon, Peter de Craon: *CPR 1396–1399*, 550, 553.

[3] *Foedera*, viii. 75–7; Haydon, F. S. (ed.), *Continuatio Eulogii Historiarum* (RS, 1863); *Traison et Mort*, 27.

[4] *Hist. Angl.* ii. 232.

again with favour, and that he intended to waste its resources from bases outside the kingdom.[5] For the people of London and the Home Counties at least, the estrangement was real enough. Since the autumn of 1397 Richard's discrimination against them had been all too apparent. London and the sixteen counties of southern England felt the full weight of royal displeasure, being forced to compound for the king's pardon to the tune of £1,000 or 1,000 marks.[6] By contrast, there was the notoriously prodigal favour Richard showered on the men of Cheshire, several hundred of whom he recruited into a royal bodyguard. The new principality of Chester which he created was no more than the 'inner citadel' of a potentially immense provincial power-base, embracing the principality of Wales, a cluster of Marcher lordships under royal control, and, ultimately, the vast Lancastrian inheritance. Between 1397 and 1399 the centre of political gravity was shifting westwards and northwards, to Coventry or Lichfield, if not to Shrewsbury or Chester. At Holt castle on the Welsh border, he amassed great treasure. Augmenting the hoard confiscated from the earl of Arundel, he transferred wagon-loads of bullion and jewels from the capital to this regional fastness.[7]

The events of the late 1390s raise a number of issues about the politics of Richard II, and not least about his view of his dominions. His repudiation of London and his movement into the provinces naturally prompt a consideration of Richard's knowledge of his kingdom, his experience of the wider realm, and his geopolitical sense. It is important to attempt to reconstruct his political world. Given that the late fourteenth century is generally regarded as a time of nation-building in England, a time of increasing integration and centralization, his involvement with outlying regions and his concern with Ireland demand fuller exploration. His reign, in fact, underlines the need to provide some counterbalance to the traditionally Westminster-centred view of English history. Even more strikingly, it is an object-lesson in the need, now increasingly acknowledged, to set English politics in a wider British, and indeed European, framework.[8] Richard was

---

[5] *Annales*, 239–40.

[6] C. M. Barron, 'The Tyranny of Richard II', *BIHR* 41 (1968), 1–18.

[7] Tout, *Chapters*, iv. 59; R. R. Davies, 'Richard II and the Principality of Chester, 1397–1399', in *Reign of Richard II*, 256–79; C. Given-Wilson, 'Wealth and credit, public and private: the Earls of Arundel 1306–1397', *EHR* 106 (1991), 17.

[8] e.g. J. Gillingham, *The Angevin Empire* (London, 1984), esp. introd. and ch. 4; R. R. Davies (ed.), *The British Isles, 1100–1500: Comparisons, Contrasts and Connections* (Edinburgh, 1988); S. Ellis, 'Crown, Community and Government in the English Territories', *History*, 71 (1986), 187–204.

a Plantagenet, the duke of Aquitaine as well as the lord of Ireland, and a prince concerned with his standing in Christendom. It would be unwise to set too narrow bounds to the political imagination of Richard II.

Although he was born in Bordeaux in 1367, Richard was more thoroughly English than any of his Plantagenet forebears. The son of Edward the Black Prince and Joan of Kent, he was actually the first king since the Norman Conquest of wholly English parentage, and to speak English as his first language. Brought to England on the death of his older brother in 1371, he could have had little or no memory of Aquitaine, and showed curiously little desire to visit France. His adult experience of continental Europe was limited to a few weeks in the neighbourhood of Calais. By contrast, there were few kings who travelled more extensively around England and Wales, and none since John who visited Ireland. Though he took as wives European princesses, Anne of Bohemia and Isabella of France, and assiduously cultivated his European reputation, it is possible to overestimate the cosmopolitanism of his court. In the course of his reign Englishmen from all corners of his kingdom thronged his court and prospered in his service, not least in the late 1390s. Even if Francophile in his personal tastes, Richard almost certainly had some role in the sponsorship of English literature.[9]

Needless to say, when Richard came to the throne in 1377 his horizons were very limited. He was brought up in a narrow world, the circle of royal palaces and lodges whose central axis was the Thames. Still, his milieu was as much defined by people as place. His father was prince of Wales, duke of Cornwall, and earl of Chester, with lands and connections throughout the realm. Furthermore, he was a man of European repute, a doyen of chivalry, most of whose public life had been spent in harness in France and Spain. Not surprisingly, the Black Prince's household, in terms of composition and outlook, reflected the breadth of his interests and reputation. When his father died in 1376, Richard was invested with his titles and lordships, all of which he was to retain as king of England. What was perhaps of more immediate consequence was that he inherited the services of a group of knights and clerks with uncommonly wide experience. A number were French-born, most notably 'the gentle knight' Sir Guichard d'Angle, his first tutor. Others were from the provinces: Sir Baldwin

---

[9] G. Mathew, *The Court of Richard II* (London, 1968), esp. chs. 7 and 8; M. J. Bennett, 'The Court of Richard II and the Promotion of Literature', in B. A. Hanawalt (ed.), *Chaucer's England: Literature in Historical Context* (Minneapolis, 1992), 3–20. For a more sceptical view, see V. J. Scattergood, 'Literary Culture at the Court of Richard II', in *English Court Culture*, 29–43.

Raddington from Somerset, Sir John Devereux from Herefordshire, and Sir David Cradock from Cheshire. If there was a common thread in their careers it was experience in south-west France. Their frame of reference did not pivot on London.

After his accession to the throne, if not earlier, there was presumably an attempt to indoctrinate Richard in the traditions of English kingship. The splendour of his coronation in 1377 and the ceremonial round which suddenly became a fact of his life reinforced such lessons. The young king early acquired a taste for history as well as pageantry, and it was of a national sort. He was described as 'a great searcher out of antiquities relating to his royal ancestors', and the Westminster Chronicle records two occasions in 1385 when he, seemingly on impulse and at night, visited the abbey, once to show the king of Armenia the royal insignia used at his coronation.[10] He had a book of the 'miracles' of Edward II compiled and, when a prisoner in the Tower of London in 1399, was heard to recount the names and histories of kings who had suffered at the hands of their subjects since the first settlement of England.[11] His devotion to the cult of Edward the Confessor was deep and enduring, culminating in the king's adoption of the Confessor's arms in a sort of heraldic marriage in 1395. His interest in the cults of other English saints, most particularly royal saints like St Ethelbert of Kent, St Etheldreda of Ely, St Edward King and Martyr, and above all St Edmund King and Martyr, is likewise well documented.[12]

The king might be forgiven, though, if he failed to develop a sentimental attachment to London. The capital was disease-ridden and turbulent. In 1378 concern both about the plague and the anticlerical temper of the city led to Parliament being convened in distant Gloucester. The Peasants' Revolt of 1381 added to London's unpleasant associations for the impressionable young king. A great deal is made of his personal triumph in outfacing the rebels at Mile End and Smithfield. It is perhaps as appropriate to speculate on his reaction to reports that Londoners had opened the gates to the rebels and joined them in lynching the king's ministers and pillaging royal palaces. Meanwhile Richard was by degrees learning about a larger England. The Gloucester Parliament of 1378 involved what was his first

---

[10] *Annales*, 299; *Westm. Chron.* 130–3, 154–7.

[11] F. Devon (ed.), *Issues of the Exchequer* (London, 1837), 259; Adam of Usk, 30.

[12] J. H. Harvey, 'The Wilton Diptych: A Re-Examination', *Archaeologia*, 98 (1961), 5–6; H. C. Maxwell-Lyte, *Historical Notes on the Use of the Great Seal of England* (London, 1926), 225; A. H. Davis (ed.), *William Thorne's Chronicle of St. Augustine's Abbey, Canterbury, now rendered into English* (Oxford, 1934), 674; J. B. Sheppard (ed.), *Literae Cantuarienses: The Letter Books of the Monastery of Christ Church, Cambridge*. iii (RS, London, 1889), 36–40.

progress into the provinces. Presumably he was shown Edward II's tomb in Gloucester, and had his interest in him kindled at this stage.[13] After the collapse of the rebellion in the summer of 1381 he was taken in a show of royal authority to St Albans and other centres of revolt.

In the early 1380s Richard began to assert his own personality. While he continued to favour the palaces and hunting-lodges of the Thames valley, he started to undertake more extensive tours through the realm. In May and June 1393 he took Queen Anne on a leisurely pilgrimage to Walsingham, spending time at Bury St Edmunds, Thetford, and Norwich, then crossing by way of Cambridge, Ely, and Peterborough to Nottingham, where he held a council in early August prior to heading north to York. There is the first unfavourable notice of what became his lifelong habit of descending on monasteries, and requiring them to maintain his large, and often unruly, retinue.[14] In 1384 he held a Parliament at Salisbury, and toured through the southern counties, attending a wedding at Arundel castle.[15] In May 1385 he sent Sir John Clanvowe, one of his most trusted knights, into south and west Wales 'with special mandate to act on the King's behalf in examining the conditions of those parts'.[16] The expedition against Scotland later in the year was more obviously significant. He established himself first at York, then pushed northwards through Durham and Newcastle upon Tyne. At the head of what Walsingham termed 'an imperial army', he crossed the Scottish border and advanced as far as Edinburgh.[17] If the chronicles are right, the young king had a wiser head for strategy than his uncle, John of Gaunt, who allegedly proposed penetration across the Forth. The expedition over, Richard hurried back to Westminster where, even before going to his lodgings, he visited the shrine of St Edward and the other relics placed there by his predecessors.[18]

Certainly the king extended his knowledge of his realm and his people. Hitherto, most of the king's courtiers and retainers had been southerners. C. Given-Wilson has noted a marked geographical expansion of recruitment from 1389, but there are grounds for believing that this trend was

---

[13] As early as 1383 the abbot of Gloucester was granted a favour in return for celebrating masses for Edward II's soul on his anniversaries: *CPR 1381–1385*, 273; E. Perroy (ed.), *Diplomatic Correspondence of Richard II* (Camden So., 3rd ser. 48, London, 1933), 210.

[14] *Hist. Angl.*, ii. 96–7; *Westm. Chron.* 42–3. The costs of entertaining the royal entourage, which included the earl of Nottingham, John Holand, the duchess of Brittany, the countess of Pembroke, and lords and ladies 'in multitudine copiosa', at Ely 4–6 July 1383 appear in Bishop Arundel's household accounts: Cambridge University Library, Ely Records, D5/7A.

[15] *Westm. Chron*, 66–7, 88–9.   [16] *CPR 1381–1385*, 575.

[17] *Hist. Angl.* ii. 133.   [18] *Westm. Chron.* 126–33.

established between 1385 and 1387.[19] The king's experience in the Scottish campaign of 1385 was perhaps critical. There is reason to suppose that he felt that the royal retinue was wholly overshadowed by the immense following of the duke of Lancaster. When it came to taking stock of his own forces, he cannot but have been aware of how vital to his honour was the turnout of men from the palatinate of Chester.[20] Over the following years there is certainly evidence of a larger vision of the sources of royal power. The appointment of his favourite, de Vere, to key positions in the earldom of Chester and the lordship of Ireland in 1385 testifies to an interest in exploiting more systematically his credit in the wider realm. In the course of 1386, a time of mounting hostility towards the court, the king had occasion to be reminded of the fund of loyalty and military power in his palatinate. During the great invasion scare in the summer, men from Cheshire and Wales were prominent among the troops deployed in the environs of London, attracting unfavourable attention for their depredations on the civilian population.[21]

A wider awareness of the realm on the king's part is clearly evident in the dramatic events of 1387. After the establishment of a continual council to supervise the king late in 1386, Richard left the capital early in the new year, and after heading north to York began an extensive perambulation of the Midlands. To his critics, it was an erratic gyration and presumably involved some measure of spontaneity and improvisation. Yet there is reason to believe that Richard's movements were rather more purposeful than has generally been supposed.[22] Of course, it is well enough recognized that he was actively seeking to harness the loyalties of the provinces against his baronial opponents. In addition to recruiting men in the Midlands and the north-west, agents were sent into East Anglia to raise men for the royal retinue. The outcome of this strategy was the

---

[19] Given-Wilson, *The Royal Household and the King's Affinity: Service, Politics and Finance in England 1360–1413* (New Haven, 1986), 220–1. Reliance on the date at which men were formally retained by the king can be somewhat misleading, especially given the necessarily informal arrangements which must have prevailed in 1386–7.

[20] N. B. Lewis, 'The Last Summons of the English Feudal Levy, 13 June 1385', *EHR* 73 (1958); P. Morgan, *War and Society in Medieval Cheshire 1277–1403* (Manchester, 1987), 186–7.

[21] Knighton, ii. 213 ff. The king's recruitment of Cheshire men to go in his service 'towards the parts of London' in Oct. might well be more attributable to the political situation than the French threat: Cheshire RO, DLT, Liber C, fo. 181.

[22] The itinerary has been reconstructed by Anthony Tuck, who concluded that 'the progress was coherent, if prolonged' with 'none of the aimless wandering and rapid moves suggested by the chroniclers': J. A. Tuck, *Richard II and the English Nobility* (London, 1973), 227–8, 109.

army recruited by de Vere in Cheshire and the north-west that marched on London in December 1387. The eventual débâcle at Radcot Bridge should not be allowed to detract from the importance to the king of this initiative.

The impression that the king's time in the provinces was no more than a frantic manœuvre to rustle up military support is not entirely appropriate. Though poorly documented, the royal entourage at this time was neither small nor undistinguished. The act book of the Lichfield cathedral chapter provides a valuable glimpse of the court in progress. On 29 June, the feast of Sts Peter and Paul, the king and queen attended Richard Scrope's installation as bishop. The list of the prelates, lords, and knights in attendance is virtually a list of the key members of the 'court' party: the archbishops of York and Dublin; the bishop of Chichester; the dukes of Ireland, York, and Suffolk; Lords Basset, Beaumont and Zouche; Simon Burley, John Beauchamp, John Golafre, and other knights. The king held a great feast in the bishop's palace, 'then the King's palace', to which he invited all the clergy and leading citizens of Lichfield.[23] Earlier in the month the court had been based in Coventry. The king was so taken with the city that he allegedly granted its mayor the mayor of London's privilege of having a gilded sword carried before him.[24] The councils the king held at Shrewsbury around 21 August and at Nottingham on 25 August must likewise have been majestic occasions. The questions he put to the chief justices at the two sessions, bearing on his regality and his prerogative powers, must surely attest a thoughtfulness, indeed an ideological underpinning, to his strategy at this time.[25]

The king's formal declaration of his majority in 1389 brought the crises and upheavals of 1386-8 to a sudden, if somewhat anticlimactic, end. For a number of years Richard ruled with a degree of statesmanship and moderation. Presiding over a distinguished court and a broadly based council, he settled back into a more tranquil routine, with lengthy stays at Windsor, Woodstock, Sheen, Eltham, and Langley. This period of relative stability

---

[23] Lichfield Joint RO, Dean and Chapter Act Books I, fo. 15.

[24] Knighton, ii. 235. Richard's close association with Coventry would seem to date back at least to 1385. According to an early tradition, he visited the city immediately after his return from Scotland to lay the foundation stone of the Carmelite convent on 9 Sept. 1385: W. Dugdale, *The Antiquities of Warwickshire* (2nd edn., London, 1730), 207.

[25] S. B. Chrimes, 'Richard II's Questions to the Judges, 1387', *Law Quarterly Review*, 72 (1956), 365-90. The king was attended at Nottingham by the archbishops of York and Dublin; the bishops of Durham, Chichester, and Bangor; the duke of Ireland; and the earl of Suffolk: Knighton, ii. 236-40. In mid-Sept. the royal party was lodged at Leicester abbey: Knighton, ii. 240.

lasted in some degree until the death of Queen Anne in the summer of 1394, when he had Sheen, their favourite palace, razed to the ground, and proceeded to throw himself into a major expedition to Ireland. Even so, there were in the early 1390s many signs of restlessness. In the summer of 1390 he assembled in Gloucester an eminent group of bishops and canon lawyers to consider reports of miracles at his great-grandfather's tomb.[26] He spent most of the summer of 1390 in the north Midlands, at Leicester and Nottingham, and early in 1391 he returned to the west, lingering 'now at Gloucester, and now at Bristol'.[27] Most notably, of course, there was his quarrel with London in 1392. Relations between court and capital had been strained for some time, and Richard had a range of grievances, real and imagined. Suddenly, though, he took the extreme step of transferring Chancery and King's Bench to York. The mayor, sheriffs, aldermen, and a further twenty-four citizens of second rank were ordered, 'under pain of forfeiture of life and limb' before the king at Nottingham on 29 June. London's liberties were overridden, and a Household knight, first Sir Edward Dallingridge, then the more hard-nosed Sir Baldwin Raddington, was appointed as its warden. The stage was set for Londoners to treat for the restoration of their liberties, which involved the payment of £10,000 to the Crown. In the final act in the charade of 'reconciliation' the king and queen were treated to a magnificent reception by the city on 21 August.[28]

The king was clearly looking outwards from London and the Home Counties. Even if he had no serious design to advance York as an alternative centre of government, he was certainly based in his northern capital for most of the summer of 1392. He held court again at York at Easter 1396.[29] In the mid-1390s the king spent time, and frequently transacted important business, at Nottingham, Stamford, Coventry, Winchester, and other provincial centres. It was likewise a period of documented expansion in the geography of recruitment in the royal household.[30] It is possible to trace the beginnings of a number of regional initiatives on the part of the court. In the West Country there was the increasing endowment of his half-brother, John Holand, earl of Huntingdon, in part from Crown office

[26] *Westm. Chron.* 436–9.   [27] Ibid. 440–3, 454–5.

[28] C. M. Barron, 'The Quarrel of Richard II with London 1392–1397', in *Reign of Richard II*, 173–201.

[29] J. H. Harvey, 'Richard II and York', in *Reign of Richard II*, 202–15. I am grateful to Dr N. Saul for allowing me to see his forthcoming paper 'Richard II and York: The Evidence of the King's Itinerary', in which he demonstrates that, contrary to Harvey's findings, Richard did not spend Christmas 1395 at York.

[30] Given-Wilson, *Royal Household and King's Affinity*, 220–1.

and the resources of the duchy of Cornwall but in part, too, at the expense of the Courtenays and other local magnates.[31] In the north there was a more complex reordering, with Richard first working to advance the Nevilles as a counterbalance to the Percys, and then perhaps subjecting the northern nobility to a royal lieutenant such as the duke of Lancaster or the duke of Aumale.[32] Then there was his expedition to Ireland, planned, of course, before Queen Anne's death. It involved, first of all, a progress westwards, with staging-posts at Gloucester and Hereford. He spent most of September in south Wales, visiting Cardiff and making a pilgrimage to St Davids.[33] After a show of force in Ireland, he received the submission of a succession of Gaelic 'kings' and chieftains, and celebrated Christmas 1394 and Easter 1395 'with great solemnity' in Dublin.[34]

Even at this stage it is thus instructive to see Richard's view of his domains as British rather than narrowly English. The strength and splendour of the English monarchy, after all, was held to subsist not in its geographical integrity and political cohesion but in its wide dominions and dependent peoples. It is well known that Richard sought to exalt the Crown by honouring kinsmen and favourites with grandiose titles: dukedoms became more common, and the marquisate was introduced into England.[35] In 1397, as 'entire emperor of his realm of England', the king legitimated his Beaufort cousins, raising the eldest to the peerage first as the earl of Somerset then as marquis of Dorset.[36] There are hints that the creation of client-principalities might from time to time have been contemplated. His ultimate intentions with regard to the principality of Chester cannot be ascertained. Thinking of this sort, though, may have lain behind the elevation of de Vere as duke of Ireland in 1386, the similar proposal in favour of Thomas of Woodstock in 1389, and the belief in some quarters in 1399 that he intended to have the duke of Surrey crowned as king of

---

[31] M. Cherry, 'The Courtenay Earls of Devon: The Formation and Disintegration of a Late Medieval Aristocratic Affinity', *Southern History*, 1 (1979), 90–2.

[32] J. A. Tuck, 'Richard II and the Border Magnates', *Northern History*, 3 (1968), 46–52; id., 'The Emergence of a Northern Nobility 1250–1408,' *Northern History*, 22 (1986), 14–17.

[33] Tout, *Chapters*, iii. 487 n.   [34] *Annales*, 173.

[35] C. Given-Wilson, *The English Nobility in the Late Middle Ages: The Fourteenth-Century Political Community* (London, 1987), 47–54. There are hints of other creations that were still-born, not least in 1385 when Henry Knighton believed that Sir Simon Burley had been created earl of Huntingdon, and the Westminster Chronicler thought that John Neville of Raby had been created earl of Cumberland: Knighton, ii. 205; *Westm. Chron.* 126–7. The novel creation in 1387 of a 'barony by patent' in favour of John Beauchamp of Kidderminster is likewise noteworthy: Given-Wilson, *English Nobility*, 63. See above, p. 119, for the significance of these intended creations.

[36] *RP* iii. 343; Given-Wilson, *English Nobility*, 50.

Ireland.[37] In Gaelic Ireland, and in the wider Celtic fringe, there were already chieftains who boasted royal titles. The submission of the Gaelic 'kings' in 1394–5, and their deference to his 'most exalted crown', implied a model of high-kingship or king-emperorship which Richard could not have failed to find flattering and congenial.[38] It would be interesting to know whether he encouraged his favourite, William Scrope, to use the title of king of Man.[39]

Richard II's attitude towards Aquitaine and his continental lordships can be seen to fit this general pattern. Despite being born in Bordeaux, he had no special attachment to the duchy of Aquitaine. From the 1380s he was contemplating proposals for its alienation from the Crown to endow John of Gaunt or some other English prince.[40] While this proposition was essentially a part of the peace process with France, it is worth seeing it, too, as of a piece with the proposals for a dukedom of Ireland.[41] It is tempting to attribute to Richard II a vision of his dominions akin to that of his Angevin ancestors: a loose 'empire' of principalities, duchies, and lordships, continental and insular, subject in some fashion to his Crown. The profile he cultivated in Christendom was more grandiose than his accommodations with France might otherwise indicate. The Flemish ambassadors who in 1382 acknowledged him as overlord of Flanders cannot have failed to flatter the youthful king, and Richard himself offered to take Flanders under his protection in 1390. John de Montfort, duke of Brittany, came to England in 1398, made a pact with Richard, and was reinvested with the earldom of Richmond.[42] William duke of Guelders and William of Ostrevant, the heir of the count of Holland, were more firmly in the English orbit, paying court to Richard and becoming his vassals. In 1396 Rupert count palatine

[37] As marquis of Dublin, de Vere had been granted in return for homage all royal lands and rights in Ireland: Tout, *Chapters*, iii. 397. For the proposal of 1389, see *Westm. Chron.* 378–9. For the plan to crown Surrey, see Adam of Usk, 36, 190.

[38] In general see E. Curtis, *Richard II and Ireland 1394–1395 and the Submission of the Irish Chiefs* (Oxford, 1927); D. Johnston, 'Richard II and the Submission of Gaelic Ireland', *Irish Historical Studies*, 22 (1980), 1–20.

[39] He is styled *rex Manniae* in a Chancery document recording the homage of the bishop of Llandaff to Richard II in the king's chamber at Havering atte Bower on 14 June 1396: PRO C270/25/27. For the most part he styled himself *dominus Manniae*: e.g. BL Harley Charter 56.A.22. After his elevation to the English peerage in 1397, the title of earl of Wiltshire was clearly preferred.

[40] The alienation of Aquitaine in favour of John of Gaunt was first proposed in 1375: J. J. N. Palmer, *England, France and Christendom, 1397–1399* (London, 1972), ch. 2.

[41] In 1389 plans to make the king's uncles duke of Aquitaine and duke of Ireland were linked, at least in the mind of one chronicler: *Westm. Chron.* 378–9.

[42] M. Jones, *Ducal Brittany 1364–1399: Relations with England and France during the Reign of John IV* (Oxford, 1970), 140, 194–5.

of the Rhine and duke of Bavaria likewise performed homage and became his pensionary.[43]

In considering Richard II's last years it is essential to adopt an European framework. In 1395 and 1396 the king became a focus for the ambitions and hopes of men who looked to peace and reconciliation of Christendom as a prelude to a counter-assault on the Turks and the ultimate recovery of the Holy Land. By this stage the emperor-elect Wenceslas (Wenzel), Richard's own brother-in-law, was a drunken sot, while Charles VI of France was subject to bouts of madness. Richard had much to commend him. His desire for peace with France was genuine and well known, and a final pacification could provide the basis for a healing of the schism of the western Church. From the mid-1380s, when he had been flattered into bestowing largesse on the so-called king of Armenia, he had doubtless been fantasizing about such a role. Philippe de Mézières's *Epistre au Roi Richart* and Robert the Hermit's missions to England worked in the same direction. The king's marriage to the 8-year-old daughter of Charles VI of France in 1396 was a stage in the realization of great possibilities. As the news of the defeat of the French chivalry at Nicopolis spread across Europe and as German opposition to Wenceslas mounted, Richard seemed to be drawn to a higher destiny. His half-brother, John Holand, earl of Huntingdon, was commissioned by the Roman pope to lead troops into Italy as 'Conservator of Roman Liberties'. There were serious moves to elect Richard as Holy Roman Emperor in place of Wenceslas. The dean of Cologne led a mission to this end in the summer of 1397, and over the following months Richard assiduously cultivated German allies.[44] In the circumstances it is possible to give some credence to the reported opinion that Richard's candidature was impaired only by his inability to rule his own subjects.[45]

From the autumn of 1397 the king acted like a man frantically seeking to set his own house in order. Even as he set about destroying his aristocratic opponents, he committed himself to the construction of a royalist power-base in the provinces. On 25 September he raised the earldom of Chester to the dignity of a principality, and set about the recruitment in the region of a massive retinue, including a select bodyguard of several hundred archers. In important senses, though, Cheshire was merely the

[43] J. J. N. Palmer, 'English Foreign Policy 1388–1399', in *Reign of Richard II*, esp. 79–86.

[44] *CPR 1396–1399*, 219, 220, 247; D. M. Bueno de Mesquita, 'The Foreign Policy of Richard II in 1397: Some Italian Letters', *EHR* 56 (1941), 633; Harvey, 'Richard II and York', 213–14.

[45] *Annales*, 199.

centrepiece of a larger territorial reordering. Richard was, after all, prince of Wales, and was not entirely unmindful of its resources. The grant to William Scrope, earl of Wiltshire and lord of Man, of key offices in Chester and north Wales, and lordship of Anglesey, made for a remarkable concentration of power around the Irish Sea. If Cheshire remained the 'inner citadel' of Ricardian power, neighbouring districts were drawn in to form thick curtain walls. In addition to Flintshire, the Shropshire lordships of the attainted earl of Arundel, including Holt castle, were incorporated into the principality of Chester. The earl of March's sudden death in 1398 brought the lands of another powerful Marcher lord under royal control. Finally, the acquisition of control of the Lancastrian estates early in 1399 offered the prospect of a broad belt of royalist power from south Wales across to Yorkshire.[46] All in all, it appeared an unassailable power-base from which to rule England. The orientation towards Ireland was likewise evident. The final subjection of his Irish lordship would demonstrate conclusively his mastery of his lands.[47]

His policy involved a repudiation of the traditional heart of the kingdom. The king claimed that he was not safe in his capital, and his movements in 1398–9 recall his movements in 1387. When at Westminster or Canterbury, his unruly Cheshire bodyguard was very much in evidence. The Westminster Parliament of autumn 1397 was reconvened in the new year at Shrewsbury, and through most of 1398 he perambulated the west and north Midlands, favouring with his presence Bristol, Coventry, Lichfield, Nottingham, Shrewsbury, and Chester.[48] Over Christmas 1398 the king held court at Lichfield, occupying the splendid episcopal palace and entertaining on a grand scale.[49] It was to these regional centres that a stream of foreign noblemen and churchmen came to seek him out. Among the king's guests at Shrewsbury was a chamberlain of the king of France, at Bristol the duke of Brittany, at Lichfield the kinsman of the emperor of Constantinople and the papal envoy.[50] When the king had his treasure

---

[46] Davies, 'Richard II and Principality of Chester', esp. 273–5. For developments in the north Midlands, see S. K. Walker, *The Lancastrian Affinity 1361–1399* (Oxford, 1990), 230–2.

[47] For Richard's careful monitoring of Irish affairs between 1395 and 1399, see D. Johnston, 'The Interim Years: Richard II and Ireland, 1395–1399', in J. F. Lydon (ed.), *England and Ireland in the Later Middle Ages: Essays in Honour of Jocelyn Otway-Ruthven* (Blackrock, 1981), 175–95.

[48] Tout, *Chapters*, iv. 33–5.

[49] *Vita*, 151. Earlier in 1398, on 8 Sept. the king, along with the archbishops of Canterbury, York, and Dublin; the bishops of Salisbury, Exeter; Hereford, Chichester, and Bangor; the dukes of York, Aumale, Exeter, and Surrey; and the earls of Worcester, Salisbury, Wiltshire, and Gloucester had attended the installation of Bishop Burghill at Lichfield: Lichfield Joint RO Dean and Chapter Act Books I, fos. 52ᵛ–53ʳ.

[50] Corpus Christi College, Cambridge, MS 339, fo. 48ᵛ; *CPR 1396–1399*, 361; *Vita*, 151.

taken from the Tower of London to Holt castle, and took some of the regalia from Westminster abbey on his expedition to Ireland, there was widespread and justified alarm in most of England.

Needless to say, Richard's grand schemes were stillborn. During his absence in Ireland his exiled cousin, Henry of Bolingbroke, returned to claim first the duchy of Lancaster and ultimately the Crown. Landing at Ravenspur, he swept across the Midlands, rapidly making himself master of the kingdom. After treating with the duke of York and other members of the regency council at Berkeley, he hastened north towards Chester, cutting Richard off from his formidable power-base. In the course of August 1399 the geography of the Ricardian politics was wholly inverted. Richard hurried back from Ireland, leaving most of his men and baggage in Dublin and south Wales as he made his frantic dash towards his castles in north Wales. He surrendered at Flint and became a prisoner at Chester. At Lichfield, on the road back to London, there was a bid to free him by Welsh loyalists.[51] His return to the capital was ignominious and, according to one tradition, he was brought back in disguise to save him from the mob. After his death his body was openly displayed in St Paul's London, and then taken for burial to Langley, not the magnificent tomb he had prepared at Westminster.

II

Given the vicissitudes of the time, it is hard to obtain a clear focus on the thinking that informed Richard's policies. While it is tempting to discern a strong geopolitical sense, it is obviously necessary to be cautious in attributing modern strategic thinking to rulers in the Middle Ages. In the absence of accurate maps and population figures, let alone geographical and statistical habits of mind, the safer assumption has tended to be that kings and nobles, even merchants and scholars, had a fairly nebulous view of the realm. Yet there is a danger in erring too far on the side of caution and condescension. The 1370s saw a series of experiments in taxation, including a parish tax and the notorious poll-tax, which indicate an increasing capacity to conceptualize the realm and its resources. With regard to cartography, there is still extant the Gough Map.[52] There is no reason to suppose that it represented the pinnacle of English cartography, but it would have met Richard's needs—and, for that matter, Bolingbroke's in his coup of 1399.

[51] *Traison et Mort*, 211–12.
[52] *Facsimile of the Ancient Map of Great Britain in the Bodleian Library, Oxford. A.D. 1325–50* (Ordnance Survey, 1935). Richard Exeter, monk of Westminster, and possible author of the Westminster Chronicle, owned maps of England and Scotland: *Westm. Chron.*, pp. xli–xlii.

At the same time there are signs that the king was seeking, in an age of increasing centralization around London, to resist any tendency towards a narrow conception of the locus of royal authority. It cannot be said, of course, that he was lacking a sense of royal place. His commitment to Westminster was sustained and deeply felt: Westminster Hall and his tomb, effigy, and portrait, in the abbey are, apart from the Wilton Diptych, his only significant surviving monuments.[53] Yet his kingship obstinately transcended place. He declined to put down roots, and he was prepared to have the palace of Sheen, whose amenities he had developed at enormous cost, razed to the ground. He probably felt that he was in a sense the kingdom, just as he allegedly stated that the laws of England were in his mouth and breast.[54] The privileged status of London, not least in respect of its claim to be the king's 'chamber,' was implicitly and explicitly challenged. In 1387 and in the 1390s Richard's peripatetic style was reminiscent of German imperial practice. Surrounded by his nobles and bishops he held court in his *civitates* and in abbeys of royal foundation, dignifying the ancient diocesan and monastic centres with councils and 'crown-wearing' ceremonies.[55] It is hard not to see his hand at work in the institution in March 1398 of three new feast-days in the province of Canterbury, in honour of St David, St Chad, and St Winifred.[56] A marked feature of his 'tyranny,' the subject of much deep consternation, was his moving items of his regalia, crown jewels, and valuable relics from their traditional resting-places and carrying them with him around his kingdom and lordships.

It is likewise clear that to understand Richard II's politics it is necessary to discard a rigidly and narrowly English frame of reference. It is most useful to see his Crown as comprising a congeries of lordships, with the

[53] Strangely, though, there was no place in this royal mausoleum for his immediate family: his father lay at Canterbury, his mother was buried at Stamford, and his elder brother, whose body he had brought back from Bordeaux, was reinterred at Langley. Regrettably, the shrine erected in St Paul's, London, in 1391 in honour of the Empress Elizabeth, his mother-in-law, has not survived: it was a 'very unusual imperial shrine, the like of which had nowhere been seen before': *Westm. Chron.* 516–17.

[54] *RP* iii. 419. For Richard's remark, see above, p. 46.

[55] With regard to the major feasts, he spent Christmas 1394 and Easter 1395 at Dublin, Easter 1396 at York, Christmas 1397 at Lichfield, Easter 1398 in Bristol or thereabouts, and Christmas 1398 at Lichfield.

[56] The constitution noted that the saints were buried at St David's cathedral, Lichfield cathedral, and Shrewsbury abbey. Richard's personal interest is suggested by the facts that he had recently visited all three shrines, and that the new observances languished until reinstated by Henry V. It may be significant, too, that Convocation coupled the constitution with a constitution augmenting observances for St Thomas of Canterbury. D. Wilkins (ed.), *Concilia Magnae Britannicae et Hiberniae*, 4 vols. (London, 1737), iv. 234–6; BL Cotton Charter XV/12.

peripheries and the core on a sort of continuum. His interest in adding to the dignity of his Crown by exalting the status of the dependent lordships has already been touched on. The need to set this sort of thinking in the larger framework of western Europe or, more properly, Christendom is evident enough. Richard's provincial politics and international concerns need to be seen as different sides of the same coin. In the *Epistre au Roi Richart* appealing for peace with France as a prelude for a crusade to liberate the Holy Land, Philippe de Mézières apostrophized, 'O gentle and thrice noble King of Great Britain, Prince of Wales and North Wales, Lord of Great Ireland and King of Cornwall'.[57] Significantly, too, he marvelled at Richard's achievement in Ireland in 1394, 'in bringing under his lordship, without bloodshed, a race of people as savage and uncivilised as the Irish', and saw it as evidence of God's grace and of Richard's readiness 'for the peace of his Christian brothers, for the union of the Church, and finally, for the enterprise of the holy passage'.[58] It was doubtless all music to his ears. In this sense, as in others, Richard was the last of the Plantagenets. Like them, he saw the English Crown as the core of a grander and more glorious 'British' imperium.

In making his base in the Midlands and the Welsh borderlands, and in his expeditions to Scotland and Ireland, Richard clearly demonstrated a practical engagement with the wider realm. In his perambulations around the cathedrals and monasteries of the west Midlands, and in his sojourns in cities like Bath, Chester, and Cardiff in the late 1390s, he may well have been putting himself more in touch with British, and indeed Arthurian, tradition. The concept of Britain in the fourteenth century was, after all, as much a confection of myth and prophecy as it was of cartography. It drew on the whole corpus of what was termed the 'matter of Britain', which embraced the myth of Brutus and New Troy, the career of Constantine and the legend of King Arthur, the Britons, Saxons, and Normans, and the prophetic writings of Merlin and Gildas. Richard's interest in royal antiquities, documented at least with respect to his Plantagenet and Anglo-Saxon forebears, make it inconceivable that he was unaware of this glorious past. At the same time there is every reason to suppose that he reflected deeply on this tradition and derived from it a sense of his own destiny. Oddly enough, Richard liked to present himself as prudent, and what he

---

[57] Mézières time and again apostrophizes him as king of Great Britain, though in the body of the letter he more often describes him as king of England: *Philippe de Mézières' Letter to Richard II: A Plea made in 1395 for Peace between England and France*, ed. and trans. G. W. Coopland (Liverpool, 1975), 101. For a discussion of the MS, see below, pp. 249–51.

[58] Mézières, *Letter to Richard II*, 65.

seems to have been claiming, especially in the phrase 'prudent as Homer', was the sort of wisdom which drew on the past to provide a vision of the future.[59] According to Thomas Walsingham, he fell under the influence of pseudo-prophets, who mendaciously attributed to him whatever prophecies could bear a favourable interpretation, especially, it seems, those that presented him as a future emperor and the greatest prince in the world.[60] The most celebrated prophecy was perhaps that associated with the holy oil of St Thomas of Canterbury, allegedly discovered by Richard in the Tower of London. It told of an English king anointed with this oil who after achieving victory over his enemies would liberate the Holy Land and drive the pagans from Babylon.[61]

What needs stressing is that Ireland had a place in this world of myth, history, and prophecy. According to Geoffrey of Monmouth's *History of Britain*, King Arthur had launched his glorious career in Christendom with the conquest of Ireland, and, predictably enough, prophecies about an English king who would eventually win back the Holy Land picked up on this point. Thus *The Verses of Gildas* foretold an outstanding career of success for 'our King now ruling' which would begin with a successful expedition to Ireland undertaken after a grave crisis.[62] The career is outlined in intoxicating detail. After the conquest of Ireland, the king would defeat the Scots and suppress revolt in Gascony. On his return to England, he would honour the lords who sought his grace but exile the malcontents. The king would conquer France, march through Spain and north Africa, subdue Egypt, and advance triumphantly on Babylon. After the recovery of the Holy Land, and after the pope had thrice offered to crown him, he would finally accept coronation as the emperor of the world.[63] This sort of fantasy even appears outside the prophetic tradition. A letter-book or formulary composed in the late 1390s is very revealing of the way in which the Irish campaign had fed the imagination of a clerk. He begins a series of model French letters with a letter dated 13 October 1395 from the king to John of Gaunt to enquire about the state of Ireland. In his reply, Gaunt assured the king of the loyalty of the Irish and reported a massive victory over the Scots. In a further letter to an earl, his nephew, Gaunt announced a major expedition, conducted with Irish assistance, against the

[59] Bennett, 'Court of Richard II', 16.   [60] *Annales*, 233–4.
[61] T. A. Sandquist, 'The Holy Oil of St Thomas of Canterbury', in id. and M. R. Powicke (edd.), *Essays in Medieval History presented to Bertie Wilkinson* (Toronto, 1969), 330–44, esp. 332, 337–9.
[62] J. R. S. Philipps, 'Edward II and the Prophets', in W. M. Ormrod (ed.), *England in the Fourteenth Century: Proceedings of the 1985 Harlaxton Symposium* (Woodbridge, 1986), 194.
[63] Ibid.

Wilton Diptych & Ireland 1394/5

King of Scots. The earl in turn responded with news of his father, Gaunt's brother, who was 'in the parts of Babylon' with a very fine company. The army had torched the land around Alexandria and won a great victory in an open field near Cairo. Many Saracens had been slain, and the sultan of Babylon had been taken prisoner, 'to the great honour of our lord liege the king' and 'all the chivalry of England'.[64]

If Walsingham is at all creditworthy, it is hard to imagine that Richard II was kept unaware of *The Verses of Gildas*. The version in British Library, Arundel MS 57 appears to relate to Edward II, but given Richard's identification with his great-grandfather, the association would have heightened rather than diminished his interest in it. Much of the detail, including the king's having a French queen, actually accords remarkably well with Richard's position in the mid- and late 1390s. How far this sort of fantasy may have shaped his policy towards Ireland is another matter. There is no hint of it in the records relating to the Irish campaign of 1394–5 or, for example, in Creton's account of the expedition of 1399. Further, it is hard to credit that the crudely belligerent role cast for him would have been to his taste. Still, there is a clear sense in which Ireland was important to him, and deeply and inexplicably important. In 1394–5 he assumed and then impaled the arms of St Edward the Confessor, acts of great personal significance, allegedly on account of Ireland's reverence for the saint.[65] The basis of this reverence is obscure, but the impression is that Richard was exploiting a tradition about the peace-loving king, perhaps even a prophecy about a bloodless conquest of Ireland. It was this achievement, after all, that Mézières saw as a clear sign that God had marked Richard out for his role as peacemaker and crusader. It may well help inform the Wilton Diptych, which survives as a compelling testimony to the grandeur of the king's conception of his role in the mid-1390s.[66] This prophetic, even millenarian, vision may provide a context for other odd details recorded by chroniclers: the king's carrying his regalia, including the

---

[64] BL Harleian MS 3988, fos. 39–41. In this fantasy the victor over the sultan of Babylon would appear to be Edmund of Langley, duke of York. It is worth noting that in 1395 he was the leading English member of Philippe de Mézières's new crusading order, the Order of the Passion: M. V. Clarke, 'The Wilton Diptych', in L. S. Sutherland and M. McKisack (edd.), *Fourteenth-Century Studies* (Oxford, 1937), 288.

[65] Froissart, xv. 180. For Richard's patronage of the cult of St Edward, see above, p. 42; below, pp. 259, 261–2, and 268–9.

[66] D. Gordon, *Making and Meaning: The Wilton Diptych* (London, 1993), esp. 59–60. Recent restoration has revealed a miniature of an island painted on the boss of the standard handed by the king to the Virgin Mary. The assumption has been that it represents England: ibid. 57–8. It could equally well, if not more appropriately, represent Ireland. For other comments on the Diptych, see above, pp. 10–13; below, pp. 265–70.

ampulla containing the holy oil of St Thomas of Canterbury, to Ireland; his alleged intention to call a Parliament in Dublin and create his nephew king of Ireland; and his alleged talk of laying down the Crown of England, presumably in preparation for higher honours.[67]

All in all, Richard clearly had a vision of his realm which was richer, broader, and more transcendental than the nation-state whose increasing definition and integration have been assumed to be the main concerns of English kings from the later Middle Ages on. Political circumstances encouraged Richard to look outwards from London, to cultivate power-bases in the provinces, and ultimately to make regional centres his headquarters. His tilt at the pretensions of London may have originated in pique, but may well have been nourished by a growing awareness of a larger British identity. His kingship may have been peripatetic and regionally based in the late 1390s, but it was universalist in ambition. Drawing inspiration from the 'matter of Britain', and from the auspicious challenges and opportunities in Christendom, he was willing to be flattered into considering, if not into actively pursuing, a grand crusading vision. What he had in mind when he left for Ireland in 1399, apart from a resolve to suppress rebellion, can never be known. Within a month he had to return in haste to Wales and England to face insurrection, betrayal, deposition, and death. Suffice it to say that in the late 1390s Ireland was no mere sideshow: its pacification appears to have been central to some larger design.

[67] Adam of Usk, 36 and 190; C. L. Kingsford (ed.), *Chronicles of London* (Oxford, 1905), 52.

10

Richard II and the House of Luxemburg

Anthony Tuck

In January 1377 the Anglo-French peace negotiations, which had got under way at Bruges in the summer of 1374, finally broke down. No agreement had proved possible on the issues dividing the two sides, and all that they could achieve was a prolongation of the general truce until 24 June 1377. Charles V made one last effort in May 1377, with a series of proposals which the English envoys agreed to place before Edward III and return to Bruges with a response by 1 August. However, Edward III died on 21 June 1377; the English never kept their appointment at Bruges, and the war began again on 24 June.[1]

The breakdown of the Bruges negotiations and the resumption of the war necessitated, so far as the English were concerned, a renewed search for allies amongst those rulers of western Europe, particularly in the Empire, the Low Countries, and the Iberian peninsula, who might share England's interest in countering French power. In the early months of 1377 English attention was directed particularly towards the Iberian peninsula. During the Parliament of January 1377 the chancellor had warned that the French king, supported by the king of Castile and the Scots, was planning to attack England by land and sea in the coming summer.[2] England's ineffective naval response has been discussed in some detail by James Sherborne;[3] but the diplomatic reponse in the early months of 1377 was firmer. In English eyes one of the keys to effective countermeasures against Franco-Castilian naval

---

[1] E. Perroy (ed.), 'Anglo-French Negotiations at Bruges, 1374–1377', *Camden Miscellany*, xix (London, 1952), 64–8, 81–5.
[2] *RP* ii. 362.
[3] 'The English Navy: Shipping and Manpower 1369–1389', *Past and Present*, 37 (1967), 163–75; 'The Cost of English Warfare with France in the Later Fourteenth Century', *BIHR* 50 (1977), 135–50.

power was the group of ports in Normandy which formed part of the inheritance of Charles II of Navarre, and of which Cherbourg was the most significant. An English envoy, Sir Edward Berkeley, spent most of 1377 in Navarre, and although we have no first-hand account of his mission its results in all probability figured in the confession of Charles of Navarre's chamberlain, Jacques de Rue, who was captured and arrested by the French in the early months of 1378.[4] Although Rue's confession was extracted under torture, it is probably true in all essentials, though some of his more lurid admissions, such as that Charles of Navarre had plotted to poison the French king, may perhaps be discounted. The French king reacted by sending troops to seize Charles's castles in Normandy, though they failed to take Cherbourg, and Charles now sought to bring his negotiations with England to a successful conclusion. Froissart suggests that Charles himself visited London in June 1378,[5] but whether or not the visit took place the English and Navarrese reached agreement in a treaty that was ratified on 1 August 1378. Charles agreed to lease Cherbourg to Richard II for a period of three years, and in return Richard II's government agreed to send 500 men-at-arms and 500 archers to help Charles in his war against the king of Castile.[6] During the Anglo-Navarrese contacts of 1377–8, if Jacques de Rue's confession is to be trusted, the two sides discussed a number of marriage proposals as well as a military alliance.[7] Perhaps the most significant of these proposals was that for a marriage between Richard II himself and a Navarrese princess. Indeed, the evidence of the confession suggests that the English were very keen for such a marriage: they gave the Navarrese the impression that the hand of their princess would be valued even above that of the emperor's daughter Anne of Luxemburg, whom the emperor had proposed as a bride for Richard II in 1377.[8] However, much of this

---

[4] *Chronique des Règnes de Jean II et de Charles V*, ed. R. Delachenal, 4 vols. (Paris, 1910–20), ii. 286–305; M. Secousse (ed.), *Receuil de pièces servant de preuves aux Mémoires sur les Troubles excités en France par Charles II dit le Mauvais Roi de Navarre et Comte d'Evreux*, 2 vols. (Paris, 1755), ii. 375; P. E. Russell, *The English Intervention in Spain and Portugal in the Time of Edward III and Richard II* (Oxford, 1955), 255–61; R. Delachenal, *Histoire de Charles V*, 5 vols. (Paris, 1909–31), v. 180–97.

[5] Froissart, ix. 57–60. *Foedera*, vii. 196–7: safe conduct for the king of Navarre, valid for a year, to come to England, dated 31 May 1378. Russell, *English Intervention*, 258; Delachenal, *Charles V*, 5, 197–213.

[6] *Foedera*, vii. 201–2.

[7] *Chronique de Jean II et de Charles V*, ii. 289–90; Secousse (ed.), *Receuil de pièces*, 381.

[8] E. Perroy, *L'Angleterre et le grand schisme d'occident* (Paris, 1933), 136–7 n. 1, 137. See also the confession of Jacques de Rue, Secousse (ed.), *Receuil de pièces*, 381–2 and the discussion in N. Saul, *Richard II* (London, 1977), 83. The English bargaining position in Navarre might well have been strengthened by letting it be known that the emperor's daughter had been proposed as a bride for Richard. However, the emperor remained on good terms with France at least until after his visit to Paris in Jan. 1378.

may have been intended to ensure that Charles of Navarre could be persuaded to lease Cherbourg; Froissart said that 'li Englès désiroint moult
à estre seigneurs' of the fortress,[9] and once the lease had been agreed English
relations with Navarre cooled somewhat. Richard II's lieutenant in
Aquitaine, John lord Neville, dragged his feet over assembling the force
promised to Navarre, and when it finally set out for Navarre at the end
of October 1378 under the command of Sir Thomas Trivet it probably
numbered far fewer men that had originally been agreed. The war with
Castile, however, went badly for Charles of Navarre; by the Treaty of
Briones in March 1379 he had to agree to dispense with the services of
all English or Gascon mercenaries, and to promise that 'no child of his
would marry an English prince'. If the proposal for an Anglo-Navarrese
marriage alliance had been a serious proposition in 1377 and 1378, the
Treaty of Briones effectively put an end to it.[10]

For the English, the negotiations with Navarre in 1377 gave them what
was, in all probability, their chief objective: the lease of Cherbourg. The
Treaty of Briones might make any future English intervention in the Iberian
peninsula more difficult, for Navarre was effectively neutralized by the
treaty, but in the opening years of Richard's reign the eyes of the English
government were more firmly set on countering French aggression in the
north, and the acquisition of Cherbourg strengthened that 'barbican' on
the other side of the Channel which Richard Scrope persuaded Parliament in 1378 was worth paying for.[11]

Cherbourg was an important acquisition, but the reassertion of traditional English diplomacy following the renewal of the war with France
in 1377 was soon to be focused on the Empire and the Low Countries
rather than the Iberian peninsula or Charles of Navarre's Norman inheritance. Shortly after Richard II's accession, the emperor, Charles IV of
Luxemburg, had written to the council in England suggesting a marriage
between his daughter Anne and the young king of England.[12] It does not
seem that either side took the proposal very seriously at this stage. The
English rejected it, and on the imperial side there is no reason to suppose
that it marked a decisive departure from the pro-French stance which the
House of Luxemburg had maintained since the time of Charles's father
John II who had died fighting against the English at Crécy in 1346. In the
last year of Charles IV's life, the maintenance of good relations with France
seems to have been uppermost in his mind. In January 1378 he visited Paris

---

[9] Froissart, ix. 59.
[10] Russell, *English Intervention*, 270–1; Perroy, *Grand Schisme*, 212 n. 1.
[11] *RP* iii. 34, 36.   [12] Perroy, *Grand Schisme*, 136; Saul, *Richard II*, 83.

and in a series of meetings and ceremonies, reported in highly favourable terms by the French official chronicler, he reiterated his support for the French king.[13]

After dinner on 8 January 1378, Charles V of France assembled his counsellors and treated his guest to a lengthy denunciation of the English, accusing them of being unwilling to make peace despite the success of French armies since 1369. He sought the emperor's verdict on the peace terms which had been put forward at Bruges: the emperor accepted that Charles's analysis of the Anglo-French dispute was correct and suggested that, although the English might sue for peace when the war was going against them, they would break their agreement if they regained the upper hand. This general declaration of support, however, did not satisfy Charles V, and on the following day, after the emperor had taken counsel with his advisers, the two rulers met again. This time the emperor told Charles V that he regarded himself and his family as allies of the king of France, though he did not go as far as formally renewing the Franco-Luxemburg alliance.[14] Charles V had to be content with this: the lavish reception he had given the emperor probably served to ensure that the emperor would not respond in the immediate future to any overtures from England. However, behind the emperor's favourable rhetoric there was little of real substance, and indeed it is unlikely that the English problem was at the forefront of the emperor's mind.

The emperor's most immediate concern in 1378 was probably the succession to the Hungarian and Polish Crowns. King Louis I (the Great) of Hungary, who had also succeeded to the throne of Poland in 1370, had no male heir, but his wife Eizabeth of Bosnia had given birth to three daughters, Catherine in 1370, Mary in 1371, and Jadwiga (Hedwig) in 1373. Louis became a father late in life, and the marriage of his daughters, together with the destiny of his two kingdoms, became an issue of some importance almost as soon as they were born. Neither in Poland nor in Hungary did Louis have an entirely free hand, for a settlement of the succession issue would require the agreement of the nobility of each country. In Poland, the personal union with Hungary had been unpopular with the nobility. Few of the Polish nobles had any objection in principle to an Angevin succession in Poland, but they expected their monarch to reside in the kingdom and they were therefore unlikely to accept that both the Polish and the Hungarian Crowns should devolve upon one of the three daughters

---

[13] *Chronique de Jean II et de Charles V*, ii. 210–75.
[14] This discussion is based on the account, ibid. 246–65, and Delachenal, *Charles V*, v. 61–119.

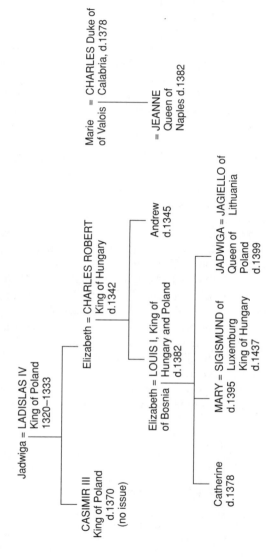

FIG. 10.1. Genealogical table showing succession to the Polish and Hungarian Crowns

of King Louis. The question was further complicated by Louis's claim to be the heir of Queen Jeanne of Naples, whose territories included Provence, long coveted by the French kings. One historian has suggested that Louis intended each of his daughters to inherit one of the crowns which he wore or claimed, and that Catherine, the eldest, was destined for Naples, were he able to regain his right there with the help of France and the papacy.[15] Even if such a neat solution was in Louis's mind, however, it was never formally agreed; papal support for Louis's right in Naples was not forthcoming and the idea was in any case rendered nugatory by Catherine's death in 1378. The succession to the inheritance of Louis of Hungary was to become an issue with ramifications well beyond central Europe.

As king of Bohemia and lord of Silesia and Brandenburg, the emperor could not remain indifferent to the fate of the Hungarian and Polish Crowns, and the dynastic ambitions of the House of Luxemburg were now focused on the acquisition of at least part of Louis I's inheritance. In 1372, when Mary of Hungary was barely 1 year old, the emperor had begun negotiations for her marriage to his second son Sigismund, with the expectation that either Poland or Hungary (or possibly both) would thus pass into the Luxemburg orbit. On 6 December 1374 Pope Gregory XI issued the dispensation necessary for the betrothal to take place.[16] Some months before the issue of the papal dispensation for the betrothal of Mary and Sigismund, the French and Hungarian courts had opened negotiations for the marriage of Louis I's eldest daughter Catherine to Charles V's second son Louis count of Valois (later duke of Orléans).[17] In April 1374 a Hungarian embassy led by the bishop of Zagreb left Buda for Paris, and on 10 August the marriage treaty was concluded. For Charles V, the main significance of the marriage treaty was that Catherine would receive as her dowry the right which her father claimed to the Crown of Naples and the

---

[15] B. Hóman, *Gli Angioini di Napoli in Ungheria 1290–1403*, trans. from Hungarian by L. Zambra and R. Mosca (Rome, 1938), 431. See also G. Léonard, *Les Angevins de Naples* (Paris, 1954), 444–6. In the peace treaty which followed Louis I's unsuccessful invasion of the kingdom of Naples in 1352, Louis renounced his claim to the kingdom in return for an indemnity of 300,000 florins; but Louis later declined to accept the indemnity and in the 1370s still regarded his claim to Sicily as valid, even though it was not accepted by the papacy. Léonard, *Angevins*, 364–5, 446.

[16] E. Jarry, *La Vie politique de Louis de France, duc d'Orléans* (Paris, 1889), 9.

[17] *Chronique des Quatre Premiers Valois*, ed. S. Luce (Paris, 1862), 249; Jarry, *Vie politique*, 4–14; N. Valois, 'Le Project de mariage entre Louis de France et Catherine d'Hongroie et le voyage de l'Empereur Charles IV a Paris', *Annuaire-Bulletin de la Société de l'Histoire de France*, 30 (1893), 209–23; Delachenal, *Charles V*, v. 88–90.

counties of Provence and Piedmont.[18] This, however, depended on papal confirmation of Louis of Hungary's right in Naples and, despite the persuasive efforts of a Hungarian embassy which visited Gregory XI at Avignon later in 1374, the pope refused to issue the necessary confirmation.[19] The negotiations between Charles V and Louis of Hungary continued: over the autumn and winter of 1377–8 the two sides exchanged embassies, and we are informed of the outcome of the negotiations in a letter which Charles V wrote to Louis of Hungary in late January or early February 1378.[20] Louis of Valois and Catherine were to be married when Catherine reached marriageable age. Louis's right in Naples was to be safeguarded even if the marriage were childless and Catherine predeceased him, and Provence was to become a hereditary fief of the house of Valois. Charles also asked Louis to obtain from the Hungarian nobility recognition of Catherine as future queen of Hungary. Although there is no doubt that Provence was important to Charles, the establishment of a cadet branch of the House of Valois on the Hungarian throne was now perhaps an objective of some independent significance, not least perhaps because there was no realistic prospect of Catherine becoming queen of Naples.

The Hungarian embassy to Paris coincided with the visit of the emperor, and there is no doubt that the two monarchs discussed the question of the Polish and Hungarian succession.[21] The proposed marriage between Louis of Valois and Catherine raised fears in the emperor's mind about the Polish succession, for Catherine, as the eldest daughter, might well claim right in Poland as well as in Hungary. The emperor evidently asked Charles V to accept a Luxemburg succession in Poland and in effect to renounce any right that Louis of Valois might acquire in Poland by virtue of his marriage to Catherine. Charles felt unable to give the clear guarantee that the emperor sought and, in his letter to Louis of Hungary a few weeks later, declared that he would not accept the Luxemburg title to Poland without consulting Louis and obtaining his approval.[22] Despite the outward cordiality of his relations with the emperor, Charles V was not willing simply to concede the enhancement of Luxemburg power that would follow from Mary's and Sigismund's accession in Poland.

[18] Jarry, *Vie politique*, 7–8. For the text of the treaty and subsequent clarifications see ibid. 369–82. See also M. de Ferdinandy, 'Ludwig I von Ungarn (1342–1382)', in S. B. Vardy, G. Grosschmid, and L. S. Domonkos (eds.), *Louis the Great, King of Hungary and Poland* (New York, 1986), 37. He stresses the importance of the Mediterranean in the Valois–Anjou alliance.
[19] Ibid. 7–8.   [20] Printed by Valois, 'Projet de mariage', 221–2.
[21] Delachenal, *Charles V*, v. 88–90.   [22] Valois, 'Projet de mariage', 221–2.

Hungary and Poland were thus more pressing concerns of the emperor in 1378 than England or the Anglo-French dispute. Despite the efforts of Charles V no formal alliance between France and the Empire was concluded and the French king had to be content with a general declaration of support and a promise by Charles's son and heir Wenceslas, who travelled to Paris with his father, that he would maintain the *entente* with France after his father's death.[23] The emperor did not wish to commit himself to a formal alliance with France when his main concern lay in the east, but it was even less likely that he would respond favourably to any overtures from England after the rejection of his proposal for a marriage between Anne and Richard II in the previous year.

While he was in western Europe, there was one remaining problem for the emperor to settle. His younger brother Wenceslas duke of Brabant had no heirs and the succession to the duchy was a matter of great interest for England, France, and the emperor. The duchy had come to Wenceslas by his marriage to Jeanne, eldest of the three daughters of John III of Brabant, and the emperor naturally hoped that the duchy (together with the duchy of Limburg) would now devolve permanently on the House of Luxemburg. Charles V for his part hoped that the duchy would pass to Jeanne's niece Margaret, heiress of Flanders and wife of Philip duke of Burgundy, Charles V's brother: in these circumstances Brabant would move firmly into the French orbit. Since the collapse several years earlier of Edward III's proposal to marry Margaret of Flanders to his own son Edmund of Langley, the English had no dynastic interest in the Brabançon succession but every reason to oppose the eventual union of Flanders and Brabant under a cadet branch of the House of Valois. England and the emperor thus had a common interest in the fate of Brabant, and in 1378 Wenceslas of Brabant concluded a treaty with his brother and suzerain the emperor under which, if he died without issue, the duchy would pass to his nephew Wenceslas king of the Romans.[24] It was highly likely, however, that the French would seek to prevent this treaty being implemented when it came to the point and that the Franco-Imperial *entente* would thereby be weakened. Indeed, the succession both in Brabant and in central Europe offered the potential for conflict between Valois and Luxemburg ambitions.

All this, however, lay in the future. During the last months of the emperor's life he was preoccupied with two more pressing, and inter-

[23] *Chronique de Jean II et de Charles V*, ii. 248–58, 264–5.

[24] H. Laurent and F. Quicke, 'Les Origines de l'État Bourguignon: L'Accession de la Maison de Bourgogne aux duchés de Brabant et de Limbourg, 1383–1407', *Memoires de l'Académie Royale de Belgique*, 41/1 (1939), 63–117.

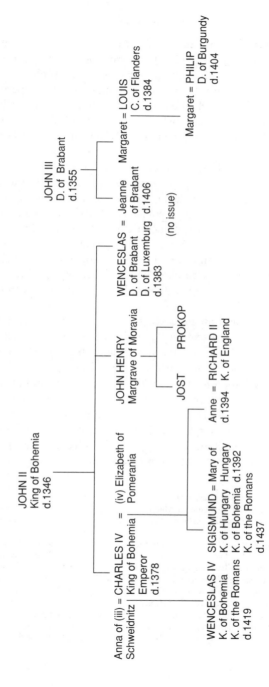

FIG. 10.2. Genealogical table of the House of Luxemburg

related, problems. His son and heir Wenceslas had been nominated king of the Romans at an imperial diet in July 1376,[25] but the emperor was anxious to obtain recognition from Pope Urban VI of his son's title, to pave the way towards his eventual coronation as emperor. The emperor's task, however, was made more difficult by the outbreak of schism within the papacy when the conclave of rebel cardinals elected Robert of Geneva as Pope Clement VII in September 1378, and Clement took up residence at Avignon.

The emperor rejected the claims of Clement VII and recognized Urban VI as the canonically elected pope: with his overriding concern for papal confirmation of Wenceslas's title, he could do little else but accept Urban, resident in Rome. If such a stance entailed a breach with France, it served to indicate once again that the emperor's priority remained the retention of the imperial succession within his own dynasty and the advancement of the dynasty's interests in central Europe. Recognition of Urban VI was virtually the final act of the emperor's life: he died on 29 November 1378 and in the last weeks of his life he urged his son Wenceslas to maintain his allegiance to Urban.[26]

Wenceslas IV, who now inherited the Crown of Bohemia but not all the other lands of the Luxemburg dynasty, has had little sympathy from historians.[27] His conflicts with the Bohemian nobles, which twice led to his capture and imprisonment, his deposition as king of the Romans in 1400, and his abdication in favour of his brother Sigismund in 1410 perhaps bear out these strictures, at least as far as the years after 1390 are concerned. In 1378, however, he gave every appearance of following his father's policies of support for the Roman pontiff and safeguarding the interests of the Luxemburg dynasty, primarily in central Europe. Yet he had to do so with resources which in no way matched his commitments[28]

---

[25] B. Jarrett, *The Emperor Charles IV* (London, 1935), 234.

[26] N. Valois, 'Le Grand Schisme en Allemagne de 1378 à 1380', *Römische Quartalschrift*, 8 (1893), 116–17; P. Stacul, *Il Cardinale Pileo da Prato* (Rome, 1957), 102; Perroy, *Grand Schisme*, 130–6.

[27] Wenceslas inherited Bohemia; Sigismund was given Brandenburg; Charles IV's youngest son received Gorlitz, while his nephew received Moravia. This division had been made some years before Charles IV died; Jarrett, *Charles IV*, 236. Stacul described Wenceslas as more interested in hunting than canon law in *Cardinale Pileo*, 116. Perroy called him 'indolent, young, inexperienced' in *Grand Schisme*, 158. R. Vaughan referred to his 'periodic drunkenness' in *Philip the Bold* (London, 1962), 54.

[28] Bohemia possessed important silver-mines, but there is some doubt about how profitable they were in the last quarter of the 14th cent. See M. M. Postan and H. J. Habakkuk (edd.), *The Cambridge Economic History of Europe*, 8 vols. (2nd edn. Cambridge, 1966–89), ii. 722–3.

and at a time when the dynasty's traditional understanding with France came under severe pressure. Hence, perhaps, the overtures to England which were soon to follow.

The outbreak of the schism coincided with the death in 1378 of Louis of Hungary's eldest daughter Catherine, who had been betrothed to Louis of Valois. For Charles IV in the last months of life, and now for Wenceslas IV, this created a situation which, like the schism, offered the threat of a direct conflict of interest with France. For Charles V, the obvious move might have been to activate a clause in the 1374 marriage treaty which provided for Louis of Valois to marry another of Louis of Hungary's daughters in the event of Catherine's death.[29] However, the outbreak of the schism made such an alliance unlikely. In a joint declaration in June 1379, Louis I and Wenceslas proclaimed their adhesion to Urban VI. Louis's decision may have been motivated at least in part by his enmity towards Queen Jeanne of Naples, with whom the Clementist cardinals had considerable influence. As we have seen, Louis still maintained his claim to Naples, and he had never been satisfied that Queen Jeanne had accepted her share of responsibility for the murder in 1345 of his brother Andrew, who had been her second husband.[30] However, the French made efforts to persuade Louis to transfer his allegiance to Clement VII. These efforts came to nothing, and for the moment the idea of a Franco-Hungarian marriage alliance seemed dead. Indeed, the biographer of Louis of Valois suggested that in 1381 Charles VI's court proposed that Louis should marry a daughter of the duke of Lancaster.[31] Only in the very different circumstances of 1383 in Hungary did the marriage of Louis to Mary of Hungary seem, for a short time, a viable proposition.

Wenceslas IV's immediate task in 1379, however, was to bring the German princes into the Urbanist camp and prevent the schism acting as a means for the weakening of what authority he possessed in Germany as king of the Romans and for the extension of French influence into the western parts of Germany. Wenceslas summoned an imperial diet to meet at Frankfurt in February 1379.[32] Charles V sent ambassadors there in the

---

[29] Valois, 'Project de mariage', 220; Jarry, *Vie politique*, 7–8, 11, 22, 369–82. In a clarification of the 1374 treaty, issued by Louis I in 1375, he had excluded those of his daughters who were already betrothed: thus Mary could not in Louis's eyes be a candidate for marriage to Louis of Orleans (Jarry, *Vie politique*, 382).

[30] Léonard, *Angevins*, 346–7.

[31] Jarry, *Vie politique*, 361–2; Froissart, xiii. 111–12, where the proposal is mentioned, but in a context that implies it was put forward later than 1381, possibly in 1385 or 1386.

[32] T. Lindner, *Deutsche Geschichte unter den Habsburgern und Luxemburgern, 1273–1437*, 2 vols. (Stuttgart, 1893), ii. 108.

hope that they might persuade some of the German princes to adhere to the Clementist cause, but the French ambassadors were shunned as schismatics and scarcely given a hearing. The diet appeared to go very much Wenceslas's way. Most of the German princes agreed to recognize Urban VI, but the superficial unity of the diet concealed misgivings amongst some German princes, particularly those from the Rhineland and the Low Countries, about Wenceslas's support for Urban.[33]

A number of historians have seen Pileo da Prato, the cardinal archbishop of Ravenna as one of the main influences on the young Wenceslas, and have argued that he played a leading role in the negotiations with England which now ensued.[34] On 20 May 1379 Wenceslas wrote to Richard II proposing an Anglo-Luxemburg alliance which would form the nucleus of an anti-Clementist league.[35] There is no explicit evidence that Wenceslas proposed a marriage between his half-sister Anne and Richard at this stage, though Édouard Perroy thought that it was probable.[36] However, in March 1379 Michael de la Pole, Sir John Burley, and George Felbrigg had set out for Italy with the power to arrange a marriage between Richard and Catherine, daughter of Bernabò Visconti of Milan. From Milan de la Pole and Burley proceeded to Rome, and according to Perroy it was then that the Anglo-Milanese negotiations broke down.[37] Perroy suggested that the idea of an Anglo-Luxemburg marriage was put to de la Pole and Burley by the pope, who flattered them that it would be a distinguished match for Richard and that it would offer some hope of a coalition against Charles V of France. Whatever the truth of this, it is possible that there had been direct contact between Wenceslas and English envoys at the Frankfurt diet in February 1379, before de la Pole and Burley reached Milan or Rome. The biographer of Anne of Luxemburg suggested that de la Pole himself may have met Wenceslas at the Frankfurt diet in February 1379. Perroy argued that this could not be so, but there is reason to believe that some English envoys may have been present at the diet.[38] Preliminary

---

[33] Perroy, *Grand Schisme*, 132–6; Valois, 'Grand Schisme en Allemagne', *passim*.

[34] Perroy, *Grand Schisme*, 134–6; Stacul, *Cardinale Pileo*, 119–21, 134–5.

[35] Perroy, *Grand Schisme*, 140; Stacul, *Cardinale Pileo*, 119–21.

[36] Perroy, *Grand Schisme*, 140 n. 4.   [37] Ibid. 138–9.

[38] C. Hofler, *Anna von Luxemburg* (Vienna, 1871), 129; Perroy, *Grand Schisme*, 141 n. 2; Valois, 'Grand Schisme en Allegmagne', 120 n. 3. The suggestion that English envoys may have been present at the February diet rests on a letter from the papal nuncio Perfectus de Malatesti, abbot of Sitria, to the Franciscan Peter of Aragon, son of James II of Aragon. Malatesta states that 'procuratores regis Anglie' attended the diet and that French envoys attended to make the case for Clement VII (J. Weizsäcker (ed.), *Deutsche Reichstagsakten unter König Wenzel*, 3 vols. (Munich, 1867)), i. 264–5. The problem with this evidence is that Malatesta may have confused or telescoped the Feb. and Sept. diets. Peter of Aragon received the letter on 3 Nov. 1379, but as Weizsäcker points out (ibid. i. 264–5 nn. 1 and 2), the date of the letter suggests that it relates to the Sept. diet, but the contents to the Feb. diet.

soundings about an Anglo-Luxemburg alliance might well have been made there, for it is not necessary to believe that the proposal was concocted in Rome. None the less papal encouragement was an important factor in the negotiations with Wenceslas which now ensued. De la Pole and Burley met Wenceslas, probably at Prague in October, and the two sides evidently agreed to proceed with negotiations. In June 1380 an English embassy was dispatched to Prague, and over the autumn and winter of 1380–1 negotiations between the two sides went ahead smoothly.[39]

In the circumstances of 1379–80, very different from those in which the emperor Charles IV had been fêted in Paris, an Anglo-Luxemburg alliance had some advantages for both sides. For England it would mark the effective revival of her traditional friendly relationship with the Empire, which had not survived the election of Charles IV as emperor. The English evidently hoped for an alliance with Wenceslas against France and that Wenceslas could be persuaded to abandon the House of Luxemburg's traditional alignment with France. The alliance would be sealed by a marriage between Richard and a princess of one of the leading dynasties in Europe, whose new head had aspirations to the imperial crown which his father had worn. The eventual failure of the House of Luxemburg to establish a permanent position for itself amongst the leading dynasties of Europe should not blind us to its power and prestige at the end of the fourteenth century. Charles IV had been a dominant figure in the politics and culture of central Europe throughout his long reign. His heir Wenceslas was now confirmed by papal bull as king of the Romans and might eventually expect to have the imperial crown placed upon his head by the pope. He was already king of Bohemia, and his family had an interest in the succession to the kingdoms of Poland and Hungary, as well as the duchy of Brabant—of great concern to England. Were Wenceslas to succeed his uncle as duke of Brabant, an Anglo-Luxemburg alliance might ensure the survival of some English influence in the Low Countries despite the marriage of Margaret of Flanders to Philip of Burgundy. Whatever Wenceslas's personal failings, the Luxemburg star must have seemed in the ascendant in 1379. Pope Urban VI was no doubt correct when he tried to persuade de la Pole and Burley that a Luxemburg marriage conferred more prestige and status on Richard than marriage to the daughter of the ruler of Milan.

If the advantages to England of an alliance with the House of Luxemburg were obvious, it is less clear what Wenceslas expected to get out of it. As we have seen, the main interests of the House of Luxemburg lay far away from the traditional area of English involvement in Europe, though

---

[39] Perroy, *Grand Schisme*, 140–2, 145–6.

both sides shared an interest in ensuring that Brabant did not pass to Margaret of Flanders and Philip of Burgundy. Wenceslas had no wish to commit himself to an alliance directed specifically against France, not least because his scarce resources were likely to be called upon to maintain his position in Germany and Bohemia. Indeed, it seems likely that Wenceslas's main motive in negotiating with England was financial rather than religious or political: neither the formation of an anti-Clementist league nor an anti-French coalition with England were high priorities for him. On the other hand there is clear evidence that he was short of money: in May 1380, for example, Wenceslas's chancellor, the archbishop of Prague, stated that Wenceslas was in very great debt and could no longer raise any money from the Jews of many of the cities in the Empire.[40] The English chroniclers give the same impression and evidently believed that money was the essence of the agreement.[41]

The Anglo-Luxemburg negotiations of 1379 and 1380 were watched in Paris with alarm.[42] Charles V immediately offered larger concessions than before in the hope of obtaining an Anglo-French settlement and suggested a marriage between Richard II and his younger daughter Catherine, who would bring the county of Angoulême as her dowry. This was a shrewd move, for Wenceslas was unlikely to be able to offer anything very substantial by way of dowry for Anne. However, the English were not interested in the French proposal and, as a means of bringing pressure to bear on France, they concluded an agreement with Duke John of Brittany in March 1380.[43] Despairing of the English, Charles turned to Wenceslas in the hope that he could win the hand of Anne for the dauphin, soon to be Charles VI. Wenceslas was not anxious to see his relationship with France deteriorate any further. He agreed to send an embassy to Paris and on 20 July 1380 he renewed the Franco-Luxemburg alliance, but he made it clear that he was not prepared to consider a marriage alliance.[44]

In the event neither side was seduced by French promises, and Wenceslas reached an agreement with Richard II on 2 May 1381.[45] The marriage treaty

---

[40] Stacul, *Cardinale Pileo*, 143 n. 6.   [41] *Hist. Angl.* ii. 46; *Westm. Chron.* 24.

[42] Perroy, *Grand Schisme*, 142–3; Delachenal, *Charles V*, v. 226–7; *Chronique de Jean II et de Charles V*, ii. 370.

[43] Delachenal, *Charles V*, v. 364–5; M. Jones, *Ducal Brittany: Relations with England and France during the Reign of John IV* (Oxford, 1970), 89–91. The treaty was followed by an expedition to northern France led by the earl of Buckingham, which spent the winter of 1380–1 fruitlessly besieging Nantes. John of Brittany was also negotiating with Charles VI of France. The negotiations culminated in the second Treaty of Guérande, which in effect aligned Brittany with France (Jones, *Ducal Brittany*, 91–7). The treaty marks another setback for traditional English diplomacy.

[44] Perroy, *Grand Schisme*, 144–5.   [45] *Foedera*, iv. 111–13.

embodied an agreement that there should be a 'union and league between Richard and the King of the Romans and Bohemia against schismatics' and English merchants were to enjoy the right to trade freely by land and sea in all the territories of the Empire and the Bohemian Crown. There was more substance to this commercial clause than might appear at first glance. There was little cordiality between English merchants and the merchants of the Hanse in the Baltic, and although as king of the Romans Wenceslas could expect to exercise little influence over the Hanse diet at Lübeck, his brother Sigismund's lands in eastern Brandenburg lay close to the dominions of the Teutonic Knights, whose influence over the Hanse towns of the eastern Baltic, such as Danzig, was substantial. An Anglo-Luxemburg alliance might thus produce some commercial benefits for English merchants trading there.[46] On the same day Wenceslas acknowledged a loan from Richard of 20,000 florins (about £3,500 sterling) to be repaid at Michaelmas 1382[47] and four days later Richard formally agreed to lend Wenceslas 80,000 florins (about £13,000 sterling) 'for his expenses and to support his necessities'. This money was paid to Wenceslas over the following months.[48]

The marriage was greeted without enthusiasm in England. The English chroniclers believed that the alliance was essentially a financial transaction for the benefit of the king of the Romans. Thomas Walsingham went so far as to suggest that the purpose of the visit to England of the cardinal archbishop of Ravenna in 1380 was not just to negotiate the marriage alliance but also to take out of the realm a vast sum of money.[49] This sum of money, according to Walsingham, was raised by the sale of indulgences and other rights and privileges, while the Monk of Westminster stated bluntly that Richard had bought Queen Anne.[50] The English chroniclers never viewed the queen with much favour. Her Bohemian entourage attracted criticism and even scandal when Robert de Vere, earl of Oxford repudiated his wife, a granddaughter of Edward III, and ran off with Agnes Lancecrona, one of the ladies in the household of the queen.[51] Richard's own attitude, however, seems to have been very different. Although the queen produced no heir for Richard, his relationship with her seems to have been genuinely affectionate and his outburst of destructive grief at

---

[46] For a discussion of Anglo-Hanseatic relations in the early years of Richard II's reign, see T. H. Lloyd, *England and the German Hanse, 1157–1611* (Cambridge, 1991), 56–66.
[47] *Foedera*, iv. 113.   [48] Ibid. 116.   [49] *Chron. Angl.* 283.
[50] *Westm. Chron.* 24.
[51] Ibid. 188–90, see now Saul, *Richard II*, 92–3 and n. 36. See above, pp. 40–1, for another perspective on the Bohemian connection.

her death in 1394 is well known.[52] Indeed, Richard may well have seen his marriage as giving him the status at which the pope had hinted in 1379. In 1393, for instance, he ordered masses to be said for the soul of his mother-in-law Elizabeth of Pomerania, who died that year, and the Westminster Chronicler tells us that Richard had an 'imperial shrine' of a hitherto unheard-of design constructed in St Paul's cathedral.[53]

From the diplomatic point of view, however, the alliance proved unsuccessful from the outset. Wenceslas reaped the financial reward, but otherwise he did little to breathe life into the alliance. The English made considerable efforts to persuade Wenceslas to form an anti-French coalition with them. On 16 August 1382, for instance, ambassadors were sent to Prague to negotiate an alliance which would be directed 'especially against Charles present occupant of the kingdom of France', his uncles and the kings of Castile and Scotland, but nothing of any substance came from the negotiations.[54]

Almost certainly, the English expected too much from Wenceslas. The papacy saw the Anglo-Luxemburg treaty as no more than a marriage alliance[55] and there is no reason to suppose that Wenceslas had either the resources or the will to make an effective commitment to the English cause against the French. Wenceslas was also anxious to avoid a complete rupture with France and, together with Louis of Hungary, he had continued to negotiate with Charles VI in the early months of 1381.[56] It is possible that Wenceslas's anti-Clementist fervour was waning. By now some pro-Clementist elements were beginning to make their influence felt in the court at Prague, and the German princes remained divided in their allegiance.[57]

Yet in the event the failure of the Anglo-Luxemburg alliance was not just the result of Wenceslas's lack of resources and his desire to maintain good relations with France. Nor was it a matter of English inertia.[58]

[52] *King's Works*, ii. 998; Adam of Usk, 8–9; *Vita*, 134.

[53] *Westm. Chron.* 516. Four letters from Richard II to his mother-in-law the dowager empress Elizabeth survive, all written in affectionate terms. E. Perroy (ed.), *Diplomatic Correspondence of Richard II* (Camden Soc., 3rd ser. 48, London, 1933), nos. 35, 57, 62, 140; also p. 193 note to letters 33–9. In one letter (no. 62, dated by Perroy to sometime after June 1386), Richard refers in a flattering manner to the coronation of her son (Sigismund) as king of Hungary. The success of the Luxemburg cause in Hungary would have been a source of more than merely personal satisfaction of Richard, for Sigismund's coronation ended the threat of Valois influence establishing itself there. See below, p. 223.

[54] *Foedera*, iv. 151, 163.   [55] Stacul, *Cardinale Pileo*, 142.

[56] Perroy, *Grand Schisme*, 148–9.

[57] Valois, 'Grand Schisme en Allemagne', *passim*.

[58] See e.g. J. J. N. Palmer, *England, France and Christendom, 1377–1399* (London, 1972), 57.

Rather it came about through a sequence of events in Europe between 1382 and 1384 which decisively affected the essential interests of the House of Luxemburg, revealing the English alliance as the diplomatic irrelevance that it almost certainly was for Wenceslas.

On 11 September 1382 King Louis I of Hungary died, and the long-foreseen crisis over the Hungarian succession erupted. His elder surviving daughter Mary was now potentially heiress to both the Polish and the Hungarian crowns, though her succession in both kingdoms was likely to be challenged. Mary was betrothed to Wenceslas's half-brother Sigismund, but as we have seen the Franco-Hungarian treaty of 1374 had left the way open for a marriage between Louis of Valois and another of Louis of Hungary's daughters.

The succession in Poland, however, was resolved without major or prolonged conflict. In 1379, after Catherine's death, Louis I had persuaded the Polish nobility to accept Mary as their future queen and in 1382, shortly before his own death, he had persuaded the Polish nobles to do homage to Sigismund as well, though this met with some resistance. Two months after Louis died, the Polish nobles offered to do homage to either of Louis's two surviving daughters provided she and her husband agreed to live in Poland. Even this was not acceptable to all the nobles: some felt bound by their oath to Sigismund; others favoured a native prince, the duke of Masovia. Civil war was averted only by the dowager queen Elizabeth agreeing to absolve the nobles from their oaths to Mary and Sigismund and the Polish nobles uniting around the proposal that Jadwiga, Louis's youngest daughter, should become their queen.[59] However, she was not yet 12 and her nominal husband William of Austria was unacceptable to the Poles, who found another candidate for her hand in Jagiello prince of Lithuania. With the support of the Polish nobility, Jadwiga was crowned as 'king' of Poland on 15 October 1384 and in 1386 she was maried to Jagiello of Lithuania, inaugurating the long period of dynastic union between the two countries.[60]

Thus the ambition of the House of Luxemburg to inherit the throne of Poland had come to nothing. In Hungary, however, all the ingredients for civil war seemed to be in place at Louis's death. Only a few days after

---

[59] This discussion is based on the account of events in 'Chronicon Polonorum Johannis de Czarnkow', ed. A. Bielowski in *Monumenta Poloniae Historica* (Lwów, 1872), 721–36. For a discussion of the reliability of John of Czarnkow and an analysis of the Polish succession problem after 1382, see O. Halecki, 'From the Union with Hungary to the Union with Lithuania: Jadwiga, 1374–1399', in W. F. Reddaway *et al.* (edd.), *Cambridge History of Poland* (Cambridge, 1950), 189–96.

[60] Halecki, 'Union with Hungary', 194, 195–9.

Louis died, Mary was crowned queen of Hungary, but the queen mother, Elizabeth of Bosnia, was effectively in control of much of the country, and Mary was not universally recognized as queen by the nobility. In particular, neither the queen mother nor many of the nobility seem to have been enthusiastic about Sigismund ruling Hungary as Mary's husband. Furthermore Charles of Durazzo put forward a claim to the Crown as Louis's nearest male heir, a claim which had some appeal to those Hungarian nobles who were opposed to female succession and which was strongly supported by the nobility of Croatia and Dalmatia.[61]

Faced with the threat of invasion by both Charles of Durazzo and Sigismund, the dowager queen Elizabeth turned to France for support and in 1384 opened negotiations for a marriage between Mary and Louis of Valois.[62] If this proposal had been made after Catherine's death in 1378 it would have come up against the problem that the two dynasties recognized rival popes, but in 1384 Elizabeth was desperate and the schism was not permitted to stand in the way of the negotiations. The proposal was received with enthusiasm in Paris and, if Froissart is to be believed, Jean de la Personne was sent to Buda to marry Mary in the name of Louis of Valois.[63] The proxy marriage was celebrated in April 1385 by the bishop of Győr, acting on the authority of a dispensation issued by Clement VII annulling the betrothal of Mary to Sigismund. The marriage was not recognized by those of the Hungarian nobility who adhered to Pope Urban VI and the conflict over the succession was now complicated by religious schism.[64]

In August 1385 Sigismund arrived on the Hungarian border with a mercenary army.[65] The towns of Bratislava and Nyitra accepted him without resistance and he was able to make rapid progress in face of the disunity of his opponents: when he reached Buda he and Mary were married by

[61] S. Guldescu, *History of Medieval Croatia* (The Hague, 1964), 227–32; A. de Regibus, 'Il declino degli Angioini d'Ungheria sotto Carlo III di Durazzo', *Rivista storica italiana*, 52 (1935), 369–410.

[62] Jarry, *Vie Politique*, 22–3; Hóman, 459–61; Froissart, x. 343.

[63] Hóman, *Angioini di Napoli*, 461; Jean Le Fèvre, *Journal*, ed. H. Moranvillé (Paris, 1887), 139 (Le Fèvre was bishop of Chartres and chancellor to Louis duke of Anjou: the *Journal* covers 1380–9). Froissart, x. 343–4, says that the queen of Hungary's proposal seemed 'moult haute et moult noble' to the French court.

[64] Hóman, *Angioini di Napoli*, 461.

[65] This discussion is based on Hóman, ibid. 465–6. It is significant that Froissart devotes some attention to this episode. He says that Sigismund arrived in Hungary with an army of 10,000 men, and that some of the French nobles were not unhappy that the Hungarian marriage-plan collapsed, for they said that Hungary was a far-away place 'et mal en le main pour les François' (Froissart, x. 371–4).

the archbishop of Esztergom, regardless of both the opposition of the queen mother and Mary's previous 'marriage' to Louis of Valois. When the news was brought to France the following month by one Durant Bastide, a resident of Montpellier, Jean Le Fèvre recorded in his journal that 'le frere du Roy des Romains nommé Symon a pris à fame la fille de Hongroie que devoit avoir monsegneur de Valois'.[66]

The dowager queen Elizabeth retaliated to the marriage by trying to deprive the archbishop of his see, and in face both of Charles of Durazzo's invasion of southern Hungary in October 1385 and the continuing hostility of many of the Hungarian nobility Sigismund was unable to consolidate his *coup de main*. He returned to Bohemia in the late autumn of 1385. However, Charles of Durazzo's short-lived attempt to reign as Charles II ended with his murder on 24 February 1386 and in April Sigismund returned to Hungary, this time with the support of his half-brother Wenceslas and Jost and Prokop of Moravia: the Luxemburg family now united to enforce Sigismund's claim in Hungary. For Sigismund, the price of support from his family was high: he granted Brandenburg to Wenceslas, and he raised a loan of 200,000 gold florins from his cousins Jost and Prokop of Moravia, who received as security for the loan the Hungarian border provinces of Trencsen, Nyitra, and Bratislava.[67] The resources of the Luxemburg dynasty, such as they were, were now to be used to ensure that at least part of Louis of Hungary's inheritance fell to Sigismund.

There can be little doubt that the problems in central Europe which followed Louis of Hungary's death preoccupied Wenceslas between 1382 and 1386. Wenceslas's chief councillors were all men whose position and interests lay in central Europe. The archbishop of Prague, John of Jenstein, was his chancellor; Martin canon of Olomouc was the treasurer of the household of the dowager empress Elizabeth and the nobles most prominent at his court in Prague included the duke of Teschen, the duke of Silesia, and the margrave of Moravia. These men played a leading part in the negotiation of the Anglo-Luxemburg alliance but they were likely to view the dynasty's position in central Europe as their primary concern. German historians have pointed to a conflict between Wenceslas's dynastic interests and the interests of the Empire and have suggested that his dynastic interests were taking precedence by 1385, when Wenceslas

[66] Le Fèvre, *Journal*, 187.

[67] Hóman, *Angioini di Napoli*, 466. Le Fèvre recorded events in Hungary in his *Journal*, not least because Charles of Durazzo had contested Louis of Anjou's title to the throne of Sicily. He notes Charles of Durazzo's coronation as king of Hungary (p. 235) and his murder (pp. 245–6, 248).

began to prepare for intervention in the civil war in Hungary.[68] As far as the alliance with England was concerned, it necessarily seemed of limited significance to Wenceslas when he was faced with pressing problems for his dynasty in central Europe. In the one issue over which the Anglo-Luxemburg alliance was tested—the succession to Brabant—it was found wanting largely because of Wenceslas's preoccupation with central Europe. From the English point of view, the revival of traditional diplomacy after 1376 was characterized not just by an Anglo-imperial alliance but also by the search for allies in the Low Countries. Little could be done by this time to prevent Flanders moving into the Franco-Burgundian orbit as a result of the marriage of Margaret heiress of Flanders to Philip of Burgundy: the failure of the bishop of Norwich's crusade in the summer of 1383 served merely to underline the collapse of English influence there.[69] However, English interest in the Low Countries had not traditionally been confined to Flanders. The ruler of Hainault, Holland, and Zeeland, Albert of Wittelsbach, occupied a strategic position to both the north and the south of Flanders. Relations between England and Hainault had traditionally been cordial, and in the early 1380s John of Gaunt began negotiations for a marriage between his daughter Philippa and Duke Albert's heir, William count of Ostrevant. Albert's sister Joanna was already married to Wenceslas IV and, had the marriage between the count and Gaunt's daughter taken place, it would not only have strengthened English influence in the Low Countries but would have brought the Low Countries' branch of the Wittelsbach family more firmly within the Anglo-imperial orbit.[70] Further east, the duke of Guelders, who was also heir to the duchy of Juliers, maintained the traditional pro-English stance of his family and was cultivated in the early 1380s by the duke of Teschen as the main bastion of imperial influence in the Low Countries. Indeed, it has been suggested that the duke hoped that Wenceslas IV might transfer his right in Brabant to him.[71] Thus at the death of Wenceslas of Brabant on 8 December 1383, the prospects for the advancement of Anglo-Luxemburg interests in the Low Countries were far from hopeless; yet within sixteen

[68] See for this H. Weigel, 'Männer um König Wenzel: Das Problem der Reichspolitik 1374–1384', *Deutsches Archiv für Geschichte des Mittelalters*, 5 (1942), 112–77 and id., 'König Wenzels persönliche Politik. Reich und Hausmacht 1384–1389', *Deutsches Archiv für Geschichte des Mittelalters*, 7 (1944), 153.

[69] See e.g. J. S. Roskell, *The Impeachment of Michael de la Pole Earl of Suffolk in 1386* (Manchester, 1984), 42–3.

[70] Froissart, x. 307–11; Palmer, *England, France and Christendom*, 58.

[71] Palmer, *England, France and Christendom*, 55; Laurent and Quicke, 'Origines de l'État Bourguignon', 96–7.

months Franco-Burgundian influence was in the ascendant throughout the region. For Wenceslas IV, the death of his uncle of Brabant could hardly have happened at a worse moment. Just as Luxemburg interests in central Europe seemed threatened by the instability following Louis I's death, the death of the duke of Brabant laid the way open to the expansion of Franco-Burgundian influence in the Low Countries. Wenceslas of Brabant, however, had been ruler not merely of Brabant and Limburg but also of Luxemburg. Under the Treaty of Ath in 1357, Luxemburg was to revert to the descendants of Charles IV if Wenceslas died childless. Wenceslas IV's succession in Luxemburg was uncontentious, and in August 1384 he arrived there to receive the homage of the nobility of the duchy.[72] The position in Brabant and Limburg, however, was more complex. Duke Wenceslas's right there had derived from his wife Jeanne, and under the Treaty of Ath Wenceslas and Jeanne had recognized the right of the count of Flanders to succeed in Brabant if they remained childless. With the death of the count of Flanders a few weeks after that of Duke Wenceslas, his right in Brabant passed to his daughter Margaret, wife of Philip duke of Burgundy.[73] If this right were recognized, the way would be open to the establishment of Franco-Burgundian ascendancy in Brabant and Limburg. Such an outcome was not in the interests of Wenceslas IV, Richard II, or the duke of Guelders. A complicating issue was whether Jeanne could rule Brabant and Limburg in her own right for the rest of her life. Brabant and Limburg, however, were imperial fiefs, and in principle Wenceslas had the right to regulate their succession and, in particular, to bar female succession. In practice, the effective exercise of imperial suzerainty over the two fiefs was likely to prove beyond his resources.

Initially, Wenceslas relied on the duke of Teschen to safeguard his interests in the Low Countries. In early December 1383, at the moment of Duke Wenceslas's death, the duke was in the Low Countries seeking to build up a pro-Luxemburg party there, and on 10 December he obtained the agreement of the dukes of Guelders, Juliers, and Berg to an alliance in which they undertook to uphold the honour and right of the king of the

---

[72] Laurent and Quicke, 'Origines de l'État Bourguignon', 103–5. For Wenceslas IV's itinerary in these years, see I. Hlaváček, 'Studie k Diplomatice Václava IV: Itinerář krále Václava IV (1361–1419)', *Československý Časopis Historický*, 10 (1962), 72–5. F. X. Wurth-Paquet (ed.), 'Table chronologique des chartes et diplomes relatifs à l'histoire de l'ancien pays de Luxembourg: Règne de Wenceslas II, roi des Romains et de Bohème', *Publications de la section historique de l'Institut Royal Grand-Ducal de Luxembourg* (Luxemburg, 1850), 12–22.

[73] Vaughan, *Philip the Bold*, 80, 95–6. Wenceslas of Brabant died on 8 Dec. 1383; Louis de Male, count of Flanders died on 30 Jan. 1384.

Romans. There can be little doubt that the duke expected William duke of Guelders to be the spearhead of this alliance. In March 1384 the duke of Teschen moved to Brabant and at exactly the same time Philip of Burgundy travelled there with the object of persuading Jeanne to accept the right of his wife Margaret in the two duchies. Wenceslas himself left Prague on 29 June and reached Luxemburg on 6 August.[74] Both Burgundy and the Empire were now focusing their diplomatic and financial resources on the Low Countries. Wenceslas's departure for the west at a time when the Hungarian crisis was nearing its climax was a measure of the seriousness with which he took the threat to Luxemburg interests in the Low Countries and his right as king of the Romans to regulate the succession to an imperial fief. Wenceslas remained in the Low Countries until 25 November, holding a series of meetings with the dowager duchess Jeanne and with the duke of Guelders.[75] However, Wenceslas had few weapons at his disposal apart from diplomacy. Unlike Philip of Burgundy, who was using both his own resources and the resources of the French monarchy to build up support amongst the nobility of Brabant, Wenceslas lacked the means to build up a network of clients in Brabant and could not compete with the appeal of the duke of Burgundy as a patron.[76] Whatever resources Wenceslas possessed were needed to support the dynasty's right in Hungary. Wenceslas had perforce to rely on others to maintain his interests in the Low Countries. Indeed, so desperate was he for resources to maintain the dynasty's position in central Europe that in February 1388 he mortgaged his ancestral duchy of Luxemburg to his cousin Jost Margrave of Moravia,[77] who in fact never visited the duchy. Faced, perhaps, with a choice between defending his interests in the Low Countries and supporting the Luxemburg position in Hungary, it is not surprising that Wenceslas and the Prague court chose the latter. Wenceslas remained in Bohemia throughout 1385 and in the spring of 1386 he was in Hungary. Not until 1398 did he make another visit to the Low Countries.[78]

Froissart portrayed the dowager duchess Jeanne as a pivotal figure in the diplomatic manœuvring which took place over the winter of 1383–4.

[74] Laurent and Quicke, 'Origines de l'État Bourguignon', 77–80, 98–100, 102–3; Hlaváček, 'Studie', 74.

[75] Laurent and Quicke, 'Origines de l'État Bourguignon', 106–14; Hlaváček, 'Studie', 74. Wenceslas was at Cologne in early Dec. and returned to Prague in early Jan. 1385.

[76] Laurent and Quicke, 'Origines de l'État Bourguignon', 81–6. Wenceslas attempted to raise money by the sale of fiefs in Luxemburg: e.g. in Nov. 1384 he sold his castle and lordship of Schoneck to the archbishop of Trier for 30,000 florins: Wurth-Pacquet (ed.), 'Table chronologique', 21–5.

[77] Wurth-Pacquet (ed.), 'Table chronologique', 57–8.　　　[78] Hlaváček, 'Studie', 75, 82,

In his opinion, she appreciated the threat to Franco-Burgundian interests posed by the negotiations for a marriage between Phillipa of Lancaster and the count of Ostrevant, and set herself to prevent it happening.[79] At the same time, Philip of Burgundy's embassy to Brabant apparently procured from her an agreement in principle to an eventual Burgundian succession in the duchies of Brabant and Limburg.[80] Whether Jeanne's own wishes proved more important in determining the outcome of the negotiations than Philip of Burgundy's patronage may be open to question, but by January 1385 it was clear that she was going to get her way, at least as far as the marriage of the count of Ostrevant was concerned. At a conference held at Cambrai in that month, attended by Jeanne, Philip of Burgundy, and Albert of Holland-Hainault, it was agreed that William of Ostrevant should marry Philip's daughter Margaret, and William's sister, also called Margaret, would marry Philip's eldest son John of Nevers. This double marriage was celebrated in April 1385 and was described in some detail by Froissart.[81] It has been argued that the 'Cambrai weddings' represented a substantial setback for English interests in the Low Countries. Certainly John of Gaunt was unhappy with the outcome of his suit on behalf of Philippa. According to Froissart, he sent a delegation to confront Albert of Hainault-Holland at Le Quesnoy, but the delegation received a dusty answer. Albert apparently told Gaunt's envoys that it was not Gaunt's place to concern himself with when, how, where, or to whom Albert married his children.[82]

The Cambrai weddings ensured that Burgundian rather than English influence was preponderant in Holland and Hainault, but it is not clear that they made any immediate difference to the situation in Brabant. Although in the marriage treaty between John of Nevers and Margaret of Wittelsbach John's right to succeed in Brabant through his mother Margaret of Flanders was explicitly recognized, no doubt with the ready agreement of the dowager duchess Jeanne, the Burgundian succession there could not yet be taken for granted. The loyalty of the Brabançon towns to the Burgundian cause was still doubtful and, more importantly, the duke of Guelders was making bellicose noises on Brabant's eastern border. His hostility to Burgundian claims in Brabant suggests that both Richard II and Wenceslas IV might find him a reliable ally, and the government of Richard II kept in touch with him in 1384 and 1385. It has been argued that the

[79] Froissart, x. 307–11.
[80] Laurent and Quicke, 'Origines de l'État Bourguignon', 87–9.
[81] Froissart, x. 314–15.
[82] Palmer, *England, France and Christendom*, 58. Froissart, x. 312–14.

English showed litle energy in pursuing these contacts with Guelders, and
the duke himself made no move yet. However, in September 1386 he
declared war on Jeanne of Brabant. The new regime in England which
followed the impeachment of Michael de la Pole in October 1386 concluded
an offensive alliance with him in June 1387, and in July he wrote to Charles
VI, addressing him as 'Charles who call yourself king of France', and repudiating his allegiance to him.[83] Open war between France and Guelders
broke out in September 1388 and although this ended in a truce Philip's
rights in Brabant were still insecure. Indeed, in 1397–8 Philip and the duke
of Guelders were again at war, and not until 1403 were Burgundian rights
in Brabant formally recognized. During these years both Richard II and
Wenceslas IV relied on the duke of Guelders to resist Burgundian ambitions in Brabant, and he proved the most dependable and consistently
loyal of all the Low Countries rulers whom Richard and Wenceslas dealt
with. Nor did Richard II refuse to subsidize his ally: the Anglo-Guelders
alliance of 1387 made provision for the duke to receive an annual pension
of £1,000 from Richard, which was paid at least until 1392; and the duke's
readiness to go to war against Philip ensured that Brabant remained a
major problem, and a serious distraction, for Philip for the rest of his life.[84]

Although the outcome of the negotiations which followed the death of
Wenceslas of Brabant could not in any sense be described as favourable
to England and to Wenceslas, neither were they quite as catastrophic as
has sometimes been argued. The prospect of bringing Hainault into the
English orbit had vanished, but the outcome in Brabant remained uncertain throughout the remaining years of Richard II's reign. If neither English
nor Luxemburg interests had made much headway in the Low Countries
it was not for want of trying. John of Gaunt's reaction to the failure of
the Hainault marriage negotiations suggests that he took them seriously
and had hoped for a successful outcome, while Richard II maintained
contacts with the most reliable opponent of Burgundian ambitions in the
Low Countries, the duke of Guelders. During Michael de la Pole's period
of office as chancellor, the English government may not have been either
as prompt or as generous as it should have been in supporting the duke,
but the duke's hostility to Burgundian ambitions in the Low Countries
remained strong, and the 1387 alliance provided evidence of renewed

---

[83] *Foedera*, vii. 535–8; Palmer, *England, France and Christendom*, 57–8, 91–2; for the date
of the treaty, see ibid. 103 n. 11; L. Douët d'Arcq, *Choix de pièces inédites relatives au règne
de Charles VI*, i (Paris, 1863), no. 39; Vaughan, *Philip the Bold*, 98.

[84] *Foedera*, vii. 535–8; Vaughan, *Philip the Bold*, 96–101; PRO Exchequer Issue Rolls
E.403/536 m. 11.

English interest in and commitment to the duke's cause. As far as the alliance with Wenceslas was concerned, there was little that either Richard and de la Pole or their opponents in 1387 could do to breathe life into it. Wenceslas's most pressing problems lay in the east; his mortgaging of the duchy of Luxemburg in 1388 symbolized his effective abandonment of his interests in the west, and throughout the period of the Anglo-Luxemburg alliance he lacked the resources to make any serious impact in the Low Countries. In the last analysis, perhaps Pope Urban VI was right to see the Anglo-Luxemburg alliance as merely a marriage treaty. In view of the religious divisions in Germany, Wenceslas was unlikely to join England in an anti-Clementist crusade, even if Richard II had been willing to embark on such an enterprise. Throughout his reign, too, Wenceslas had shown himself most reluctant to allow any open breach with France, even though their interests conflicted in Hungary, in Brabant, and over the papacy: for both diplomatic and financial reasons Wenceslas was in no position to offer England any effective help against France. England's return to older patterns of diplomacy after 1376 served only to show how much had changed in Europe since the 1340s; in the Low Countries Burgundian influence, underpinned by the resources not just of Philip himself but also of the French monarchy, made any effective revival of English interests there most unlikely; while the imperial dynasty was now preoccupied with its family politics in central Europe and could no longer act as an effective counterweight to French influence in the Low Countries. The events of the years between 1382 and 1385 had demonstrated that the network of alliances which England had traditionally sought to develop in north-west Europe was no longer viable, and a new policy towards France was necessary.[85]

[85] I should like to thank Professor Nigel Saul for reading and commenting on a draft of this chapter.

I I

Richard II and the Literary Arts

Patricia J. Eberle

In the literary as in the visual arts, the reign of Richard II coincides with a period of remarkable achievement. Although not all texts can be dated securely, this period includes the work of four of the most important poets in Middle English: Geoffrey Chaucer, John Gower, William Langland, and the anonymous poet of *Sir Gawain and the Green Knight*. Despite their wide variety in style and subject-matter, it is possible to find common themes among the works of these poets, including themes related to questions of kingship or governance, broadly defined.[1] Any attempt to move beyond this very general statement, however, and establish a connection between individual works and the policies or literary tastes of Richard II himself is forced to confront the scarcity of direct evidence for royal patronage of those literary works most highly valued today.[2] Literary historians who have

---

[1] J. A. Burrow, *Ricardian Poetry: Chaucer, Gower, Langland and the Gawain Poet* (London, 1992). Burrow explicitly disclaims any direct influence of Richard II on the style or subjects of these poets.

[2] G. Mathew, *The Court of Richard II* (London, 1968) argued for a distinctive court culture fostered by Richard and evident in the literature and art of the period; the essays in *English Court Culture* all raise serious questions about the value of Mathew's arguments and evidence. R. F. Green's *Poets and Princepleasers: Literature and the English Court in the Late Middle Ages* (Toronto, 1980), 3–12 and *passim*, the most comprehensive study of the subject to date, discusses the kinds of evidence available for literary patronage at the court. N. Saul's 'The King and his Court', in his *Richard II* (New Haven, 1997), 327–65 is now essential reading on the distinctive features of Richard's court. Several specialized studies discuss in more detail associations of varying kinds between Richard's court and writers such as Geoffrey Chaucer, John Gower, Thomas Usk, and Sir John Clanvowe, as well as the French poets Oton de Granson and Jean Froissart. D. Pearsall's *Life of Geoffrey Chaucer* (Oxford, 1992), 180, credits Richard with creating an environment that encouraged literature and the arts; A. J. Minnis, 'Chaucer's Shorter Poems: Social and Cultural Contexts', in *Oxford Guides to Chaucer: The Shorter Poems*, ed. A. J. Minnis with V. J. Scattergood and J. J. Smith (Oxford, 1995), 9–35, offers a judicious review of the scholarship to date and the issues involved.

addressed this problem have all been faced with the same conundrum: very few of the literary works surviving from Richard's reign can be shown to be directly connected with royal patronage, and very few of the works directly connected with royal patronage would be regarded today as literary. Perhaps because most of the works that can be connected directly to Richard's patronage are not primarily of literary interest, they have seldom been the subject of detailed analysis, and the available information on the nature and conditions of their production varies widely. An annotated list of all texts known to me which were commissioned by or addressed to Richard appears below, as a preliminary step towards an improved understanding of his patronage of writing. Not all of the works have been edited,

P. Eberle, 'The Politics of Courtly Style at the Court of Richard II', in G. S. Burgess and R. A. Taylor (edd.), *The Spirit of the Court: Selected Proceedings of the Fourth Congress of the International Courtly Literature Society (Toronto, 1983)* (Cambridge, 1985), 168–78, argues that this cultural environment was part of a larger programme linking 'magnificence' with Richard's regalist policy. In 'Court Politics and the Invention of Litrature: The Case of Sir John Clanvowe', in D. Aers (ed.), *Culture and History, 1350–1600: Essays in English Communities, Identities and Writing* (Detroit, 1992), 7–41, L. Patterson shows that socio-political tensions at Richard's court fostered a complex and densely allusive literary discourse. Others argue that the environment created by Richard's affinity in Cheshire may be connected with the sophisticated alliterative poetry associated with this region; see M. J. Bennett, 'The Court of Richard II and the Promotion of Literature', in B. A. Hanawalt, *Chaucer's England: Literature in Historical Context* (Minneapolis, 1992), 3–20 and J. M. Bowers, '*Pearl* in its Royal Setting: Ricardian Poetry Revisited', *Studies in the Age of Chaucer*, 17 (1995), 111–55. Chaucer, the most important of the poets involved and the one who most directly and continuously benefited from Richard's patronage, remains a special case. P. Strohm documents direct links between Chaucer and the king's affinity (*Social Chaucer* (Cambridge, 1989), 24–46); he also offers support for the claim, first made in the 15th cent. by John Shirley, that the envoy to an unnamed 'prince' in Chaucer's balade 'Lak of Stedfastnesse' was addressed to Richard and was connected, if indirectly, with Chaucer's appointment as clerk of the king's works on 12 July 1389 (*Hochon's Arrow: The Social Imagination of Fourteenth-Century Texts* (Princeton, 1992), 57–74). This appointment, however, like the others which Chaucer received from Richard, was no sinecure (Pearsall, *Chaucer*, 210), and there are no extant records of direct payment for Chaucer's poetic services even if, as L. D. Benson argues, *The Parliament of Fowls* may have been written to celebrate the betrothal of Richard and Anne of Bohemia ('The Occasion of *The Parliament of Fowls*', repr. in T. M. Andersson and S. A. Barney (edd.), *Contradictions: From Beowulf to Chaucer* (Aldershot, Hants., 1995), 175–97. John Lydgate (*Fall of Princes*, prologue, i. 330) claimed that Chaucer's *Legend of Good Women* was written at the request of Queen Anne, and one version of the prologue to that work urges that it be given to 'the quene . . . at Eltham or at Shene' (F Prologue, 496–7); for a review of scholarship on its possible relationship to Richard's court, see *The Riverside Chaucer*, 3rd edn., ed. L. D. Benson (Cambridge, 1987), 1059–65 and, for discussion of possible allusions to Richard himself see D. Wallace, *Chaucerian Polity: Absolutist Lineages and Associational Forms in England and Italy* (Stanford, 1997), 365–70. Although Chaucer was connected to the royal affinity for most of his writing career, and although many references, direct and indirect, to Richard and political issues current in his reign, have been found in his writings, none of his extant works were dedicated to or commissioned by the king. For an important discusson of Richard's books, see above, pp. 43–4.

and, of those that have, some modern editions are not widely available. Given these limitations, the main purpose of the present study is to call attention to the value these works have for an understanding of the political significance of Richard II's patronage of letters. The focus of interest here is on the image of the king that emerges from the works addressed to him. It is true that the evidence these works provide for Richard's own interests and views is problematical; for most of them, we have no way of knowing how much the king actually read, and still less what he thought of what he did read. Moreover, in works of this kind, the truth value of the direct addresses and references to the king cannot be expected to be high; like most works soliciting the favour of a patron, they portray Richard not as he was but as he liked to imagine himself. The task the writers set themselves in their addresses to the king is not the reflection of reality but what is now called the social (or better, textual) construction of reality.[3] As such, however, these works do have something to tell us about the image of kingship Richard was trying to project, at least in so far as it was perceived by those who attempted to reflect it in their own writing. Although the royal patron addressed by these works is only an image, it is an image that provides valuable insights into the idea of royal prerogative as it was understood by Richard and his adherents.

The works for which we have evidence of a connection with Richard's patronage are a diverse lot, and the evidence for the connection varies in reliability. If the list were limited to the extant presentation manuscripts known to have been commissioned by Richard, it would be very short; only one presentation manuscript of a commissioned work, Bodley 581, has been securely identified, and even in this manuscript it is not clear that all of the texts included were directly commissioned by the king. For the purposes of this study, however, the list can be made somewhat longer: it includes all works addressed or presented to the king in the hopes of attracting his favour, whether or not they succeeded in their attempt. (Works like 'Richard the Redeless' that make no pretence of attracting the royal favour and address the king as a rhetorical ploy are omitted here as belonging to another kind of enquiry.) Since the list is meant to stimulate

[3] On the praise of rulers as a literary tradition, see O. B. Hardison, *The Enduring Monument: A Study of the Idea of Praise in Renaissance Literature* (Chapel Hill, NC 1962). On the 'social construction of reality' see P. L. Berger and T. Luckmann, *The Social Construction of Reality: A Treatise in the Sociology of Knowledge* (New York, 1967). For a detailed account of language used to describe and praise Richard in other kinds of documents, together with an account of its political significance, see N. Saul, 'Richard II and the Vocabulary of Kingship', *EHR*, 110 (1995), 854–77.

further work on the subject, it also gives references to modern editions and discussions of each work. The order is roughly chronological, given the problems of dating individual works.

1. *Processus factus ad coronacionem domini regis Anglie Ricardi secundi post conquestum anno regni sui primo* (1377).[4] Beginning with an account of various magnates and citizens suing in the Court of Claims for the right to serve their king at his coronation, and including a description of the ceremonies and festivities surrounding the coronation service as well as the service itself, the *Processus* seems designed not only to maintain a record of coronation serjeanties but also to commemorate for posterity the image of a loyal nobility faithfully and harmoniously supporting the dignity of the Crown. The manuscript of the *Processus* in the Public Record Office states explicitly that John of Gaunt delivered this account of the proceedings 'by his own hands' to be enrolled in Chancery, and the image of kingship it presents appears to reflect Gaunt's views. The speeches recorded make clear that, even in cases of primarily symbolic importance, the distribution of patronage depended on a delicate balance of hereditary right and royal prerogative; the text repeatedly stresses that, where hereditary rights are ambiguous or contested, it is the prerogative of the king to appoint serjeanties according to his own pleasure.

It is often argued that the coronation ceremonies made a lasting impression on the young Richard. Evidence for this argument is provided by a copy of the *Processus* which is included in a manuscript compiled in 1386 for Richard II (BL MS Cotton Nero D. VI, fos. 65–9, discussed below); the *Processus* recorded at the order of John of Gaunt was evidently designed not merely as a matter of public record, but as a memorial of royal dignity to be kept before the eyes of the king himself.

2. A letter of advice addressed to Richard II in some 600 lines of Latin elegiac verse (*Vox Clamantis*, bk 6, chs. 8–18) by John Gower. The first version of the letter (*c.*1382), which he describes as written 'in praise of the king' (6. 6. 587), mixes conventional advice to princes with praise

---

[4] L. G. W. Legg (ed.), *English Coronation Records* (London, 1901), 131–50 (Fr. and Lat.), 150–68 (trans.), ed. from the MS in PRO CR I Ric. II. mem. 45. See also H. G. Richardson and G. O. Sayles, 'Early Coronation Records', *BIHR* 13 (1935), 129–45, which lists other MSS of the *Processus*, 131 n. 1, and describes the *Processus* as 'drawn up under the personal supervision of John of Gaunt', 132–3. Although records of a Court of Claims before a coronation exist as early as 1236, and a record of the proceedings in 1327 was deposited in Chancery, there is no precedent for the the the fully articulated and detailed *Processus* of 1377. The 1327 document is printed in H. G. Richardson and G. O. Sayles, 'Early Coronation Records 5: Some Coronation Serjeanties', *BIHR* 14 (1937), 1–8.

of a sort calculated to appeal particularly to Richard, including a lengthy portrait of his father the Black Prince.[5] Although he altered the text at a later date, in this version Gower refers to criticisms of Richard's government only to defend the young king against his detractors.[6] In addition to matters common in the tradition of advice to princes, Gower addresses more topical and controversial issues, such as the relation between the king and the law, and the nature and composition of the King's Council; while stressing the king's personal obligation to obey the moral law, Gower subscribes to an exalted view of royal prerogative, telling the king, 'You are above the laws. . . . Your wrath is death; you can do what is not allowed.'[7] It is precisely because his prerogative is so all-encompassing, Gower argues, that Richard is morally bound to set his subjects the example of a supremely law-abiding and righteous king. Even at this relatively early date, Gower is also advocating personal rule; chapter 9 addresses the problem of counsel by placing the responsibility for the selection and dismissal of counsellors solely in the hands of the king and advocates that the king ought to 'annihilate completely as traitors to the realm' those counsellors who betray his trust.

In the ongoing discussions over the extent to which Richard had access to, or interest in, theories of kingship, this letter has been overlooked, but it may well be that it was known to Richard himself. Gower's account of the royal commission for his *Confessio Amantis* claims that the king recognized him and requested 'some new thing', a suggestion that he knew one of Gower's earlier poems; if so, the letter in the *Vox*, directly addressed to him, is the work he is most likely to have known.

---

[5] John Gower, *The Complete Works*, ed. G. C. Macaulay, iii. *The Latin Works* (Oxford, 1902), 247–66. Macaulay suggests a reference to the king's marriage as a basis for the date (p. xxx). After the accession of Henry IV, Gower dedicated a revised version of the *Vox*, together with his account of events leading up to Richard's deposition, to Thomas Arundel, archbishop of Canterbury; in the later version, the letter to Richard is revised to remove some of the praise, and to insert a new note of strong criticism of his early conduct. For a trans. of the letter, see John Gower, *The Major Latin Works*, ed. and trans. E. W. Stockton (Seattle, 1962), 233–49. For a discussion of the dating and versions of the letter, and an analysis of it in context of the tradition of the *speculum regis*, see M. Wickert, *Studies in John Gower*, trans. R. J. Meindl (Washington, 1981), 6–11, 133–55. Wickert suggests (197–200) that an early version of the *Vox* may have been planned as a *speculum* for Richard, concluding with the letter addressed directly to him. Of the MSS of the unrevised text, Wickert suggests that Oxford, Bodleian MS Laud 719 (which does not include the *Visio* of the Peasants' Revolt that appears at the beginning of all other versions) is the closest to the version Richard is likely to have seen. For other comments on Gower's works, see above, pp. 54, 63–4.

[6] See the lines introducing the letter: bk. 6, ll. 555–60, beginning 'Stat puer immunis culpe'.

[7] 'Tu super es iura . . . Est mors ira tua, potes id quod non licet' *Vox*, 6. 6. 613–15.

3. *Confessio Amantis*, by John Gower (begun *c*.1385, first version completed after 1390 and before 1393).[8] A learned and imposing poem of more than 30,000 lines in Middle English octosyllabics, divided into eight books, and subdivided into sections introduced with Latin verses, the *Confessio* draws on three literary traditions: the *Roman de la Rose* is the basis for the vision of a lover confessing his sins to Genius, priest of Venus, which frames the whole; the penitential manual is the model for the discussion of the seven deadly sins with illustrative *exempla* which forms the body of the work; and the *Secretum Secretorum*, which Aristotle supposedly wrote for Alexander the Great, is evoked as the source for the long digression on advice to rulers which fills the whole of book 7. The work as a whole can be read as an extended discussion of the issues raised in the letter to Richard in the *Vox Clamantis*,[9] combining an exalted view of royal prerogative with an equally exalted ideal of the moral and religious virtues required of the king.

Gower's very circumstantial and detailed account of the royal commission, describing his encounter with the royal barge while boating on the Thames, has been occasionally questioned but is now widely accepted as factual.[10] Although no presentation manuscript to the king has survived, Gower concludes the poem by making a verbal presentation, restating his desire to express what he calls his 'ligance' to the king by fulfilling his request, and announcing, 'This povere bok heer I present Unto his hihe worthinesse' (8. 3050*–3051*).

4. The manuscript of the *Vie du Prince Noir* by the Chandos Herald, now at the University of London (MS 1, *c*.1385).[11] Both the poem itself

---

[8] John Gower *The English Works*, ed. G. C. Macaulay, 2 vols. (London, 1900). On the problems of dating the version dedicated to Richard II, see ibid. 24, and P. Nicholson, 'The Dedications of Gower's *Confessio Amantis*', *Mediaevalia*, 10 (1984), 159–80. The two MSS closest to the version that would have been presented to Richard are Oxford, Corpus Christi College MS 67 and Bodleian MS Laud 609. A revised version of the poem removed the account of the royal commission in the prologue, and replaced it with a dedication to Henry of Lancaster. A. I. Doyle describes the Ellesmere MS of this version of the poem (now Huntington Library, EL 26 A. 17) as 'presumably a presentation from the author', 'English Books In and Out of Court', *English Court Culture*, 170.

[9] For a discussion of the *Confessio* as belonging to the tradition of advice to princes, see R. A. Peck, *Kingship and Common Profit in Gower's* Confessio Amantis (London, 1978).

[10] Green, *Poets and Princepleasers*, 62; he notes that absence of records of royal payment for literary commissions is common (ibid. 5–7), and cites a number of works, known to have been royal commissions, for which presentation copies have not survived. See also Nicholson, 'Dedications' for a review of the evidence. The discussion in Saul, 'Richard II and the Vocabulary of Kingship' sheds light on the political significance of Gower's use of terms like 'ligance' and 'obeissance' in his addresses to Richard.

[11] D. B. Tyson (ed.), *Beihefte zur Zeitschrift für Romanische Philologie* (Tübingen, 1975).

and this manuscript have been associated with Richard's patronage.[12] What we know of Richard's devotion to his illustrious father from other sources makes this a likely attribution.[13] Two telling references to Richard reinforce the association. The only mention of his elder brother Edward is a brief reference to his death, while Richard's own birth is recounted in highly coloured, romantic terms. At the moment of the departure of the Prince for what will be his famous victory at Nájera, the grief of the Princess Joan is so great that she gives birth to the child she is carrying. The prince expresses his joy in words meant to be prophetic for his newborn son as well as his own military venture, 'Behold a right fair beginning' (l. 2102). Again, in the description of the death of the prince, detailed attention is given to two affecting scenes in which he commends his son Richard, first to all who have served him in battle (ll. 4119–38), and then to his father the king and his brother the duke of Lancaster, as well as all the other magnates (ll. 4139–52); all pledge their faith to the dying prince to serve Richard and maintain him in 'his right' (l. 4148). This image of the loyal magnates pledging their faith to the young Richard parallels several passages in the *Processus*, and shows how chivalric idealism could be mustered to support the ideology of monarchy.

5. An untitled treatise in French (*c.*1386) on the rules and procedures for conducting judicial combat in the High Court of Chivalry, written in French by Thomas of Woodstock, duke of Gloucester and constable of the realm.[14] As Woodstock himself claims, it represents the first attempt to make a written record of rules for this court.[15] Although the court was commonly called 'the Court of the Constable and Marshal', Woodstock refers to it repeatedly as a court subject to the king's 'souveraine jurisdiccion'

---

[12] The initial at the beginning of the text contains the arms of England and the illumination bears similarities to BL MS Bodley 581. See J. J. G. Alexander, 'Painting and Manuscript Illumination for Royal Patrons in the Later Middle Ages', in *English Court Culture*, 145 for the argument that the MS was a presentation copy to Richard, and cf. L. F. Sandler, *Gothic Manuscripts, 1285–1385*, ed. J. J. G. Alexander, 2 vols. (Oxford, 1985), ii. 175, 177. D. B. Tyson, in the introd. to her edn. (see n. 11, above), suggests that the poem may have been commissioned by Richard, but argues that the London Univ. MS is a defective copy of the original text, which has not survived.

[13] See Scheifele, in ch. 12, below. Saul, *Richard II*, 344–5, describes the court of the Black Prince as a 'major influence' on Richard.

[14] Ed. Sir T. Twiss in *The Black Book of the Admiralty*, 4 vols. (RS, London, 1871), i. 300–29. Twiss refers to one 15th-cent. MS used in the preparation of his edn. of the French text (BL Add. MS 28, 534). He does not mention the existence of a copy of the work in BL, MS Cotton Nero D. VI, a MS prepared for Richard, and dated by its contents after 1386. Goodman dates it 'before 1390', *The Loyal Conspiracy* (London, 1971), 77.

[15] G. D. Squibb, *The High Court of Chivalry: A Study of the Civil Law in England* (Oxford, 1959), 14, 23, 187.

(p. 300), since the combat takes place in the king's presence (p. 302) and
the king has power to intervene in the proceedings or suspend them entirely
at his pleasure. The Constable, he says, is only the king's 'vicaire general'
(p. 304), and he submits his treatise to the king for his approval, to examine, correct, and amend it as he should see fit (pp. 302, 304).

Richard II apparently accepted and approved the treatise, because it
was included in a manuscript collection made for him (BL MS Cotton
Nero D. VI, discussed below), and, as Squibb notes, it became authoritative for the High Court of Chivalry.[16] The question has been raised as to
whether, in interrupting the trial by battle between Hereford and Norfolk
in 1398, Richard was aware of the 'authoritarian principles' on which the
Court of Chivalry was based;[17] Woodstock's treatise would have been
sufficient to give him an authoritative basis for his actions in this case.

6. BL MS Cotton Nero D. VI (after 1386, the date of the latest datable
item), an untitled collection of a variety of historical records, and accounts
of ceremonial procedures, in French and Latin.[18] It contains two works
discussed above: the *Processus* (fos. 65–9), together with an account of his
coronation service (fos. 70–1), and the treatise on the Court of Chivalry
(fos. 82–4), together with related materials on the office of Earl Marshal
of England: a letter from Richard II appointing Thomas Mowbray, earl of
Nottingham, marshal in 1386 (fo. 85); a list of the names of the lords
of Mowbray (fo. 2); an account of the duties and offices of Thomas of
Brotherton, marshal of England from 1316 (fo. 85), and a description of
the office of the marshal in time of peace (fos. 86–8). A number of other
documents concern the war with France: a collection of treaties and agreements made with the French during the reign of Edward III (fos. 4–28);
a letter of Edward III concerning disputed territories on the continent,
dated 1 February 1366 (fos. 29–30); a record of the appointment of the
Black Prince to the principality of Aquitaine made 19 July 1362 (fo. 31);
a record of a treaty, dated 1254, in which King Alfonso X, king of Castile,
renounces all claim to Gascony in favour of King Henry III (fo. 56b); a
peace proposal made by John II, king of France (fos. 36–56). Another group
of documents deals with Richard's campaign in Scotland: a copy of the
'estatuz, ordenances et custumes' made between the king and John duke

---

[16] Ibid. 14.
[17] J. A. Tuck, *Richard II and the English Nobility* (London, 1973), 203, 209.
[18] V. J. Scattergood, 'Literary Culture at the Court of Richard II', in *English Court Culture*, 33 lists it as one of the books owned by Richard. See also Sandler, *Gothic Manuscripts*, ii. 175 for a description of the illumination of the manuscript, associating it with BL MS Bodley 581 and the London Univ. Library MS of the *Vie du Prince Noir*.

of Lancaster, Thomas earl of Essex (i.e. Woodstock), and others, at Durham July 17, 1385 (fos. 89–91); the 'ordenances' of war in Scotland in 1385 (fo. 91); a copy of the truce with Scotland made at Berwick in 1357 (fos. 61–4), and an account of the campaign of Edward I in Scotland in 1296 (fos. 93–4). One other item, loosely related to the interest in historical precedent demonstrated throughout the collection, is an outline of history beginning with Noah but focusing on English kings, and ending with the accession of Richard II (fos. 76–82).

Even this summary list of the contents suggests that Richard's interest in history, attested by Walsingham,[19] was not simply antiquarianism. In juxtaposing a collection of records of his own expedition to Scotland with an account of the expedition of Edward I, the text presents Richard as self-consciously playing a role in history, a role reinforced by the history of kings which concludes with his reign. Despite its miscellaneous character, this collection suggests an awareness on Richard's part that he was, by his own actions, making history as well as following historical precedents.

7. *De primis regalibus ornamentis regni Angliae* (*c.*1387–9), by William Sudbury, a Benedictine monk of Westminster abbey, who held a doctorate of divinity from Oxford. The treatise addresses a question raised by Richard II himself, 'whether the regalia of [his] reign are the regalia of King Alfred and take their origin from him' (p. 38).[20] In the course of a discussion of the origins and history of the regalia, the treatise also offers a lengthy discussion of Westminster abbey as the 'royal seat [*sedes regia*]' and, following the tradition established by King Edward the Confessor, the place of conservation of the regalia. The regalia are described as both signs (*insignia*) of the sacrament of coronation and the means by which the king takes on 'the royal dignity, which among and above all the riches, pleasures, and honours of this world takes first place, supereminently at the very highest point'.[21] At the same time, the regalia are presented as

---

[19] See *Hist. Angl.* i. 239 describing Richard II's interest in the holy oil of Canterbury: 'Rex Ricardus curiose perscrutatus [res] a progenitoribus sibi relictas'. For an account of the role of the Scots expedition, together with the later Irish campaigns, as part of an attempt to create an image of Richard modelled on that of his father, see J. L. Gillespie, 'Richard II: King of Battles?', in id. (ed.), *The Age of Richard II* (New York, 1997), 139–63.

[20] The treatise circulated as part of *Ricardi de Cirencestria Speculum Historiale*, ed. J. E. B. Mayor, 2 vols. (RS, London, 1863–9), ii. 26–39. The date has been assigned by J. A. Robinson, 'An Unrecognized Westminster Chronicler, 1381–1394', *Proceedings of the British Academy*, 3 (1907–8), 61–92, who also discusses what is known about Sudbury. On Sudbury and his background, see also B. F. Harvey, 'The Monks of Westminster and the University of Oxford', in *Reign of Richard II*, 108–30.

[21] 'regiam . . . dignitatem, quae inter omnes et super omnes huius mundi divitias, delicias, et honores supereminenter in culmine residet principatus', 30.

signs of the traditional privileges of the abbey, as the coronation site, the repository of the regalia, and the shrine of the image of sacred kingship as represented by Edward the Confessor.

By thus appealing to the king's interest in the regalia and devotion to Edward the Confessor, the treatise succeeded in gaining his goodwill and increasing his patronage to the abbey. In 1383 Richard had seized the temporalities of the abbey in retaliation for the community's violation of a writ forbidding them to pursue their dispute with the incumbents of St Stephen's chapel at the court of Rome. In September 1389, however, Sudbury drafted a letter to Pope Urban VI on the king's behalf, asking for confirmation of the traditional privileges of the abbey.[22] When the dispute between the abbey and St Stephen's again reached a crisis in December 1389, and the abbot again sought aid from Rome, the king intervened this time on behalf of the abbey, as the *Westminster Chronicle* puts it, 'out of his desire to keep his church [*ecclesiam suam*] from harm or loss' (pp. 378–9). It looks very much as though the treatise on the regalia played a role in persuading Richard to identify the interests of the royal prerogative with the privileges of the abbey as his church; a similar association of ideas appears in the formal portrait of the king that was hung in the abbey, portraying Richard in regal majesty and wearing the robes of state that are part of the regalia discussed in such detail by Sudbury.[23]

8. Cambridge, St John's College, MS A. 7 (after 1388), a collection of statutes of England, selected from the reigns of Henry III to Richard II;

[22] It is likely that included with this letter was an addition to the regalia Richard had arranged at the urging of the monks of the abbey. At his coronation in 1377, one of the royal coronation slippers had been lost, presumably when the newly crowned king was carried through the streets on the shoulders of Sir Simon Burley; the loss was duly noted in the abbey records, with the comment, 'King Richard must be told', Robinson, 'Unrecognized Chronicler', 71. In Mar. 1390 the king sent to the abbey 'a pair of red velvet shoes, with fleurs-de-lis worked on them in pearls, which had been blessed by Urban VI shortly before his death [on 15 Oct. 1389]', to be preserved with the rest of the coronation regalia (*Westm. Chron.* 414–15).

[23] The well-known passage in which the *Westm. Chron.* 326–7, praises Richard as an ardent defender of the privileges of the abbey, was probably written after Sudbury's treatise, and may attest to its influence on Richard's attitudes. The treatise may also be associated with Richard's other benefactions to the abbey; *King's Works*, i. 151. Richard's donations to the abbey's construction were exceeded only by those of Henry III, and Barbara Harvey calls the foundation of Richard II and Anne of Bohemia one of the three 'major royal foundations' of the medieval period; *Westminster Abbey and its Estates in the Middle Ages* (Oxford, 1977). For a detailed account of Richard's patronage of the abbey see N. Saul, 'Richard II and Westminster Abbey', in J. Blair and B. Golding (edd.), *The Cloister and the World: Essays in Medieval History in Honour of Barbara Harvey* (Oxford, 1996), 196–218. Cf. above, pp. 90–1.

the latest statute recorded is dated 1 December 1388 (fos. 154^r–156^v). Each section begins with a historiated initial portraying the king in whose reign the statutes which follow were made. The last portrait shows a kneeling clerk presenting a book to Richard II, seated on the royal throne (fo. 133).[24] According to J. W. Sherborne, a number of the statutes included, such as the ordinances of 1311, suggest that Richard was investigating precedents for 'crown–magnate hostilities'.[25] The contents of the manuscript await a detailed study.[26] The care with which it was prepared and illuminated demonstrates that Richard II's interest in statute law was not confined to the questions raised with his judges in 1387.

9. Oxford, MS Bodley 581 (*c.*1391), an untitled collection of four treatises: *De quadripartita regis specie* (fos. 1^r–3^r), a treatise on the selection of counsellors and the distribution of largesse, adapted from the *Secretum Secretorum*;[27] *Physionomia Aristotelis* (fos. 3^r–5^v), another excerpt from the *Secretum*, where physiognomy is advocated as a scientific basis for the selection of counsellors to the king; *Sompniale Danielis* (fos. 6^r–8^v), a treatise on the interpretation of images seen in dreams;[28] and the *Libellus geomancie* (fos. 9^r–89^v), a handbook of geomancy, elaborately illuminated, complete with a table of the properties of the geomantic 'figures' each

---

[24] The MS is described in M. R. James, *Descriptive Catalogue of the Manuscripts in the Library of St. John's College, Cambridge* (Cambridge, 1913), 8–9. The illumination is described in detail in Sandler, *Gothic Manuscripts*, ii. 179, where the text is dated 'close to 1388' since there are 24 blank ruled folios left at the end, presumably for recording statutes after 1388. For a discussion and reproduction of the portrait of Richard, see S. Whittingham, 'The Chronology of the Portraits of Richard II', *Burlington Magazine*, 113 (1971), 15.

[25] 'Aspects of English Court Culture in the Later Fourteenth Century', in *English Court Culture*, 22.

[26] Prof. R. I. Schneider of York University, Toronto, is preparing a monograph on the uses of portraits of Richard II, which will include extensive study of this MS (as well as of BL MS Cotton Nero D. VI); portions of this work have been presented in lectures to the Society of the White Hart at the International Congress of Medieval Studies, held annually at Western Michigan University. For an account of this MS, together with a reproduction of the historiated initial depicting Richard receiving the presentation copy, see Saul, *Richard II*, 237 and pl. 12; Saul dates the MS 'probably around 1390' and describes it as 'a kind of manifesto for the reassertion of royal power'.

[27] J.-P. Genet (ed.), *Four English Political Tracts of the Later Middle Ages* (Camden Soc., 4th ser. 18, London, 1977), 22–39. See Saul, *Richard II*, 386–7, for a discussion of a passage on 'disobedience' in the MS that is clearly related to Richard's own ideology of the importance of obedience for the peace of the realm. See also above, pp. 52–3.

[28] Richard's interest in this treatise may have been inspired by his tutor, Sir Simon Burley, whose library in 1388 included a copy of it in French: for Burley's copy see V. J. Scattergood, 'Two Medieval Book Lists', *Library*, 23 (1968), 236–9, and M. V. Clarke, 'Forfeitures and Treason in 1388', in L. S. Sutherland and M. McKisack (edd.), *Fourteenth Century Studies* (Oxford, 1937), 121.

illustrated with an image showing its principal attributes.[29] On the last
folio (89ᵛ) appears a table of the planets governing all the hours of the
day and night. The geomantic handbook is described as expressly commissioned by Richard himself in March 1391,[30] and a portrait of a king,
presumably Richard appears in the historiated capital at the beginning of
the treatise.[31]

Because it is the only work for which we have internal evidence that
the text was both commissioned by and presented to Richard, this handbook of geomancy has given rise to speculations concerning the nature
and extent of his interest in what is often described as 'occult science'.[32]
The recent study by Thérèse Charmasson[33] makes clear that many of
Richard's contemporaries regarded geomancy as an authoritative form of
divination, because it was based on fundamental principles common to
astronomy and mathematics as well as astrology and because it reflected the
widely held view of the cosmos as a network of interacting influences, em-
anating in the first instance from the heavenly bodies.[34] These influences
could be called 'occult' in the technical sense because they were 'hidden'

---

[29] Sandler describes the illumination of the MS and links it with two other MSS associated with Richard, BL MS Cotton, Nero D. VI, and Univ. of London MS 1, as well as with
the Litlyington Missal (Sandler, *Gothic Manuscripts*, ii. 175–6).

[30] 'Ad consolacionem mocionemque specialem dominice incarnacionis 1391 mo, mense
marcii' (fo. 9ᵛ); transcribed in Genet (ed.), *Political Tracts*, 22.

[31] Another copy of the *Libellus geomancie*, BL MS Royal, 12 C. 5, also describes itself in
similar terms as 'the book of Richard II which he had made by his own command [*motu pro-
prio*], in the fourteenth year of his reign' (fo. 3ᵛ), and it includes all the geomantic material,
complete with the illustrated figures. Genet suggests that this MS was also made for Richard, but he mistakenly dates it 'in the second year of his reign' Genet (ed.), *Political Tracts*.
22, n. 2. Sandler notes that the quality of illumination is inferior to that of Bodley 581,
and the historiated initial portraying Richard is absent from this MS (Sandler, *Gothic
Manuscripts*, 175–6).

[32] On the basis of the MSS H. M. Carey describes Richard II as 'the first English king
to have taken a positive interest in the occult sciences', 'Astrology at the English Court in
the Later Middle Ages', in P. Curry (ed.), *Astrology, Science, and Society: Historical Essarys*,
(Woodbridge, 1987). A fuller account of MS Bodley 581, in the context of Richard's other
interests, appears in H. M. Carey, *Courting Disaster: Astrology at the English Court and
Universitty in the Later Middle Ages* (London, 1992), 92–116.

[33] T. Charmasson, *Recherches sur une technique divinatoire: La Geomancie dans l'occident
médiéval* (Geneva, 1980), 122, 136, 204, 206–7, 296, and 312 discuss Oxford MS Bodley 581
in the context of other handbooks.

[34] On the concept of 'influence', see E. Grant, 'Medieval and Renaissance Scholastic
Conceptions of the Influence of the Celestial Region on the Terrestrial', *Journal of Medieval
and Renaissance Studies*, 17 (1987), 1–23; J. D. North, 'Celestial Influence: The Major Premiss
of Astrology', in P. Zambelli (ed.), *'Astrologi hallucinati': Stars and the End of the World in
Luther's Time* (Berlin, 1986), 45–100.

(*occultus*) from ordinary sense-perception, but they were not considered supernatural,[35] and they were associated with one of the most basic forces in the natural world, the force of number. On the basis of a full study of a large number of medieval geomantic manuscripts, Charmasson characterizes it as a ' "learned" method of divination, more learned even than astrology, known especially in intellectual circles of translators, professors, and doctors as well as in the courts of princes and kings'.[36]

Far from offering evidence that Richard 'wanted to learn something about the occult sciences',[37] the *Libellus geomancie*, in the form that Richard commissioned it, presupposes that Richard himself is already learned in the theory and practice of geomancy. It does not describe how to form the initial configuration of random marks while meditating on a given question, and it does not describe the complex procedures necessary to transform this configuration into the standard geomantic schema of fifteen 'houses'. It assumes a knowledge of how to derive, from the initial configuration of random dots, the sixteen possible geomantic 'figures' comprised of arrangements of dots in four rows, each consisting of one or two dots. Without knowledge of these procedures, the *Libellus* would be useless, for the bulk of the work is dedicated to an account of the sixteen figures and their twenty-seven different kinds of attributes, together with a set of questions which may be appropriately asked: for example, whether a journey should be undertaken, a siege raised, or a proposed marriage contracted.

Compared to more rudimentary presentations of the material in some of the other manuscripts surveyed by Charmasson, Richard's handbook of geomancy is remarkable for its systematic presentation of a large amount of material needed by the experienced practitioner; in addition to

---

[35] Astronomical calendars often include tables of the ruling planets and signs as well as the position of the moon, evidence that the influence of the heavenly bodies was taken as a fact of nature. Richard's mother, Princess Joan, owned an astronomical calendar made for her in 1380 by John Somer, a Franciscan (BL Royal MS 2 B. 8), and Nicholas of Lynn, a Carmelite, dedicated his *Kalendarium* to John of Gaunt, patron of his Order, at whose request it was made; see Nicholas of Lynn, *The Kalendarium*, ed. S. Eisner (Athens, Ga.: 1980). Both calendars circulated widely, and were used for a variety of purposes, both religious and secular. For an account of the distinction between the natural and the supernatural in the period, which would make geomancy a form of natural divination, see B. Hansen, 'Science and Magic', in D. C. Lindberg and A. G. Debus (edd.), *Science in the Middle Ages* (Chicago, 1978), 483–506.

[36] 'Elle est restée, essentiellement, une methode divinatoire "savante," davantage meme que l'astrologie, surtout repandue dans les milieux intellectuels (traducteurs, professeurs, medicins) et dans les cours princières ou royales', *Recherches*, 270.

[37] Carey, 'Astrology', 44; Carey gives a more detailed and nuanced account of Richard's interest in the various arts now called occult or superstitious in *Courting Disaster*, 95–9.

a variety of tables and schematic presentations of material it includes a thumb index of the geomantic figures for ease of consultation. It is also noteworthy for its elaborate justification of the validity of geomancy, claiming that the art presupposes an understanding of the basic principles of astrological influence and that it has the endorsement of William of Moerbeke and Albertus Magnus.[38]

In his preface, the compiler emphasizes that it is a learned science, and commends Richard in the highest terms for his learning in commissioning the work.[39] In prefixing to this work excerpts from the *Secretum Secretorum*, the compiler was making a natural connectioh, since the *Secretum* repeatedly stresses the importance of the influences of the stars and advises the ruler to do nothing without the counsel of those skilled in astrology.[40] The fundamental concern of the *Secretum*, how a ruler can maintain and increase his power over his subjects, is also addressed in *Libellus*; in the preface, the compiler cites the saying attributed to Ptolemy, 'Vir sapiens dominabitur astris', implying that the ruler who is wise enough to have power over the influences of the heavens, through the art of geomancy, will have enhanced power in other matters as well. In commissioning a handbook of geomancy, Richard was demonstrating not only his learning in an abstruse divinatory art but also his interest in legitimating and maintaining his power as king.

   10. *Concordia facta inter regem Riccardum II et civitatem Londonie* (1393), a Latin poem in elegiac couplets, by Richard Maidstone (d. 1396), commemorating the royal entry pageant held in London on 21 August 1392, to celebrate the reconciliation of the famous quarrel between Richard

---

[38] Moerbeke compiled a geomancy in 1276 (Charmasson, *Recherches*, 157). Albertus, referred to here as 'Doctor Parisiensis', is credited with the authorship of 'De licitis et illicitis' (i.e. *Speculum astronomiae*, fo. 9ʳ, col. 1). The *Speculum astronomiae* presents an ambivalent view of geomancy; it does exempt geomancy from the kind of criticism levelled at hydromancy and other forms of divination, saying that it does not involve idolatry, but it also groups geomancy with those forms of divination that 'do not deserve to be called sciences'; see S. Caroti, M. Pereira, and S. Zamponi (edd.), *Speculum astronomiae*, NS 10 of P. Zambelli (gen. ed.), *Quaderni di storia e critica della scienza* (Pisa, 1977), 48. For a discussion of the authorship of this work, B. M. Ashley, 'St. Albert and the Nature of Natural Science', in id., *Albertus Magnus and the Sciences: Commemorative Essays 1980* (Toronto, 1980), 72–102.

[39] The dedication describes Richard as 'regnorum Anglie et Francie regis nobilissimi, qui non tantum validissimos armorum et utriusque legis viros sublimando gubernat, immo scienciarum subtilium fructus dulcedinem ad ipsius et sue gentis providam gubernacionem gustare non desistit propter astronomice science longissimam ac difficilem cognicionem, ad quam presens vita vix sufficere valet' (fo. 9ᵛ) (transcribed in Genet (ed.), *Political Tracts*, 23).

[40] 'nichil penitus facias sine consilio viri periti in arte astrorum' in the version of the *Secretum Secretorum* with commentary by R. Steel, F. Delorme, *et al.* in *Opera hactenus inedita Rogeri Baconi*, ed. eid., 16 vols. (Oxford, 1920), v. 60.

and the city.[41] The work is explicitly dedicated to Richard,[42] and it offers an interpretation of the pageant designed, like the pageant itself,[43] to win his favour by presenting an interpretation of the reconciliation that would enhance royal prerogative. For example, when Richard approaches the gates of the city, the keeper appears before him to offer him the keys, holding the point of a sword towards his own throat, and addressing the king in the words of 'an abject captive':

Behold! O King, whose authority is much to be feared, loved, and reverenced, behold! The humble citizens prostrated at your feet return themselves and all they have to you. By these keys and this sword, the city proclaims that it now freely surrenders and comes ready to be subject to your will . . . Let not the most beautiful walls in the kingdom be rent nor torn, for they are the king's own and whatever is within them. (ll. 137–40)[44]

The rest of the keeper's speeches continue in this vein, combining ever more elaborate panegyrics on the power of the king with increasingly abject professions of obedience from his subjects. As the king is given a series of elaborate and expensive gifts, the poem reports the words of the keeper on their significance: 'they are given in sign that the citizens now yield

---

[41] No presentation copy is extant; the sole extant copy is in Oxford, Bodleian MS *e Musaeo* 94, fos. 8ᵛ–11ᵛ (*c*.1400), a miscellany containing other Latin works by Maidstone as well. The poem appears in T. Wright (ed.), *Political Poems and Songs relating to English History*, 2 vols. (RS London, 1859), i. 282–99 and in C. R. Smith, '*Concordia facta inter regem Riccardum II et civitatem Londonie* per Fratrum Riccardum Maydiston, Carmelitam, Sacre Theologie doctorem, anno domini 1393: Edited with Introduction, Translation, and Notes', Ph.D. thesis, Princeton, 1972, the edn. cited here. Smith dates the work and discusses its role in the 1392 quarrel with London; see also C. M. Barron, 'The Quarrel of Richard II with the City of London, 1392–1397', in *Reign of Richard II*, 173–201. For a detailed account of the pageant recorded in this poem and a discussion of its underlying ideology and its relationship to other pageants, see G. Kipling, 'Richard II's "Sumptuous Pageants" and the Idea of the Civic Triumph', in *Pageantry in the Shakespearean Theater* (Athens, Ga., 1985), 83–103. See Strohm, *Hochon's Arrow*, 107–11 for an analysis of the role assigned to Queen Anne in the pageant and the poem, and a suggestion of its relevance for an understanding of the role of Alceste in Chaucer's *Legend of Good Women*. Maidstone was a Carmelite with a doctorate of theology from Oxford (Merton College), who wrote tracts against the Wyclifites as well as a commentary on the Song of Songs, and who served as confessor to John of Gaunt.

[42] 'Hinc tibi, Ricarde, duplante iugo michi iuncte, | (Nomen et omen habes, sic socium meus es) | Gaudia visa michi Trenovantum nuper in urbe,| Actus amicicia, glisco referre modo' (ll. 9–12), ed. Smith, '*Concordia*', 161–2; Wright (ed.), *Political Poems*, ii. 282.

[43] For contemporary accounts of the pageant, see H. Suggett (ed.), 'A Letter Describing Richard II's Reconciliation with the City of London, 1392', *EHR* 62 (1947), 209–13; *Hist. Angl.* ii. 207–11; Knighton, ii. 319–21, and the excerpt from Oxford, Bodleian MS Ashmole 793 printed in R. Withington, *English Pageantry: An Historical Introduction*, 2 vols. (Cambridge, Mass. 1918), i. 129–30.

[44] Smith, '*Concordia*', 180–1; Wright (ed.), *Political Poems*, ii. 286. For the pageant, see above, pp. 152–3.

themselves—bodies, riches, the Trojan citadel, their all. May the life and death of each of them be in your hands, and may the royal sceptre freely rule its own citizens' (ll. 213–16).[45] The political implications of this pageantry are obvious. These speeches parallel one of the charges made against Richard at his deposition, the claim that he said 'the lives of every one of his lieges and their lands, tenements, goods, and chattels are his at his pleasure'.[46] Even if, as some historians have argued, Richard did not actually make this statement in his own person, Maidstone and the contrivers of the pageant evidently thought he would look with favour on these words in the mouths of his subjects. The pageant as a whole, and the poem that commemorates it, echo and extend the kind of profession of 'ligeance' found in Gower's *Confessio Amantis* into a fully articulated doctrine of obedience to a Solomonic (even Christlike) king.

11. A book of the miracles associated with the tomb of Edward II, made with a view towards establishing his sainthood (1395).[47] Although the preparation of the book may have begun as early as 1385, it was not sent until 1395, when an Issue Roll entry dated 24 April records payment to Pierre Merk and Jacques Monald for conveying it to the pope. The book is not extant, but its commissioning demonstrates Richard's ongoing interest in royal sainthood (also attested in his devotion to Edward the Confessor), perhaps in this case as a way of vindicating a king who, like himself, was confronted with rebellious barons. Perroy sees the volume as an attempt at 'elevating royal prestige and sanctifying the prerogatives of the sovereign', and John M. Theilmann examines this theme in detail, as it applies to Richard.[48]

12. *De duodecim errores et hereses Lollardorum* (1395), a treatise designed as a systematic refutation of twelve Lollard propositions affixed to the doors of Westminster hall during the sessions of Parliament from 27 January to 15 February 1395, written by Roger Dymmok, Dominican friar, Doctor of Divinity (Oxford), and prior of the Black Friars at Boston. The treatise

---

[45] Smith, '*Concordia*', 188–9; Wright (ed.), *Political Poems*, ii. 289.

[46] 'Quod vita cujusque ligei sui, ac ipsius Terre, Tenementa, Bona, & Catella sunt sua ad voluntatem suam', *RP* iii. 420; trans. in A. R. Myers (ed. and trans.), *English Historical Documents*, iv. *1327–1485* (London, 1969), 411.

[47] See E. Perroy, *L'Angleterre et le grand schisme d'occident* (Paris, 1933), 341–2. J. M. Theilmann, 'Political Canonization in the Reign of Richard II', *JBS* 29 (1990). Dr Theilmann, who kindly allowed me to read the typescript of this article, notes that in 1383 Richard exempted the abbots of St Peter's, Gloucester from the duty of attending Parliament, in return for celebrating mass for the soul of Edward II on his anniversary, and that he wrote to Urban VI in 1385, or possibly as late as 1389, requesting his canonization.

[48] Perroy, *Grand Schisme*, 301; Theilmann discusses in detail the political implications of royal canonization. For Richard's concern with the process, see also above, p. 86.

is addressed to Richard, and its modern editor argues persuasively, on the basis of the illumination, that the manuscript at Cambridge (Trinity Hall MS 17) was a copy presented to the king in May 1395, after he returned from Ireland.[49]

The work begins with a lengthy dedication to Richard in terms that recall allusions in Bodley 581 to the wisdom of the king, and Maidstone's portrait of Richard as a young Solomon.[50]

Because 'a wise king [*rex sapiens*] is the support of the people' [*Sapientia* 6 : 26], whenever divine providence plans to raise up a people or a kingdom, or to free them from past suffering, He provides for them leaders or kings who are diligent, wise, and forceful and assiduous zealots for the divine law.

After a long list of these wise kings, including Moses, Samuel, and David as well as Solomon and extending to a selection of more modern rulers such as Alexander, Charlemagne, and Arthur, he then turns to Richard: 'So, in modern times . . . [God] has put forward to regal dignity your serenity and regal magnificence.'[51] For Dymmok, royal *sapientia* is a sign of divinely granted power, and he praises Richard's wisdom repeatedly as a sign that God has appointed him to defend the Church against the Lollard heretics.

A number of the arguments Dymmok uses to enlist Richard's support turn on the claim that some of the Lollard propositions aim at undermining

---

[49] Roger was the eldest son of Sir John Dymmok, a retainer of John of Gaunt who is recorded in the *Processus* of Richard's coronation as appointed to serve as Champion of England *jure uxoris*. Roger Dymmok, *Liber Contra XII errores et hereses Lollardorum*, ed. H. S. Cronin (London, n.d. [1921]); the Trinity MS is the basis for the edition, which also cites readings in three other extant MSS. The programme of illumination of this MS includes a portrait of Richard in the initial (fo. 1ʳ), with two white harts gorged with gold crowns in the lower margin, a second historiated initial portraying John the Baptist, Richard's patron saint (fo. 8ʳ), and paired images of Pope Sylvester and the Emperor Constantine (fo. 13ʳ), which the editor suggests may reflect Richard's campaign to be elected to the Empire. For a reproduction of this initial, Whittingham, 'Chronology', pl. 24. A. I. Doyle suggests that the illumination of this MS closely resembles that of the Ellesmere *Confessio Amantis* (which he thinks was made under Gower's supervision for Henry of Bolingbroke in 1393), as well as a copy of the *Ordo coronacionis* presently in Pamplona; 'English Books In and Out of Court', *Court* 170.

[50] Cf. Maidstone, *Concordia*, 'Talis adolescens toto non restat in orbe, | Qui sciat ut Salomon regna tenere sua.' (ll. 37–8); C. R. Smith, '*Concordia*', 168; Wright (ed.), *Political Poems*, ii. 283.

[51] 'Et quia rex sapiens stabilimentum efficiatur populi, quando diuina prouidencia gentem uel regnum exaltandum disponit uel a retroactis miseriis liberandu, reges siue duces eidem preficit industrios, sapientes, et strenuos ac legis diuine assiduos zelatores . . . Sic, diuina fauente clemencia, uestram serenitatem ac magnificenciam regalem, prediffinito sapiencie sue consilio, in nostro regno Anglie ad regiam promouit dignitatem modernis temporibus' (*XII Errores*, 5 (my trans.)).

the royal prerogative. For example, he claims that in posting their document on the door of Westminster hall, the king's property, the Lollards are guilty of the crime of *lèse majesté* ('magnum crimen lese magestatis', p. 27). In a similar way, in their argument against war, the Lollards are arrogating royal prerogative to themselves, since it belongs not to private persons but to the 'auctoritas principis' to declare war (p. 262). Moreover, princes have the right to compel their subjects to support the war with their goods or persons (p. 264); since, even in time of peace, they may even compel their subjects to provide for 'necessities' (p. 265). Even displays of 'magnificence' which the Lollards would condemn are necessities to a king, Dymmok maintains, citing Solomon as a precedent, for 'peace cannot be preserved among so many adversaries without a great abundance of riches' (p. 266).[52] Dymmok does not go so far as Maidstone in advancing the claim of the king to the goods of his people, but he evidently believes an argument of this kind will attract Richard to his cause, and he sees an elegantly illuminated presentation manuscript as an effective way of gaining the king's attention.[53]

13. An untitled volume of Froissart's collected poems on love and morality, expensively bound and elaborately illuminated, presented by Froissart himself to Richard in 1395.[54] The manuscript is not extant,[55] and no record of any gift from the king to Froissart has survived. There is no

[52] For a discussion of Dymmok's lengthy defence of royal magnificence as a vindication of the style of Richard's court, see Eberle, 'Politics of Courtly Style', 168–78, and Saul, *Richard II*, 355–7.

[53] The direct impact of Dymmok's lobbying is not easy to assess, since Richard was a known defender of orthodoxy. Walsingham (*Hist. Angl.* ii. 216–17), apparently believed that the so-called 'Lollard knights' were behind the posting of the propositions, saying that Richard required them to take oaths not to support the Lollard cause, and that he threatened them with death if they ever violated their oaths; Cronin, in his edn. of the *Liber Contra XII*, 9 ff. disputes the value of Walsingham's account. For a full discussion of Richard's orthodoxy and piety, see Saul, *Richard II*, 293–326. For Richard and the Lollards, see above, pp. 91–4.

[54] When Froissart first describes the volume, he says that he had a MS made, illuminated, and bound containing, 'tous les traitties amoureux, et de moralite que ou terme de XXXIII ans je avoie . . . fais et compiles', a more comprehensive collection than is usually assumed from his later, briefer description of the volume, where in response to a question from Richard on the subject of poems, he replies simply, 'D'amours'. See Froissart, XV. 141, 167.

[55] In 'Chaucer and Internationalism', E. Salter discusses the difficulty of identifying MSS from medieval descriptions and, as an example, calls attention to one that sounds similar to the volume Froissart presented to Richard: a large book 'de Tretes amoireus et moralitez et de carolles franceis bien esluminez' found among the books confiscated from Thomas duke of Gloucester in 1397, D. Pearsall and N. Zeeman (edd.), *English and International: Studies in the Literature, Art, and Patronage of Medieval England* (Cambridge, 1988), 244.

good reason to doubt Froissart's account, however,[56] and the loss of this valuable book demonstrates the danger of assuming that our records of Richard's manuscripts, even of elaborate presentation copies, are at all complete. Froissart's account of the information he acquired at Richard's court concerning the ongoing negotiations between England and France, as well as Richard's campaign in Ireland, reveals how the occasion of his royal presentation afforded him direct access to material he could use in his chronicles, as well as enhancing his credibility as a historian of events in England. Froissart's example suggests that, with literary as well as other forms of patronage, direct access to the inner circle of the king was itself considered a valuable reward.

14. *Epistre au Roi Richart* (1395), a treatise attempting to persuade Richard to end the war with France, marry the daughter of Charles VI, and join with him in ending the Schism and promoting a crusading order, the Order of the Passion of Jesus Christ dedicated to the recapturing of the kingdom of Jerusalem, written by Philippe de Mézières, former chancellor of Cyprus, adviser to Charles VI, and since 1367 originator and promoter of this proposed Order.[57] This treatise, presented to Richard on behalf of Charles VI, was only one of many attempts by Mézières to enlist Richard's support of the Order.[58] As Mézières points out (pp. 32, 105),

---

[56] J. W. Sherborne cast doubt on the authenticity of this account: 'Charles VI and Richard II', in J. J. N. Palmer (ed.), *Froissart: Historian* (Woodbridge, 1981), 62. For a rebuttal of these doubts, and a detailed discussion of Froissart's account of Richard, G. B. Stow, 'Richard II in Jean Froissart's *Chroniques*', *JMH* 11 (1985), 333–45, esp. 333 and 343 n. 2. Cf. the comments above, p. 34, supporting the account's authenticity.

[57] BL MS Royal 20 B. 6, the unique MS, a presentation copy to Richard, is richly illuminated and includes a miniature (fo. 2) depicting the author's presentation of the book to the enthroned king. *Philippe de Mézières' Letter to Richard II: A Plea Made in 1395 for Peace between England and France*, ed. and trans. G. W. Coopland (Liverpool, 1975), includes an introd. and notes, as well as a colour reproduction of the miniature.

[58] For a full account of Philippe's attempts to attract the patronage of Richard II for his Order, see J. J. N. Palmer, *England, France and Christendom, 1377–1399* (London, 1972), 180–210 and de Mézières, *Letter* 9–34, *passim*. In addition to the *Epistre* itself, Charles VI addressed a letter to Richard, which anticipates some of the arguments of the *Epistre* (and which may have been drafted by Mézières), on the subject of the proposed peace and crusade, dated 15 May 1385, and received a favourable reply from Richard. Both letters are preserved in Oxford, All Souls MS 182 (as well as in BL MS Cotton Cleopatra D. 3 and Harley 3988), printed in M. D. Legge (ed.), *Anglo-Norman Letters and Petitions* (Oxford, 1941), 242–8. Perroy raises doubts about the authenticity of these letters in *Grand Schisme*, 364, but John Palmer argues that they should be accepted as authentic, 'The Background of Richard II's Marriage to Isabel of France', *BIHR* 44 (1971); 8–10. Within the text of the *Epistre* itself, Mézières refers to frequent oral communications to Richard concerning the Order by means of Robert the Hermit, and to 'the book called *La sustance abregie* of the said Order of Chivalry, which the Old Solitary, humbly and devotedly, handed to your beloved brother, the Count of Huntingdon, to give to you so that you might know the blessings which could result from

the *Epistre* does not repeat the descriptions of the Order which were sent to Richard earlier; its purpose is rather to present a series of arguments designed to give the Order special appeal for Richard himself. The treatise takes the form of an extended interpration of a dream in which Richard II appears in the guise of 'a marvellous lodestone' while Charles VI is 'miraculous balm'. The most important attribute of the lodestone is its power, and this power is described as the 'genius' (*engin*, p. 86) of Richard, glossed as his wisdom and his ability to attract not only the love of his subjects but even the love of his enemies the French. This genial power is both a gift of God and a sign that God has appointed him to a special providential role. Richard's divinely granted power has most recently been demonstrated in the Irish campaign, where he succeeded in peacefully subjecting 'a race of people as savage and uncivilised as the Irish, who live with the wild creatures in the mountains, and also the men of the islands, who, with little form of government, depend on the fortune of the sea' (pp. 65, 139).[59]

Another argument, designed to appeal to Richard's views on the merits of strong monarchy, is based on an allegorical contrast between two gardens. Continued war will result in a garden of horror, a place of famine and suffering where there is no justice, love, law or order, and where the strong devour the weak. Peace, however, will create a delectable orchard, where the people will prosper materially and spiritually under the rule of a king who represents 'authority and the common good'; in this garden, all private ownership of property is abolished because the king serves as a 'father' to his people and has complete responsibility for their welfare (pp. 54–62, 127–36).

Whether or not Maude Clarke was correct in suggesting that Richard commissioned the Wilton Diptych as a symbolic statement of his

the establishment of this Order' (*Letter*, 32–105). *La sustance* has been described by A. Molinier, 'Description de deux manuscripts contenant la règle de la *militia passionis Jhesu Christi* de Philippe de Mézières', *Archives de l'Orient Latin* (Brussels, 1964), 346–7, and in A. H. Harmdy, 'Philippe de Mézières and the New Order of the Passion', *Bulletin of the Faculty of Arts*, 18 (1964), 1–105 [not seen]. M. V. Clarke discussed the MS in L. Sutherland and M. McKisack (edd.), *Fourteenth Century Studies* (Oxford, 1937), 288–92 and pls. 2, 3, and 4.

   [59] This view of the Irish campaign as bringing civilization to the savage was evidently one promoted by Richard's inner circle, since it echoes the account of the campaign reported to Froissart in 1395, Froissart, XV. 168–81; cf. the similar but briefer reference to Richard's Irish campaign in the letter from Charles VI, Legge (ed.), *Anglo-Norman Letters and Petitions*, 242. For an account of the role played by the Irish campaign in the construction of an image of Richard as a chivalric leader, see J. L. Gillespie, 'Richard II: Chivalry and Kingship', in id. (ed.), *Age of Richard II*, 115–38.

willingness to join the Order and participate in the crusade,[60] he did agree to marry the daughter of Charles VI, and conclude the peace; the analysis of J. J. N. Palmer suggests that Philippe de Mézières's campaign, culminating in his *Epistre*, played an important role in the negotiations.[61]

It is important to emphasize that this list is not meant as a complete account of all works given to, or owned by, Richard II. It is limited to those which sought or received his patronage and, even within these limits, it omits works for which I have not been able to find any record of patronage. For example, *The Forme of Cury* (BL MS Add. 5016) is described in the headnote as 'compiled of the chef Maister Cokes of kyng Richard the Se[cu]nde. . . . by assent and auysement of Maisters and [i.e. of] phisik and philosophie that dwellid in his court,' but although it describes Richard as 'the best and ryallest vyaundier of alle cristen kynges' it does not give any clear sign of seeking or receiving his patronage.[62] Likewise omitted is the celebrated Belleville Breviary (BN MS lat 10483–4), which Richard received as a gift from Charles VI on the occasion of his marriage to his daughter Isabella.[63] J. J. G. Alexander considers 'only a presumption' the possibility that the *Liber regalis* (Westminster abbey, MS 38), an illuminated copy of the coronation order, may have belonged to Richard, and the circumstances of its commissioning are still unknown.[64] A more likely candidate for inclusion is the *Westminster Chronicle*; Antonia Gransden describes Richard as 'the patron of the Westminster chronicler', and the work might well repay further study, in connection with Sudbury's treatise on the regalia.[65] There may well also be other works, unknown to me, which have been proposed as associated with the patronage of Richard II.

Even with its admitted limitations, this list makes it possible to see some intriguing interconnections among these works, which suggest that some of Richard's interests and preoccupations were known to the writers. The frequent references to and adaptations from *Secretum Secretorum*, for

---

[60] M. V. Clarke, 'The Wilton Diptych', *Burlington Magazine*, 58 (1931), 292; cf. Palmer, *England, France and Christendom*, 242–4; and Scheifele, below, pp. 267–8.

[61] Palmer, *England, France and Christendom*, 187–8. For comments on the *Epistre* and its author, see above, pp. 197, 201.

[62] Printed in C. B. Hieatt and S. Butler (edd.), *Curye on Inglisch* (London, 1985), 93–145 with introd., 20–30, discussing its relationship to early MSS of recipes. Sherborne, 'Aspects of English Court Culture', 33, suggests that this was one of the books that Richard owned.

[63] Alexander, 'Painting and Manuscript Illumination', 147.

[64] Ibid. 146; cf. Sandler, *Gothic Manuscripts*, ii. 182.

[65] A. Gransden, *Historical Writing in England*, 2 vols. (London, 1982), ii, 177–9.

example, suggest that this was a tradition of advice to princes in which
Richard had an interest; although it is not a work of political theory as
such, the *Secretum* assumes a strong personal monarchy is the most desir-
able form of government and offers advice on a variety of means by which
a king can maintain and extend his power.[66] The divinely appointed role
of the king to intervene in history is repeatedly stressed, most notably by
those, like Sudbury, Dymmok, and Mézières, who wish him to intervene
in favour of their own causes. Richard's interest in the history of English
kings and the associated ceremonies and regalia appears in several of the
documents as well as in the history of the regalia itself. Closely associated
with this interest is that of gaining access to or establishing authoritative
sources, whether they be statutes, rules for conducting judicial combat in
the Court of Chivalry, records of the coronation or the 1392 pageant, or
rules for divination by dreams or geomancy. The encyclopaedic character
of Gower's *Confessio* may also be a response to Richard's known interest
in what was believed to be authoritative information. Although few of these
works are directly concerned with political theory or practice, a large number of those who seek his patronage take occasion to voice support for
the royal prerogative in its various manifestations, or advocate directly an
extension of the royal powers.

   The image of kingship that results from such a variety of works is surprisingly consistent. Of the two traditional attributes of kingship, *sapientia*
and *fortitudo*, the emphasis repeatedly falls on *sapientia*.[67] The 'wisdom'
attributed to Richard in these texts is not confined to literacy in three
languages, knowledge of canon and civil law, and expertise in the more
arcane reaches of astrology; it is not a form of knowledge attainable through
book-learning alone, though such learning is evidently taken to be a sign
of this special divine gift. The repeated invocation of the figure of Solomon in these texts suggests that this wisdom is viewed both as a sign of
divine favour and as a legitimation of royal power. Literacy and mastery
of difficult subjects like astrology are not sources but signs of this kind
of wisdom. Wisdom in this sense is conceived as conferring authority on
personal rule.

----

[66] An elaborately illuminated trans. of the *Secretum Secretorum* (BL Add. MS 47680) and
a companion volume offering supplementary moral advice (*De nobilitatibus, sapientiis, et pru-
dentiis regum* (Oxford, Christ Church MS 92)) were made in 1326–7 for Edward III by Walter
of Milemete, king's clerk, but both MSS are unfinished, and it is unlikely that Edward ever
received them (see Sandler, *Gothic Manuscripts*, ii. 90–4).

[67] On the importance of *sapientia* in medieval texts discussing the image of the prince, see
B. Guenée, *States and Rulers in Late Medieval Europe*, trans. J. Vale (Oxford, 1985), 67–80.
See also Saul, *Richard II*, 356–7, 464–5.

The political implications of this kind of wisdom are evoked in several of these texts. The compiler of Bodley MS 581, for example, in a section he has added to his sources, notes that the prudent ruler should apply his wisdom to the selection of his council, testing them carefully and preferring those who are willing to undergo loss of personal honour and even corporal punishment rather than to permit the derogation of the honour or prerogative of their ruler in any respect.[68] In Maidstone's poem, wisdom is the very basis of prerogative itself; the poem concludes with the image of Richard sitting in Solomonic judgement on the erring City of London, demonstrating his wisdom not only in pronouncing their guilt and accepting their pleas for forgiveness but also in his stern reminder to them to 'take heed in the future for the wrath of their king'.[69] For Dymmok, it is the wisdom of Richard II which not only makes possible an understanding of the scholastic arguments against the Lollards, but also authorizes the king to punish them as traitors. Gower devotes the longest digression by far in his *Confessio Amantis*, the whole of book 7, to expounding the manifold nature of the royal wisdom, and his concluding description of Richard in the last section of the recension of the poem dedicated to him (book 8, section iv) portrays him as demonstrating all the virtues associated with wisdom in his commitment to seek peace both at home and abroad.

In attributing this kind of wisdom to Richard and associating it with a style of personal rule which would today be called paternalistic, those who sought and received his literary patronage may well have been reflecting an image in the mind of the king himself. What may justly be regarded as the last text commissioned by Richard, the epitaph that appears on his tomb in Westminster abbey, evokes a parallel image of a wise king in the self-portrait of the opening sentences:

Prudens et Mundus—Ricardus jure Secundus, per fatum victus—jacet hic sub marmore pictus. Verax sermone—fuit, et plenus ratione: Corpore procerus—animo prudens ut Omerus.[70]

---

[68] 'Prudens igitur gubernator sapienter investigare debet qui regni sui proceres, discreciores et nobiliores exstiterint. . . . ipsum preferentes, qui citius honorum ammissionem et penam corporalem sustinerent quam ipsius honorem seu prerogativum in aliquo derogarent, tales enim in consiliarios suos eligere debet' (Genet (ed.), *Political Tracts*, 38).

[69] 'Vos ideoque cavete deinceps principis iras' (l. 521: Smith, '*Concordia*', 222; Wright (ed.), *Political Poems*, i. 299). In response to these words, the people of London are portrayed as rejoicing and renewing their abject professions of submission: 'Gaudet at hec turba; prostrata ruit, jacet humo' (l. 541).

[70] Royal Commission on the Ancient and Historical Monuments and Constructions of England, *An Inventory of the Historical Monuments in London*, 5 vols. (London, 1924–30), i. 30.

12

Richard II and the Visual Arts

Eleanor Scheifele

While Richard II's beleaguered reign was silenced in 1399, his image of kingship has not only endured but prevailed. As the patron of the Westminster hall roof and the Wilton Diptych, Richard has been accorded a stature beyond which even his own ambitions might have conceived.[1] Recently, though, scholars have begun to diminish this acclaim by questioning the presumption of a distinct Ricardian court style.[2] A call has since been made to determine the degree of continuity between Richard's court and that of his grandfather Edward III, especially concerning the number of commissions, formal types, expenditures, and artists employed. Under this revision, the splendour once attributed to Richard's patronage has somewhat dimmed. New large-scale architectural construction and sculptural projects were rare, and now fewer illuminated manuscripts can be ascribed with certainty to his direct commission or even to his private collection.[3] Further, it appears that he often employed artists and formal designs that were inherited from Edward III. Even his alleged extravagance, for

---

The material presented in this chapter is derived from several conference papers delivered from 1987, principally at the International Congress on Medieval Studies, Kalamazoo, Michigan. The author acknowledges the invaluable debt to the comments of the discussants and listeners.

[1] For handsome illustrations of Richard's commissions, many in colour, the reader is referred to the well-documented exhibition catalogue, D. Gordon, *Making and Meaning: The Wilton Diptych* (London, 1993).

[2] G. Mathew, *The Court of Richard II* (London, 1968); *English Court Culture*; K. Staniland, 'Court Style, Painters, and the Great Wardrobe', in W. M. Ormrod (ed.), *England in the Fourteenth Century* (Woodbridge, 1986), 236–46.

[3] V. J. Scattergood, 'Literary Culture at the Court of Richard II', in *English Court Culture*, 29–43; J. J. G. Alexander, 'Painting and Manuscript Illumination for Royal Patrons in the Later Middle Ages', ibid. 141–62.

which he was censured, may not have actually exceeded that of his grand-father. Thus the revisionist view has assessed that Richard's court style was not substantially distinct from that of Edward III, and that Richard himself seems to have displayed little initiative or personal involvement in his commissions.

The present chapter does not challenge the new material evidence but rather the conclusions drawn from it concerning Richard's lack of style-consciousness. A consideration of the symbolic content and function of the works of art suggests to the contrary that he was personally involved in the selection of forms, symbols, and physical sites for his commissions and that he was keenly aware of their political potential to further his image of kingship. To be sure, there is strong evidence for discerning a continu-ity of court style, but such traditionalism need not evince a paucity of vision or the lack of a consciousness of style. It may signify quite the opposite. Richard had a keen antiquarian interest in all things Plantagenet, which was acknowledged by his contemporaries and which might have been reflected by his adoption of a certain retrospective style. Continuity of style with the court of Edward III also offered a political potential: stylistic hered-ity could express dynastic heredity. By presenting a modicum of formal difference, Richard could give visual evidence for his claim of legitimacy to the throne of his grandfather.

Without question Richard II is recognized to have been most interested in the sumptuary arts and in ceremonial pomp.[4] Conventionally banners and streamers functioned as political and social signboards to declare iden-tity and rank. Intended often for public audiences, these banners presented quite traditional designs of heraldic arms, emblems of patron saints, or per-sonal/fraternal/guild devices. Under the patronage of first Edward III and then Richard, personal dress was exploited as a comparable surface for political posturing and employed similar iconography for its patterning.[5] Edward's focus was decidedly feudal, international, and at times satirical. He promoted his Order of the Garter and his claim to the French throne and title of 'Rex Anglie et Rex Francie', the latter by portraying himself in the French coronation robe and by quartering the heraldry of England

---

[4] Mathew, *Court of Richard II*, 38–52; F. Palgrave (ed.), *The antient Kalendars and invent-ories of his Majesty's Exchequer* (etc.), 3 vols. (London, 1836), iii. 315–18, records the invent-ory of Richard's possessions (clothing, jewellery, plate) taken after his deposition, which testifies to Richard's personal splendour.

[5] K. Staniland, 'Clothing and Textiles at the Court of Edward III, 1342–1352', in *Col-lectanea Londiniensis: Studies Presented to Ralph Merrifield* (London and Middlesex Archeo-logical Society, Special Papers, 2; 1978), 223–34; id., 'Court Style', 236–46; S. M. Newton, *Fashion in the Age of the Black Prince: A Study of the Years 1340–1365* (Woodbridge, 1980).

(gold lions-leopardy on a red ground) with that of France Ancient (gold fleurs-de-lis on a blue ground).[6] Richard further exploited the political potential of clothing, but with a marked redirection of focus back to the English throne and more personally back to Richard himself. In distinction, he almost exclusively portrayed himself in the state robe of England, not France, which often bore his personal devices rather than heraldic arms, thereby linking him more personally with the official robe. On a grand scale the Westminster abbey portrait depicts Richard enthroned in a blue tunic, emblazoned with his personal device of the crowned initial R, and enveloped in a red robe with an ermine tippet. Such official dress appears repeatedly in the various manuscript portraits of Richard,[7] where he is enthroned and in possession of the regalia (crown, sceptre, and orb). From Edward III, Richard inherited the quartered arms with which he began to link the arms of Edward the Confessor (gold cross patonce and five martlets on a blue ground) and ultimately impaled them by perhaps 1395.[8] Rarely, however, did Richard use heraldry alone as a full decorative pattern,[9] preferring instead his personal devices of the crowned initial R or the recumbant white hart crown-collared and chained (as depicted in the Wilton Diptych), or a combination thereof (as seen on his Westminster abbey tomb effigy).

By far though, it was the white hart that became the symbol most closely identified with Richard, its provenance and inherent import well reflecting and promoting his self-image and that of his court. For the Smithfield tournament in October 1390, the device of the white hart was introduced as the king's personal livery and was emblazoned on the English team's surcoats, armour, shields, and tack.[10] Even more spectacular,

[6] E. Danbury, 'English and French Artistic Propaganda during the Hundred Years War: Some Evidence from Royal Charters', in C. Allmand (ed.), *Power, Culture, and Religion in France, c.1350–c.1550* (Woodbridge, 1989), 75–97.

[7] Most notable illuminated portraits are Oxford: Bodleian Library MS Ashmole 1831; MS Bodley 581, fo. 9ʳ; London: BL Cotton MS Nero D VII, fo. 7; Westminster Abbey, MS 38, fos. 1ᵛ, 20, 29, 33ᵛ; Cambridge: Trinity Hall, MS 17, fo. 1; St John's College, MS A.7; Shrewsbury: Guildhall, Corporation Muniments, Box 1, no. 24.

[8] J. H. Harvey, 'The Wilton Diptych: A Re-examination', *Archaeologia*, 98 (1961), 5–6.

[9] An exception may be the now lost altarpiece, between 1382–94, for the English College in Rome, which apparently depicted Richard in a robe that was entirely emblazoned with heraldic devices (perhaps for the benefit of the international audience in Rome). For discussions and reconstructions, see S. Petrasancta, *Tesserae Gentilitiae* (Rome, 1638), 677–78; C. Coupe, 'An Old Picture', *Month*, 84 (1895), 229–42; Harvey, 'Wilton Diptych', 1–24; D. Gordon, 'A New Discovery in the Wilton Diptych', *Burlington Magazine*, 134 (1992), 662–7.

[10] *Vita*, 122; S. Lindenbaum, 'The Smithfield Tournament of 1390', *Journal of Medieval and Renaissance Studies*, 20 (1990), 1–20; R. L. Storey, 'Liveries and Commissions of Peace, 1388–1390', in *Reign of Richard II*, 131–52.

before the jousts began there was a procession in London of twenty knights in golden chains led by twenty ladies, all forty of whom wore the red livery with the chained white hart,[11] thereby bedecked in Richard's favourite colours of red and white. He later repeated this ceremonial pageant for the January 1397 coronation of his child bride Isabella.[12]

Richard did not invent the symbol of the white hart, nor its royal and chivalric contexts.[13] For an earlier London tournament, Edward III had staged a similar procession of knights and ladies (but without the white hart imagery). As for the hart itself, Richard's father, the Black Prince, had a bed-covering that displayed the hart encircled with the arms of Kent and Wake, suggesting that the device derived from Richard's mother, Joan of Kent.[14] The white hart also had a continental connection. The French version, the *cerf volant*, was slightly different in form but not in meaning; it was white and crown-collared but it also had wings and was rampant.[15] As early as 1380, the coronation year of Charles VI, the hart became the personal device of the French king when, according to Juvénal des Ursins, Charles was said to have captured a white hart at Senlis, which bore on its crown-collar the inscription 'CAESAR HOC MIHI DONAVIT'.[16] In 1389 the French hart made its ceremonial debut for Queen Isabella of Bavaria's royal entry into Paris, when in the form of an automaton (a mechanical model with movable eyes, limbs, and wings) it took up a sword nearby and held it erect as the queen passed by.[17] Charles VI's capture of the hart in the year of his coronation, the inscription on its collar, and the ceremonial introduction of it at a coronation all demonstrate his knowledge of the hart's symbolism. According to the legend of Caesar's deer, the chain and crown-collar identified the hart as the *cervus reservatus*, whose recapture was a pledge of dynastic continuity, legitimacy, and renewal.[18]

---

[11] Lindenbaum, 'Smithfield Tournament', 4 and n. 5.

[12] PRO E101/403/5 records payments for forty red garments embroidered with the white hart; Harvey, 'Wilton Diptych', 7 and n. 3; Gordon, *Making and Meaning*, 51.

[13] M. Bath, 'The Iconography of the Collared Deer', in K. Varty (ed.), *Proceedings of the International Colloquium Beast Epic, Fable, and Fabliau* (Glasgow, 1976), 73–80; id., 'The White Hart, the *cerf volant*, and the Wilton Diptych', in J. Goossens and T. Sodman (edd.), *Third International Beast Epic, Fable and Fabliau Colloquium* (Cologne, 1981), 25–42; id., 'Imperial *renovatio* symbolism in the Très Riches Heures', *Simiolus*, 17 (1987), 5–22.

[14] N. H. Nicolas, 'Observations on the Origin and History of the Badges and Mottoes of Edward Prince of Wales', *Archaeologia*, 31 (1846), 364.

[15] H. M. Legros, 'Les Cerf volants supports des armes de Charles VI', *Revue des études historiques*, 97 (1930), 1–4; C. Beaune, 'Costume et pouvoir en France à la fin du Moyen Âge; Les Devices royales vers 1400', *Revue des sciences humaines*, 183 (1981), 125–46.

[16] Bath, 'White Hart', 27 and n. 5.   [17] Ibid, 32.

[18] Id., 'The Legend of Caesar's Deer', *Medievalia et Humanistica*, 9 (1979), 53–66.

The political implications of Caesar's deer would also have held special appeal for Richard, and for his symbolic defence of his dynastic legitimacy. Further, Richard's deliberate choice of the Smithfield tournament to introduce his livery may also have been motivated by the additional significance of the white hart as a symbol of chivalric honour and prowess, as is expressed by the royal hunt of the white hart in Arthurian romances, such as *Erec and Enide*. The image that Richard created at Smithfield, of the captured chained white hart emblazoned on the chained red knights, was no hollow pomp but, rather, explicit political posturing in which life was made to imitate art. With this one symbol, he could proclaim his dynastic continuity and legitimacy to the Crown, invoke the manifold significances of Caesar's deer, and strengthen support for his court. Obviously such rich symbolism was worth repeating, for the chained white hart appears many times and in many forms throughout his reign,[19] most notably in the Wilton Diptych where it is emblazoned on Richard's red mantle and worn as a livery badge by the king and the eleven angels.

Such self-conscious political symbolism was not restricted to secular dress or banners. Letters patent of 8 May 1389 record that Richard commissioned a complete set of red vestments for the abbot and convent of Westminster, by which Edward the Confessor was to be perpetually honoured on his feast-days as the young king's predecessor.[20] While the chasuble is no longer extant, the orphrey scheme was described in some detail. One border displayed hierarchically the images of the Trinity and Mary, then St Edward King and Confessor, then St Edmund King and Martyr, and last the arms of the Confessor, Richard, and Anne of Bohemia; juxtaposed on the other border were the images of Mary, then John the Baptist, then the abbot, and last the same arms linked. The precise selection of these figures reflects the purpose for the commission, its intended recipient, and its patron Richard. Sts Edward and Edmund were national royal symbols and their inclusion may have served to signify the young king's royal ancestors. The juxtaposition of the Baptist and the Confessor may have served to express their favoured status as Richard's personal saints. Last, the inclusion of the king's heraldry linked with the Confessor's identified him with the commission, with his succession from Edward, and with its dynastic implications.

---

[19] For the numerous and varied white hart images in Richard's court, Gordon, *Making and Meaning*, 49–50.

[20] J. W. Legg, 'On an Inventory of the Vestry in Westminster Abbey, taken in 1388', *Archaeologia*, 52 (1890), 280–1. For Richard and the cult of St Edward, see above, pp. 41–3, 90–1, and 203.

In contrast with these sumptuary arts, Richard is perceived to have been the least personally involved in new large-scale public works, since few architectural initiatives can be ascribed to his direct patronage with the exception of the new palace in Windsor Park, *c*.1394–6.[21] As successor to the prolific building projects of Henry III, Edward I, and Edward III, there remained perhaps little practical need or justification for Richard to commission additional structures. Rather the young king chose to enlarge, renovate, and decorate a few select monuments, which included the palace at Westminster and the personal residences of Edward III, Westminster abbey as the coronation site with its Plantagenet tombs (including those of his grandparents), and Canterbury cathedral with its tomb of his father, the Black Prince. From a historical perspective then, Richard was outproduced and outspent by his royal ancestors, which has fuelled the modern judgement of a lack of comparable architectural interest on his part.[22]

However, physically less may be symbolically more. Continuity of form and place can proclaim a continuity of rule, whereas new constructions in a new style and at new sites can evoke a public perception of a new and distinct court. Richard's interest in architecture bespeaks an awareness and exploitation of this potential. Further, the image of the Crown in perpetuity was signified by his concentration on those sites which most clearly represented the full dynastic cycle, from the coronation to the court in residence to the royal necropolis. A personal statement was also added by his attention to the commissions and sites that were of special interest to his father and grandfather.

If Richard was less a patron of new architectural construction, he was more a patron of architectural decoration and symbolic space. Nowhere is this interest more evident than with his renovation and embellishment of Westminster hall, particularly in the carpentry of its new open-timber roof.[23] While the synthesis of the hammerbeam bracket system with the arch-brace-and-collar was unique at this time, each form had been used independently before and within Richard's personal sphere, most notably

[21] Mathew, *Court of Richard II*, 32–7; H. M. Colvin, 'The "Court Style" in Medieval English Architecture: A Review', in *English Court Culture*, 129–39; id., in *King's Works*, i. 161–292.

[22] J. W. Sherborne, 'Aspects of English Court Culture in the Later Fourteenth Century', in *English Court Culture*, 1–27; Mathew, *Court of Richard II*, 32–7; Colvin, 'Court Style', 129–39, who presents a less harsh assessment.

[23] Colvin, in *King's Works*, i. 527–33; L. T. Courtenay, 'The Westminster Hall Roof and its Fourteenth Century Sources', *Journal of the Society of Architectural Historians*, 43 (1984), 295–309; id. and R. Mark, 'The Westminster Hall Roof: A Historiographic and Structural Study', *Journal of the Society of Architectural Historians*, 46 (1987), 374–93.

by Edward III for his great Hall of St George at Windsor castle, *c*.1362.[24] Richard's distinct contribution to these inherited forms was to add a multilayered, self-reflective gloss. For this new decorative veneer he selected only those symbols that would promote his legitimacy and royal power: the white hart, his heraldic arms linked with the Confessor's, angels bearing his heraldry, statues of the past Plantagenet kings, together with his own likeness. The import of these symbols was then heightened by their repeated use and precise placement—at the prime visual power points which mark the union of the two formerly separate truss systems, the distinction between the solid stone wall and the open carpentry vault, and between the inherited architectural shell and Richard's new rhetorical space. The king's personal device of the chained white hart lodged is stamped, so to speak, continuously along the string-course that girds the interior space and pronounces the union of the masonry wall with the new timber roof. The arms of Richard and the Confessor alternate on the crowned corbels that mark the springing of the vault. Then from above, heavenly angels with heraldic shields project from the hammerbeam terminals and define the fusion of the two truss systems. Recent analysis by L. Courtenay has determined that these visual power points are no mere ornament as had previously been thought.[25] Rather, as the true load-bearing supports and stress-stabilizers for the vault, the corbels and beam terminals are the real structural power points. Richard's renewal of Westminster Hall reveals a predilection to blur the real with the fictive and to confuse substance with symbol; such a tendency is witnessed in his other commissions and perhaps also in his political policies and personal character.

Into this rhetorical space were to have been placed at least thirteen stone statues of Plantangenet kings from Edward the Confessor to Richard himself.[26] Monumental figures in full regalia with orbs, sceptres, and generous crowns, they most likely were intended to stand in front of Richard's personal and heraldic devices on the wall and under the heavenly sanction of the angels hovering in the vault above. Today the series stands incomplete and the exact placement of each figure is uncertain, yet quite evident is their symbolic import as dynastic witnesses for Richard's kingship. Formal sources and comparisons for such a series may be found in choir screens which were decorated with similar statues of kings and which were to provide a secular reflection in stone of Christ's royal

---

[24] Id., 'Westminster Hall', 308–9.   [25] Id., and Mark, 'Westminster Hall', 392–3.
[26] Colvin, in *King's Works*, i. 528. Dr Courtenay delivered a paper on the sculptural programme and its meaning for the Fourteenth International Congress on Medieval Studies, May 1979, Kalamazoo, Mich.

genealogy from King David, as read from the *pulpitum*.[27] In stained glass, the programme of the royal window in Canterbury cathedral may have provided an extensive listing of Richard's progenitors.[28]

A most personal dynastic statement was made by the king's commission of the double effigy tomb at Westminster abbey for himself and Anne of Bohemia.[29] Much state ceremony and politically charged symbolism has traditionally marked the funeral of a king or queen, which often has found more permanent expression in the tomb design and the site selection. Richard did not miss such an opportunity. In 1395 he contracted for a double tomb to be installed in the westernmost bay on the south side of the chapel of Edward the Confessor (necessitating the removal of an earlier occupant). By sheer physical proximity to the Confessor's shrine, Richard could express continuously his personal association. A coincidence of date may have motivated the young king's lifelong devotion: the Confessor was believed to have been buried at Westminster on 6 January 1066, while on the same day in 1367 a new king, Richard II, was born (thereby linking the death of the old king and the birth of the new king into a compressed symbol of the Crown eternal). Speculation aside, dynastic linkage with the Confessor was represented quite tangibly by the insertion of Richard's double tomb within the pre-existing necropolis series of select Plantagenet kings and queens (Henry III and Eleanor, Edward I, and Edward III and Philippa). Visual continuity was maintained by Richard's use of gilt-bronze for his effigies to match the earlier tombs and to complete the glittering radiance about the Confessor's shrine. Specific linkage with Edward III was expressed by the placement of Richard's tomb directly adjacent to that of his grandfather and by the stylistic consonance of both tomb chests.[30] Hereditary descent may also have been signified by the choice of emblems that were powdered on Richard's state robe: Richard himself is represented by his crowned initial R and the white hart lodged, his grandfather by the device of the clouds with the rising sun, and his Plantagenet lineage by the broom-cods (*planta genista*).[31]

---

[27] Sir W. St.-John Hope, 'Quire Screens in English Churches, with Special Reference to the Twelfth-Century Quire Screen formerly in the Cathedral Church of Ely', *Archaeologia*, 68 (1916–17), 43–110; id., 'Images of Kings in the Cathedral Church of Salisbury', *Wiltshire Archaeological and Natural History Magazine*, 39 (1917), 505–6.

[28] M. H. Caviness, *The Windows of Christ Church Cathedral Canterbury* (Oxford, 1981), 227–48.

[29] PRO E101/473/7 records the tomb contract; see also *Foedera*, vii. 797. For modern discussions, see Colvin, in *King's Works*, i. 477–90; and Gordon, *Making and Meaning*, 63 n. 9.

[30] J. H. Harvey, *Henry Yevele, c.1320–1400* (London, 1944), 35.

[31] J. G. Nicolas, 'Observations on the Heraldic Devices discovered on the Effigies of Richard II and his Queen in Westminster Abbey', *Archaeologia*, 29 (1842), 32–59. For the interpretation of the broom-cod motif as a possible reference to the Plantagenet dynasty (*planta*

Yet Richard's double tomb incorporates several elements that are quite distinct and unprecedented. The profusion of personal devices that appear on Richard's effigy is in stark contrast to the unpatterned robe of Edward III's image, evincing the young king's predilection for densely layered, over-stated, personal symbolism. A further distinction in form and import is witnessed by the arrangement of the effigies' hands (now missing) and the inclusion of the regalia. According to the contract, Richard and Anne were not to clasp their hands conventionally in gestures of prayer for divine recep-tion, but rather were to join their right hands in a show of marital devo-tion and were to hold in their left hands royal sceptres in evidence of their sovereignty. The orb was then to be placed between them and crowns at their heads. This exceptional inclusion of the regalia reflects the manifold political import of Westminster abbey itself as the depository for the bod-ies of the past Plantagenet kings, the repository for the actual regalia, and the ceremonial site for the coronation of the new king. By placing his regalian portrait within this charged context, Richard defended his hereditary claim to the Crown and its prerogatives; a birthright that was witnessed by the past English kings and demonstrated then and still now by Richard's pos-session of the regalia. Divine reception was then invoked by the painted testor (now in ghostly ruin) above the king and queen, which depicts the Enthroned Majesty and the Coronation of the Virgin.[32] Last at either end of the testor are two sets of angels who stand in a paradisial mead and bear the heraldic shields of Richard and Anne.

To this regalian image of kingship, Richard bonded his most personal symbol—his own portrait—thereby linking symbolically the institution of the Crown with the individual who wears it.[33] According to all accounts, the king was considered to be quite handsome with smooth fair skin, arched eyebrows, languid eyes, straight nose, high cheekbones, golden wavy hair, and later a small double-pointed beard and thin moustache.[34] The tomb

genista), and its reference to Charles VI of France, see Harvey, 'Wilton Diptych', 8–10; R. W. Lightbrown, *Medieval European Jewelery* (London, 1992), 269 ff; Gordon, *Making and Meaning*, 51–3.

[32] E. W. Tristram, *English Wall Painting of the Fourteenth Century* (London, 1955), 199–200. For Richard's patronage of Westminster abbey, see above, pp. 90–1.

[33] Such visual bonding of the king's body natural (portrait) with the king's body cor-porate (regalia) may touch on the concept of the 'King's Two Bodies'; E. Kantorowicz, *The King's Two Bodies: A Study in Medieval Political Theology* (Princeton, 1957); R. Giesey, 'Inaugural Aspects of French Royal Ceremonials', in J. Bak (ed.), *Coronations* (Berkeley and Los Angeles, 1990), 34–45.

[34] S. Whittingham, 'The Chronology of the Portraits of Richard II', *Burlington Maga-zine*, 113 (1971), 12–21; Harvey, 'Wilton Diptych', 1–24; Gordon, *Making and Meaning*, 22–4, who reports that infra-red reflectography of Richard's portrait profile reveals that an area

effigy displays these features but in a rather stylized manner. Prior to his reign, portraiture in England had been used only sporadically, while in France Charles V had made extensive use of it within a variety of official but also narrative contexts.[35] In contrast with both traditions, Richard was distinctly single-focused. He almost exclusively portrayed himself enthroned in a frontal hieratic pose, in possession of the regalia, and alone or within the symbolic company of past English kings, or divine personages, or both.[36] Such a constancy of image may have been inspired by a personal interest in symbolic physiognomy. One of the few manuscripts known to have been made at Richard's request was a collection of treatises (Oxford, Bodleian Library, MS Ashmole 581), dated 1391, which dealt with the qualities of the Wise Ruler and the various means by which they could be discerned.[37] Included was a short treatise on physiognomy, *Phisionomia Aristotelis* (fos. 3^r–5^r), which explained the art of interpreting character, especially wisdom (*res sapiens*), from a person's/king's facial features. Also included in this manuscript (as an exemplar of the Wise Ruler?) was an illuminated portrait of Richard (fo. 9^r), enthroned, cloaked in the blue state robe with ermine tippet, and invested with the sceptre and crown.

A comparable portrait is presented by the much-restored panel painting of Richard II in Westminster abbey, but on a far more public scale than the manuscript illuminations.[38] Silhouetted against a gold background, the young king is enthroned, crowned, and vested in the state robe emblazoned with the crowned initial R. In his right hand he holds the

had been left, which at a later stage was painted with Richard's anachronistically youthful image, suggesting that the portrait was delayed until a suitable model could be provided. No such delay would have been necessary for a contemporary image of the king. For his appearance, see also above, pp. 27–8.

[35] For English portraiture, see W. A. Shaw, 'The Early English School of Portraiture', *Burlington Magazine*, 65 (1934), 171–84: A Hepburn, *Portraits of the Later Plantagenets* (Woodbridge, 1986); R. Ormond, *The Face of Monarchy: British Royalty Portrayed* (London, 1977). For the French practice at the courts of Charles V and VI, see C. R. Sherman, *The Portraits of Charles V of France (1338–1380)*, (New York, 1969); A. Hepburn, *The Royal Image* (Berkeley and Los Angeles, 1991).

[36] E. Danbury, 'The Decoration and Illumination of Royal Charters in England, 1250–1509: An Introduction', in M. Jones and M. Vale (edd.), *England and her Neighbours, 1066–1453* (London, 1989), 157–79; id., 'Artistic Propaganda', 75–97; see above, n. 7 for a listing of some of the images.

[37] Scattergood, 'Literary Culture', 41–2; H. Carey, *Courting Disaster: Astrology at the English Court and University in the Later Middle Ages* (New York, 1992), 92–116.

[38] Hepburn, *Portraits*, 13–26; Tristram, *English Wall Painting*, 196–8; G. Scharf, 'The Westminster Portrait of Richard II', *Fine Arts Quarterly Review*, NS 2 (1867), 27–63; W. R. Lethaby, 'The Westminster Portrait of Richard II', *Burlington Magazine*, 65 (1934), 220–2.

cross-mounted orb, while in his left he grasps the sceptre. The display of these royal ensigns is reversed from the depiction in the royal charters, but it echoes the intended arrangement for the tomb and the impression from the Great Seal. By the strict frontality of the pose, Richard also appears as the secular reflection of Christ in Majesty, thereby visually assuming the role of the *vicarius Christi*, as confirmed by his elevation to royal and quasi-sacerdotal power at the coronation and unction. With this commission as well, the physical context may have played a determining role. There is little doubt that the painting was intended for Westminster abbey, but its precise placement and function are less certain. Most compelling is the theory that the panel once decorated the back of the royal pew, which may have been located in the stall on the south side of the choir.[39] Two accounts from the *Westminster Chronicle* record that in 1390 and again in 1392 for the feast-day of the Translation of Edward the Confessor, 13 October, Richard apparently sat crowned in the choir, while the queen 'took her place on the north side' (presumably then the king sat opposite her on the south side).[40] Here one should recall Richard's earlier gift of the chasuble to the abbot, which was to be worn on the Confessor's feast-days as a symbol of Richard's dynastic heritage. In direct proximity with this vestment, the panel portrait would have manifested Richard's constant devotion to Edward and asserted his birthright.

Of greater celebrity and controversy is the Wilton Diptych, the last commission under discussion. As this painting has recently been cleaned and technically investigated, and well documented in an exhibition, catalogue, and symposium in 1993 by D. Gordon of the National Gallery,[41] only those aspects that are most pertinent to this study of Richard's consciousness of style are presented here. For over a century the Diptych has resisted scholarly attempts to interpret its meaning and purpose, with the debate centred on reconciling historical reality with political symbolism. Based on the heraldry and Richard's adoption of the white-hart livery and broom-cod collar, the painting is now dated securely to the years from 1395 to

[39] Hepburn, *Portraits*, 13–26; Lethaby, 'Westminster Portrait', 220–2; F. Sandford, *The History of the Coronation . . . of James I* (London, 1687), 102–3, who illustrates an engraving that depicts the panel in the choir.

[40] *Westm. Chron.* 450.

[41] Gordon, 'New Discovery', 662–7; id., *Making and Meaning*. For the symposium also held at the Gallery, 5–6 Nov. 1993, 'The Wilton Diptych and Court Art in the Reign of Richard II', see the summary report by P. Binski in *Kunstchronik* (Apr. 1994), 188–90. Another symposium, 'The Wilton Diptych: Image, Meaning, and Context', was held on 9 Apr. 1994 at the University of Massachusetts, Amherst; for the listing of speakers, see *Avista Forum*, 8 (1994), 15. For discussions of the Diptych, see also above, pp. 10–13, 203.

1399.[42] Yet the youthful, unbearded portrait of the king and the unusual
number of eleven angels have suggested an earlier reference to Richard's
coronation in 1377, when he was 11 years old.[43] Speculations have also
focused on the possible significances of the banner, the Passion symbols,
and the liveried angels. Yet the apparent enigma of these elements and
their combined meaning fades when they are viewed within the company
of other Ricardian commissions and when the coexistence and compres-
sion of multiple symbolic references is recognized. All the now familar symbols and predilections that characterize Richard's patronage are repeated
in the Diptych, albeit in a more concentrated form. Closed, the panels display the chained white hart lodged and the impaled arms of Richard and
the Confessor, while open they present Richard's crowned image (here in
profile) linked with the figures of Edward the Confessor and Edmund the
Martyr, John the Baptist, the Virgin and Child, and celestial angels bearing Richard's device (here wearing his livery badge rather than holding
his heraldic shield).

Open, the Diptych forms a single composition that reads as an
Epiphany—as the three priestly kings in Adoration of the Christ Child.[44]
Tradition places the foremost king in a kneeling pose, while the two others
stand behind displaying their gifts. A standing attendant may hold the
gift for the first king. In the Diptych, Richard plays the role of the first
king, with John the Baptist as his aide. All three saints then display their
attributes as gifts of homage to Christ: the Baptist with the Agnus Dei,
the Confessor with the royal ring, and Edmund with his arrow of martyr-
dom. These attributes correspond with the symbolic import of the Magi's
gifts: divinity (frankincense), royalty (gold), and mortality (myrrh).[45] The
feast-day of Epiphany on 6 January celebrates the royal and sacerdotal
acknowledgement of Christ's claim to the throne of David as augured
by his birth. Richard was born on this feast-day in 1367, and thus he was

---

[42] M. V. Clarke, 'The Wilton Diptych', *Burlington Magazine*, 58 (1931), 283–94, first determined the later dating, based on the heraldic evidence. The recent scientific investigation
of the Diptych confirms that the heraldic emblems are contemporary with the painted
panels; Gordon, *Making and Meaning*, 74–81.

[43] Richard's youthful portrait was first linked to his coronation by M. Conway, 'The Wilton
Diptych', *Burlington Magazine*, 55 (1929), 209; also for Gordon's recent finding regarding
the making of the portrait, see above, n. 34.

[44] The Epiphany reference was first noted by Conway, 'Wilton Diptych', 210, and
W. G. Constable, 'The Date and Nationality of the Wilton Diptych', *Burlington Magazine*,
55 (1929) 41.

[45] The writings of Gregory the Great are the chief source for the symbolism of the Magi's
gifts, see e.g., *Homilia XL in Evangelia*, lib. 1 (*Patrologiae cursus completus*, series latina, ed.
J.-P. Migne (Paris, 1844–64), lxxvi. 1112–1113).

born into a symbolic semblance with Christ, to which he made reference throughout his troubled reign. Such a personal association may have inspired the choice of the Epiphany scheme as well as the reciprocal roles played by Christ and Richard. The saints/Magi seem to present yet one more gift with which to honour Christ—that of Richard himself—and in feudal fashion Christ shows his acceptance by exposing his foot to be ceremonially kissed. Richard then gestures in an attitude of expectation (not exclusively of prayer) for he is about to receive a gift himself. At the divine command, the angel who is nearest to Christ and who points directly towards Richard, will invest the young king with the sovereign banner of St George (the white standard charged with a red cross and surmounted by an orb).

Often perceived as a pivotal linking device for the Diptych, the banner has been the focus of much scholarly interest.[46] One theory has associated it with Philippe de Mézières's call for a crusade and with his Order of the Passion, based on the exceptional inclusion of the Passion symbols in Christ's halo (the Crown of Thorns and three nails) and the identification of the banner as that of the crusading Order or of Christ's Resurrection.[47] John Palmer has further suggested that the angels are wearing the secular livery badges of Richard II, and the broom-cod collars of Charles VI to show the divine support of these monarchs' ambitions to undertake a crusade to the Holy Land.[48] But Mézières's crusading banner differs significantly from that in the Diptych, as it was to be white and charged with a red cross but with a black quatrefoil in the centre impressed with a gold Agnus Dei;[49] in contrast, no Agnus Dei appears in the centre of the Diptych's banner.[50] Recent cleaning and technical examination of the panel, however, has revealed some startling discoveries, which raise new questions concerning the meaning of the banner. Originally it was surmounted

---

[46] The association of the banner with crusading was first proposed by G. Scharf, *Description of the Wilton House Diptych* (London, 1882), 65 ff.

[47] Associations with Philippe de Mézières' crusading Order of the Passion were developed by Clarke, 'Wilton Diptych', 283–94; J. J. N. Palmer, *England, France and Christendom 1377–1399* (London, 1972), 242–4. For this crusade and Philippe de Mézières, see *Philippe de Mézières' Letter to King Richard II*, ed. and trans. G. W. Coopland (Liverpool, 1975), ed.'s introd., pp. ix–xxxiv; A. H. Hamdy, 'Philippe de Mézières and the New Order of the Passion', *Bulletin of the Faculty of the Arts*, 18 (1964) 1–105. See also above, pp. 197, 201, and 249–52.

[48] Palmer, *England, France and Christendom*, 243.

[49] *La su(b)stance de la Chevalerie de la Passion de Jhesu Crist en Francois*, c.1389–94, Oxford, Bodleian Library, Ashmole MS.813, fo. 4ʳ; *Epistre au Roi Richart*, c.1395, BL Royal MS.20.B.VI, fos. 1ᵛ and 35ʳ. For the transcription of the texts, see Hamdy, 'Philippe de Mézières', 86, which describes the banner (Ashmole MS.813).

[50] Clarke, 'Wilton Diptych,' 294, acknowledged that the banner in the *Diptych* does not display an Agnus Dei, but Christ's emblem is carried by John the Baptist.

by a four-armed cross atop a small orb; later a second, larger orb was painted over the cross.[51] Evidently, then, this original form of the banner fused the cross-staff of Christ's banner with the orb-surmounted banner of St George and thereby fused the sacred image of Christ's salvation with the secular image of Richard's sovereignty. On this second orb was painted a scene which Gordon has interpreted as a small map depicting a green island with a white turreted castle, trees, a blue sky, and a silver sea upon which sails a small boat.[52] Gordon then speculates that this map may signify the island of Britain and further that it may be similar to the 'globe or pat-terne of England' that Richard presented to the Virgin as her dowry in the now lost altarpiece in Rome, dated between 1382 and 1394.[53] If such may be the case, then this observation would present yet another example of Richard's recycling of symbols. However, the banner is not the only gift that is presented to the Heavenly Court. Richard himself is presented by the saints/Magi, suggesting that while the banner may signify the sovereignty of England, Richard signifies the individual who exercises its power and prerogatives. Both Richard and the banner are presented to Christ, who then signals his divine sanction of Richard's kingship by bless-ing the banner and returning it to the young king's outstretched hands. Perhaps the dual symbolism of the original banner was intended to rep-resent the transformation of the secular banner by Christ's blessing.

In addition, the banner may refer to the date when Richard was knighted and actually received the sovereign banner, on 23 April 1376, the feast-day of St George. Such a chivalric investiture was the first ceremonial step towards royal investiture at the coronation. Further events in Richard's advent to the throne may be signified by the specific selection, placement, and astrological import of the three saints who stand behind him.[54] At the panel's far left is Edmund on whose feast-day, 20 November 1376, Richard was invested as prince of Wales. At the far right is the figure of the Baptist on the vigil of whose feast-day, 16 July 1377, Richard received the crown. Last in the centre is Edward the Confessor, on whose feast-day, 10 December 1377, Richard convened his first Parliament.[55] Sts Edward and Edmund also stand in their now familar role as Richard's dynastic forebears and, together with the Baptist (and the Virgin), they repeat the

[51] Gordon, 'New Discovery', 664.
[52] Ibid. 664–6; and id., *Making and Meaning*, 57–8.
[53] Id., 'New Discovery', 665–7; id., *Making and Meaning*, 58; see also above, n. 9, for the Rome altarpiece. Cf. above, p. 12.
[54] S. J. Ferris, 'The Iconography of the Wilton Diptych', *Minnesota Review*, 7 (1967), 342–7 suggested this possible symbolic reference to key dates in Richard's ascendency to the throne.
[55] *RP* ii. 361–3.

decorative scheme of the Westminster abbey chasuble. Their precise placement in the painting may also allude to the architectural alignment of their chapels with the coronation site at Westminster abbey: the Confessor's chapel and shrine are in the centre with the chapels of Edmund and the Baptist flanking it to the north and south.[56] It has been further proposed that these three saints may be portraits of Richard's immediate forebears: the Black Prince is John the Baptist, Edward III is the Confessor, and Edward II is Edmund the Martyr—an appealing theory but one difficult to substantiate.[57]

Both panels are further linked by the liberal peppering of coronation symbols and white hart badges. Quite explicit is the display of crowns in appropriately varied guises: Richard wears the English royal crown as do Sts Edmund and Edward, Christ wears his Crown of Thorns, and the angels wear their coronas of red and white roses (rather than divine haloes).[58] Christ's Crown of Thorns may thus present a dual symbolism, signifying both his Majesty and Passion; a duality which seems to be also expressed by the frontispiece illumination from the *Epistre au Roi Richart*, where Christ's Crown of Thorns is flanked by the secular royal crowns of England and France.[59] Further, Richard's decidedly youthful self-portrait in the Diptych should still be considered a reference to his coronation in 1377, but as a symbolic not literal record. Additional references to a yet more recent event may also have been intended by the same crown imagery, Richard's youthful appearance, and the angels' sporting of the white hart badges. At the opening of the Revenge Parliament of 1397, Richard declared that he had restored the 'crown of his youth' that had been denied him by the Appellants in the Merciless Parliament.[60] At the close of the 1397

---

[56] F. Wormald, 'The Wilton Diptych', *Journal of the Warburg and Courtauld Institutes*, 17 (1954), 200.

[57] J. Evans, 'The Wilton Diptych Reconsidered', *Archaeological Journal*, 105 (1948), 1–5; M. Galway, 'The Wilton Diptych: A Postscript', *Archaeological Journal*, 107 (1950), 9–14; Harvey, 'Wilton Diptych', 191–203 nn. 1 and 4. Wormald, 'Wilton Diptych', 191–203, rejected this theory yet the question of emblematic portraiture was raised again by Nigel Morgan at the 1993 National Gallery symposium and by C. T. Wood at the 1994 Amherst symposium; see above, n. 41.

[58] Gordon, *Making and Meaning*, 80, says that scientific analysis of the Diptych has determined that the 'red lake pigments have faded', so the coronas which now appear to be pink and white would originally have been red and white.

[59] BL Royal MS.20.B.VI, fo. 1ʳ; the letter to King Richard by Philippe de Mézières, proposing a joint crusade with Charles VI, *c*.1395; *de Mézières' Letter*, 1–72. The Passion significance, rather than royal symbolism, of this frontispiece has been emphasized; Palmer, *England, France and Christendom*, 243; Gordon, *Making and Meaning*, 60 and pl. 17.

[60] *RP* iii. 347–85; *Annales*, 209–25; Adam of Usk, 9–23; F. S. Haydon (ed.), *Eulogium Historiatum sive Temporis*, 3 (RS, 1863), 373–9. For the 11 peerage creations on 25 Sept. 1397, *RP* iii. 355.

Parliament, eleven nobles, who received more elevated titles, renewed their coronation oaths of fealty at the Confessor's shrine in Westminster, and who were themselves invested with Richard's livery. In the Diptych then, Richard's crowned anachronistic portrait may symbolize the renewal of the 'crown of his youth' and the restoration of his sovereign prerogatives. Perhaps here also the curious ambiguity of the banner may have been intended to fuse the emblem of Christ's Resurrection and victory (over death) with Richard's renewal and victory (over the Appellants) into a reciprocal acknowledgement of royal power.

The eleven liveried angels also suggest not one significance but rather compress several references. The number eleven seems to have held special meaning for Richard, as it could signify his age at his coronation, the regnal year when he lost his prerogatives (1388), and the restoration of his power in 1397 with the eleven newly entitled nobles. The white hart badges worn by the angels and by Richard proclaim the renewal and continuity of his sovereignty, as signified by the legend of Caesar's deer, confirmed by Christ's blessing, and declared officially in Parliament. Furthermore, the depiction of liveried angels may not have been intended as a purely secular or sacrilegious image.[61] The hart was not exclusively a secular symbol, for it also was associated with Christ as a symbol of Christian devotion (referring to Psalm 41 : 2), and as a divine messenger (as the cruciferous stag of Sts Eustace and Hubert).[62] Rich in symbolism, the hart livery in the Diptych could signify the angels' and Richard's devotion to Christ as the source of salvation, and as the source of Richard's divine authority to rule. The white hart devices might then demonstrate a reciprocal fealty given to both kings, to Christ, as well as to his chosen vicar on earth, Richard.

Perhaps, then, the Wilton Diptych was made soon after the Revenge Parliament in glorification of Richard's renewed regal authority, which had been augured by his birthright on Epiphany in 1367, confirmed ceremonially at his coronation in 1377, and restored in Parliament in 1397. A possible occasion or purpose for such a commission may have been Richard's birthday in 1398, based on the choice of the Epiphany composition that unites all the component symbols, by the emphasis on gift-giving by and to Richard, and by the encapsulation of Richard's life from his birth to the present.[63]

---

[61] Gordon, *Making and Meaning*, 58, reviews the dual roles (religious and secular) played by angels in the ceremonies and commissions of Richard.

[62] Bath, 'White Hart', 58–9.

[63] Gordon, *Making and Meaning*, 59–62, reviews earlier theories.

In conclusion, the court style of Richard II suggests that he was highly conscious of style and personally involved in his commissions. The retrospective element so evident in his patronage was a symbol itself, which like the white hart, could be used to demonstrate dynastic continuity. The distinction of Richard's commissions lies not in their individual parts —few of which he created—but rather in their unity of conception and self-conscious reflection. The king's most celebrated work, the Wilton Diptych, is a consummate example of Ricardian image-making, which repeated inherited forms and symbols, compressed time-references, and conflated the personal with the official, the secular with the sacred, and the real with the ideal. For Richard, his patronage of the visual arts was no mere ostentatious display of wealth or hollow pomp but, rather, a highly concentrated defence of his dynastic legitimacy. The inconsistency and inconstancy that seem to have plagued Richard's policies and relations with the nobles are not evident in his visual commissions, where to the contrary Richard presented a dazzling and eternal image of kingship. The personal tragedy for the young king was that he was more a man of symbol than of substance, and thus more successful in fashioning a visual image of kingship than in sustaining its gritty reality.

Bibliography

UNPRINTED SOURCES

Manuscripts

Bodleian Library: Cotton Charter XV/12; Harley Charter 56 A 22; MS Arundel 68; MS Harley 3988.

Cambridge University Library: D5/7A, Ely Diocesan Records, Bishop Arundel's Household Expense Rolls.

Cheshire Record Office: DLT, Liber C.

Corpus Christi College, Cambridge: MS 339.

Cumbria Record Office: DRC 1/2, Register of Thomas Appleby, bishop of Carlisle, 1363–95.

Lichfield Joint Record Office: Dean and Chapter Act Book 1.

Public Record Office: C.47 Chancery Miscellanea; C.270; DL.28 Duchy of Lancaster, Various Accounts; E.28 Exchequer, Treasury of Receipt, Council and Privy Seal Records; E.101 Exchequer, King's Remembrancer, Accounts Various; E.403 Exchequer Issue Rolls; SC.8 Ancient Petitions.

Westminster Abbey Muniments: 6226; 9473.

Dissertations

Alexander, A. F., 'The War with France in 1377', Ph.D. thesis (London, 1933).

Barron, C. M., 'The Government of London and its Relations with the Crown', Ph.D. thesis (London, 1970).

Bolton, J. L., 'Alien Merchants in England in the Reign of Henry VI', B.Litt. thesis (Oxford, 1971).

Bradley, H., 'Italian Merchants in London', Ph.D. thesis (London, 1992).

Briggs, C. F., 'The English Manuscripts of Giles of Rome's *De Regimine Principum* and their Audience, 1300–1500', Ph.D. thesis (Chapel Hill, NC, 1993).

Davies, R. G., 'The Episcopate in England and Wales, 1375–1443', Ph.D. thesis (Manchester, 1974).

Fryde, E. B., 'Edward III's War Finance, 1337–1341: Transactions in Wool and Credit Operations', D.Phil. thesis (Oxford, 1947).

Mott, R. A. K., 'A Study in the Distribution of Patronage 1389–1399', Ph.D. thesis (Leeds, 1974).

Rigby, S. H., 'Boston and Grimsby in the Middle Ages', Ph.D. thesis (London, 1982).

PRINTED SOURCES

Primary Sources

Basin, T., *Histoire de Charles VII*, ed. and trans. C. Samaran, 2 vols. (Paris, 1933–44).

Bielowski, A. (ed.), 'Chronicon Polonorum Johannis de Czarnkow', *Monumenta Poloniae Historica* (Lwow, 1872).

Bower, Walter, *Scotichronicon*, ed. D. E. R. Watt, vols. 1–6, 8 (Aberdeen, 1987–95).

Brie, F. W. D. (ed.), *The Brut or The Chronicles of England* (2 vols., EETS, London, 1906–8).

Calendar of Close Rolls.

Calendar of Fine Rolls.

Calendar of Patent Rolls.

Caroti, S., Pereira, M., and Zamponi, S., *Speculum astronomiae* (P. Zambelli (gen. ed.), *Quaderni di storia e critica della scienza*, NS 10, Pisa, 1977).

Chambers, R. W., and Daunt, M. (edd.), *A Book of London English 1384–1425* (Oxford, 1931).

Chastellain, G., *Œuvres*, ed. Kervyn de Lettenhove, 8 vols. (1863–6).

Childs, W. R., *The Customs Accounts of Hull 1453–1490* (Yorkshire Archaeological Soc. Record Ser., 144, Leeds, 1984).

Chrimes, S. B., and Brown, A. L. (edd.), *Select Documents of English Constitutional History 1307–1485* (London, 1961).

Cirencester, Richard of, *Speculum historiale de gestis regum Angliae*, 2 vols. (RS, London, 1863–9).

Clarke, M. V., and Denholm-Young, N. (edd.), 'The Kirkstall Chronicle, 1355–1400', *BJRL*, 15 (1931).

Clarke, M. V., and Galbraith, V. H. (edd.), 'Dieulacres Chronicle', *BJRL*, 14 (1930).

Clayton, M. (ed.), *Catalogue of Rubbings of Brasses and Incised Slabs* (London, 1968).

Coopland, C. W. (ed. and trans.), *Philippe de Mézières' Letter to King Richard II: A Plea Made in 1395 for Peace between England and France* (Liverpool, 1975).

Creton, J., 'A French Metrical History of the Deposition of Richard II', Webb, J. (ed. and trans.), *Archaelogia*, 20 (1824).

Cronin, H. S. (ed.), *Rogeri Dymmok, Liber Contra XII errores et hereses Lollardorum* (London, 1921).

Crowder, C. M., *Unity, Heresy and Reform 1378–1460. The Conciliar Response to the Great Schism* (London, 1977).

Curtis, E., 'Unpublished Letters from Richard II in Ireland, 1394–1395', *Proceedings of the Royal Irish Academy*, 37 (1927).

Davies, J. S. (ed.), *An English Chronicie of the Reigus of Richard II, Henry IV, Henry V, and Henry VI, 1377–1461* (Camden Soc., London, 1856).

Davis, A. H. (ed.), *William Thorne's Chronicle of St Augustine's Abbey, Canterbury* (etc.) (Oxford, 1934).

Day, M., and Steele, R. (edd.), *Mum and the Sothsegger* (EETS, London, 1936).

Delachenal, R. (ed.), *Chronique des Règnes de Jean II et de Charles V*, 4 vols. (Paris, 1910–20).

Eisner, S. (ed.), *The Kalendarium of Nicholas of Lynn* (Athens, Ga., 1980).

Facsimile of the Ancient Map of Great Britain in the Bodleian Library, Oxford, A. D. 1325–50 (Ordinance Survey, 1935).

Favent, T., *Historia Mirabilis Parliamenti*, McKisack, M. (ed.), *Camden Miscellany XIV* (London, 1926).

Foedera, conventiones, litterae (etc.), Rymer, T. (ed.), 20 vols. (London, 1704–35); Clarke, A. *et al.* (edd.), 4 vols. in 7 parts (Record Comm., London, 1816–69).

Froissart, J., *Oeuvres complètes . . . Chroniques*, Lettenhove, K. de (ed.), 25 vols. in 26 parts (Brussels, 1867–77).

Galbraith, V. H. (ed.), *The St Albans Chronicle 1406–1420* (Oxford, 1937).

Gamez, Guttiere Diez de, *El Vitorial: Crónica de Don Pero Niño, Conde de Buelna*, ed. J. de M. Carriazo (Madrid, 1940).

Genet, J.-P. (ed.), *Four English Political Tracts of the Later Middle Ages* (Camden Soc., 4th ser. 18, London, 1977).

Given-Wilson, C. (ed. and trans.), *Chronicles of the Revolution, 1397–1400: The Reign of Richard II* (Manchester, 1993).

Gower, John, *The Complete Works*, ed. G. C. Macaulay, 4 vols. (EETS, Oxford, 1899–1902).

—— *The English Works*, ed. G. C. Macaulay, 2 vols. (London, 1900; repr. 1957).

—— *The Major Latin Works*, ed. and trans. E. W. Stockton (Seattle, 1962).

Haydon, F. S. (ed.), *Continuatio Eulogii Historiarum* (RS, London, 1863).

Hector, L. C., and Harvey, B. F. (edd.), *The Westminster Chronicle 1381–1394* (Oxford, 1982).

Hieatt, C. B., and Butler, S. (edd.), *Curye on Inglisch* (London, 1985).

Hudson, A. (ed.), *Selections from English Wycliffite Writings* (Cambridge, 1978).

Ingram, R. W. *Records of Early English Drama: Coventry* (Toronto, 1981).

Kimball, E. G. (ed.), *Oxfordshire Sessions of the Peace in the Reign of Richard II* (Oxford Record Soc. 53, London, 1983).

Kingsford, C. L. (ed.), *Chronicles of London* (Oxford, 1905).

Klausner, D. N. (ed.), *Records of Early English Drama: Herefordshire and Worcestershire* (Toronto, 1990).

Legg, L. G. W. (ed.), *English Coronation Records* (London, 1901).

Legge, M. D. (ed.), *Anglo-Norman Letters and Petitions* (Oxford, 1941).

Lumby, J. R. (ed.), *Chronicon Henrici Knighton*, 2 vols. (RS, London, 1889–95).

Manzalaoui, M. A. (ed.), *Secretum Secretorum: Nine English Versions*, I (EETS, London, 1977).

Ricardi de Cirencestria Speculum Historiale, ed. J. E. B. Mayor, 2 vols. (RS, London, 1863–9).

Molenaer, S. P. (ed.), *Li Livres du Gouvernement* (New York, 1899).

Moranvillé, H. (ed.), *Journal de Jean Le Fèvre* (Paris, 1887).

Morse, R. (ed.), *St. Erkenwald* (Cambridge, 1975).

Myers, A. R. (ed. and trans.), *English Historical Documents. iv. 1327–1485* (London, 1969).

Nichols, J. (ed.), *A Collection of the Wills of the Kings and Queens of England* (London, 1780).

Nicolas, N. H. (ed.), *Proceedings and Ordinances of the Privy Council of England*, 7 vols. (London, 1834–7).

O'Connor, S. J. (ed.), *A Calendar of the Cartularies of John Pyel and Adam Fraunceys* (Camden 5th ser. 2, London, 1993).

Palgrave, F. (ed.), *The antient Kalendars and inventories of his Majesty's Exchequer* (etc.), 3 vols. (Record Comm., London, 1836).

Perroy, E. (ed.), *Diplomatic Correspondence of Richard II* (Camden Soc., 3rd ser. 48, London, 1933).

—— (ed.), 'Anglo-French Negotiations at Bruges, 1374–1377', *Camden Miscellany, xix* (London, 1952).

Petitot, C. B. (ed.), 'Le Livre de faictz du bon messire Jehan le Maingre dit "Boucicaut" ', *Collection complète des mémoires relatif à l'Histoire de France*, 2 vols. (Paris, 1819–26).

Riley, H. T. (ed.), *Annales Ricardi Secundi et Henrici Quarti*, in J. de Trokelowe (etc.), *Chronica et Annales* (RS, London, 1866).

—— (ed.), *Historia Anglicana*, 2 vols. (RS, London, 1863–4).

—— (ed. and trans.), *Memorials of London and London Life in the XIIIth, XIVth and XVth Centuries 1276–1419* (London, 1868).

Secousse, M. (ed.), *Receuil de pièces servant de preuves aux Mémoires sur les Troubles excités en France par Charles II dit le Mauvais Roi de Navarre et Comte d'Evreux*, 2 vols. (Paris, 1755).

Sharpe, R. R. (ed.), *Calendar of Letter-Books of the City of London, Letter Books A–L*, 11 vols. (London, 1899–1912).

Sheppard, J. B. (ed.), *Literae Cantuarienses: The Letter Books of the Monastery of Christ Church, Canterbury*, 3 vols. (RS, London, 1887–9).

Steel, R., and Henderson, T. (edd.), *Three Prose Versions of the Secreta Secretorum* (EETS, London, 1898).

—— Delorme, F. *et al.* (edd.), *Opera hactenus inedita Rogeri Baconi*, 16 vols. (Oxford, 1909–40).

Stow, G. B. (ed.), *Historia Vitae et Regni Ricardi Secundi* (Philadelphia, 1977).

Strachey, J., *et al.* (edd.), *Rotuli Parliamentorum*, 7 vols. (London, 1767–83).

Suggett, H., 'A Letter describing Richard II's Reconciliation with the City of London, 1392', *EHR* 62 (1947).

Taylor, F., and Roskell, J. S. (edd.), *Gesta Henrici Quinti* (Oxford, 1975).

Taylor, J. (ed.), *The Kirkstall Abbey Chronicles* (Thoresby Soc. 42, Leeds, 1952).

Thomas, A. H., and Jones, P. E. (edd.), *Calendar of Select Pleas and Memoranda of the City of London, AD 1323–1482*, 6 vols. (Cambridge, 1926–61).

Thompson, E. M. (ed.), *Chronicon Angliae, 1328–1388* (RS, London, 1874).

—— (ed.), *Chronicon Adae de Usk, 1377–1421* (London, 1904).

Toulmin Smith, L., and Brentano, L. (edd.), *English Guilds: The Original Ordinances of More than One Hundred Early English Guilds* (EETS, London, 1870).

Tyson, D. B. (ed.), *Beihefte zur Zeitschrift für Romanische Philologie* (Tübingen, 1975).

Weizsacker, J. (ed.), *Deutsche Reichstagsakten unter König Wenzel*, 3 vols. (Munich, 1867).

Wilkins, D. (ed.), *Concilia Magnae Britanniae et Hiberniae*, 4 vols. (London, 1737).

Williams, B. (ed.), *Chronicque de la traison et mort de Richart Deux Roy Dengleterre* (London, 1846).

Wright, T. (ed.), *Political Poems and Songs relating to English History*, 2 vols. (RS, London, 1859–61).

Secondary Sources

Alexander, J., and Binski, P. (edd.), *Age of Chivalry: Art in Plantagenet England, 1200–1400* (London, 1987).

Alexander, J. J. G., 'Painting and Manuscript Illumination for Royal Patrons in the Later Middle Ages', *in English Court Culture*.

—— (ed.), *A Survey of Manuscripts Illuminated in the British Isles*, 5 vols. (London, 1986).

Allmand, C., *Henry V* (London, 1992).

Ashley, B. M., 'St Albert and the Nature of Natural Science', in id., *Albertus Magnus and the Sciences: Commemorative Essays 1980* (Toronto, 1980).

Aston, M. E., 'The Impeachment of Bishop Despenser', *BIHR* 38 (1965).

—— *Thomas Arundel* (Oxford, 1967).

—— 'Richard II and the Wars of the Roses', in *Reign of Richard II*.

—— 'Lollardy and Sedition, 1381–1431', in ead. *Lollards and Reformers* (London, 1984).

Atwater, D., *A Dictionary of Mary* (London, 1957).

Backhouse, J., 'Founder of the Royal Library: Edward IV and Henry VII as Collectors of Illuminated Manuscripts', in *England in the Fifteenth Century: Proceedings of the 1986 Harlaxton Symposium* (Woodbridge, 1987).

Baker, R. L., *The English Customs Service 1307–1343: A Study of Medieval Administration* (Philadelphia, 1961).

Baldwin, J. F., *The King's Council in England during the Middle Ages* (Oxford, 1913).

Barber, R. V., *The Tournament in England 1100–1400* (Woodbridge, 1986).

Barron, C. M., 'The Tyranny of Richard II', *BIHR* 41 (1968).

—— 'Richard Whittington: The Man behind the Myth', in A. E. J. Hollaender, and W. Kellaway (edd.), *Studies in London History presented to Philip Edmund Jones* (London, 1969).

—— 'The Quarrel of Richard II with London, 1392–1397', in *Reign of Richard II*.

—— *Revolt in London: 11th to 15th June 1381* (London, 1981).

—— 'The "Golden Age" of Women in Medieval London', in K. Bate, A. Curry, C. Hardman, and P. Noble (edd.), *Medieval Women in Southern England* (Reading, 1989).

Barron, C. M., 'The Deposition of Richard II', in *Politics and Crisis*.

Bartos, F. M., *Cechy v dobe Husove 1378–1415* (Prague, 1947).

Bath, M., 'The Iconography of the Collared Deer', in K. Varty (ed.), *Proceedings of the International Colloquium Beast Epic, Fable, and Fabliau* (Glasgow, 1976).

—— 'The Legend of Caesar's Deer', *Medievalia et Humanistica*, 9 (1979).

—— 'The White Hart, the *cerf volant*, and the Wilton Diptych', in J. Goossens and T. Sodman (edd.), *Third International Beast Epic, Fable and Fabliau Colloquium* (Cologne, 1981).

—— 'Imperial *renovatio* Symbolism in the Très Riches Heures', *Simiolus*, 17 (1987).

Beardwood, A., *Alien Merchants in England, 1350 to 1377* (Cambridge, Mass., 1931).

Bean, J. M. W., *The Decline of English Feudalism 1215–1540* (Manchester, 1968).

Beaune, C., 'Costume et pouvoir en France à la fin du Moyen Âge: Les Devices royales vers 1400', *Revue des sciences humaines*, 183 (1981).

Bennett, M. J., 'The Court of Richard II and the Promotion of Literature', in B. A. Hanawalt (ed.), *Chaucer's England: Literature in Historical Context* (Minneapolis, 1992).

Binski, P., 'Reflections on *La estoire de Seint Aedward le rei*: Hagiography and Kingship in Thirteenth Century England', *JMH* 16 (1990).

Bird, R., *The Turbulent London of Richard II* (London, 1949).

Black, A., *Political Thought in Europe 1250–1450* (Cambridge, 1992).

Bloch, M., *The Royal Touch*, trans. J. E. Anderson (London, 1973).

Bolton, J. L., *The Medieval English Economy 1150–1500* (London, 1980).

Bonney, M. M., 'The English Medieval Wool and Cloth Trade: New Approaches for the Local Historian', *Local Historian*, 22 (1992).

Branner, R., 'Westminster Abbey and the French Court Style', *Journal of the Society of Architectural Historians*, 23 (1964).

Bray, J., 'Concepts of Sainthood in Fourteenth-Century England', *BJRL* 66 (1984).

Bridbury, A. R., *Economic Growth: England in the later Middle Ages* (2nd edn., Brighton, 1975).

—— *Medieval English Clothmaking* (London, 1982).

Broker, N., and Prest, G., 'Effigy', *Connoisseur*, 116 (1945).

Brown, A. L., 'The Reign of Henry IV: The Establishment of the Lancastrian Dynasty', in S. B. Chrimes, R. A. Griffiths, and C. D. Ross (edd.), *Fifteenth Century England, 1399–1509* (Manchester, 1972).

—— 'Parliament, *c.*1377–1422', in R. G. Davies, and J. H. Denton (edd.), *The English Parliament in the Middle Ages* (Manchester, 1981).

—— *The Governance of Late Medieval England, 1272–1461* (London, 1989).

Brown, C., and Robbins, R. H., *The Index of Middle English Verse* (New York, 1943).

Brown, R. A., Colvin, H. M., and Taylor, A. J., *The History of the King's Works: The Middle Ages*, 2 vols. (London, 1963).

Bueno de Mesquita, D. M., 'The Foreign Policy of Richard II in 1397: Some Italian Letters', *EHR* 56 (1941).

Burrow, J. A., *Ricardian Poetry: Chaucer, Gower, Langland and the Gawain Poet* (London, 1992).

Carey, H. M., 'Astrology at the English Court in the Later Middle Ages', in P. Curry (ed.), *Astrology, Science, and Society: Historical Essays* (Woodbridge, 1987).

Carpenter, D., 'King, Magnates and Society: The Personal Rule of King Henry III, 1234–1258', *Speculum*, 60 (1985).

Carus-Wilson, E. M., *Medieval Merchant Venturers* (2nd edn., London, 1967).

—— and Coleman, O., *England's Export Trade, 1275–1547* (Oxford, 1963).

Caspary, G. E., 'The Deposition of Richard II and the Canon Law', in S. Kuttner, and J. J. Ryan (edd.), *Proceedings of the Second International Congress of Medieval Canon Law* (Vatican, 1965).

Catto, J. L., 'Religion and the English Nobility in the Later Fourteenth Century', in H. Lloyd-Jones, V. Pearl, and B. Warden (edd.), *History and Imagination* (London, 1981).

—— 'Religious Change under Henry V', in G. L. Harriss (ed.), *Henry V: The Practice of Kingship* (Oxford, 1985).

Caviness, M. H., *The Windows of Christ Church Cathedral Canterbury* (Oxford, 1981).

Charmasson, T., *Recherches sur une technique divinatoire: La Geomancie dans l'occident mediéval* (Geneva, 1980).

Cherry, M., 'The Courtenay Earls of Devon: The Formation and Disintegration of a Late Medieval Aristocratic Affinity', *Southern History*, 1 (1979).

Cheyette, F., 'Kings, Courts, Cures and Sinecures: The Statute of Provisors and the Common Law', *Traditio*, 19 (1965).

Childs, W., 'Finance and Trade under Edward II', in *Politics and Crisis*.

Chorley, P., 'English Cloth Exports during the Thirteenth and Early Fourteenth Centuries: The Continental Evidence', *Historical Research*, 61 (1988).

Chrimes, S. B., 'Richard II's Questions to the Judges, 1387', *Law Quarterly Review*, 72 (1956).

Clarke, M. V., 'The Wilton Diptych', *Burlington Magazine*, 58 (1931).

—— *Fourteenth Century Studies*, ed. L. S. Sutherland, and M. McKisack (Oxford, 1937).

—— and Galbraith, V. H., 'The Deposition of Richard II', *BJRL* 14 (1930).

Clay, R. M., *The Hermits and Anchorites of England* (London, 1914).

Cokayne, G. W. (ed.), *Complete Peerage of England, Scotland, Ireland, Great Britain and the United Kingdom, Extant, Extinct or Dormant*, 12 vols. (London, 1910–59).

Coleman, J., *English Literature and History, 1350–1400* (London, 1981).

Coleman, O., 'The Collectors of Customs in London under Richard II', in A. E. J. Hollaender, and W. Kellaway (edd.), *Studies in London History* (London, 1969).

Colvin, H. M., 'The "Court Style" in Medieval English Architecture: A Review', in *English Court Culture*.

280 *Bibliography*

Constable, W. G., 'The Date and Nationality of the Wilton Diptych', *Burlington Magazine*, 55 (1929).

Conway, M., 'The Wilton Diptych', *Burlington Magazine*, 55 (1929).

Cooper, I. M., 'Westminster Hall', *Journal of the British Archaeological Association*, 1 (1936).

Coupe, C., 'An Old Picture', *Month*, 84 (1895).

Courtenay, L. T., 'The Westminster Hall Roof and its Fourteenth Century Sources', *Journal of the Society of Architectural Historians*, 43 (1984).

—— and Mark, R., 'The Westminster Hall Roof: A Historiographic and Structural Study', *Journal of the Society of Architectural Historians*, 46 (1987).

Crowder, C. D. M., *Unity, Heresy and Reform 1378–1460: The Conciliar Response to the Great Schism* (London, 1977).

—— 'Peace and Justice around 1400: A Sketch', in J. G. Rowe (ed.), *Aspects of Late Medieval Government and Society* (Toronto, 1986).

Dahmus, J. H., 'Richard II and the Church', *Catholic Hist. Rev.* 39 (1953).

—— *William Courtenay, Archbishop of Canterbury, 1381–1396* (Philadelphia, 1966).

Danbury, E., 'English and French Artistic Propaganda during the Hundred Years War: Some Evidence from Royal Charters', in C. Allmand (ed.), *Power, Culture and Religion in France, c.1350–c.1550* (Woodbridge, 1989).

Davies, R. G., 'Thomas Arundel as Archbishop of Canterbury, 1396–1414', *Journal of Ecclesiastical History*, 24 (1973).

—— 'Alexander Neville, Archbishop of York, 1374–1388', *Yorkshire Archaeological Journal*, 47 (1975).

—— 'Richard II and the Church in the Years of Tyranny', *JMH* 1 (1975).

—— 'The Episcopate and the Political Crisis in England of 1386–1388', *Speculum*, 51 (1976).

—— 'The Attendance of the Episcopate in English Parliaments, 1376–1461', *Proceedings of the American Philosophical Society*, 129/1 (1985).

—— 'Lollardy and Locality', *TRHS*, 5th ser. 41 (1991).

Davies, R. R., 'Richard II and the Principality of Chester, 1397–1399', in *Reign of Richard II*.

—— *Lordship and Society in the March of Wales 1282–1400* (Oxford, 1978).

—— (ed.), *The British Isles, 1100–1500: Comparisons, Contrasts and Connections* (Edinburgh, 1988).

Delachenal, R., *Histoire de Charles V*, 5 vols. (Paris, 1909–31).

Deuchler, F., 'Philipp der Gute von Burgund als Auftraggeber-Vermutungen zum Bern Tausend-blumenteppisch', *Jahrbuch des Bern Historischen Museums in Bern*, 45–6 (1968).

Doyle, A. I., 'English Books In and Out of Court from Edward III to Henry VII', in *English Court Culture*.

Du Boulay, F. R. H., *Germany in the Later Middle Ages* (London, 1983).

—— and Barron, C. M. (edd.), *The Reign of Richard II: Essays in Honour of May McKisack* (London, 1971).

Duls, L. D., *Richard II in the Early Chronicles* (The Hague, 1975).

Dunbabin, J., 'Government', in J. H. Burns (ed.), *The Cambridge History of Medieval Political Thought c.350–c.1450* (Cambridge, 1988).

Dvorakova, V. et al., *Gothic Mural Painting in Bohemia and Moravia, 1300–1378* (Oxford, 1964).

Dyer, C., *Standards of Living in the Later Middle Ages: Social Change in England, c.1200–1520* (Cambridge, 1989).

Eberle, P. H., 'The Politics of Courtly Style at the Court of Richard II', in G. S. Burgess, and R. A. Taylor (edd.), *The Spirit of the Court: Selected Proceedings of the Fourth Congress of the International Courtly Literature Society* (Toronto, 1983).

Edwards, J. G., *The Second Century of the English Parliament* (Oxford, 1975).

Ellis, S., 'Crown, Community and Government in the English Territories', *History*, 71 (1986).

Emden, A. B., *A Biographical Register of the University of Oxford to A.D. 1500*, 3 vols. (Oxford, 1957–9).

Evans, J., 'The Wilton Diptych Reconsidered', *Archaeological Journal*, 105 (1948).

—— 'Le Diptyque de Wilton', *L'Œil*, 24 (1956).

Ferris, S. J., 'The Iconography of the Wilton Diptych', *Minnesota Review*, 7 (1967).

Fisher, J. H., *John Gower: Moral Philosopher and Friend of Chaucer* (London, 1965).

Foran, E. A., 'Robert de Waldeby, O. S. A.', *Irish Ecclesiastical Record*, 5th ser. 16 (1921).

Fryde, E. B., 'The English Farmers of the Customs', *TRHS*, 5th ser. 9 (1959).

Galbraith, V. H. (1930). See *Clarke, M. V.*

—— 'Thomas Walsingham and the St Albans Chronicle', *EHR* 47 (1932).

—— 'A New Life of Richard II', *History*, 26 (1942).

—— 'Good Kings and Bad Kings in English Medieval History', *History*, 30 (1945).

Galway, M., 'The Wilton Diptych: A Postscript', *Archaeological Journal*, 107 (1950).

Genet, J. P., 'Ecclesiastics and Political Theory in Late Medieval England: The End of the Monopoly', in R. B. Dobson (ed.), *The Church, Politics and Patronage* (Gloucester, 1984).

Giesey, R., 'Inaugural Aspects of French Royal Ceremonials', in J. Bak (ed.), *Coronations* (Berkeley and Los Angeles, 1990).

Gilbert, A. H., 'Notes on the Influence of the *Secretum Secretorum*', *Speculum*, 3 (1928).

Gillespie, J. L., 'Richard II's Cheshire Archers', *Transactions of the Historic Society of Lancashire and Cheshire*, 125 (1975).

Gillingham, J., *The Angevin Empire* (London, 1984).

—— 'Crisis or Continuity? The Structure of Royal Authority in England 1369–1422', in R. Schneider (ed.), *Das Spätmittelalterliche Königtum Im Europäischen Vergleich* (Sigmaringen, 1987).

Given-Wilson, C., 'Richard II and his Grandfather's Will', *EHR* 93 (1978).

—— *The Royal Household and the King's Affinity: Service, Politics and Finance in England 1360–1413* (New Haven, 1986).

Given-Wilson, C., *The English Nobility in the Late Middle Ages: The Fourteenth Century Political Community* (London, 1987).

—— 'Wealth and credit, public and private: The Earls of Arundel, 1306–1397', *EHR*, 106 (1991).

—— 'Royal Charter Witness Lists 1327–1399', *Medieval Prosopography*, 11 (1991).

—— 'Richard II, Edward II and the Lancastrian Inheritance', *EHR*, 109 (1994).

Goodman, A., 'Sir Thomas Hoo and the Parliament of 1376', *BIHR*, 41 (1968).

—— *The Loyal Conspiracy* (London, 1971).

—— 'John of Gaunt: Paradigm of the late Fourteenth Century Crisis', *TRHS*, 5th ser. 37 (1987).

—— *John of Gaunt: The Exercise of Princely Power in Fourteenth-Century Europe* (London, 1992).

Gordon, D., 'A New Discovery in the Wilton Diptych', *Burlington Magazine*, 10 (1992).

—— *Making and Meaning: The Wilton Diptych* (London, 1993).

Gransden, A., 'Propaganda in English Medieval Historiography', *JMH*, 2 (1975).

—— *Historical Writing in England, c.1307 to the Early Sixteenth Century*, 2 (London, 1982).

—— 'The Westminster Chronicles, 1381–1394', *Nottingham Medieval Studies*, 28 (1984).

Grant, E., 'Medieval and Renaissance Scholastic Conceptions of the Influence of the Celestial Region on the Terrestrial', *Journal of Medieval and Renaissance Studies*, 17 (1987).

Gras, N. S. B., *The Early English Customs System* (Cambridge, Mass., 1918).

Graus, F., 'Das Scheitern von Königen: Karl VI., Richard II., Wenzel IV.', R. Schneider (ed.), *Das Spätmittelalterliche Königtum Im Europäischen Vergleich* (Sigmaringen, 1987).

Gray, H. L., 'The Production and Exportation of English Woollens in the Fourteenth Century', *EHR*, 39 (1924).

Green, R. F., 'King Richard II's books revisited', *Library*, 5th ser. 31 (1976).

—— *Poets and Princepleasers: Literature and the English Court in the Late Middle Ages* (Toronto, 1980).

Griffiths, R. A., 'The Crown and the Royal Family in Later Medieval England', R. A. Griffiths and J. W. Sherborne (edd.), *Kings and Nobles in the Later Middle Ages* (Gloucester, 1986).

Guenée, B., *States and Rulers in Later Medieval Europe*, trans. J. Vale (Oxford, 1985).

—— *Between Church and State: The Lives of Four French Prelates in the Late Middle Ages*, trans. A. Goldhammer (Chicago, 1987).

Guldescu, S., *History of Medieval Croatia* (The Hague, 1964).

Halecki, O., 'From the Union with Hungary to the Union with Lithuania: Jadwiga, 1374–1399', in W. F. Reddaway *et al.* (edd.), *Cambridge History of Poland* (Cambridge, 1950).

Hallam, E. M., *Capetian France, 987–1328* (London, 1980).

Hamdy, A. H., 'Philippe de Mézières and the New Order of the Passion', *Bulletin of the Faculty of the Arts*, 18 (Alexandria, 1964).

Hanawalt, J. (ed.), *Chaucer's England: Literature in Historical Context* (Minneapolis, 1992).

Hansen, B., 'Science and Magic', in D. C. Lindberg and A. G. Debus (edd.), *Science in the Middle Ages* (Chicago, 1978).

Hardison, O. B., *The Enduring Monument: A Study of the Idea of Praise in Renaissance Literature* (Chapel Hill, NC, 1962).

Harriss, G. L., 'The Commons' Petition of 1340', *EHR* 78 (1963).

—— *King, Parliament and Public Finance in Medieval England to 1369* (Oxford, 1975).

—— 'The Formation of Parliament, 1272–1377', in R. G. Davies and J. H. Denton (edd.), *The English Parliament in the Middle Ages* (Manchester, 1981).

—— 'Theory and Practice in Royal Taxation: Some Observations', *EHR* 97 (1982).

—— (ed.), *Henry V: The Practice of Kingship* (Oxford, 1985).

—— *Cardinal Beaufort: A Study of Lancastrian Ascendancy and Decline* (Oxford, 1988).

—— 'Political Society and the Growth of Government in Late Medieval England', *Past and Present*, 138 (1993).

Harvey, B. F., 'The Monks of Westminster and the University of Oxford', in *Reign of Richard II*.

—— *Westminster Abbey and its Estates in the Middle Ages* (Oxford, 1977).

Harvey, J. H., *Henry Yevele, c.1320–1400* (London, 1944).

—— 'The Wilton Diptych: A Re-Examination', *Archaeologia*, 98 (1961).

—— 'Richard II and York', in *Reign of Richard II*.

Harvey, M., 'The Letter of Oxford University on the Schism, 5 February 1399', *Annuarium Historiae Conciliorum*, 6 (1974).

—— 'The Power of the Crown in the English Church during the Great Schism', in S. Mews (ed.), *Religion and National Identity* (Oxford, 1982).

Hatcher, J., *English Tin Production and Trade before 1500* (Oxford, 1973).

Heath, P., 'Richard II, 1377–1399: The Clergy under Attack', in id., *Church and Realm, 1272–1461* (London, 1988).

Heaton, H., *The Yorkshire Woollen and Worsted Industries* (2nd edn., Oxford, 1965).

Hector, L. C., 'An Alleged Hysterical Outburst of Richard II', *EHR* 68 (1953).

Henneman, J. B., 'The Military Class and the French Monarchy in the Late Middle Ages', *American Hist. Rev.* 83 (1978).

Hepburn, A., *Portraits of the Later Plantagenets* (Woodbridge, 1986).

—— *The Royal Image* (Berkeley and Los Angeles, 1991).

Hlavacek, I., 'Studie k Diplomatice Vaclava IV: Itinerar krale Vaclava IV (1361–1419)', *Ceskoslovensky Casopis Historicky*, 10 (1962).

Hofler, C., *Anna von Luxemburg* (Vienna, 1871).

Holmes, G., *The Good Parliament of 1376* (Oxford, 1975).

Holmes, P. J., 'The Great Council in the Reign of Henry VII', *EHR* 101 (1986).

Homan, B., *Gli Angioni di Napoli in Ungheria* (Rome, 1938).

Hope, Sir W. St.-John, 'Quire Screens in English Churches, with Special Reference to the Twelfth-Century Quire Screen formerly in the Cathedral Church of Ely', *Archaeologia*, 68 (1916–17).

—— 'Images of Kings in the Cathedral Church of Salisbury', *Wiltshire Archaeological and Natural History Magazine*, 39 (1917).

Horrox, R., *Richard III: A Study of Service* (Cambridge, 1989).

Housley, N., 'The Bishop of Norwich's Crusade', *History Today*, 33 (1983).

Howgrave-Graham, R. P., 'The Earlier Royal Funeral Effigies: New Light on Portraiture in Westminster Abbey', *Archaeologia*, 98 (1961).

Jack, R. I., 'Entail and Descent: The Hastings Inheritance 1370–1406', *BIHR* 38 (1965).

James, M. K., *Studies in the Medieval Wine Trade* (Oxford, 1971).

Jarrett, B., *The Emperor Charles IV* (London, 1935).

Jarry, E., *La Vie politique de Louis de France, duc d'Orléans* (Paris, 1889).

Johnston, D., 'Richard II and the Submission of Gaelic Ireland', *Irish Historical Studies*, 22 (1980).

—— 'The Interim Years: Richard II and Ireland, 1395–1399', in J. F. Lydon (ed.), *England and Ireland in the Later Middle Ages: Essays in Honour of Jocelyn Otway-Ruthven* (Dublin, 1981).

Jolliffe, J. E. A., *Angevin Kingship* (2nd edn., London, 1963).

Jones, M., *Ducal Brittany 1364–1399: Relations with England and France during the Reign of John IV* (Oxford, 1970).

Jones, P. J., 'Communes and Despots: The City State in Late Medieval Italy', *TRHS*, 5th ser. 15 (1965).

Jones, R. H., *The Royal Policy of Richard II: Absolutism in the Later Middle Ages* (Oxford, 1968).

Jones, W. R., 'Bishops, Politics, and the Two Laws: The *Gravamina* of the English Clergy, 1237–1399', *Speculum*, 41 (1966).

Kantorowicz, E., *The King's Two Bodies: A Study in Medieval Political Theology* (Princeton, 1957).

Keen, M. H., *Chivalry* (New Haven, 1984).

Keene, D., 'A New Study of London before the Great Fire', *Urban History Yearbook 1984* (London, 1984).

Kerling, N. J. M., *Commercial Relations of Holland and Zeeland with England from the Late 13th Century to the Close of the Middle Ages* (Leiden, 1954).

Kingsford, C. L., *English Historical Literature in the Fifteenth Century* (Oxford, 1913).

Kipling, G., *The Triumph of Honour* (Leiden, 1977).

—— 'Richard II's "Sumptuous Pageants" and the Idea of the Civic Triumph', in D. M. Bergeron (ed.), *Pageantry and the Shakespearean Theatre* (Athens, Ga., 1985).

Kirby, J. L., 'The Issues of the Lancastrian Exchequer and Lord Cromwell's Estimates of 1433', *BIHR* 24 (1951).

Knowles, M. D., *The Religious Orders in England*, 3 vols. (Cambridge, 1948–59).

Lacey, K., 'The Production of "Narrow Ware" by Silkwomen in Fourteenth and Fifteenth Century England', *Textile History*, 18 (1987).

Laurent, H., and Quicke, F., 'Les Origines de l'État Bourguignon: L'Accession de la Maison de Bourgogne aux duchés de Brabant et de Limbourg, 1383–1407', *Mémoires de l'Académie Royale de Belgique*, 41/1 (1939).

Legg, J. W., 'On an Inventory of the Vestry in Westminster Abbey, taken in 1388', *Archaeologia*, 52 (1890).

Legros, H. M., 'Les Cerfs volants supports des armes de Charles VI', *Revue des études historiques*, 97 (1930).

Leonard, G., *Les Angevins de Naples* (Paris, 1954).

Lethaby, W. R., 'The Westminster Portrait of Richard II', *Burlington Magazine*, 65 (1934).

Levine, M., *Tudor Dynastic Problems 1460–1571* (London, 1973).

Lewis, N. B., 'The "Continual Council" in the Early Years of Richard II, 1377–1380', *EHR* 41 (1926).

—— 'The Last Summons of the English Feudal Levy, 13 June 1385', *EHR* 73 (1958).

Lindenbaum, S., 'The Smithfield Tournament of 1390', *Journal of Medieval and Renaissance Studies*, 20 (1990).

Lindner, T., *Deutsche Geschichte unter den Habsburgern und Luxemburgern, 1273–1437*, 2 vols. (Stuttgart, 1893).

Lipson, E., *The Economic History of England, i. The Middle Ages* (12th edn., London, 1959).

Lloyd, T. H., *The Movement of Wool Prices in Medieval England* (*EcHR* suppl. 6, Cambridge, 1973).

—— *The English Wool Trade in the Middle Ages* (Cambridge, 1977).

—— 'Overseas Trade and the English Money Supply in the Fourteenth Century', in N. J. Mayhew (ed.), *Edwardian Monetary Affairs (1279–1344)* (Oxford; British Archaeological Reports, 36; 1977).

—— *Alien Merchants in England in the High Middle Ages* (Brighton, 1982).

—— *England and the German Hanse, 1157–1611* (Cambridge, 1991).

Lobel, M. D. (ed.), *The City of London from Prehistoric Times to c.1520* (Oxford, 1989).

Loomis, R. S., 'The Library of Richard II', in E. B. Atwood, and A. A. Hill (edd.), *Studies in Language, Literature and Culture of the Middle Ages and Later* (Austin, Tex., 1969).

Lunt, W. E., *Financial Relations of the Papacy with England, 1327–1534* (Cambridge, Mass., 1962).

Lydon, J. F., 'Richard II's Expeditions to Ireland', *Journal of the Royal Antiquaries of Ireland*, 93 (1963).

McFarlane, K. B., *Lancastrian Kings and Lollard Knights* (Oxford, 1972).

—— *The Nobility of Later Medieval England* (Oxford, 1973).

McHardy, A. K., 'The English Clergy and the Hundred Years War', in W. J. Shields (ed.), *Studies in Church History*, xx (Oxford, 1983).

McKenna, J. W., 'Popular Canonization as Political Propaganda: The Cult of Archbishop Scrope', *Speculum*, 45 (1970).

—— 'How God became an Englishman', in id. and D. J. Guth (edd.), *Tudor Rule and Revolution* (Cambridge, 1982).

McNiven, P., 'The Betrayal of Archbishop Scrope', *BJRL* 54 (1971–2).

—— *Heresy and Politics in the Reign of Henry IV* (Woodbridge, 1987).

Mathew, G., *The Court of Richard II* (London, 1968).

Maxwell-Lyte, H. C., *Historical Notes on the Use of the Great Seal of England* (London, 1926).

Mews, S., 'The Power of the Crown in the English Church during the Great Schism', in id. *Religion and National Identity* (Oxford, 1982).

Mills, M., 'The Collectors of Customs', in J. F. Willard, W. Morris, J. R. Strayer, and W. H. Dunham, Jr. (edd.), *The English Government at Work, 1327–1336*, 3 vols. (Cambridge, Mass., 1940–50).

Molinier, A., 'Description de deux manuscripts contenant la règle de la *militia passionis Jhesu Christi* de Philippe de Mézières', *Archives de l'Orient Latin* (Brussels, 1964).

Morgan, D. A. L., 'The King's Affinity in the Polity of Yorkist England', *TRHS*, 5th ser. 23 (1973).

—— 'The Cult of St George *c.*1500: National and International Connotations', in J.-M. Cauchies (ed.), *L'Angleterre et les pays bourguignons: Relations et comparaisons* (XVᵉ–XVIᵉ s.) (Centre Européen d'Études Bourguignonnes (XIVᵉ–XVIᵉ s.), Neuchâtel, 1995).

Morgan, P., *War and Society in Medieval Cheshire, 1277–1403* (Manchester, 1987).

—— 'Henry IV and the Shadow of Richard II', in R. E. Archer (ed.), *Crown, Government and People in the Fifteenth Century* (Stroud, 1995).

Mott, R. A. K., 'Richard II and the Crisis of July 1397', in I. Wood, and G. A. Loud (edd.), *Church and Chronicle in the Middle Ages: Essays presented to John Taylor* (London, 1991).

Munro, J. H., *Wool, Cloth, and Gold: The Struggle for Bullion in Anglo-Burgundian Trade, 1340–1478* (Toronto, 1972).

—— 'Monetary Contraction and Industrial Change in the Late-Medieval Low Countries, 1335–1500', in N. J. Mayhew (ed.), *Coinage in the Low Countries (880–1500)* (Oxford; British Archaeological Reports, Informational Series 54; 1979).

—— 'Industrial Transformations in North-West European Textile Trades, *c.*1290–*c.*1340: Economic Progress or Economic Crisis?', in B. M. S. Campbell (ed.), *Before the Black Death: Studies in the 'Crisis' of the Early Fourteenth Century* (Manchester, 1991).

Nicholas, D., 'The English Trade at Bruges in the Last Years of Edward III', *JMH* 5 (1979).

Nicholson, P., 'The Dedications of Gower's *Confessio Amantis*', *Mediaevalia*, 10 (1984).

Nightingale, P., 'Capitalists, Crafts and Constitutional Change in Late Fourteenth-Century London', *Past and Present*, 124 (1989).

North, J. D., 'Celestial Influence: the Major Premiss of Astrology', in P. Zambelli (ed.), *'Astrologi hallucinati': Stars and the End of the World in Luther's Time* (Berlin, 1986).

Norton-Smith, J., 'Textual Tradition, Monarchy and Chaucer's *Lak of Stedfastnesse*', *Reading Medieval Studies*, 8 (1982).

Oman, C., *The Great Revolt of 1381*, ed. E. B. Fryde (new edn., Oxford, 1969).

Orme, N., *From Childhood to Chivalry* (London, 1984).

—— 'Sir John Speke and his Chapel in Exeter Cathedral', *Trans. Devon Association for the Advancement of Sciences*, 118 (1986).

Ormond, R., *The Face of Monarchy: British Royalty Portrayed* (London, 1977).

Ormrod, W. M., 'The English Crown and the Customs, 1349–1363', *EcHR*, 2nd ser. 40 (1987).

—— *The Reign of Edward III: Crown and Political Society in England 1327–1377* (London, 1990).

—— 'The Crown and the English Economy, 1290–1348', in B. M. S. Campbell (ed.), *Before the Black Death: Studies in the 'Crisis' of the Early Fourteenth Century* (Manchester, 1991).

—— 'Political Theory in Practice: The Forced Loan on English Overseas Trade of 1317–18', *Historical Research*, 64 (1991).

Page, W. (ed.), *The Victoria History of the Counties of England: Hertfordshire*, 4 vols. (London, 1902–23).

Palais, H., 'England's First Attempt to Break the Commercial Monopoly of the Hanseatic League, 1377–1380', *American Hist. Rev.* 64 (1959).

Palmer, C. F. R., 'The King's Confessors', *Antiquary*, 22 (1890).

Palmer, J. J. N., 'England and the Great Western Schism, 1388–1399', *EHR* 83 (1968).

—— 'The Last Summons of the Feudal Army in England (1385)', *EHR* 83 (1968).

—— 'The Impeachment of Michael de la Pole in 1386', *BIHR* 42 (1969).

—— 'The Parliament of 1385 and the Constitutional Crisis of 1386', *Speculum*, 46 (1971).

—— *England, France and Christendom, 1377–1399* (London, 1972).

—— 'The Authorship, Date, and Historical Value of the French Chronicles on the Lancastrian Revolution', *BJRL* 61 (1978–9).

—— 'Charles VI and Richard II', in id. (ed.), *Froissart: Historian* (Woodbridge, 1981).

Partner, P., 'William of Wykeham and the Historians', in R. Custance (ed.), *Winchester College: Sixth-Centenary Essays* (Oxford, 1982).

Pearsall, D., and Zeeman, N. (edd.), *English and International: Studies in the Literature, Art, and Patronage of Medieval England* (Cambridge, 1988).

Peck, R. A., *Kingship and Common Profit in Gower's* Confessio Amantis (London, 1978).

Perroy, E., *L'Angleterre et le grand schisme d'occident* (Paris, 1933).

—— *The Hundred Years War* (London, 1965).

Petrasancta, S., *Tesserae Gentilitiae* (Rome, 1638).

Philipps, J. R. S., 'Edward II and the Prophets', in W. M. Ormrod (ed.), *England in the Fourteenth Century: Proceedings of the 1985 Harlaxton Symposium* (Woodbridge, 1986).

Plenderleith, H. J., and Maryon, H., 'The Royal Bronze Effigies in Westminster Abbey', *Antiquaries Journal*, 39 (1959).

Post, J. B., 'The Obsequies of John of Gaunt', *Guildhall Studies in London History*, 5 (1981).

Postan, M. M., and Power, E. E. (edd.), *Studies in English Trade in the Fifteenth Century* (London, 1933).

—— and Habakkuk, H. J. (edd.), *The Cambridge Economic History of Europe*, 8 vols. (2nd edn., Cambridge, 1966–89).

Powell, J. E., and Wallis, K., *The House of Lords in the Middle Ages* (London, 1968).

Power, E. E., *The Wool Trade in English Medieval History* (Oxford, 1941).

Prestwich, M., *War, Politics and Finance under Edward I* (London, 1972).

—— *Edward I* (London, 1988).

Ramsay, J. H., *The Genesis of Lancaster, 1307–1399*, 2 vols. (Oxford, 1913).

—— *A History of the Revenues of the Kings of England*, 2 vols. (Oxford, 1925).

Reddaway, T. F., and Walker, L. M., *The Early History of the Goldsmith's Company 1327–1509* (London, 1976).

Regibus, A. de, 'Il declino degli Angioni d'Ungheria sotto Carlo III di Durazzo', *Rivista storica italiana*, 52 (1935).

Richardson, H. G., 'Heresy and the Lay Power under Richard II', *EHR* 51 (1936).

—— and Sayles, G. O., 'Early Coronation Records', *BIHR* 13 (1935).

—— —— 'Early Coronation Records 5: Some Coronation Serjeanties', *BIHR* 14 (1937).

Rickert, E., 'King Richard II's Books', *Library*, 4th ser. 13 (1933).

—— *Chaucer's World* (New York, 1948).

Rigby, S. H., 'The Customs Administration at Boston in the Reign of Richard II', *BIHR* 58 (1985).

Robinson, J. A., 'An Unrecognized Westminster Chronicler, 1381–1394', *Proceedings of the British Academy*, 3 (1907–8).

Rogers, A., 'Henry IV, the Commons, and Taxation', *Mediaeval Studies* 31 (1969).

Roskell, J. S., *Parliament and Politics in Late Medieval England*, 3 vols. (London, 1981–3).

—— *The Impeachment of Michael de la Pole Earl of Suffolk in 1386* (Manchester, 1984).

Ross, C. D., 'Forfeitures for Treason in the Reign of Richard II', *EHR* 71 (1956), 560–75.

Rosser, G., *Medieval Westminster 1200–1540* (Oxford, 1989).

Roth, F., *The English Austin Friars, 1249–1538*, 2 vols. (New York, 1961–6).

Royal Commission on the Ancient and Historical Monuments and Constructions of England, *An Inventory of the Historical Monuments in London*, 5 vols.
(London, 1924–30).

Russell, P. E., *The English Intervention in Spain and Portugal in the Time of Edward
III and Richard II* (Oxford, 1955).

Sabine, E., 'Butchering in Medieval London', *Speculum*, 8 (1933).

—— 'City Cleaning in Medieval London', *Speculum*, 12 (1937).

Sandford, F., *The History of the Coronation . . . of James I* (London, 1687).

Sandler, L. F., *Gothic Manuscripts, 1285–1385*, ed. J. J. G. Alexander, 2 vols.
(Oxford, 1985).

Sandquist, T. A., 'The Holy Oil of St Thomas of Canterbury', in id. and M. R.
Powicke (edd.), *Essays in Medieval History presented to Bertie Wilkinson*
(Toronto, 1969).

Saul, N. E., 'The Commons and the Abolition of Badges', *Parliamentary History*,
9 (1990).

—— 'Richard II and the Vocabulary of Kingship', *EHR* 110 (1995).

—— 'Richard II and Westminster Abbey', in W. J. Blair, and B. Golding (edd.),
The Cloister and the World: Essays in Medieval History presented to Barbara Harvey
(Oxford, 1995).

—— *Richard II* (London, 1997).

Scattergood, V. J., 'Two Medieval Book Lists', *Library* 23 (1968).

—— 'Literary Culture at the Court of Richard II', in *English Court Culture*.

—— and Sherborne, J. W. (edd.), *English Court Culture in the Later Middle Ages*
(London, 1983).

Scharf, G., 'The Westminster Portrait of Richard II', *Fine Arts Quarterly Review*,
NS 2 (1867), 27–63.

—— *Description of the Wilton House Diptych* (London, 1882).

Shaw, P., 'The Black Prince', *History*, 24 (1940).

Shaw, W. A., 'The Early English School of Portraiture', *Burlington Magazine*,
65 (1934).

Sherborne, J. W., 'Indentured Retinues and English Expeditions to France
1369–1380', *EHR* 79 (1964).

—— 'The English Navy: Shipping and Manpower 1369–1389', *Past and Present*,
37 (1967).

—— 'Charles VI and Richard II', in J. J. N. Palmer (ed.), *Froissart: Historian*
(Woodbridge, 1981).

—— 'Perjury and the Lancastrian Revolution of 1399', *Welsh Hist. Rev.* 14
(1988).

—— 'The Defence of the Realm and the Impeachment of Michael de la Pole in
1386', in *Politics and Crisis*.

Sherman, C. R., *The Portraits of Charles V of France (1338–1380)* (New York, 1969).

Squibb, G. D., *The High Court of Chivalry: A Study of the Civil Law in England*
(Oxford, 1959).

Stacul, P., *Il Cardinale Pileo da Prato* (Rome, 1957).

Staniland, K., 'Clothing and Textiles at the Court of Edward III, 1342–1352', *Collectanea Londiniensis: Studies presented to Ralph Merrifield* (London and Middlesex Archeological Society, Special Papers, 2; 1978), 223–340.

—— 'Court Style, Painters, and the Great Wardrobe', in W. M. Ormrod (ed.), *England in the Fourteenth Century: Proceedings of the 1985 Harlaxton Symposium* (Woodbridge, 1986).

Starkey, D., 'The Age of the Household: Politics, Society, and the Arts *c*.1350–*c*.1550', in S. Medcalf (ed.), *The Later Middle Ages* (London, 1981).

—— (ed.), *The English Court from the Wars of the Roses to the Civil War* (London, 1987).

Steel, A. B., *Richard II* (Cambridge, 1941).

—— *The Receipt of the Exchequer, 1377–1485* (Cambridge, 1954).

—— 'The Collectors of Customs at Newcastle upon Tyne in the Reign of Richard II', in J. Conway Davies (ed.), *Studies presented to Sir Hilary Jenkinson* (London, 1957).

—— 'The Collectors of the Customs in the Reign of Richard II', in H. Hearder, and H. R. Loyn (edd.), *British Government and Administration* (Cardiff, 1974).

Storey, R. L., 'Liveries and Commissions of the Peace, 1388–1390', in *Reign of Richard II*.

—— 'Clergy and Common Law in the Reign of Henry IV', in R. F. Hunnisett and J. B. Post (edd.), *Medieval Legal Records in Memory of C. A. F. Meekings* (London, 1978).

—— 'Episcopal Kingmakers in the Fifteenth Century', in R. B. Dobson (ed.), *The Church, Politics and Patronage in the Fifteenth Century* (Gloucester, 1984).

Stow, G. B., 'Richard II in Thomas Walsingham's Chronicles', *Speculum*, 59 (1984).

—— 'Richard II in Jean Froissart's *Chroniques*', *JMH* 11 (1985).

—— 'Chronicles versus Records: The Character of Richard II', in J. S. Hamilton and P. J. Bradley (edd.), *Documenting the Past: Essays to George Peddy Cuttino* (Wolfeboro, NH, 1989).

—— 'Richard II in John Gower's *Confessio Amantis*: Some Historical Perspectives', *Medievalia*, 16 (1993).

Strohm, P., *Hochon's Arrow* (Princeton, 1992).

Swanson, R. N., *Church and Society in Late Medieval England* (Oxford, 1989).

Taylor, J., 'Richard II's Views on Kingship', *Proceedings of the Leeds Philosophical and Literary Society*, 14 (1970–2).

—— *English Historical Literature in the Fourteenth Century* (Oxford, 1987).

—— 'The Good Parliament and its Sources', in *Politics and Crisis*.

—— and Childs, W. (edd.), *Politics and Crisis in Fourteenth-Century England* (Gloucester, 1990).

Theilmann, J. M., 'Political Canonization and Political Symbolism in Medieval England', *JBS* 29 (1990).

Thomson, J. A. F., *The Transformation of Medieval England 1370–1529* (Harlow, 1983).

Thompson, J. M., *The Carthusian Order in England* (London, 1930).

Tout, T. F., *Chapters in the Administrative History of Mediaeval England*, 6 vols. (Manchester, 1920–33).

Trevelyan, G. M., *England in the Age of Wycliffe* (London, 1899; repr., with introd. by J. A. Tuck, 1972).

Tristram, E. W., *English Wall Painting of the Fourteenth Century* (London, 1955).

Tuck, J. A., 'Richard II and the Border Magnates', *Northern History*, 3 (1968).

—— 'The Cambridge Parliament, 1388', *EHR* 84 (1969).

—— *Richard II and the English Nobility* (London, 1973).

—— *Crown and Nobility, 1272–1461* (London, 1985).

—— 'The Emergence of a Northern Nobility, 1250–1408', *Northern History*, 22 (1986).

Tyson, D. B. (ed.), *Beihefte zur Zeitschrift für Romanische Philologie* (Tübingen, 1975).

Ullmann, W., 'The University of Cambridge and the Great Schism', *Journal of Theological Studies*, NS 9 (1958).

—— *Principles of Government and Politics in the Middle Ages* (4th edn., London, 1978).

Unwin, G. (ed.), *Finance and Trade under Edward III* (Manchester, 1918).

Vale, J., *Edward III and Chivalry: Chivalric Society and its Context, 1270–1350* (Woodbridge, 1982).

Valois, N., 'Le Project de marriage entre Louis de France et Catherine d'Hongroie et le voyage de l'Empereur Charles IV à Paris', *Annuaire-Bulletin de la Société de l'Histoire de France*, 30 (1893).

—— 'Le Grand Schisme en Allemagne de 1378 à 1380', *Romische Quartalschrift*, 8 (1893).

Vaughan, R., *Philip the Bold* (London, 1962).

Veale, E. M., *The English Fur Trade in the Later Middle Ages* (Oxford, 1966).

Waley, D., *Later Medieval Europe* (London, 1964).

Walker, S. K., 'Lordship and Lawlessness in the Palatinate of Lancaster, 1370–1400', *JBS* 28 (1989).

—— *The Lancastrian Affinity 1361–1399* (Oxford, 1990).

Waugh, W. T., 'The Great Statute of Praemunire, 1393', *EHR* 37 (1922).

Weigel, H., 'Manner um König Wenzel: Das Problem der Reichspolitik 1374–1384', *Deutsches Archiv für Geschichte des Mittelalters*, 5 (1942).

—— 'König Wenzel's personliche Politik, Reich und Hausmacht 1384–1389', *Deutsches Archiv für Geschichte des Mittelalters*, 7 (1944).

Weske, D., *Convocation of the Clergy* (London, 1937).

Whittingham, S., 'The Chronology of the Portraits of Richard II', *Burlington Magazine*, 113 (1971).

—— 'The Date of the Wilton Diptych', *Gazette des Beaux Arts*, 98 (1981).

Wickert, M., *Studies in John Gower*, trans. R. J. Meindl (Washington, 1981).

Wilkinson, B., *Constitutional History of Medieval England 1216–1399*, 3 vols. (1948–58).

Wilkinson, B., *Studies in the Constitutional History of the Thirteenth and Fourteenth Centuries* (2nd edn., Manchester, 1952).
—— *Constitutional History of England in the Fifteenth Century, 1399–1485* (London, 1964).
Wilks, M., 'Royal Priesthood: The Origins of Lollardy', in id., *The Church in a Changing Society* (Uppsala, 1978).
Williams, G. A., *Medieval London from Commune to Capital* (London, 1963).
Wilson, C. *et al.*, *Westminster Abbey* (London, 1986).
Withington, R., *English Pageantry: An Historical Introduction*, 2 vols. (Cambridge, Mass., 1918).
Wood, C. T., 'Richard II and the Wilton Diptych', in id., *Joan of Arc and Richard III* (Oxford, 1988).
Wormald, F., 'The Wilton Diptych', *Journal of the Warburg and Courtauld Institutes*, 17 (1954).
Wright, G. S., 'A Royal Tomb Program in the Reign of St Louis', *Art Bulletin*, 55 (1974).
Wurth-Paquet, F. X. (ed.), 'Table chronologique des chartes et diplomes relatifs à l'histoire de l'ancien pays de Luxembourg: Règne de Wenceslas II, roi des Romains et de Bohème', *Publications de la section historique de l'Institut Royale Grand-Ducal de Luxembourg* (Luxemburg, 1850).

Electronic data base

European State Finance Database (Univ. of Leicester). deposited (1993), Economic and Social Research Council Data Archive, Univ. of Essex, which may be consulted via *JANET*; e-mail: ARCHIVE@UK.AC.Essex.

Index